TYPOS

THE TYPOLOGICAL INTERPRETATION
OF THE OLD TESTAMENT
IN THE NEW

by
LEONHARD GOPPELT

Translated by
DONALD H. MADVIG

Foreword by
E. EARLE ELLIS

WILLIAM B. EERDMANS PUBLISHING COMPANY
GRAND RAPIDS, MICHIGAN

Translated from *Typos: Die typologische Deutung des Alten
Testaments im Neuen,* copyright © C. Bertelsmann Verlag, 1939
This edition published through special arrangement
with Gütersloher Verlagshaus Gerd Mohn, Germany,
and sponsored by the Institute for Biblical Research

Library of Congress Cataloging in Publication Data

Goppelt, Leonhard, 1911-1973.
Typos, the typological interpretation of the Old
Testament in the New.

Translation of: Typos, die typologische Deutung
des Alten Testaments im Neuen.
Originally presented as the author's thesis
(doctoral—Erlangen, 1939)
Includes indexes.
1. Typology (Theology) 2. Bible. N.T.
—Relation to the Old Testament. I. Title.
BS478.G6513   220.6'4   81-17284
ISBN 0-8028-3562-7   AACR2

CONTENTS

FOREWORD

I

The interpretation of the OT in the church has been a matter of controversy almost from the beginning. As a number of writers have argued,[1] and the present book most clearly demonstrates, a typological understanding of Scripture governed the interpretation of NT writers and continued to be followed, more or less closely, by Ireneus of Lyon[2] (ca. A.D. 125-195) and by the patristic school of Antioch. There were, however, other views bidding for acceptance. Most prominent among them was an allegorical approach to the OT, fostered by Origen (ca. A.D. 185-254) and the school of Alexandria,[3] which largely dominated the church's exposition of Scripture throughout the Middle Ages.

Professor Goppelt clearly distinguishes the allegorical hermeneutic from typology,[4] but he gives less attention to two more extreme interpretations of the OT in early Christianity. Marcion (ca. A.D. 100-160) rejected the OT entirely, regarding it as the instrument of an evil deity,[5] and according to Clement of Alexandria some of Marcion's followers or a similar sect urged that whatever the OT taught, one should do the opposite.[6] This attitude, however, was not present in the NT period with which Goppelt is concerned. At the other extreme were the Judaizers, some of whom required believers to observe Jewish ritual laws and others who endorsed a Jewish political messianism. The first type surfaces in the NT as a faction within "the circumcision party," who are opposed

---

1. Cf. the literature and discussion in E. E. Ellis, *Prophecy and Hermeneutic in Early Christianity* (Tübingen/Grand Rapids, 1978) 165-69.

2. His doctrine of ἀνακεφαλαίωσις is not mere "recapitulation" but, like typology, contains elements of both correspondence and escalation. Cf. G. Wingren, *Man and the Incarnation. A Study in the Biblical Theology of Irenaeus* (Edinburgh, 1959) 125f., 192ff.

3. Cf. R. P. C. Hanson, *Allegory and Event. Origen's Interpretation of Scripture* (Richmond, 1959).

4. See below, pp. 42-58.

5. Ireneus *Adv. haer.* 1.27.2.

6. Clement of Alexandria *Strom.* 3.4.34f. (on Exod 20:13), cited by Hanson, *Allegory and Event*, 138, although it is not clear to me that the reference ἄλλοι τίνες is to Marcionites.

by the NT apostles and prophets.[7] The second type, the political Judaizer, is a less certain entity. Political liberation was a popular understanding of OT messianic texts in the first and second centuries.[8] It was an interpretation that brought disastrous results and one that Jesus clearly rejected, although some of his would-be followers apparently sought to make him a political Messiah.[9] If, as a few scholars have thought, some early Christians were tempted to a political Judaizing, that is, an interpretation of the dawning of the kingdom of God in terms of Israel's liberation from Rome,[10] there is very little evidence for it.

Unlike allegorical exposition, the typology of the NT writers represents the OT not as a book of metaphors hiding a deeper meaning but as an account of historical events and teachings from which the meaning of the text arises. Unlike a Judaizing hermeneutic, typology views the relationship of OT events to those in the new dispensation not as a "one-to-one" equation or correspondence, in which the old is repeated or continued, but rather in terms of two principles, historical correspondence and escalation. The inadequacy of a Judaizing hermeneutic lay *inter alia* in its failure to understand the latter principle in relating the OT to the new dispensation. In typology, however, the OT type not only corresponds to the NT antitype but also is complemented and transcended by it. The priniple of escalation is perhaps most clearly developed in Goppelt's treatment of the church as the "spiritual" Israel.[11]

II

Professor Goppelt's elucidation of a typological interpretation of Scripture is, for at least two reasons, significant for current biblical studies. First, the hermeneutical question continues, through the work of Brevard Childs, Peter Stuhlmacher, and others,[12] at the forefront of the scholarly analysis of Scripture. Second, and perhaps more important, the competing alternatives to typological exegesis that were present in the early church and the surrounding Judaism are also, under other names, present in the church today.

Contemporary biblical scholars do not, of course, advocate allegorical interpretation as such. However, some of them, in their depreciation of the historical

---

7. Acts 15:5; 21:20f.; Mark 7:18f.; Gal 2:12-14; Col 2:8-18; Titus 1:10-14. Cf. Ellis, *Prophecy and Hermeneutic*, 80-128, 230-36.

8. E.g., Acts 5:36f.; 21:38; Josephus *Ant.* 20.5.1 §§97-99; 20.8.6 §§167-72; 1QM 5:1; 1QSb 5:20-28; *y. Ta'an.* 4, 5 (= 68d); cf. CD 7:19; 4QTestim 9-13; 1QM 11:6f.; T.Judah 24:1-6.

9. Cf. Matt 4:8ff.; 12:28; 26:51f.; John 18:36; cf. also John 6:15; M. Hengel, *Was Jesus a Revolutionist?* (Philadelphia, 1971).

10. Cf. the intensely argued but unsuccessful thesis of S. G. F. Brandon, *The Fall of Jerusalem and the Christian Church* (2d ed.; London, 1957) 88-125, 202ff.

11. See below, pp. 140-51; cf. pp. 17f., 199.

12. B. S. Childs, *Introduction to the Old Testament as Scripture* (Philadelphia, 1979); P. Stuhlmacher, *Vom Verstehen des Neuen Testaments* (Göttingen, 1979); idem, *Historical Criticism and Theological Interpretation of Scripture* (Philadelphia, 1977).

meaning of the text and in their use of biblical words, concepts, and stories as symbols or myths for deeper meanings, do manifest essential features of an allegorical approach.[13]

The revival of a Marcionite attitude toward the OT, which may have resulted from a distortion of the law/gospel dialectic of traditional Lutheranism,[14] is a rather curious phenomenon in the modern church. It apparently first came to explicit expression in Adolf von Harnack's book on Marcion to which Goppelt calls attention.[15] Harnack, a leading representative of the older liberal theology, called for an outright ejection of the OT from the Christian canon. The history-of-religions school, with which Harnack had his differences, for other reasons also tended to give the OT a secondary role and to depreciate its significance for understanding the origin of NT teachings.[16] Through W. Heitmüller, J. Weiss, and W. Wrede this school decisively shaped the thought of R. Bultmann and his pupils. Bultmann was not far from Harnack's viewpoint, writing that *"to the Christian faith the Old Testament is no longer revelation* as it has been, and still is, for the Jews." It "is not in the true sense God's Word. So far as the Church proclaims the Old Testament as God's Word, it just finds in it again what is already known from the revelation in Jesus Christ."[17] This confessional attitude, in turn, was not without its effect on Bultmann's reconstruction of the Gospel traditions, which largely determined the direction of the older form criticism and in which OT quotations were regularly regarded as secondary accretions.[18]

One of Bultmann's pupils, G. Klein, approaches even more closely the ancient Marcionite attitude when he describes Moses the lawgiver as "the functionary of antigodly powers" and the historical realm based on him as "not merely profaned but flatly demonized."[19] Other heirs of the history-of-religions school are generally more moderate. But it is, I think, not unfair to say that in their thorough and minute attention to Greco-Roman parallels to the NT—a

---

13. Cf. the criticisms of psychological and structural exegesis by O. C. Edwards, Jr., *ATR* 59 (1977) 115-34; A. C. Thistleton, *ExpTim* 89 (1978) 329-35; B. C. Lategan, *Journal of Theology for South Africa* 25 (1978) 23-29; and B. Stancil, *Southwestern Journal of Theology* 22 (1980) 41-59; of existentialist "demythologizing" by K. Frör, *Biblische Hermeneutik* (München, 1961) 326.

14. Cf. C. E. Braaten, *History and Hermeneutics* (London, 1968) 121-25.

15. See below, pp. 3f., 61 n. 1.

16. E.g., W. Bousset, *Kurios Christos* (Nashville, 1970) 149; W. Wrede, *The Task and Methods of "New Testament Theology"* (1897) in R. Morgan, *The Nature of New Testament Theology* (London, 1973) 99, 184.

17. R. Bultmann, "The Significance of the Old Testament for the Christian Faith," *The Old Testament and the Christian Faith* (ed. B. W. Anderson; New York, 1963) 31f. On the philosophical background cf. H. J. Kraus, *Geschichte der historisch-kritischen Erforschung des Alten Testaments* (Neukirchen, 1956) 175-79.

18. R. Bultmann, *History of the Synoptic Tradition* (New York, 1963) 16ff., 26f., 47-50, 125, *et passim*. In important respects this approach can now be seen to have been mistaken. Cf. L. Hartman, *Prophecy Interpreted* (Lund, 1966); Ellis, *Prophecy and Hermeneutic*, 157ff., 247-53; R. Riesner, *Jesus als Lehrer* (Tübingen, 1981); B. Gerhardsson, *The Origins of the Gospel Traditions* (Philadelphia, 1977).

19. G. Klein, *Rekonstruktion und Interpretation* (München, 1969) 155.

necessary and important task—they are often correspondingly weak in their perception of its OT (and Jewish) antecedents.[20] Such scholarship is not necessarily Marcionite. But it does, at the least, risk losing sight of the fundamental importance of the OT and of post-OT Judaism for understanding the NT. One of the values of Goppelt's work is to demonstrate vis-à-vis the history-of-religions schools the priorities and the more significant conceptual background of the NT writers.

Judaizing interpretations of the OT did not disappear with the opponents of Paul. In a general way they are implicitly present in all movements in the church seeking to achieve salvation by good works. They appear, for example, in the imposition of regulations about food and drink and days or in attitudes toward ministries and sacraments that do not recognize the proper distinctions—the escalation—between OT orders and rituals and their NT counterparts.[21] Such efforts to facilitate individual salvation were pretty effectively addressed by the *sola fide*, *sola gratia* theology of the Reformation, however one may judge the acceptance and implementation of Reformation insights in the doctrine and praxis of various sectors of the post-Reformation church.

Somewhat different is a phenomenon that may be termed political Judaizing, the attempt to facilitate societal salvation, the coming of the kingdom of God, along the lines of the Jewish "messianic" revolt under Bar Cochba and similar figures in the first and second centuries. Like the Judaizing in early Christianity this understanding of the OT also fails to observe the proper distinctions between the acts and ordinances of God in the Old Covenant and those in the New. Certain elements in the medieval church and in the modern "social gospel" movement have affinities with political Judaizing but cannot really be identified with it. The political status, papal armies, and the Crusades of the institutional church in the Middle Ages did rest in part on earlier OT analogies between the church and the institutions of Israel.[22] But they were not aimed toward achieving eschatological salvation. Conversely, the social gospel of American liberalism, which did promote a salvation by works with eschatological goals,[23] had little direct connection with any OT hermeneutic known in Judaism, but was more an amalgam of the messianic ideals of the Puritans and the scientific, evolution-

---

20. For example, H. D. Betz's *Galatians* (Hermeneia; Philadelphia, 1979) reflects this imbalance, as C. K. Barrett (*Int* 34 [1980] 417) has noted.

21. Cf. Gal 2:14 (ἰουδαΐζειν); 4:10; Matt 12:5f.; Rom 2:28f.; 14:3ff.; Col 2:16; E. Hatch, *The Organization of the Early Christian Churches* (Oxford, 1881) 137ff.; T. Greenwood, *Cathedra Petri* (8 vols. in 3; London, 1856-59) 1. 147-52, 159.

22. Cf. A. D. Nock in *CAH* 12 (1938) 445f. Hatch, *Organization* 138; Greenwood, *Cathedra Petri*; *Apos. Const.* 2.25, middle: Bishops "are to the laity prophets, rulers, governors and kings."

23. Cf. W. Rauschenbusch, *The Righteousness of the Kingdom* (Nashville, 1968); K. Cauthen, *The Impact of American Religious Liberalism* (New York, 1962) 84-107, 147-68. In criticism cf. H. J. Cadbury, *The Peril of Modernizing Jesus* (New York, 1937); J. G. Machen, *Christianity and Liberalism* (Grand Rapids, 1946) 117-56.

ary optimism of the Victorians.[24] These two phenomena fall short, then, of reflecting a truly Judaizing interpretation. However, in liberation theology one does encounter what may properly be termed a Judaizing tendency in the modern church.

Attempts to hasten the coming of the kingdom of God by political revolution were initiated by the Münster Rebellion (1535) during the Reformation and again by the Fifth Monarchy Men of Oliver Cromwell's England.[25] In the present century they have been based upon Marxist analysis[26] and accompanied by a passion to obtain "economic justice" for the poor. Our concern here is not to query the methods or the general theological implications of liberation theology[27] but, much more limited, to contrast briefly its biblical interpretation with that of the work of Goppelt.

"The distinctively Jewish . . . element in the traditional religious inspiration of Marxism is the apocalyptic vision of a violent revolution. . . . [Marx's] Messianic Kingdom is conceived as a Dictatorship of the Proletariat. But the salient features of the traditional Jewish apocalypse protrude through this threadbare disguise, and it is actually the pre-Rabbinical Maccabaean Judaism that our philosopher-impressario is presenting in modern Western costume. . . ."[28] This incisive summation by Arnold Toynbee of the influence of Marx's Jewish heritage strikes, I believe, close to the mark even though it is not a matter that can be specifically documented. Marx's latter-day disciples among the liberation theologians are in this respect not untrue to their mentor when they use Marxist ideology to interpret the OT.[29] In doing so, they suppose that they have discovered a new thing. The question arises, however, whether they have not in fact fallen back essentially into a Jewish political hermeneutic already current in the first century that, from the standpoint of Jesus and the NT, would be regarded as a Judaizing interpretation of Scripture.

The "horizontal" interpretation of liberation and the minimizing of God's intervention to achieve it, writes Andrew Kirk, "overestimates man's unaided

24. Representative were, for example, the writings of G. A. Coe, "Salvation by Education," *American Protestant Thought: The Liberal Era* (ed. W. R. Hutchison; New York, 1968) 117-26; idem, *A Sociological Theory of Religious Education* (New York, 1917), whose index has the entry: "Kingdom of God, see *Democracy*" (p. 359).

25. They based their views on an interpretation of Dan 2:44.

26. Or, in the view of some, they replaced the Gospel of Mark with the gospel of Marx. Cf. Cadbury, *Peril*, 203. Expressing this view more precisely, they read Mark through Marxian spectacles and used it to serve Marxist ideology.

27. For an appreciative analysis and critique cf. J. A. Kirk, *Liberation Theology* (London, 1979), esp. 143-208; more critically, H. T. Hoekstra, *The World Council of Churches and the Demise of Evangelism* (Wheaton, 1979) 63-131; E. R. Norman, *Christianity and the World Order* (Oxford, 1979).

28. A. J. Toynbee, *A Study of History* (10 vols.; London, 1939-54) 5. 178f.

29. E.g., G. Gutierrez, *A Theology of Liberation* (Maryknoll, New York, 1973) 153-212; J. P. Miranda, *Marx and the Bible* (Maryknoll, New York, 1974). For a wider literature see Kirk, *Liberation Theology*, 228-37.

capability to effect real and lasting change . . . and ends, not infrequently, in an illusory 'triumphalism.' "[30] This is a fair characterization of liberation theology. Its concern for subjugated people, like that of the messianic pretender Bar Cochba, is entirely to be commended. But in terms of its biblical hermeneutic it must be classified as a reactionary, philosophical manifestation of an ancient error of salvation by works. For that the words of Augustine are not inappropriate: "It is because the philosophers will not believe in this beatitude [of eternal life] which they cannot see that they go on trying to fabricate here below an utterly fraudulent felicity built on virtue filled with pride and bound to fail them in the end."[31]

In contrast to a Marxian approach Goppelt's typological exegesis explains the NT fulfillment of OT promises of liberation as acts of God within history that, at the same time, sovereignly select and go beyond the human political processes of this age. It thus implicitly distinguishes between "salvation history" and "general history,"[32] a distinction that liberation theology rejects. The rejection is perhaps best expressed in the words of Gustavo Gutierrez: "[There] are not two histories, one profane and one sacred, 'juxtaposed' or 'closely linked.' Rather there is only one human destiny, irreversibly assumed by Christ, the Lord of history."[33] Goppelt does not address the broader issue of the relationship between the two dimensions of history,[34] a question that is crucial for liberation theology. But within the limits of his topic he does pose an alternative to Judaizing exegesis, no less than to allegorical and Marcionite interpretations of the Bible, that will be of interest to all who are concerned to structure their theology within biblical categories.

III

The typological approach followed by Goppelt has been criticized for its attitude toward history. First, it is suggested that the NT's typological interpretation of the OT is not a true "historical" understanding but only a "reading back" of the interests of the NT writers. The criticism immediately gives rise to a further question, the nature of historical knowledge. During the eighteenth and nineteenth centuries it was thought that the study of history, including biblical history, was an objective science and that the past could be reconstructed "as it actually

---

30. Kirk, *Liberation Theology*, 152.

31. Augustine *City of God* 19.4, end (trans. *Fathers of the Church Vol. 24*, ed. J. De Ferrari; New York, 1954, 201f.).

32. Goppelt stands generally within a "salvation history" hermeneutic. Cf. L. Goppelt, *Theology of the New Testament* (Grand Rapids, 1981) 1. 276-81.

33. E.g., Gutierrez, *Theology*, 163ff.

34. For that cf. O. Cullmann, *Salvation in History* (London, 1967); briefly, Ellis, *Prophecy and Hermeneutic*, 153ff.; idem, *The Gospel of Luke* (New Century Bible; repr. Grand Rapids, 1981) 15-18.

happened." Today there is a greater recognition of the subjective factors that influence every historian's representation of the past.[35] As the reconstruction of a historian, history *is* interpretation since any reading, say, of the OT texts, no less than the typological, is done through interpretive spectacles. While it can be plausibly argued that the OT writers themselves had in view a future significance of the things they were relating,[36] this is not necessary for the argument that such a significance was placed in them by God as the NT claims.[37] Typological exegesis assumes a divine sovereignty over history, an assumption that admittedly not everyone is prepared to accept. But it may, nonetheless, be a defensible assumption.

A second criticism of a typological approach addresses this presupposition of divine sovereignty. Karl Popper labels as "historicism" the doctrine that "there are specific historical laws which can be discovered, and upon which predictions regarding the future of mankind can be based."[38] He brilliantly critiques this view of history as it is expressed in Hegelianism and Marxism, a critique that is pertinent to modern biblical studies. As we have seen above, a Marxist historicism heavily influences the biblical views of the liberation theologians. Also, through the theories of J. Wellhausen and F. C. Baur, a kind of Hegelian captivity has long afflicted the study of the OT and NT.[39] Indeed, virtually no nineteenth-century Continental theology escaped the pervasive influence of the Berlin master. Even those who reacted against Hegel's philosophy, such as Soren Kierkegaard and Karl Marx, were in some respects influenced by him.[40] The theology of "salvation history," as represented by J. C. K. von Hofmann,[41] was also not unaffected. But does a theistic, biblical view of history, which affirms a divine purpose and sovereignty in human affairs and which is assumed by a "salvation history" typological interpretation of the OT, as such fall under the strictures upon historicism?

Professor Popper thinks that it does and, unlike C. S. Lewis,[42] does not seem to be aware of the distinction between the two situations. His comments on the

---

35. Cf. B. J. F. Lonergan, *Method in Theology* (2d ed.; New York, 1973) 197-234; A. Richardson, *History, Sacred and Profane* (London, 1964) 83-183.

36. Cf. G. von Rad, *Old Testament Theology* (2 vols.; London, 1962-65) 2. 319-429.

37. E.g., Matt 4:14; John 13:18; Acts 13:27; Rom 15:4; 1 Cor 10:11; Gal 4:24ff.; Heb 8:5; 10:1. Cf. E. E. Ellis, *Paul's Use of the Old Testament* (repr. Grand Rapids, 1981) 126-35.

38. K. R. Popper, *The Open Society and its Enemies* (2 vols.; 5th ed.; London, 1980) 1. 8f.

39. Cf. Kraus, *Geschichte*, 178f., 239f.; W. F. Albright, *History, Archeology and Christian Humanism* (London, 1965) 36f., 136-40; E. E. Ellis, "Dating the New Testament," *NTS* 26 (1980) 494ff.; H. Harris, *The Tübingen School* (Oxford, 1975) 25ff., 155-58; W. G. Kümmel, *The New Testament: The History of the Investigation of its Problems* (Nashville, 1972) 132f.

40. Cf. N. Thulstrup, *Kierkegaard's Relation to Hegel* (Princeton, 1980); Popper, *Open Society*, 2. 318f.

41. J. C. K. von Hofmann, *Interpreting the Bible* (repr. Minneapolis, 1972); cf. Kraus, *Geschichte*, 207f.

42. C. S. Lewis, "Historicism," *Christian Reflections* (London/Grand Rapids, 1967) 100-13.

topic reflect a shift in his definition of historicism and a misunderstanding of the relationship between divine sovereignty and human freedom as it is represented by the Scriptures and by more perceptive Christian theologians. As a rationalist—or what Goppelt calls a Cartesian[43]—thinker Popper has no place for revealed truth, much less for the truth of logical antinomies. He apparently is not aware that in a theistic view of history divine sovereignty and human freedom and responsibility operate as a *concursus* in which neither is sacrificed and neither forcibly conformed to the other. For him "the rationalist attitude toward history in its emphasis on our supreme responsibility for our actions" and the conception of divine purpose and predetermination of the course of history are mutually exclusive.[44] But a proper Christian attitude toward history affirms the biblical revelation that both are true and that here, as in other matters, reality transcends the reasoning of autonomous man.[45]

As Popper initially defined historicism—"historical laws which can be discovered" by human reason—it does not apply to a theology of salvation history or to a typological interpretation of Scripture. For in such a case the plan of history is in the hands of God and is not subject to human discovery or prediction. Even God's decisive act in sending Jesus the Messiah is perceived only by a divine disclosure.[46] Furthermore, except in its broadest outline the plan is revealed only in retrospect. Only in the light of the NT fulfillment is the typological significance of an OT personage, event, or institution made clear. Equally, only as the events of the consummation of the age occur will the relevant prophecies concerning them be fully understood. If in the light of the ministry, death, and resurrection of the Messiah the gifted Christian is able to perceive these events somewhat more specifically than the faithful of the OT, he can do so also only in general terms such as those in the Apostles' Creed. Certain current events and anticipations may signal fulfillments of prophecies.[47] But the pages of church history encourage the prudent Christian more to hopeful expectation than to flat affirmations about them. The fulfillment of God's purpose, like the gradual focusing on a screen of a previously unseen picture, always brings surprises even as it unveils its perfect correspondence and coordination with the foregoing reality and plan.

---

43. Goppelt, *Theology*, 1. 272; cf. H. Thielicke, *The Evangelical Faith* (3 vols.; Grand Rapids, 1974-82) 1. 30-65, for a critique of an epistemology controlled by Cartesian assumptions and for its implications for biblical interpretation (esp. pp. 64f.).

44. Popper, *Open Society*, 2. 259-80, 279.

45. Cf. M. Luther, *The Bondage of the Will* (tr. J. I. Packer and O. R. Johnson; Westwood, New Jersey, 1957) 74-108, and Packer's introduction, 45-57; B. B. Warfield, "Predestination," *Dictionary of the Bible* (5 vols.; ed. J. Hastings; Edinburgh, 1904) 4. 47-63 = *Biblical and Theological Studies* (Philadelphia, 1952) 270-329; G. Florovsky, "The Predicament of the Christian Historian," *God, History and Historians* (ed. C. T. McIntire; New York, 1977) 428-42.

46. Matt 16:17; 11:25ff.; 13:11; cf. Luke 9:45; 24:31; Rom 10:17; 16:25f.; 1 Cor 2:9f.; 1 Pet 1:10ff.; 2 Pet 1:20f.

47. E.g., the return of Jerusalem to the Jews (cf. Luke 20:24) and their turning en masse to the Messiah (cf. Rom 11:25-32).

IV

An important feature of *Typos* is its illumination of the wide-ranging unity of the NT writers' understanding of the OT.[48] This has been criticized by those who view the NT as a collection of competing and even contradictory theologies. Since the criticism is levelled rather broadly both against Goppelt and against any approach to the NT as a unified body of teaching, it may be worthwhile to look at its source and validity.

The loss of a sense of the unity of the NT has been characteristic of some circles of scholarship for almost two centuries. In part it was the result of the general "secularization of the European mind"[49] with a consequent rejection of the revelatory character of Scripture, or, in the words of T. W. Manson, with a consequent failure to interpret the Bible as the word of God.[50] The determination to treat the Bible as a purely human product, combined with the self-assurance of the eighteenth century's "absolute man,"[51] produced not only antipathetic interpretations of biblical texts but also the conviction that these interpretations were "scientific" results that had virtually the character of facts. Largely unrecognized was what the rabbis long before knew and, indeed, developed into a fine art:[52] contradictions in Scripture are the result of interpretation (or of superficial reading), and what one interpreter could bring forth another could resolve. The meaning of ancient texts no less than other aspects of historical knowledge is never free from the subjective factors with which the interpreter comes to and pursues his task. What appears probable to one interpreter will be improbable to another. The failure of the historical-critical method, after two hundred years, to achieve an agreed meaning for any substantive biblical passage underscores that fact and makes a more modest attitude incumbent upon all biblical scholars.

Perhaps more important in promoting the tendency to set one NT passage or writer against another was a dialectical *Denkmethode* that became an important factor in Continental biblical criticism of the nineteenth century. Although it is as old as Plato, and in modern theology may have some roots in the law/gospel dichotomy of traditional Lutheranism,[53] it appears to be largely the legacy of the philosophy of Hegel, who by "his powerful dialectical methods [was able] to draw real physical rabbits out of purely metaphysical silk hats."[54] Clearly,

---

48. E.g., see below, pp. 194f.

49. Cf. O. Chadwick, *The Secularization of the European Mind in the Nineteenth Century* (Cambridge, 1975), esp. pp. 179-88, 193-97, 212-26.

50. Cf. T. W. Manson in C. W. Dugmore, *The Interpretation of the Bible* (London, 1944) 92-107.

51. Cf. K. Barth, "Man in the Eighteenth Century," *Protestant Theology in the Nineteenth Century* (London, 1972) 33-79, esp. pp. 37-41.

52. Cf. N. A. Dahl, "Contradictions in Scripure," *Studies in Paul* (Minneapolis, 1977) 159-77.

53. E.g., Galatians against James; cf. Braaten, *History and Hermeneutics*, 107f. Luther, however, apparently did not regard James as a part of his NT canon. Cf. M. Reu, *Luther and the Scriptures* (Columbus, Ohio, 1944) 38-48.

54. Popper, *Open Society*, 2. 27.

dialectic can be an important tool, as it is in Plato's *Dialogues*, for defining an issue; and it can be useful in highlighting the unique contribution of a biblical passage or writer vis-à-vis another. But the highly antithetical Hegelian form in which it appears, implicitly or explicitly, in NT studies often exaggerates and distorts the texts and ignores the (far more likely) complementary character of the different perspectives that NT writers bring to an issue.

In calling attention to the unity of the NT writings, *Typos* does not lose an awareness of their diversity. If one is prepared to grant the prophetic credentials of the NT authors, that unity may be attributed to the Holy Spirit who speaks his message through their various voices, giving different responses to different situations. However, even if one takes a different confessional attitude, Goppelt's approach is quite in accord with the historical origin of these documents. For they are the product of a cooperative and relatively close-knit segment of early Christianity.

In the first two centuries after Christ a stream of writings poured forth from those professing to be followers of Jesus. They represented the most diverse interpretations of the OT and of the meaning of Christianity itself. Apart from the NT all that are extant were, with a few exceptions,[55] written after the first century, and the hypothesis that some had (Christian) *Vorlagen* contemporary with the canonical writings has thus far not been established.[56] Nevertheless, the NT itself bears witness to other Christian writings of various sorts.[57] Some of them are attributed to a competing Judaizing-gnosticizing mission,[58] and probably others from that or similar groups can be inferred. One need only compare the vast literary output of a similar and contemporary Jewish apocalyptic sect, the Qumran community—unknown until 1947—to raise the probability of extensive literary activity among the first followers of Jesus. It is not unlikely, then, that the NT represents a select group from a larger and more diverse body of Christian literature from the apostolic period.

Considerable evidence from both the NT and second-century witnesses suggests that the whole canonical corpus was produced by relatively few apostolic circles—Pauline, Petrine, Johannine, Jacobean, and Matthean—within a generation or two of the resurrection of Jesus.[59] The individual authors led or worked

---

55. E.g., *1 Clement*; *Didache*; perhaps *Barnabas*, *Shepherd of Hermas*, and *Odes of Solomon*. Cf. the discussion in J. A. T. Robinson, *Redating the New Testament* (London, 1976) 312-35; J. H. Charlesworth in *John and Qumran* (ed. J. H. Charlesworth; London, 1942) 109.

56. E.g., the *Gospel of Thomas*; cf. E. Yamauchi, *Pre-Christian Gnosticism* (Grand Rapids, 1973) 89-94; Ellis, *Prophecy and Hermeneutic*, 206, 251 n. 57.

57. Cf. Luke 1:1; Acts 18:27; (Rom 16:26); 1 Cor 7:1.

58. 2 Cor 3:2; cf. 2 Thess 2:2; 3:17; Ellis, *Prophecy and Hermeneutic*, 80-128, 221-36.

59. Pauline: Luke, Acts, the Pauline letters, Hebrews; Petrine: Mark, 1 Peter (2 Peter); Johannine: John, 1-3 John, Revelation; Jacobean: James, Jude (2 Peter); Matthean: the Gospel of Matthew or its *Vorlage* may be closely associated with the Jacobean mission. Cf. J. B. Mayor, *Epistle of James* (London, 1892) lxxxii ff. for the parallels.

within one or more of these circles and, for their mutual benefit, gave and received and used (oral and) written traditions from other circles.[60] The NT representation that the leaders of these groups cooperated with each other, even as they pursued their separate missions and distinctive emphases, is historically entirely credible.[61] And current reconstructions that view these circles and the NT writings coming from them as antithetical expressions of Christian theology are little more than echoes of F. C. Baur's Hegelian model, interpretations that mold the texts in accordance with a preconceived philosophical mind-set.[62] Over against this approach Goppelt is quite justified in presenting the NT interpretation of the OT as a cohesive and compatible theological perspective.

V

Since Goppelt wrote this volume in 1939, important discoveries have been made, particularly the library at Qumran, that will require a modification of some of his arguments. For example, in the light of the Qumran *1 Enoch* 37–71 can no longer be used with any confidence as a pre-Christian witness, and, in general, Goppelt's discussion of the typological significance of the titles given to Jesus will need to be supplemented. Also, the importance of NT midrash as a vehicle to convey its typological exposition was relatively unexplored when *Typos* was written.[63] However, to some extent the original work has already been updated by Goppelt himself in his dictionary article on τύπος[64] and in the essay appended to the present edition; and, in the light of recent form criticism,[65] his analysis of the Gospels stands on firmer critical ground than when it was penned. It would be beyond the scope of this preface to detail the recent works that bear upon the thesis of *Typos*.[66] But Goppelt's thorough treatment has not been

---

J. A. T. Robinson, *Redating*, makes a fairly strong case for putting it all before A.D. 70, even if a question mark may be placed at a few points in his argument. Cf. Ellis, "Dating." Also still in point is J. B. Lightfoot's perceptive critique of a Scottish devotee of F. C. Baur's school in *Essays in Supernatural Religion* (London, 1893) 90-96, 101f., 251-71.

60. E.g., traditions behind the four Gospels; behind 2 Peter and Jude; traditions on the Lord's Supper in the Gospels and in 1 Cor 11; church order in the Jerusalem church and in the Pastorals and 1 Cor 11:3-16; 14:33ff.; traditions on wisdom in 1 Cor 2:6-16 and Jas 3:13-18.

61. E.g., Acts; Gal 1:18f.; 2:1, 9; 1 Cor 3:22-4:1; 9:5; 2 Pet 3:15. Cf. Ellis, *Prophecy and Hermeneutic*, 3-22, 122-28, 235f.

62. Cf. J. B. Lightfoot's criticism of Baur's approach in "St. Paul and the Three," *Galatians* (London, 1896) 295 n., 309 n., 334 n., 354 n., 355, 363 n.); *The Apostolic Fathers* (5 vols.; London, 1890) 1/1. 357f.; 2/1. xi f.; *Essays*, 24f., 64, 82, 90-96, 101f., 151, 251. Cf. Ellis, *Prophecy and Hermeneutic*, 86-95.

63. See below, pp. 61-106. Cf. J. T. Milik, *The Books of Enoch* (Oxford, 1976) 89-98; Ellis, *Prophecy and Hermeneutic*, 151-62.

64. *TDNT* 8. 246-59.

65. See n. 18.

66. One may point to a few titles and the literature found there that directly address typology in the NT: D. L. Baker, *Two Testaments: One Bible* (Downers Grove, Illinois, 1977) 239-70; D. Daube, *The Exodus Pattern in the Bible* (London, 1963); Ellis, *Prophecy and Hermeneutic*,

superseded and has stood the test of time remarkably well. In its basic thesis it is as appropriate and significant for current biblical criticism as it was for its original audience. It represents historical scholarship at its best, utilizing to the full tools of research and the contributions of other scholars and at the same time striving, almost always successfully, to avoid imposing modern assumptions and interests upon the biblical text.

The NT's understanding and exposition of the OT lies at the heart of its theology, and it is primarily expressed within the framework of a typological interpretation. *Typos* will, therefore, provide an excellent prolegomenon to the study of NT theology. Standing between the seminal work in typology of J. C. K. von Hofmann and the broader canvas of O. Cullmann's *Salvation in History*,[67] it will fill an important place in the theological education of the English-speaking reader. For it unfolds a hermeneutical perspective that will deepen one's understanding of the biblical message and offers important insights into the way in which Jesus and his apostles and prophets interpreted his acts and teachings. For those who believe, as I do, that their interpretation is the foundation and key to any legitimate contemporary expression of Christianity, this volume will be essential reading.

In correspondence with Dr. Goppelt shortly before his death he gladly gave me his permission to seek a translator and publisher for an English edition of *Typos*.[68] I proceeded to do this through the recently organized Institute for Biblical Research, which had a standing committee to encourage such translations as a service to our discipline and to our colleagues. Dr. Donald Madvig accepted an invitation to translate the book under the sponsorship of the Institute, and, although encountering a number of delays, worked faithfully to bring it to a successful fulfillment. He has given us a version that is both sensitive to Goppelt's meaning and eminently readable. For this sacrificial labor—and the role of a translator is precisely that—we are all in his debt.

It is fitting to close this preface with an expression of thanks to Bill Eerdmans for his willingness to bring this important work to the English-speaking public and for the cooperative spirit in which he carried out the task. In this as in his other publications he continues to render an exceedingly important service both to evangelical Christianity and to the scholarly world at large. For this we all are grateful to him.

E. Earle Ellis

165-69; idem, *Paul's Use*, 126-35; R. T. France, *Jesus and the Old Testament* (London, 1971) 38-80; A. T. Hanson, *Studies in Paul's Technique and Theology* (Grand Rapids, 1974) 225-57; G. W. H. Lampe and K. J. Woollcombe, *Essays on Typology* (London, 1957); G. Reim, *Studien zum alttestamentlichen Hintergrund des Johannesevangeliums* (Cambridge, 1974) 262-68; C. Westermann, ed., *Essays on Old Testament Hermeneutics* (Atlanta, 1960).

67. Von Hofmann, *Interpreting the Bible*; Cullmann, *Salvation in History*.

68. Letters of 23 February and 7 August 1973.

AUTHOR'S PREFACE TO THE
GERMAN REPRINT

This is a study of the interpretation of Scripture that is characteristic of the NT. It was written nearly 30 years ago in the light of the prevailing discussion of the way in which the OT was to be interpreted and how it could continue to be used. The reception of this book by OT scholarship was more productive than could have been expected. A new objective in hermeneutics was encountered and confirmed by this book. This objective was to interpret the OT (totally apart from any historical analysis) the way it is interpreted in the NT where it is applied to the Christ event. Today this new hermeneutical approach has found mature expression in numerous publications, especially Gerhard von Rad's *Old Testament Theology* and the Neukirchener Kommentar zum Alten Testament.

The influence of this new approach in OT theology is evident in the more recent systematic studies. Moreover, it poses a question for NT scholarship. Under the influence of the history-of-religions method and of kerygmatic theology, at least in German-speaking circles, the NT references to the OT are largely ignored as antiquated scriptural evidences. Now a branch of OT research that can no longer be ignored considers these references to be legitimate and fundamentally in accord with the OT. This use of the OT to interpret the Christ event permeates the NT and is central to it; consequently, unless NT scholars want to overlook an essential aspect of the NT's understanding of itself, they cannot continue to ignore it.

The following study of the typological use of the OT in the NT is important for the current discussions in NT research, especially since no more recent treatment has been published to take its place. Chapter X, "Apocalypticism and Typology in Paul," is an attempt show how the discussion of this topic has been carried forward by scholars since this book was written. Although a number of questions have arisen in the meantime and are not considered in this book, it will provide intelligent readers with a basic introduction to the subject with which it deals and to the relevant exegetical material. If a revision were to be made, it would have to include the literature that has been published in the meantime, as well as a history-of-traditions analysis of the texts and a discussion of the implications of the history of religions. I will have to defer this immense task because of more urgent matters. This is why I was glad to consent to the proposal of the Wissenschaftlichen Buchgesellschaft, Darmstadt, that a reprint be published. In the form in which it has served OT scholarship, this book can now confront NT research with many unresolved questions.

L. GOPPELT
Hamburg, September 1965

PREFACE

In this study we will examine the principal form of the NT's interpretation of Scripture and the way the NT understands itself in the light of redemptive history. In the Introduction we will show how this study is related to the current ecclesiastical and theological discussions and will indicate its objective and outline.

This treatise was submitted to the theological faculty of Erlangen in the winter semester of 1938-39 as a doctoral dissertation.

I owe special thanks to Professor D. Strathmann of Erlangen for suggesting this study and to Professor D. Althaus of Erlangen for his friendly interest in it and particularly for including it in this series.

L. GOPPELT
Erlangen, September 1939

Chapter One

INTRODUCTION

The new ecclesiastical and theological consciousness of our time has given rise to a new search for the proper way to interpret the OT.[1] A comparison of the views of Vischer, Hirsch, and Eichrodt will provide a summary of the situation. The presupposition that these writers have in common is the historical-critical method which has been practiced for 150 years. The crucial question, however, does not deal with the particular findings of this research. It is concerned with the general assessment of the nature of the OT faith that historical criticism has set forth more clearly than ever before. The fundamental question that divides the various schools of thought is about the relationship of the OT to Jesus Christ. There are even differences of opinion concerning what the NT says about Christ in this regard.

Vischer asserts, "The Old Testament tells us *what* the Christ (i.e., the Messiah

---

1. On the rise of this new search for the "correct interpretation" of the text, see E. von Dobschütz, *Vom Auslegen insonderheit des Neuen Testaments* (Halle, 1922; 2d ed. 1927); E. Fascher, *Von Verstehen des Neuen Testaments* (Giessen, 1930). For the (rather unproductive) debate about "pneumatic" exegesis in the years 1925ff., especially 1927, see F. Torm, *Hemeneutik des Neuen Testaments* (Göttingen, 1930) 18 n. 3; *Theologisches Literaturblatt* 51 (1930) cols. 243ff. A. Oepke, *Geschichtliche und Übergeschichtliche Schriftauslegung* (Gütersloh, 2d ed. 1947).

On the contemporary debate about the interpretation of the OT that received its external stimulus primarily from W. Vischer's *The Witness of the Old Testament to Christ* and from the popular attacks on the OT, see J. Begrich and M. Doerne, *Das Alten Testament in der Christlichen Predigt* (Dresden, 1936); W. Eichrodt, "Zur Frage der theologischen Exegese des Alten Testaments," *TBl* 17 (1938) col. 76; R. Hermann, "Deutung und Umdeutung der Schrift," *Theologia Militans* 12; V. Herntrich, *Theologische Auslegung des Alte Testaments* (Göttingen, 1936); M. Müller, *Das Alte Testament* (Leipzig, 1937); M. Noth, "Zur Auslegung des Alten Testaments," *Deutsches Pfarrerblatt* (1937) Nos. 21ff.; G. von Rad, "Das Christuszeugnis des Alten Testaments, eine Auseinandersetzung mit W. Vischers gleichnamigem Buch," *TBl* 14 (1935) col. 265; idem, "Gesetz und Evangelium, Gedanken zu dem Buch von E. Hirsch," *TBl* 16 (1937) col. 42; idem, "Fragen der Schriftauslegung im Alten Testament," *Theologia Militans* 20 (1938) (a reply to this: H. Hellbardt, "Auslegung der Schrift oder Deutung der Religionsgeschichte?" *Deutsches Pfarrerblatt* [1935] 354); H. Schreiner, *Das Alten Testament in der Verkundigung* (Schwerin, 1937); H. Strathmann, "Zum Ringen um das Verständnis des Alten Testaments," *TBl* 15 (1936) col. 257; A. Weiser, "Die Theologischen Aufgabe der alttestamentlichen Wissenschaft," *Deutsche Theologie* 2 (1935) 299.

of Israel, as He is called in the OT)[2] is, the New, *who* He is—and indeed in such a manner as to make it clear that he alone knows Jesus who recognizes Him as the Christ, and he alone knows what the Christ is who knows that He is Jesus."[3] Through his death Christ has united the believers of both the Old Covenant and the New into one church of which it can be said, "One faith and one hope, one Lord and Mediator, one God and Father of all" (pp. 19f.). When the NT proclaims that the promise has been fulfilled, it does not mean that what was promised has now taken the place of the promise, but only that the promise has become complete and unambiguous (p. 24). Accordingly, Vischer discovers that throughout the Pentateuch "in the primeval history as well as in the patriarchal sagas, in the narratives of the Exodus as well as in the social and ritual laws, not merely is there a prediction of Christ, but there is a life with Him and a faith in Him that has essentially the same content as life and faith in the New Testament."[4] Vischer follows no definite method in his interpretation because "the discovery is the gift of God" (p. 32). He usually proceeds typologically and sometimes allegorically, but always with a claim to general evidence (p. 28). Frequently he supplies the meaning of a particular passage directly from the NT interpretation. Vischer speaks of the faith of Abraham, Joseph, and Moses as is done in Hebrews 11 (pp. 146, 164, 167f.). Genesis 14 is interpreted on the basis of Hebrews 7 (pp. 132f.), and the story of the crossing of the Red Sea is interpreted on the basis of 1 Corinthians 10 (p. 177). Vischer goes far beyond anything indicated in the NT in his discovery of prefigurations of Christ (pp. 146f., 157, 167). Like Luther, he holds that the person with whom Jacob fought was none other than Jesus Christ (p. 153).

The opinion of Hirsch is quite different.[5] He states, "We must interpret the OT in its entirety as a document from a religion of law that has been annulled by Christian faith. We can no longer foster the illusion, as the NT and Luther do, that Abraham, the Prophets and the Psalms represented a truly Christian layer in the OT that, inasmuch as it was faith in something promised (as we understand promise and faith), was fulfilled in conformity with the gospel and in the gospel, but was concealed in a legalistic religion that contradicted the gospel" (p. 26). The God who is proclaimed by the OT is not the Father of Jesus Christ, but is the classical expression of the non-Christian idea of God from which we have all come (see pp. 27ff.). It is not the historical interrelationship alone that gives the OT abiding significance for us, but the fact that it forms the greatest historical contrast to the NT (p. 83). Only as we experience the conflict between law and gospel do we belong to the gospel (p. 82; cf. pp. 79-84). The OT was able to gain and to keep its place in the canon of the Christian church

---

2. W. Vischer, *The Witness of the Old Testament to Christ* (London, 1949) 26.
3. Ibid., 7.
4. W. Eichrodt, "Altes Testament," *Theologie der Gegenwart* 29 (1935) 123.
5. Emanuel Hirsch, *Das Alte Testament und die Predigt des Evangeliums* (Tübingen, 1936).

because of a violent and revolutionary reinterpretation that began with Christ, but it is one we can no longer follow (p. 27; cf. pp. 67-71).

Finally, Eichrodt sees the task of OT theology as being *"to understand the realm of OT belief in its structural unity and, by examining on the one hand its religious environment and on the other its essential coherence with the NT, to illuminate its profoundest meaning"* (1. 31).[6] Although he has a very positive attitude toward the results of previous research, he wants to break the tyranny of historicism and publish—for the first time in 25 years—an OT theology that interprets the OT as a structural unity and not as the result of successive phases of religion (pp. 27f.). Moreover, Eichrodt wants to take seriously the conviction that the OT points beyond itself and only comes to rest in the NT, and that the NT leads back to the main contents of the OT (1. 26). *"That which binds together indivisibly the two realms of the Old and New Testaments—different in externals though they may be—is the irruption of the Kingship of God into this world and its establishment here.* This is the unitive fact because it rests on the action of one and the same God in each case; that God who in promise and performance, in Gospel and Law, pursues one and the selfsame great purpose, the building of his Kingdom" (1. 26; cf. pp. 385-87). In contrast to Vischer, Eichrodt's interpretation does not simply proceed from the letter of the canon, but takes into consideration what OT research has discovered about the place of individual sayings in history. For him, Christ is not already present in man's communion with God in the OT; he is its consummation and fulfillment. Both Eichrodt and Vischer work on the principle that the Bible does not proclaim a closed system of teaching, but "a real God becoming manifest in history" (1. 503).

From this point of view, the present debate is merely a new chapter in the struggle to properly interpret the OT that can be traced to the beginnings of the church. It has been given its distinctive character by historical criticism and it became involved in this particular problem about 100 years ago in the reaction against the theology of the Enlightenment.[7] Harnack has shown great insight in his examination of Marcion's thesis in the light of the history of the interpretation of the OT in the church and has demonstrated that Marcion confronted the church with an important question that has never been solved adequately.[8] This is not

6. W. Eichrodt, *Theology of the Old Testament* (Philadelphia, 1961-67); see W. Eichrodt, "Zur Frage," *TBl* 17 (1938) cols. 76ff.

7. The contemporary views have closer or more remote antecedents in the nineteenth century: Schleiermacher's position (see his *Glaubenslehre*, § 12 and § 132), of course, is the view of Harnack and Hirsch. A Christological interpretation of the OT was sought by J. A. Kaune (*Christus im Alten Testament* [1818]), R. Stier, E. Hengstenberg (*Christology of the Old Testament* [Edinburgh, 1836-39], etc. (see A. Hartmann, *Die enge Verbindung des Alten Testaments mit dem Neuen* [Hamburg, 1831] 650ff.; L. Diestel, *Die Geschichte des Alten Testaments in der christlichen Kirche* [Jena, 1869] 620ff.). Hofmann and Delitzsch were also seeking "a new way to teach an old truth."

8. A. Harnack, *Marcion, Das Evangelium vom fremden Gott* (Leipzig, 1924); cf. N. Bonwetsch, "Das Alte Testament in der Geschichte der Kirche," *Allgemeine Evangelische Lutheranische Kirkenzeitschrift* 56 [1923] cols. 50ff., 60ff.).

only true for syncretism and the philosophy of religion, which have always been offended by the OT when studying Christianity (in recent years as well as in the first centuries), but it is also true for serious Christocentric theology. In any era the interpretation and exposition of the OT is closely interrelated with the general theological climate. Harnack, in his interpretation of the nature of Christianity, described the development in the following manner: By accepting the OT, Christianity became a syncretistic religion; the church of the pure gospel must exclude the OT from its canon.[9]

Out of this situation an urgent question arises. How did Jesus and the early church interpret the book that they made the Holy Scripture of Christendom? If every interpretation of Scripture reflects the theological climate whether or not it is bound to the current thought forms, then this is a valid and important question for anyone who wants to base his views on Christianity. Even Harnack and Hirsch consider it important to be in agreement with the basic thrust of the NT, though not with its explicit statements.[10] In the present discussion, however, this question is usually handled in a superficial manner. The few thorough treatments that exist are concerned almost exclusively with some particular phenomenon in the early church, primarily Jesus or Paul, and most of them were carried out long ago. Without exception they indicate that typology is the method of biblical interpretation that is characteristic of the NT.[11] This is the subject we are going to investigate. By surveying the way typology has been defined and used in the church's interpretation of Scripture and in its hermeneutics, and by reviewing earlier studies of the way typology is used in the NT, we will attempt to arrive at a more precise definition of our task.

Typology and the typological method have been part of the church's exegesis and hermeneutics from the very beginning. Obviously this is due to the influence of the NT and it is attested by the writings of the Apostolic Fathers[12] and the pictures in the catacombs.[13] So far as we can tell, Paul was the first to use the Greek word τύπος (adj. τυπικός) as a term for the prefiguring of the future in prior history.[14] God dealt in a typical way (τυπικῶς) with Israel in the wilder-

---

9. Harnack, *Marcion*, 215-33. His well-known thesis is: "To cast away the Old Testament in the second century was an error which the church rightly rejected; to retain it in the sixteenth century was a fate which the Reformation was unable to escape; but for Protestantism to conserve it as a canonical document after the nineteenth century is a sign of religious and ecclesiastical paralysis" (p. 217).

10. For Harnack's opinion of the interpretation of the OT in the NT, see *Marcion*, 223 (Jesus), 198-201 (Paul), 203 (Hebrews), 204-6 (John); and idem, "Das Alten Testament in den Paulinischen Briefen und in den Paulinischen Gemeinden" (SPAW, 1928).

11. See below, pp. 7-14.

12. *1 Clem.* 12:7; cf. chaps. 40–41; on *Barnabas*, see below, pp. 203-5; the term is used in *Barn.* 7:3, 7, 10f.; 8:1; 12:2, 5f.; 13:5 (in *Hermas* the term is used for the symbols in his *Visions*: *Vis.* 4.1.1, 2.5, 3.6).

13. Diestel, *Die Geschichte* 146ff.; E. Dinkler, "Altchristliche Kunst," *RGG* (3d ed. 1957-65) 1. 275ff. (includes additional bibliography).

14. The basic meaning of the word τύπος is probably not what is commonly given in the lexicons, "a blow" (see, e.g., B. Pape, *Griechisch-Deutsches Wörterbuch* [1906]), but, as Blu-

ness, in a manner that is a pattern for his dealing with the church in the last days. The fortunes of Israel are types (τύποι) of the experiences of the church (1 Cor. 10:11, 6; cf. Rom 5:14). It cannot be demonstrated that the word had this meaning prior to Paul, and in Barnabas, Hermas, and Justin this usage has become firmly established.[15] The meaning originated in biblical thought. Allegorizing, which appears alongside typology in the church's interpretation of Scripture and is found sporadically in the NT, had previously been employed by

---

menthal (*Hermes, Zeitschrift für klassische Philologie* 63 [1928] 391ff.) has shown, "a concave image" or the (visible) "impression" (produced by a blow or by pressure) (BAG [2d ed. rev. by F. Gingrich and F. Danker, 1979] 289; Stephanus, *Thesaurus Graecae Linguae* [Paris, 1848ff.] 7 col. 2586). Blumenthal then developed the following principal meanings: (1) the impression of a mold (the stamping of a coin, a statue as the casting from a mold, a piece of type); (2) deformity, rude form (from which the concept of inaccuracy and crudeness has come to be associated with the word); (3) abstract: a universal, a type (in the colloquial sense), an inexact reproduction. In late Greek the word became a technical term in various fields; see Preisigke, *Wörterbuch der griechischen Papyrusurkunden* (Berlin, 1924ff.) 2. 626.

15. H. Lietzmann, *An die Korinther I* (HNT; Tübingen, 1949) on 1 Corinthians 10. That the word was not used with this meaning before Paul can be verified by an examination of the lexicons: Stephanus, *Thesaurus* 7 cols. 2586ff.; Pape, *Griechisch-Deutsches Wörterbuch* 2. 1162; Preisigke, *Wörterbuch* 2. 626; J. Moulton and G. Milligan, *The Vocabulary of the Greek Testament* (London, 1914ff.) 645; BAG, pp. 829f.

The word is not used with this meaning in the LXX or Philo, and it has no precise Hebrew equivalent. In the few places where the word appears in the LXX it has the following meanings that correspond to general Greek usage: (1) pattern, model (a) literally of the figures of furnishings of the sanctuary in Exod 25:40 (תַּבְנִית, (b) in an ethical sense in 4 Macc 6:14; (2) idol, Amos 5:26 (צֶלֶם); cf. τυποῦν used of the form of an idol, Wis 13:13; Sir 38:30; (3) the outline of a document, 3 Macc 3:30; (4) a legal regulation, Gen 47:26; Exod 12:43 (etc.).

Philo uses the word frequently. Apparently he associates the following basic concepts with it. τύπος is the impression made in wax by pressing with a stamp. From this come the following meanings: (1) the impression of a mold (a) (impression in a metaphorical sense) mark, (b) imprint, character, feature, (c) form, outline; (2) (the impression in terms of its substance) copy, likeness, plastic image; (3) (the impression in terms of the nature of its being made) the inferior, repeatable, or effaceable mark, e.g., the individual in contrast to the class.

On the use of the term in Philo's "vertical" typology, see below, pp. 51f.; in that connection one must also take into account *Op. Mund.* 157, a passage that is often presented as a parallel to the technical use of the word in the NT: "Now these (the figures of the story of the Fall) are no mythical fictions . . . but modes of making ideas visible (i.e., typical examples, δείγματα τύπων) bidding us resort to allegorical interpretation guided in our renderings by what lies beneath the surface"; cf. *Ebr.* 36 (and *Som.* 1.73)

As the Hebrew equivalent in rabbinic usage Billerbeck mentions (on 1 Cor 10:6 and on Rom 5:14) the (Massoretic) סִימָן (סִימָנָא) = "token" of a coming event (=σημεῖον). But, as the examples quoted show (see Str-B 2. 140; 3. 226), this word has another meaning that is more suitable for the Greek word σημεῖον from which it is derived linguistically; τύπος in its fullest sense is not merely the token, but the anticipatory presentation of an eschatological event. This is true also of the Hebrew word אוֹת, which means "omen" or "symbol" and approaches the meaning of τύπος in various ways (cf. Isa 8:18; 66:19; Ezek 14:8; cf. Sir 44:16); the LXX appropriately translates אוֹת with σημεῖον.

Of course the typology of the NT is not bound by this terminology. The NT has no unambiguous hermeneutical terminology (see below, p. 177). For example, in Heb 9:9; 11:19 and *Barn.* 6:10; 17:2 παραβολή is used with the same meaning as τύπος. In Gal 4:24 Paul designates a typological interpretation as ἀλληγορούμενα, as J. Gerhard has observed (*Loci Theologici* [ed. J. F. Cotta; Tübingen, 1762] 1. 69, quoted in Hartmann, *Die enge Verbindung*, 632). NT usage, therefore, cannot be the standard for our choice of terminology. It seems to have had an effect on the threefold division of the *sensus mysticus* by the later divines.

the Stoics in their interpretation of myths and was passed on to the church largely through the writings of Alexandrian Jews. The Alexandrian Christians, whose most outstanding representative was Origen, made allegorizing predominant in the church's exposition of Scripture.[16] The literal sense was emphasized in the sober exegesis of the Christians in Antioch. They advocated typology as a suitable middle ground between the wooden literalness of Jewish exposition and allegorical fictions, but they were not able to win out.[17] In the West, Hilary, Ambrose, Augustine, and Jerome were influenced by Alexandria.[18] Their very arbitrary exegesis, which made use of both allegorical and typological interpretation, was the authoritative model for the Middle Ages.[19] At the beginning of the Protestant Reformation, Luther broke away from the idea of a fourfold meaning of Scripture and the subordination to tradition that was found in medieval exegesis.[20] He repudiated allegory and embraced typology.[21] Jesus is his authority for interpreting the OT as the model or pattern for Christ and his church. Even in orthodox exegesis, the NT is the reason why typology remained a last witness to a historical understanding of revelation. Lutheranism's hermeneutical expert, M. Flacius, approved of allegory also, but with greater reserve.[22] Salomo Glassius, a student of J. Gerhard, was the authority in later orthodoxy.[23] In addition to the *sensus literalis*, he acknowledged a *sensus mysticus* or *spiritualis* and defined its three subdivisions as follows: "It is an allegory when the Holy Spirit intends that the historical events of Scripture refer to a mystery or some spiritual doctrine. It is a type when hidden things, whether present or future, are presented under the external events or prophetic visions, when events in the OT prefigure or foreshadow events in the NT. It is a parable when something or event is related to or applied to some other spiritual entity."[24] The

---

16. Diestel, *Die Geschichte*, 34ff.

17. Ibid., 129ff.

18. Ibid., 78, 80, 82.

19. Ibid., 157.

20. K. Holl, *Luther* (Tübingen, 1932) 544ff. On the significance of Luther for the advancement of the art of exposition, see ibid., 550ff.

21. On Luther's attitude toward the OT see J. Hempel, "Das reformatorische Evangelium und das Alten Testament" (*Luther-Jahrbuch*, 1932); Georg Merz, "Gesetz Gottes und Volksnomos bei Martin Luther" (*Luther-Jahrbuch*, 1934); T. Knolls, "Luther und das Alte Testament" (*Allgemeine Evangelische Lutheranische Kirkenzeitschrift* 70 [1937] cols. 100ff. and 126ff.); G. Schmidt, "Luther und das Alte Testament" (*Einzeldruck der "Jungen Kirchen"* 25); H. Steinlein, "Wie stand Luther zum Alten Testament?" (*Luthertum*, 1937, Heft 6 and 7); V. Herntrich, "Luther und das Alte Testament" (*Luther-Jahrbuch*, 1938).

22. M. Flacius, *Clavis scripturae sacrae* (Basel, 1567); Diestel, *Die Geschichte*, 252; cf. K. Schwartz, *Die Theologische Hermeneutik des Matthias Flacius Illyricus* (diss., Erlangen, 1933) 9f., 28ff.

23. Diestel, *Die Geschichte*, 365 and 375ff.; S. Glassius, *Philogia sacra*, 1623 (examples of the typological interpretation in orthodox exegesis are given by Diestel, *Die Geschichte*, 477f. [Lutheran], 380f., 480f. [Reformed], 535 [the federal theology of Cocceius]; 743, 752ff. with an analysis of the typological interpretation in symbolism throughout the course of the eighteenth century).

24. Diestel, *Die Geschichte*, 376 n. 22; he also gives more precise criteria for types.

fundamental difference between allegory and typology is well expressed in J. Gerhard's definition: "Typology consists in the comparison of facts. Allegory is not concerned with the facts but with the words from which it draws out useful and hidden doctrine."[25] Glassius and the later interpreters are striving to differentiate this teaching about the *sensus mysticus* from the Catholic hermeneutic, which was similar outwardly.[26] It is not concerned with a multiple sense of Scripture, but with the one sense intended by the author of Scripture, the Holy Spirit.[27] In the nineteenth century after the overthrow of the Enlightenment, the example of the NT induced church theologians to once again seek a typological interpretation of the OT.[28]

The typological use of the OT in the NT has always provided an example of a more profound interpretation of the OT and has motivated the search for a meaning that goes beyond the literal grammatical-historical explanation. What have been the results of this research in the past? Strictly speaking, modern methods of investigation were not employed in studying the NT use of Scripture until the eighteenth century.[29] Since that time no special study of this problem has been published. Of course, the general subject of the NT use of Scripture is treated more or less thoroughly in every commentary and NT theology. It has seldom been studied by itself, however, and even then only in the form of an appendix. In general, these studies are arranged according to the development of biblical theology, for that is the only framework in which they can be presented in a unified manner. We will limit ourselves to a survey of a few representative works that will be indicative of the discussions and labors of the past and will help us understand the problem with which we are dealing. From time to time we will attempt to show how scholars have evaluated the role of typology in the NT's use of the OT, the nature of typology, and its relationship to con-

---

25. *Loci Theologici* 1. 69 (quoted in Hartmann, *Die enge Verbindung*, 632).

26. At the present time Catholic hermeneutics refers to the "classical" exposition of Thomas (*Summa Theologica* 1 q. 1, a. 10) in defense of distinguishing a twofold meaning in Scripture: the literal sense which lies immediately in the words and is derived by explaining the literal or figurative language, and the typological sense (= *sensus realis*, *spiritualis*, *typicus*, *mysticus*), "which is based on the literal sense, in that the persons, things, and institutions that are spoken about are also divinely appointed prototypes of things in the future" (*Lexicon für Theologie und Kirche* [Freiburg, 1930ff.] 2. 337; Wetzer and Welte, *Kirchenlexikon* [Freiburg, 1888ff.] 5 cols. 1844ff.). Wetzer and Welte (col. 1854) quote Thomas's statement: "God is the author of holy Scripture and he has the power not only of adapting words to convey meanings (which even men can do), but also of adapting the things themselves. . . . That first meaning, whereby the words signify things, belongs to the sense first mentioned, namely the historical. . . . That meaning, however, whereby the things signified by the words in their turn also signify other things is called the spiritual sense; it is based on and presupposes the literal sense."

27. Diestel, *Die Geschichte*, 699ff., 628ff.

28. Ibid., 627ff.; cf. Hartmann, *Die enge Verbindung*, 650ff.

29. For earlier studies of the NT use of Scripture, see E. Böhl, *Die alttestamentlichen Zitate im Neuen Testament* (Vienna, 1878), XXI-XXII; also cf. A. Tholuck, *Kommentar zum Briefe an die Hebräer* (Hamburg, 1836), 5f.

temporary exposition of Scripture. The last concern will help to illuminate the other two.[30]

From the Jewish parallels to the NT use of Scripture that Surenhus and others have collected, the theology of the Enlightenment infers that the NT usage was basically in accord with the usage of the time and explains it, like similar culturally conditioned features of the NT, by a theory of accommodation.[31] Jesus and the NT authors, in spite of better exegetical understanding, consciously accommodated themselves to their contemporaries' way of thinking.[32] Consequently, the NT use of Scripture was not allowed to have any normative significance. Eckermann was the first to comply with the demand of Semler and Ernesti that the general grammatical-historical principles of exegesis be used in the interpretation of Scripture.[33] With the radical but superficial onesidedness characteristic of the Enlightenment, the old was exploded and the task for the future was stated. The manner and the nature of the use of Scripture in the NT must be determined by careful comparison with the interpretation of Scripture practiced in NT times. Then, together with general systematic considerations, it will become clear in what sense this use of Scripture is normative by virtue of its relationship to the heart of the NT message.

In the first third of the nineteenth century, research into this matter did not progress significantly beyond what had been done in the time of the Enlightenment. In addition to a general countermovement against the Enlightenment, an uncritical repristination sought once again to make the NT assertions about the OT normative.[34] Compared with this trend, it seemed reasonable for Döpke, in his dissertation on the hermeneutics of the NT writers, to quote numerous Jewish parallels to NT statements about the rise of Scripture in an attempt to demonstrate that these statements were culturally conditioned.[35] The practice of explaining them on the basis of the theory of accommodation was given up because the culturally conditioned nature of the revelation made it unnecessary (pp. 1-8). The NT interpretation of Scripture is essentially allegorical (p. 128); it gives a meaning to the words of a scriptural writer different from what is actually there (pp. 96f.). Allegorizing was employed by Greeks, Jews, and Christians whenever a new piety came into conflict with the religion handed down in the sacred records (pp. 103f., 125, 128). To state it more precisely, "in the NT

---

30. On the survey that follows, see J. Wach, *Das Verstehen; Grundzüge einer Geschichte der hermeneutischen Theorie im 19. Jahrhundert* (Tübingen, 1926-33); in addition, see the historical surveys in the introductions of the books discussed below.

31. See Hartmann, *Die enge Verbindung*, 521; J. Döpke, *Hermeneutik der neutestamentlichen Schriftsteller* (Leipzig, 1829) part 1 7.

32. Cf. Döpke, *Hermeneutik*, V; Tholuck, *An die Hebräer*, 7; A. Clemen, *Der Gebrauch des Alten Testaments in den neutestamentlichen Schriften* (Gütersloh, 1895) 8; Diestel, *Die Geschichte*, 642.

33. Ibid., 620, 622f., 625.

34. Ibid., 627ff.

35. Döpke, *Hermeneutik*.

a threefold use is made of the documents that come from the Jewish theocracy—
a homiletical, a typological, and a messianic" (p. 47). Therefore, solely on the
basis of form, typology was considered one kind of allegorical interpretation (cf.
pp. 156f.), a more profound, symbolical interpretation of an action (p. 173).
While the NT authors simply copy the Jews in the other kinds of interpretation,
in the case of typology, as Döpke has ably demonstrated, they had to strike out
in a new direction. No longer are they compelled to seek a universal spiritual
meaning in the ceremonial laws, as the Jewish allegorizers do; they must relate
them to the redemptive event in Christ. Döpke stopped with this superficial
observation without inquiring whether the method of interpretation would be
different when the relationship to the content is changed.

Even Hartmann's book, with its conservative theological stance, ignores such
persistent and basic questions.[36] He identifies the various kinds of Jewish exposition of Scripture by quoting many examples and from time to time he determines how extensively these same kinds of exposition were used in the NT.
In the NT, there are only a few instances of the Jewish practice of augmenting
the legal and historical part of the Torah (e.g., Acts 7:15; cf. pp. 425-514). The
procedure of developing an interpretation from the literal sense is somewhat more
common (cf. pp. 425-514), and allegorical interpretation is encountered frequently (pp. 596-630). As to form, allegory is generally defined as the search
for a more profound meaning hidden beneath the shell of the literal sense
(p. 534). Typology along with Cabbala (the only example in the NT is Rev 13:18;
pp. 669ff.) becomes a subdivision of allegory. In keeping with the kind of interpretation that was customary at that time, typology was an attempt to identify
the features in sacred history and in the characteristic elements of Mosaic worship that are preparatory for a comprehensive picture of the life and ministry of
Jesus (pp. 632f.; cf. p. 662). In contrast to what he has done in other sections
of his book, the assertion that this kind of typology is found also in Jewish
expositions is supported exclusively by reference to earlier books (p. 650).

The works of Hartmann, Döpke, and others have assembled everything that
the methods of that time were able to discover concerning the external similarities
between the NT use of Scripture and Jewish usage. We will refer to them again
in connection with this matter. On the basis of the new comprehensive theological
approach that had been achieved in the theology of accommodation and in neo-
Lutheranism, the research of the second third of the nineteenth century seeks in
various ways to discover a more profound meaning in and a new justification for
the NT use of Scripture through a more thorough grasp of the essence of the
relationship between the two Testaments.

In his well-known commentary on Hebrews, F. Bleek, following his teacher
DeWette, adopts the attitude on these questions that the only thing that can be
a direct matter of faith is the certainty that the longing for the redeemer that

---

36. Hartmann, *Die enge Verbindung*.

permeates the entire OT was fulfilled in Jesus.[37] The acceptance of the NT interpretation of individual passages cannot be a direct matter of faith because these are often based on a free rewording of the text and are restricted to Jewish exegetical tradition. "Although I demand that Christian exegetes be given the right to research these matters freely, it is still my conviction that these quotations are never used in a purely arbitrary or unfounded way. Rather, I believe that this use is based on a deeper insight into the essential ideas which are the basis of these statements . . .; because the Jewish king, like the Jewish theocracy in general, was a pattern of the Messiah and his kingdom. Hence, the Scripture author of the Old Covenant might easily attach to the person of the earthly ruler a hope that would only find its true fulfillment in the king of the New Covenant; or he might assign an epithet to that earthly ruler that can only have its full range of meaning when applied to the Messiah himself." Accordingly, in the messianic psalms, Bleek always notes the historical context and the messianic elements which point beyond that context.[38]

Following similar principles, A. Tholuck carefully illustrates the NT use of Scripture in *Das Alte Testament im Neuen Testament*, which was occasioned by his commentary on Hebrews and to which it was added as an appendix. Six editions of this essay were published between 1836 and 1877. The differences between the first and last editions reflect the progress made in critical research during this period.[39] Tholuck distinguishes between quotations that go back to direct predictions, quotations that are based on prophetic types, and quotations that are to be classified as appropriations or applications (2d ed., p. 9). He considers a quotation to be an appropriation when its wording permits it to be used as the substratum for the author's own thoughts. He uses the term "application" for "the citation of parallels with a special introductory formula" (2d ed., p. 27; 5th ed., pp. 32f.). "The difference between this category and the category of prophetic types is this: In the application of passages, the assumption that there is a God-controlled intuition (ὑπόνοια, of which the OT author need not have been conscious) is entirely dropped and the parallels are laid hold of by the author rather than being God-given" (2d ed., p. 22). It is an example of typology when the idea found in the OT event is actualized in a NT event (2d ed., p. 17; 5th ed., p. 31). Therefore, typology must not become involved in details, but must seek to compare the spirit of the OT historical narrative with the spirit of the NT event (πνευματικῶς, 1 Cor. 10:3f.) (2d ed., p. 42; 5th ed., p. 32). The types can be objects, institutions (priesthood and sacrifices), or events. They may even be OT sayings, e.g., a psalm (2d ed., p. 13; 5th ed.,

---

37. F. Bleek, *Der Brief an die Hebräer* (Berlin, 1828-40) 2. 94ff.
38. Franz Delitzsch and R. Kittel also interpret the "messianic" psalms according to this principle. H. Gressmann (*Der Messias*, Göttingen, 1929) tries to explain the "messianic elements" on the basis of parallel forms (court style). Ultimately, however, these are not formal expressions; they are anchored in the faith of the OT.
39. See the foreword to the 3d ed.

p. 29), if the facts to which the OT sayings refer have typological significance (2d ed., p. 19).

In his statements about the nature of prophecy and the nature of a type, the thinking of the idealistic philosophy of history and the thinking of redemptive history intersect more clearly than in the other writers we have discussed. "Prophecy—even direct prediction—is never an image of history that has been cast into the past out of the future by means of a concave mirror. Prophecy is that future which grows out of the past" (2d ed., p. 9; 5th ed., p. 31). Direct prediction, like a prophetic type, is based on the fact that in the history of the patriarchs and the Jewish nation there were set conditions in which patterns of the future were bound to arise spontaneously. Types exist primarily as the result of the general relationship between becoming and being, between history and spirit, as we can observe in nature and history. In the child, for example, the man is prefigured. "The truth of typological parallels is particularly clear where, from the external symbolical level of a historical sphere, an inner spiritual form of this organism emerges, like the Christian Kingdom of God emerging from the Jewish kingdom" (5th ed., p. 31). Moreover, the Christological relationship only occasionally bears a resemblance: "This kind of typological relationship (the relationship between the OT saint in Psalm 69 and Jesus) receives its full significance only if those Old Testaments saints, the same as the New Testament saints, are viewed as members of one and the same mystical Christ, who is present throughout history" (2d ed., p. 16).

In the earlier editions, Tholuck believed that he could include all NT quotations in these three classes, principally in the second, and that by demonstrating their legitimacy could prove that the NT use of Scripture is not arbitrary like rabbinic usage. In the later editions, he arranges in descending order the way Scripture was used by Jesus, by Paul, by the evangelists, and by the author of Hebrews. In Jesus' use of Scripture "the exegete of the nineteenth century will have to acknowledge the deepest insight into the spirit of those documents. Nowhere will he be able to point to a false exposition or any appearance of rabbinic artificiality" (5th ed., p. 24). "Even Hebrews retains such a high position that, by comparison, books like the Epistle of Barnabas are characterized as postapostolic works" (5th ed., p. 57).

In an even more comprehensive manner J. Hofmann undergirds the NT use of Scripture with his system of redemptive history (*Heilsgeschichte*).[40] In his opinion, the way the OT is used in the NT merely represents a sporadic application of the great continuity which exists between the two (*Interpreting the Bible*, 145), and at the same time it justifies making such applications (cf. ibid., 189). This is the touchstone for Hofmann's entire system.

The comprehensive interrelationship between the two Testaments that is the

---

40. J. Hofmann, *Weissagung und Erfüllung im Alten und im Neuen Testamente* (Nördlingen, 1841-44); idem, *Interpreting the Bible* (Minneapolis, 1959).

basis for the NT use of Scripture is described by Hofmann as follows: His basic presupposition is that "The Scripture is not a textbook teaching conceptual truths, but rather a document of an historical process" (ibid., 204; cf. *Weissagung* 1. 42, 47), i.e., the history in which salvation is gradually realized, and the accompanying statements which announce the salvation that is actualized and proclaimed in this history (ibid., 55f.; *Interpreting*, 134).

(1) The OT bears witness to the same salvation that we possess as Christians and that the NT proclaims, but only in the sense of its being something "proceeding towards its full realization" (cf. *Weissagung* 1. 39, 55). Moreover, this witness to salvation did not originate in Jesus' church like the NT witness did, but in the national community of Israel (ibid., 48f.; *Interpreting*, 133). Accordingly, the significance of the OT historical narrative is that "the history recorded in the OT is the history of salvation proceeding towards its full realization (cf. *Weissagung* 1. 54). Hence, the things recorded in the OT must be interpreted as aiming at their final goal, and thus as being of the same nature as the goal yet modified by their respective place in history. Since the course of that history and the events are determined by their goal, this goal will manifest itself in all important stages of its progress in a way which, though preliminary, prefigures it" (*Interpreting*, 135; cf. *Weissagung* 1. 52). Since the individual OT passage must be related exclusively and precisely to the NT passage which corresponds to its place in redemptive history on a higher level, all arbitrariness is precluded (*Interpreting*, 136, 145). When explaining the OT proclamation of salvation the interpreter must also determine "in what respect the content of the NT manifestation of salvation has been given a preliminary expression in the OT" (ibid., 146).[41]

(2) The NT stands on the same level of redemptive history as the Christian interpreter. He must keep in mind, however, that the church of the NT, which awaits its glorification, already prefigures the glorified church (ibid., 223ff.; cf. *Weissagung* 1. 39), and that by virtue of the connection with the OT, the NT events are antitypes, and the NT message of salvation is proclaimed in the language of the OT (*Interpreting*, 168f.). All of the NT uses of the OT fall into this category. Especially in the quotations, the connections which have been set forth between the two Testaments must hold true (ibid., 189).[42]

Hofmann divides the quotations into the following groups: (1) One series of quotations introduce NT events as the fulfillment of OT predictions. (2) Others refer to the relationship of the NT events to OT history as antitypes. (3) "Since the manifestation of the power of Jehovah which had been promised in the OT

---

41. After establishing these basic principles, Hofmann in his hermeneutic gives a brief sketch of the course and the context of OT history and of the OT proclamation of salvation and indicates how this affects the interpretation of individual passages (cf. *Interpreting the Bible*, 135-45 and 145-68). This history of prophecy is presented in detail in *Weissagung*, 1. 62ff.

42. The NT's twofold relationship in redemptive history is presented in *Weissagung* 2, also in outline in *Interpreting*, 169-80 and 180-204.

took place in the NT as the manifestation of God in Jesus Christ, everything that in this respect is told of Jesus can be introduced as the fulfillment of a passage of Scripture that deals with Jehovah" (cf. ibid., 189-204).

In defining the nature of typology, Hofmann combines concepts from idealism's philosophy of history with the philosophy of redemptive history. These ideas are prominent in a rather biased form in a small book from that time dealing with the figurative language of the Bible.[43] According to this treatise, the biblical metaphors and similes are based on a typical-allegorical philosophy of life. "As was sensed more by the ancients and has been developed scientifically in the philosophy of our century, a concept of the 'All' predominates and affects the ascending levels of creation more and more fully, so on each higher level the same thing recurs that was already present on the lower levels in undeveloped form" (p. 34). Accordingly, there are not only metaphors and similes "of the climax of creation, the kingdom of God," but there are actual types in nature and in history. His attempt to support these ideas exegetically, if only in terms of implications, shows that they are not suited to Scripture.

The essay which the English theologian Patrick Fairbairn appended to *The Typology of Scripture* should be classified with the works of these German theologians from the middle of the nineteenth century, although it contains no trace of their idealism.[44] A major part of Jesus' ministry was teaching the people, as well as the disciples, to interpret Scripture properly. The use of Scripture in the NT that can be traced to him is completely different in principle from the exegesis of the time, whether it be the exegesis of the rabbis or of Philo or even of the postapostolic church (pp. 364f.). A large number of OT passages are quoted in the NT in a simple, literal sense. Another significant portion, however, is based on more profound exegetical principles (pp. 363f.).

Careful study of the individual passages reveals that the NT use of Scripture, whenever it is not directly literal, should be considered typological rather than allegorical. An allegory is a narrative that was composed originally for the single purpose of presenting certain higher truths than are found in the literal sense, or when facts are reported for that same reason. Allegorical interpretation, therefore, is not concerned with the truthfulness or factuality of the things described. For typological interpretation, however, the reality of the things described is indispensable. The typical meaning is not really a different or higher meaning, but a different or higher use of the same meaning that is comprehended in type and antitype.[45]

The significance of the NT use of Scripture and the nature of its types are revealed more accurately by the view of OT prophecy that follows. For Fairbairn, the prophetic character of the OT is not based on its being a preliminary stage

---

43. Eduard Böhmer, *Zur biblischen Typik* (Halle, 1855).
44. P. Fairbairn, "The Old Testament in the New," *The Typology of Scripture* (New York, 1900) 363-95.
45. See below, pp. 17f.

in a process of evolution, but on the contrast between divine calling and human failure. Israel, especially the house of David, was called to realize the promise given to Abraham (Gen 12:3). Both failed. In this way God is pointing to the future. The promise can only be actualized through one who is God's Son and servant to a much greater degree than was Israel or David. The predictions of the prophets have made this way of thinking an article of faith and hope. Thus Israel is a type of Christ and his kingdom; David and his kingdom are a type also. This is no mere symbol, illustration, or simile. It is a prefiguration that must be made real on a higher level by the Messiah because both Israel and the Messiah have the same calling from God. Therefore, it is not only the words applied to Israel or to David with reference totally or in part to the future that are predictions, but also the history of Israel and of David and the stories about them (pp. 375ff.).

Concerning these efforts to find a more adequate explanation of the NT use of Scripture, Eduard Reuss asks some critical questions which are certainly justified: "From the Christian standpoint and in consideration of their respective subject matter, purpose, and method, the superiority of the apostles' hermeneutics over the hermeneutics of the Jews, especially the Alexandrians, cannot be disputed, nor can the validity of the principles be questioned, once Christendom and Judaism are recognized as stages of development in the same revelation. One might, however, debate the extent to which they were employed and the degree to which the apostles were conscious of the basis of their interpretation."[46] The views of the NT authors and the subsequent use of a modern approach to justify their methods were not distinguished sufficiently by Tholuck and Hofmann.

An important and comprehensive use of the OT in the NT was at that time viewed only with negative criticism. It was regarded as the hidden influence of the OT on the formation of the NT record. Strauss, in a monstrous exaggeration of this principle, reduces large portions of the Gospel records to fabrications by the church under the influence of the OT.[47]

Between 1880 and 1920 there was little interest in hermeneutics in general and no interest whatever in the study of NT hermeneutics.[48] Literary criticism

---

46. Eduard Reuss, *Die Geschichte der heiligen Schriften des Neuen Testaments* (Braunschweig, 3d ed. 1860), 492f.

47. D. Strauss, *The Life of Jesus, Critically Examined* (London, 2d ed. 1892). This principle had already been stated by Schelling in his lecture on the Philosophy of Art in the winter semester of 1802-03: ". . . Christ was a historical person, whose biography was written before his birth" (quoted by K. Weidel, "Studien über den Einfluss des Weissagungsweises auf die evangelische Geschichte," *TSK* 83 (1910) 84.

48. A. Clemen's book *Der Gebrauch*, which was written in that period, continues in the tradition of Tholuck and Hofmann (see pp. 13 and 252). The vigorous discussion at the turn of the century concerning Jesus and the OT centered around the question as to what extent Jesus' statements about the origin of the OT Scriptures are binding for faith. Of the literature which appeared at that time (see below, p. 61 n. 1), the book by M. Kähler (*Jesus und das Alten Testament* [Leipzig, 1896]) is still valuable. In addition to an appropriate basic and systematic solution of the problem, it contains

was reaching its zenith, the study of the Bible from the standpoint of the history of religions was developing rapidly, and form criticism was just beginning. These disciplines provide important details and presuppositions for our labor that were not available for the researches of the nineteenth century that we have been discussing.

During this time there was little interest in the problem of the OT in the NT. Consequently, E. Grafe published a small volume in which he issued a warning lest the close and integral connection between early Christianity and the OT be overlooked by persons rejoicing justifiably over newly discovered but far more incidental relationships.[49] Grafe's opinion concerning the nature of the NT use of Scripture is similar to that of Harnack and Hirsch. Early Christianity attempted "to take a collection of books consisting of very different strata and developed out of the long and changing history of a specific nation and to transform them into the documents of a new religion." Although Jesus' attitude toward the OT is naive (pp. 2-4), Paul and his disciples were able to carry out this apparently impossible task only by means of the spiritual exegesis which was customary for Jews and Greeks (p. 7). Because the Christian writers employed the exegetical methods of their time, "their interpretation was convincing even in instances where their arguments can only arouse objections in us." This is especially true of the "allegorical-typological interpretation of the OT which was exercised with great skill" (pp. 10f.). It is understandable "that the courageous Marcion did not find the true meaning in the subtle exegesis of the church" (p. 42). The use of the OT in the NT has become a part of the NT's indebtedness that is given little attention in the history of religions.[50]

Only in very recent times has the hermeneutical question been revived. The first treatment of NT hermeneutics to appear since the one published by Hofmann in 1880 (after the preparatory studies listed above, n. 1) was published by Torm in 1928.[51] Here again the NT use of Scripture is aptly characterized from the standpoint of hermeneutics: (1) By and large the literal interpretation of the OT text is retained in the NT. A definite departure from OT statements (e.g., from the Law) is not concealed by reinterpretation, but is clearly stated (p. 220). (2) In many passages, however, there is, to our way of thinking, a startling use of

---

many brilliant observations about Jesus' use of Scripture.

We are also indebted to this period for a series of monographs dealing with the literary form of the OT quotations in the NT. Eduard Böhl (*Die alttestamentlichen Zitate*) wants to free these quotations from "the stigma of rabbinical artificiality or fortuitous quotation from memory" (p. iii) by proving that they were drawn from a popular Bible that had been translated from the Septuagint into the everyday language of Palestine (p. v). The lists of passages compiled by W. Dittmar (*Vetus Testamentum in Nova* [Göttingen, 1903]), and in the Nestle's Greek Testament are a valuable preparation for our task.

49. E. Grafe, *Das Urchristentum und das Alte Testament* (Tübingen, 1907).

50. This is still the opinion of T. Häring, whose article ("Das Alte Testament im Neuen," *ZNW* 17 [1916] 213-27) is intended to be seminal as a preliminary methodological study for the consideration of this question.

51. F. Torm, *Hermeneutik*.

the OT. It is explained as follows: (a) It is possible that the NT writer has clothed his thoughts in the words of the OT, even if those words have a totally different meaning in their original context (e.g., Rom 10:5ff.; pp. 221f.). (b) What may be properly called allegorical interpretation is seldom employed (pp. 222f.). By allegory is meant a kind of exegesis, which, in addition to the literal sense of the text, and, at times, even to the exclusion of it, finds another different and supposedly deeper meaning, although the context does not indicate the presence of any figurative language (p. 213). (c) Most of these passages are to be understood as a typological use of Scripture. "What is mentioned in the OT passage— a person, an action, an event, an institution, or some other relationship—is regarded as a prefiguration or type of something in the future in which it is developed in a fuller and richer way." Allegory goes its own way regardless of the literal interpretation, while the typological use of Scripture begins with the literal meaning (p. 223). Whereas allegory is common among both Jews and Greeks, the NT has struck out in a new direction with its typological use of Scripture. Moreover, Torm differentiates between typological exegesis and a typological approach: It is typological exegesis "when the author intends to say that the OT writer had a clear conception of the future antitypes" (e.g., Matt 11:14), and it is typological in approach "when they intend to say, that it is God who wanted to use the OT prototype to prepare men to understand the future fulfillment" (e.g., the application of Psalm 69 to Jesus) (p. 225). Sometimes the relationship between type and antitype is very superficial; usually, however, it is more profound. It is "based on the fact that history repeats itself and that, particularly in the history of religions, there is often an important spiritual relationship between the persons and events of different periods" (p. 224; cf. pp. 226f.).

An article by O. Schmitz proceeds from the attitude of the NT toward the content of the OT and reaches a much deeper understanding of the nature of the NT use of Scripture: (1) The NT considers the religious customs of the OT as having been annulled.[52] They are abolished and fulfilled at the same time, because what one sought in vain to achieve through the Law and the cult is abundantly supplied in Christ (pp. 52-59).

(2) The NT accounts of OT redemptive history consistently indicate a consciousness of the continuity as well as the discontinuity and difference in the revelation of salvation. OT history is not considered as complete in itself, but always open to the future salvation, the fulfillment of that history, and as including this fulfillment in itself in the form of promise. The NT looks back and fits the NT events into the course of redemptive history in an attempt to take from them the character of mere historical facticity. "At the same time the NT looks forward in anticipation of the consummation of redemption. In this respect

---

52. O. Schmitz, "Das Alte Testament im Neuen," *Wort und Geist* (*Fest.* for K. Heim; Berlin, 1934) 49-74.

the NT is at one with the OT in spite of the fact that the NT, in contrast to the OT, is viewing things from the midpoint in the fulfillment of the saving events" (p. 64). "Thus the concepts of 'promise' and 'fulfillment' have a unique reciprocal relationship in the dialectic of redemptive history, which retains its uniform definition in the present salvation. A promise is fulfilled and yet in its fulfillment it continues to be a promise. A fulfillment far exceeds the promise and yet as fulfillment it becomes promise once more" (pp. 59-66).

(3) The use of the OT in the NT: The church did not adopt the OT "in the Palestinian manner of materializing the sacred letters nor in the Alexandrian manner of spiritualizing them. With pneumatic realism the church has drawn the consequences from the continuity in redemptive history between the fulfilling event in the present and the promising event of the biblical statement with a reckless freedom in each individual case in accordance with the immediate need. Though this process may occasionally have involved rabbinical methods of argument or allegorical exegesis, it is still true that the redemptive event in the NT is the controlling factor for the interpretation of the OT" (p. 67).

"The continuity of redemptive history in the OT and NT and the interrelationship of prophecy and fulfillment give the OT basically the character of a prototype of the NT for the church." The OT's character as prototype is not only the basis of the truly typical use of Scripture in the NT but also of all other uses (p. 69). If one wants to define its nature more precisely, then once again that curious reciprocal relationship in the dialectic of redemptive history comes to the fore. The prototype receives its full meaning from the antitype, but it has this meaning only in its own existence. This existence, however, has meaning only insofar as it prefigures the antitype (cf. 1 Corinthians 10) (pp. 71f.).

This survey of the arguments of Torm and Schmitz will suffice as an introduction to the contemporary situation of the problem we are discussing and to the related questions concerning the classification and evaluation of the nontypological use of Scripture in the NT and concerning the NT concept of prophecy and fulfillment.[53] These two questions set the boundaries for the basic issues in our study.

From the summary we have sketched here, we can define our task with greater precision and indicate the direction that will lead to its solution. We will draw upon the results of the more recent studies to determine the extent to which the OT was used typologically in the NT and especially to determine the way in which this was done.

(1) The concept of typology with which we begin may be defined and distinguished from other methods of interpretation as follows: Only historical facts— persons, actions, events, and institutions—are material for typological interpre-

---

53. For more recent studies of particular groups of NT writings, see below, p. 61 n. 1 and p. 127 n. 1. The doctoral dissertation of Jan Leunis Koole, *De overname van het Oude Testament door de Christelijk Kerk* (Amsterdam, 1938, XXIII; reviewed in *ZNW* 37 [1938] 305), was not available to me.

tation; words and narratives can be utilized only insofar as they deal with such matters. These things are to be interpreted typologically only if they are considered to be divinely ordained representations or types of future realities that will be even greater and more complete. If the antitype does not represent a heightening of the type, if it is merely a repetition of the type, then it can be called typology only in certain instances and in a limited way. This is true also when the interpreter does not view the connection between the two as being foreordained in some way, but as being accidental or deliberately contrived (a parabolic action is not a type of the event that it represents).

If those things or narratives are interpreted as the expression of a general truth so that there is a one-to-one correspondence between fact and idea, then we are dealing with symbolic meaning.

If the writer wishes to explain or describe what has happened or is literally there, it is an example of literal interpretation.

Neither the facts nor the literal sense of a passage taken as a whole is material for allegorical interpretation, but the ideas and phrases are. Viewing these metaphorically, allegory seeks to find in them, "in addition to the literal sense of the text, and, at times, even to the exclusion of it . . ." another different and presumably deeper meaning.[54] The historicity of what is reported and the literal meaning of the text are of no consequence for allegorical interpretation, but for typology they are foundational (the literal meaning, at least, is foundational also for symbolic interpretation). The allegorist, however, does not view this double meaning as something forced upon the text, but as something intended and given in the text.[55] (Grammatical-historical exegesis is a modern development. It uses the tools of modern scholarship to determine who the human author was, his point of view, and his place in history.)

Defined in this way, these terms are merely vehicles for describing the matter being considered. Therefore, it is our task to discover the viewpoint of a certain interpreter of Scripture and not to determine what, from our view of Scripture, is the *objective* method of interpretation.

The form in which a passage is included (a quotation with or without an introductory formula, stated in the actual words, an allusion, or a latent influ-

---

54. F. Torm, *Hermeneutik*, 213.

55. The following interpretations of Num 21:6ff. are presented as examples of the various methods of interpretation. (1) In Wis 16:5-7 the record is repeated in its literal meaning and the event is explained. (2) In Wis 16:8 the event is understood symbolically as the expression of the general truth that God is a helper in every emergency. With reference to 1 and 2 cf. *Mek. Exod.* on Exod 17:11, "And the Eternal said to Moses, 'Make for yourself a seraph (Num 21:8). Does a serpent kill or give life?' But while he did this, the Israelites looked and believed in the one who commanded Moses to do this, and the Holy One, blessed be he, brought about their healing. . . ." (3) In John 3:14f. the raising of the symbol of redemption is interpreted as a type of Christ's "being lifted up"; in *Barn.* 12:5-7 it is interpreted (superficially) as a prophetic type of the crucifixion. (4) Philo (*Leg. All.* 2.77-81) interprets it allegorically: "If the mind (=Israel), when bitten by pleasure, the serpent of Eve, shall have succeeded in beholding in soul the beauty of self-mastery, the serpent of Moses, and through beholding this, beholds God himself, he shall live" (2.81).

ence) and the condition of the text being quoted will be discussed only if they are significant for the particular kind of typology.

(2) To provide a proper understanding of the nature of NT typology we will preface our presentation with a survey of the way this method of interpretation was used by the Jews in NT times.[56] We will begin with the writings of late Judaism and the available studies of those writings. The opposite approach, a search for Jewish parallels to specific NT interpretations, would provide only a very incomplete picture. In our consideration of the NT, we will make use of this material which is readily available in excellent collections.

(3) In order to fully appreciate the amount of typology the NT contains, we will have to examine all the NT passages in which the influence of the OT can be detected, whether it is a quotation, an allusion, or a latent influence, to see if these are based on a typological interpretation of the OT.[57] It will not be possible to clearly distinguish between what appears to us to be typology and what was intended as typology by the NT writer. We will have to determine the latter for ourselves. Only those passages in which this preliminary examination reveals a possible typological use of Scripture can be considered in our study.

The amount of typology that is included in the other uses of Scripture in the NT and how typology should be classified among them can only be mentioned in passing, and it will not be possible to cite all of the references.

Due to the nature of our material, proof is not possible for many passages and we can only be tentative.[58] We will have to be satisfied to indicate the possibility that the author saw a typological connection in the passage. We can deal only indirectly with the exegetical discussion and the possibility that an idea

---

56. The symbolical and allegorical interpretation of mythology was well known in the Greek world, but typology was not because typology presupposes a divine history in past, present, and future. On the Hellenistic interpretation of mythology see Döpke, *Hermeneutik*, 98-104; C. Siegfried, *Philo von Alexandrien* (Jena, 1875) 7-16; P. Heinisch, *Der Einfluss Philos auf die älteste christliche Exegese* (Munster, 1909) 1-12; L. Goppelt, "Allegorie," *RGG* (3d ed. 1957-65) 1. 238ff.; F. Buchsel, "ἀλληγορέω," *TDNT* 1. 260 (bibliography); PWSup 4. 16ff.; E. Stein, "Die allegorische Scriftauslegung des Philos von Alexandrien," *ZAW* 51 (1929) 2-6; I. Heinemann, *Philons griechische und Jüdische Bildung* (*Fest.* zum 75. jahrige Bestehen des jüdischen theologischen Seminars; Breslau, 1929) 138ff. and 454ff.

Hellenism and the extrabiblical world in general knew only the conception of the return of the golden age and a cyclical view of history (see H. Gressmann, *Der Ursprung der israelitisch-jüdischen Eschatologie* [Göttingen, 1905] 197 [bibliography]; idem, *Der Messias*, 462ff.; on Vergil's Fourth Eclogue, see A. Oepke, "ἀποκαθίστημι," *TDNT* 1. 287); it knew nothing about divinely ordained types that point to a real and greater fulfillment.

So too the example of a "type" that is cited by A. Maas, "Types in Scripture," *The Catholic Encyclopedia* 15. 107-8, must be evaluated on Greek soil: "After Plutarch has informed his reader (*De fortuna Alexandri* 10) that among all the expressions of Homer the words 'both a good king, and an excellent fighter in wars' pleased Alexander most, he adds that in this verse Homer seems not merely to celebrate the greatness of Agamemnon, but also to prophesy that of Alexander."

57. Indications of the use of the OT in passages which are not explicitly quotations are such things as a reminiscence of the wording of the LXX and significant deviations from parallel accounts (in the Gospels) in agreement with OT stories.

58. Therefore, we will frequently quote the interpretations of scholars who, although they have not been working with the same question, have been led by the material to the same conclusions.

did not originate in the OT, but in the history of religions in general. The purpose of this book is to gain a general picture of the typological approach in the NT— naturally a picture which holds the particular points of view in dialectical tension—and in this way make a contribution to the general inquiry. We do not intend to discuss the various individual points of view because this could be meaningful and productive only in detailed monographs.

(4) In organizing our presentation it is very important to remember we are investigating the typological use of the OT in the NT, not the special forms or parties of early Christianity that might be deduced from it. Furthermore, we are not investigating the notion of the historical Jesus. We will restrict ourselves to the reports of the evangelists, to that which the church of Christ believed and has handed down. This is how we should be understood when in the following material we speak of Jesus' sayings and Jesus' actions. Especially in the matter of the use of the OT, it is neither possible nor meaningful to seek to distinguish carefully what can be traced directly to the historical Jesus from what has been added by the Easter faith of the church in harmony with his thought and teaching. We will investigate these matters in passages that are clear and informative.

A similar procedure is the consequence of our basic attitude in the question of sources. We always begin our study with the canonical Scriptures and, by observing the use made of Scripture, attempt to make some contribution to the question of sources. There is no other alternative, even in the treatment of the Synoptic Gospels, because no commonly recognized division of sources has been achieved, not even on the basis of the two-source theory. To work out a division of sources and provide a rationale for it would require too much space in an essay that encompasses the entire NT. Therefore, it will have to be sufficient to indicate the status of the tradition by carefully listing the parallel passages and to refer to appropriate monographs for an analysis of the subject matter.

We will organize our study according to the NT writings in such a way as to show as clearly as possible both the kind and the content of the typology found in the individual NT books. In separate sections we will deal with the NT writings that belong together because of their general character and within these main sections we will subdivide in accordance with the content of the typology.

(5) In a final section we will summarize our most important conclusions and will set forth the nature of NT typology even more clearly against the background of the *Epistle of Barnabas*, which for this purpose is especially characteristic of postcanonical writings.

Part I

TYPOLOGY IN LATE JUDAISM

In the next two chapters we will indicate the extent to which typology was used in Judaism in NT times to interpret Scripture and the nature of that typology. The sources for our study of biblical interpretation in this period will be the literature which arose between the two Testaments (ca. 150 B.C. to A.D. 100). The Jewish literature of this period is unusually varied and is customarily classified as Palestinian or Hellenistic on the basis of its relationship to Hellenism.

Because of the range of material and the difficulties involved in this study— it is necessary to consider not only the direct exposition but also the latent influence and the allusions—we will have to limit ourselves to a survey of the most important writings. In the light of what we have said already about the subject matter of typology, particular attention will have to be given to the interpretation of OT history and the cult.

Chapter Two

PALESTINIAN JUDAISM

1. THE APOCRYPHA

From the literature of Palestinian Judaism we will exclude a series of documents which are identical to books in the Christian Apocrypha[1] and make no significant contribution to our inquiry—1 (ca. 100 B.C.), 2 (ca. A.D. 70), and 3 Maccabees (ca. A.D. 40), which are a reediting of contemporary history; the stories of Judith (ca. 150 B.C.) and Tobit (ca. 100 B.C.), fictions which were created for parenetic purposes; Ecclesiasticus (the Wisdom of Ben Sira, ca. 190 B.C.) and the pseudepigraphic book of Baruch.[2]

As to the way biblical history is used in these books, it should be noted that in the Maccabean period history was utilized to build confidence that God helps his people against their enemies when they are submissive to the Law.[3] If the books of Judith and Baruch are addressing their own times by means of stories set in the Assyrian period, the time of Israel's greatest distress, then these stories are merely a literary form and not a typological approach to history.[4] Jesus the son of Sirach praises Scripture as the source of wisdom (Sir 24:32ff.) and the great personalities of Scripture are his ideals (Sirach 44–50). The small contribution this book adds to Jewish eschatology will be considered later.[5]

---

1. Wisdom and 4 Maccabees belong to Hellenistic Judaism (see below, Chap. III).

2. The customarily accepted dates are given in parentheses for general orientation. See E. Sellin, *Introduction to the Old Testament* (New York, 1923) 241-46; E. Schürer, *The History of the Jewish People in the Age of Jesus Christ* (New York, n.d.) and E. Kautzsch, *Die Apocryphen und Pseudepigraphen des Alten Testaments* (Tübingen, 1900).

3. See 1 Macc 2:26; 2:51-61; Jdt 8:26f. (LXX); 1 Macc 3:18 (cf. 1 Sam 14:6); Jdt 9:10f. (LXX) (cf. Judg 4:21; 1 Sam 14:6); Jdt 4:13f. (Vg); 2 Macc 8:19f. Introductions to prayers: 1 Macc 4:30 (cf. 1 Sam 17:49; 14:13); 2 Macc 15:22; Jdt 9:2, 7 (LXX). On the whole story of Judith cf. Judges 4–5. The same spirit pervades the use of Scripture in 3 Maccabees, which tells the story of Ptolemy IV (ca. 200 B.C.) with legendary embellishments; cf. 3 Macc 2:2-7; 6:2-8.

4. See below, pp. 36f.

5. P. Volz, *Die Eschatologie der Jüdischen Gemeinde im Neutestamentlichen Zeitalter* (Tübingen, 2d ed. 1934) 26, 58.

2. THE PSEUDEPIGRAPHA

These writings are called Pseudepigrapha because they were written by someone other than the stated author. They do not base their authority on Scripture; instead they claim to be revelations received by some famous person in antiquity.[6] Consequently, they contain almost no direct exposition of Scripture.

We will study the allusions to the OT in the apocalyptic writings,[7] which constitute the majority of the Pseudepigrapha.[8] These books actually borrow much of their material from the OT, especially historical material.[9] The way the OT is translated and applied reveals a particular understanding and interpretation of OT stories and institutions. In the apocalyptic writings the supposed author, to whom God's cosmic plan was disclosed in a special revelation, foretells the course of history period by period, most often in figurative language.[10] The dominant theme in these historical accounts is faith in God's cosmic plan in which everything from the very beginning has its prescribed place and purpose in the course of world events.[11] These accounts have been written to stimulate this faith and not simply to create confidence in the prophecies they contain. Faith, then, will sustain the saints in the present affliction. This faith is not the enthusiastic confidence in God's control of history that the Maccabeans drew from biblical history, but a serenity that is oriented toward the next world where all that is in progress here has been completed already. We do not find any typology between the individual periods of history that would be obvious to idealistic thought; but, as might be expected from what we have just said, there is a relationship between an upper and a lower world in accordance with the teaching of Philo.

OT history is used in a different way in the *Testaments of the Twelve Patriarchs*, which, in view of their general character, must be classified as apocalyp-

---

6. Ibid., 5; W. Bousset, *Die Religion des Judentums im Späthellenistischen Zeitalter* (Tübingen, 1926) 129f.

7. Noncanonical apocalyptic writings: *1 Enoch* (concerning its origin and composition see P. Volz, *Eschatologie*, 16ff.; P. Riessler, *Altjüdisches Schriftum ausserhalb der Bibel* [Augsburg, 1928] 1291f.); *2 Enoch* (first century A.D.); *Assumption of Moses* (about the time of Christ's birth); *Apocalypse of 2 Baruch* (A.D. 70-90); *Apocalypse of 3 Baruch* (?); *Apocalypse of Abraham* (ca. A.D. 100); *4 Ezra* (A.D. 96-98); *Book of Adam and Eve* (?); *Apocalypse of Moses* (?).
In addition: *Testaments of the Twelve Patriarchs* (?); *Jubilees* (?); *Ascension of Isaiah*. (The vision has been greatly revised by a Christian, but the legend of his martyrdom is of Jewish origin. See Riessler, *Altjüdisches*, 1300f.)

8. Other pseudepigrapha: the *Psalms of Solomon*, which are filled with the spirit of Pharisaism (ca. 50 B.C.), and the *Sibylline Oracles* (a collection spanning centuries, partly Jewish and partly Christian in origin; see W. Bousset, "Sibyllen und Sibyllinische Bücher," *RE* [Leipzig, 3d ed. 1896-1913] 18. 270ff.), are important only because of their eschatology. On the *Epistle of Aristeas*, see below.

9. Volz, *Eschatologie*, 5; G. F. Moore, *Judaism in the First Centuries of the Christian Era* (Cambridge, 1927-30) 2. 321.

10. See Dan 2:29-45; chaps. 7, 8, 10–11; *1 Enoch* 83–90; 93:1-10; 91:12-17; *Apocalypse of Baruch* 53–74; *Assumption of Moses* 1–6.

11. See Volz, *Eschatologie*, 6ff.

tic. These autobiographies are a rather free expansion of the Genesis narratives and are placed into the mouths of the twelve sons of Jacob. They provide examples of virtue and its resultant blessing, of vice and its appropriate punishment. The moralistic tendency of the treatment is also indicated by the warnings and admonitions that are added to the individual biographies. Consequently, the historical narrative of the Bible is filled out in the manner of a haggadic midrash in order to give ethical guidance.[12]

The book of *Jubilees* is the "classic model of this Haggadic treatment of Scripture."[13] It is included in this class of literature because of its form. It is not the way the history recorded in Genesis 1 to Exodus 12 is applied but the way it is developed that makes it distinctive and very effective. Special prominence is given to Israel's privileged position among the nations and to the eternal significance of the Law.[14]

The historical accounts in the apocalyptic writings normally conclude with a vision of the end. The eschatology in this literature is unusually varied. Ideas that belong to the expectation of an earthly Jewish-nationalistic messianic kingdom are placed alongside of and even combined with ideas that look for a superterrestrial, other-worldly, eternal kingdom of God. These elements of a nationalistic eschatology are intermingled with those of an eschatology that is individualistic and universalistic. In contrast to rabbinic eschatology the latter elements are predominant in the apocalyptic writings. The proportions are reversed with the rabbis.[15] This correlation suggests that the eschatology of the apocalyptic writings and rabbinic eschatology should be studied together.

The content of the apocalyptic writings is primarily a review of history and a hope for the future. The remainder is devoted to cosmological speculations and to instruction and exhortation.[16]

3. THE RABBINICAL WRITINGS

a. The Sources

The apocalyptic writings represent an impressive movement in late Judaism that is especially important for an understanding of NT ideas, although it did not spread beyond a rather narrow circle.[17] Palestinian Judaism was known far and

---

12. See Schürer, *History* 2/3. 114ff.; Kautzsch, *Apokryphen* 2. 458f.; Moore, *Judaism* 1. 190ff.; Volz, *Eschatologie*, 30ff.

13. Schürer, *History* 2/1. 341.

14. Ibid., 2/1. 341ff.; 2/3. 134-41; Moore, *Judaism* 1. 193-99.

15. Volz, *Eschatologie*, 4, 8, 51; Moore, *Judaism* 2. 321.

16. On cosmological speculations see, e.g., *1 Enoch* 38-44; 72-82; 108; *2 Enoch* 4-21. On instruction and exhortation see, e.g., *2 Enoch* 39-66.

17. One must not be misled by the widespread popularity of this literature among Christians. Concerning the value of apocalyptic and rabbinical literature for our knowledge of late Judaism, Volz is completely right when he says, "I do not consider it to be correct to play one off against the

wide for its study of Scripture. It is typical of the kind of exposition that was practiced in the synagogues every Sabbath and was the basis for the organization of every aspect of community life.[18] This method of interpretation was passed on to Jesus and his disciples and all the Jewish-Christian authors of the NT directly through experience, if not by formal education, as in the case of the apostle Paul.[19]

There are no records of rabbinic teaching and exegesis earlier than the end of the second century. The ideas in these writings, however, did not originate with the authors, for they are a collection of traditions that are often centuries old. The authors have added to many of the sayings information that is generally reliable and that, along with other distinguishing features, enables one to determine the date of their origin. Moreover, this method of interpretation is so bound by tradition that it has remained virtually unchanged in spite of many developments and refinements.[20] This rabbinical literature is extremely vast and diverse and spans almost a millennium. We must determine which part of this literature, in terms of its nature and date, will be most helpful in the solution of our problem.

First of all, we must distinguish between halakic and haggadic material on the basis of content. Halakah (הֲלָכָה) is that which is in common use, i.e., traditional law. Therefore, halakic exegesis consists in the derivation of legal prescriptions from the written law.[21] All other material falls in the domain of haggadah. Haggadot (הַגָּדוֹת or אַגָּדוֹת) are for the most part the historical and ethical-religious teachings that have been developed by means of a rather free adaptation of sacred Scripture.[22] Accordingly, haggadic exegesis is the treatment of sacred Scripture that aims at finding such teachings.[23]

The nature of haggadah is aptly described in the frequently quoted statement in Zunz: "The haggadah, whose aim it is to bring heaven nearer to men and to lift men up to heaven, fulfills its calling, on the one hand, by glorifying God

---

other or to emphasize the value of one at the expense of the other" (*Eschatologie*, 10; cf. G. Kittel, *Die Probleme des palästinensischen Spätjudentums und das Urchristentum* [Stuttgart, 1926] 14f.; Moore, *Judaism* 1. 127).

18. L. Zunz, *Die gottesdienstlichen Vorträge der Juden* (Berlin, 2d ed. 1892) 341ff.; Kittel, *Probleme*, 12f. On the work of the scribes, see Schürer, *History* 2/1. 320ff. He states that they were principally occupied with the Law and, therefore, were primarily lawyers. They had to formulate the Law with ever increasing accuracy, teach it to their students, and administer it in practice as judges in the court of justice. They also engaged in haggadic exegesis (pp. 326ff.), and they cared for the preservation of the text of Scripture. See also J. Jeremias, "γραμματεύς," *TDNT* 1. 740ff.; K. Rengstorf, "διδάσκω," *TDNT* 2. 139.

19. Moore, *Judaism* 1. 131.

20. Kittel, *Probleme*, 7ff.; Moore, *Judaism* 1. 131.

21. Schürer, *History* 2/1. 330ff.

22. Zunz makes a distinction between historical haggadah (the free elaboration of biblical history, *Gottesdienstlichen Vorträge*, 127ff.), ethical haggadah (e.g., Sirach; ibid., 105ff.), and exegetical haggadah (ibid., 180ff.).

23. Schürer, *History* 2/1. 339ff. On its relationship to halakah, see Zunz, *Gottesdienstlichen Vorträge*; to halakah, see ibid., 61, 334f.

and, on the other hand, by comforting Israel. Hence religious truths, moral lessons, discourses on just reward and punishment, inculcations of the laws in which the nationality of Israel is manifested, pictures of the past and future greatness of Israel, scenes and stories from Jewish history, parallels between the divine institutions and those of Israel, encomiums on the Holy Land, inspiring narratives and manifold consolations constitute the primary content of the homilies in the synagogues."[24]

This analysis of content clearly indicates that we can hope to find typological interpretation of the OT only in the haggadah. Therefore, the halakah will be excluded from our further considerations. We maintain that this branch of biblical interpretation, which was the more important one for Judaism, has no parallel whatever in the NT use of Scripture; it fell into disuse when the theocratic community and the reign of the Law collapsed.[25]

Where is haggadah found? The Mishna is a codification of the halakah that was prepared by Rabbi Judah ha-Nasi ca. A.D. 200. Only in the tractate *Pirke Aboth* and in the teachings and consolations with which several of the tractates conclude does it contain any haggadah, and it has no haggadic exegesis.[26] The situation is similar in the Tosefta, which came a little later; it contains baraita, which is halakah that is not included in the Mishna.[27] The halakic midrashim should also be classified as baraita. These have only been preserved in fragments from third-century editions. They consist of two commentaries on the books Exodus through Deuteronomy that originated in the schools of Akiba and Ishmael. Because of the nature of the content of these biblical books, the commentaries primarily present halakah; nevertheless, they also contain much haggadah because the poetic and historical portions are not overlooked.[28] The Mishna marks the end of the first period of scholarship, the Tannaite period, which spanned approximately 250 years. The Amoraim, the scholars of the following period, are bound by the tradition of the Tannaim.[29] It was through their labors on the Mishna that the Talmud gradually arose. (The Palestinian

---

24. Ibid., 362.

25. See A. Schlatter, *Das Alte Testament in der johanneischen Apocalypse* (Gütersloh, 1912) 104f., 107; see also Jeremias, "γραμματεύς," *TDNT* 1. 74. (In our study, the ceremonial law constitutes a special exception.)

26. On this and what follows see G. F. Moore, "Mischna, Talmud und Midrasch," *RGG* (2d ed. 1927-32) 4. 34ff.; F. Weber, *System der altsynagogalen palästinensischen Theologie* (Leipzig, 1880) XVff.; H. L. Strack, *Introduction to the Talmud and Midrash* (New York, 1959). In Zunz, *Gottesdienstlichen Vorträge*, there is a careful compilation of the passages referred to. On haggadah in the Mishna see ibid., 90f.; Moore, *Judaism* 1. 115ff., 156ff.

27. Zunz, *Gottesdienstlichen Vorträge*, 91f.; see Moore, *Judaism* 1. 154f.

28. Zunz, *Gottesdienstlichen Vorträge*, 87; Strack, *Introduction to Talmud*, 206ff.; Moore, *Judaism* 1. 135-48. Here is where the Mekilta of Rabbi Ishmael belongs that is frequently quoted below. It is a commentary on Exodus.

29. On the relationship of the Amoraim to the Tannaim see J. Klausner, *Die Messianischen Vorstellungen des jüdischen Volkes im Zeitalter der Tannaiten* (Berlin, 1904) 1; Strack, *Introduction to Talmud*, 3ff.

Talmud was put into writing in the fourth century, and the Babylonian Talmud ca. A.D. 500.)

In addition to halakah both Talmuds contain a large amount of haggadah—expositions, sayings, stories, sagas, parables, exhortations, etc.[30] Since the haggadah is not bound by tradition, it was not included in the collection of the Mishna. It was transmitted to future generations largely in the haggadic midrashim that were edited from the sixth century on. The exegetical midrashim are running commentaries on individual biblical books; the homiletical midrashim contain expositions of individual biblical passages.[31]

The haggadah of the Tannaim, which arose in the time of the NT, is included in our study.[32]

b. The Interpretation of Scripture in the Haggadah of the Tannaim

Because the haggadah is not obligatory, it is not bound, like the halakah, to strict rules or traditional principles of interpretation.[33] It does, however, employ the seven rules that Hillel laid down for halakic exegesis (later Ishmael reorganized them into thirteen).[34] Some of Eliezer's thirty-two rules are intended exclusively for haggadic exposition.[35] But no conclusions as to whether the rabbis interpreted Scripture typologically can be drawn from these rules that govern the logic of deduction. For this we will have to examine the content of their expositions.

Haggadic exegesis is not scientific exposition; it is the application of Scripture to the problems and phenomena of the day.[36] Nevertheless, the debates about the

---

30. Zunz, *Gottesdienstlichen Vorträge*, 98ff. These haggadic sections are included in the translations by A. Wünsche (*Der Babylonische Talmud in seinen haggadischen Bestandteilen wortgetreu übersetzt und durch Noten erläutert* [Leipzig, 1886-89]; and *Der Jerusalemische Talmud in seinen haggadischen Bestandteilen zum erstenmal ins Deutsche übertragen* [Zürich, 1880]).

31. Zunz, *Gottesdienstlichen Vorträge*, 184ff.; Moore, *Judaism* 1. 161-72.

32. W. Bacher, *Die Agada der Tannaiten* (Strassburg, 1884-90) is a collection of the haggadah of the Tannaim in chronological order together with the names of the authors. We will work from this collection supplemented with datable materials that are available from other sources. There is a chronological survey of the Tannaim (following Strack) in Volz, *Eschatologie*, XIV; cf. Schürer, *History* 2/1. 341ff.; Strack, *Introduction to Talmud*, 109ff.

33. Zunz, *Gottesdienstlichen Vorträge*, 61, 334f.

34. Strack, *Introduction to Talmud*, 93ff.

35. On Eliezer's 32 rules, see ibid., 95ff. On the rules for haggadic exegesis, see Zunz, *Gottesdienstlichen Vorträge*, 337-40; Strack, *Introduction to Talmud*, 93; Schürer, *History* 2/1. 347f. Zunz (*Gottesdienstlichen Vorträge*, 338f.) has made a collection of these and many other formal aids by which exegesis was applied to the text.

36. Zunz (ibid., 337f.) says, "This (the haggadah) is not primarily engaged in explaining the literal meaning or in rational hermeneutics, which had already been the concern of the earliest unsophisticated studies, the versions and scientific research, but in the free application of the content of the Bible to contemporary needs and opinions. Everything was brought into the confining but sacred room of the past, before which the present bowed in reverence and on which its heart depended."

I. Ziegler ("Die haggadische Exegese und der einfache Wortsinn," *MGWJ* ns 7 [1899] 149) says, "This spirit (the haggadic) which has continued to our day and which prevails even now in

meaning of individual words, phrases, and verses are evidence of an earnest struggle to discover "what is written."

The Tannaim endeavored to understand every detail in the records of Israel's history and to highlight the greatness of the past by this kind of interpretation. The two schools of that time went about this in different ways. While Ishmael wanted to interpret Scripture and the events recorded in the most simple and natural way possible, Akiba, like most of the rabbis, sought to draw from every word and letter as many secrets as he could and, as much as possible, to embellish the history with the miraculous.[37] In order to make the biblical history as full as possible, a chronology was added, anonymous persons were given names, dialogues were inserted, and various characters were combined.[38]

The Tannaim attempted to make this history more directly relevant for the times by a cautious and limited use of symbolical and allegorical interpretation, but above all by adding homiletical remarks liberally.[39] This method of interpretation that finds a meaning more profound than the literal sense is frequently compared with the typological interpretation found in the NT. For this reason we will give a few examples of it here.

Eliezer ben Hyrcanus (ca. A.D. 100) interprets the holding high of Moses' hands in Exod 17:11 as symbolic of holding fast in the future to the teaching given through Moses. And surely we are to complete the thought by concluding that this will have the same happy consequences for Israel as did the holding high of Moses' hands. An analogous interpretation was given to the letting Moses' hands fall.[40]

Two interpretations handed down by Eleazar of Modiim (died A.D. 130) are on the borderline between symbolical and allegorical interpretation. In both of these his usual conciseness of expression makes it uncertain whether his exposition is intended to be an allusion to the symbolical meaning of the events

---

Jewish pulpits seeks to discover in sacred Scripture whatever is new in contemporary thought. What marvelous familiarity with the text, what a blaze of wit, what profound absorption in the biblical word this requires will be obvious to anyone who simply reads a page of midrash carefully." He also says (p. 160), "Their exegesis was not covered with the dust of the study, having no connection with the real (outer) world and devoted only to the ingenuity of the exegete, like our exegesis of the Holy Scriptures; the haggadist speaks from the people and for the people. Every one of his interpretations has in it the authority of the common language."

37. On the controversy between Joshua ben Hananiah and Eleazar from Modiim and its counterpart in the next generation between Ishmael and Akiba, see Bacher, *Agada der Tannaiten* 1. 203ff., 215ff., 308f.; also pp. 224f.

38. On the chronology, see ibid. 1. 157f. Care was taken to protect Israel's great personages from any defamation, ibid. 1. 225 and 116.

39. This kind of homiletics, the basing of a general idea on a text by relating it to some peculiarity of that text, is "the most common kind of haggadic interpretation" (ibid. 1. 123; examples are given on pp. 123ff.).

40. *Mek. Exod.* 17:11 (J. Winter and A. Wünsche, *Ein Tannaitischer Midrasch zum Exodus* [Leipzig, 1909] 171; cf. Bacher, *Agada der Tannaiten* 1. 108). In a similar way Eleazar and Joshua ben Hananiah seek by means of symbolical interpretation to discover a deeper meaning for the measures taken in Exod 13:18 (*Mek. Exod.* 13:18; see Winter and Wünsche, *Tannaitischer Midrasch*, 75).

reported or a description of actual happenings that are hidden under the figurative form of the narrative. "Rabbi Eleazar says, 'Then came Amalek': because Amalek went in under the wings of the cloud and carried away some of the Israelites and killed them, as it says (Exod 25:18). . . ."[41] Bacher explains, "Amalek's attack is directed against the weak souls in Israel, whom he snatches from the sphere of God's protection—the supernatural protecting cloud—and kills."[42] The exposition of Exod 17:9 handed down by Eleazar continues this reinterpretation of history: " 'Tomorrow I will stand' . . . Rabbi Eleazar of Modiim says, Tomorrow we will observe a day of fasting and we will be ready because we rely on the deeds of our fathers and mothers. 'Top' [ראש] refers to the deeds of our fathers, 'hill' [גבעה] refers to the deeds of our mothers."[43] Eleazar finds another allusion to such reliance on the deeds of the fathers in the remark that Moses' hands were supported by a stone (Exod 17:12). Moses' hand becoming heavy signifies that prayer has been made difficult by the sins of Israel.[44] Accordingly, the story of the Amalekites is meant to say that Moses rescued the Israelites from destruction by the Amalekites through fasting and prayer, which were made difficult for him by Israel's sins, but were made easier by appeal to the fathers.

Eleazar expounds Exod 15:27 in a similar way: " 'And they encamped there by the water.' This teaches that the Israelites busied themselves with the words of the Torah, which were given to them at Marah."[45] Although these interpretations border on allegory, they show great reserve. The narrative is only transformed slightly; it does not fade into a universal idea as in Philo.[46]

As a kind of appendix, we include an interpretation that is considered typological by Bacher and others. Eleazar, whom we have referred to above, comments on Exod 15:27, "When the Holy One, blessed be He, created his world, he created there twelve springs corresponding to the twelve tribes of Jacob and seventy palm trees corresponding to the seventy elders."[47] He is thinking, however, of God's providence rather than his prophetic activity. But even if it were

---

41. *Mek. Exod.* 17:8, quoted from Winter and Wünsche, *Tannaitischer Midrasch*, 168.

42. Bacher, *Agada der Tannaiten* 1. 211.

43. *Mek. Exod.* 17:9, quoted from Winter and Wünsche, *Tannaitischer Midrasch*, 170.

44. *Mek. Exod.* 17:12, ibid., 172; cf. Bacher, *Agada der Tannaiten* 1. 212. On the practical aim of this interpretation, see below, pp. 36f.

45. *Mek. Exod.* 15:27, quoted from Winter and Wünsche, *Tannaitischer Midrasch*, 151.

46. There are isolated instances of allegorical interpretations of nonhistorical material; see Bacher, *Agada der Tannaiten* 1. 39 (Eccl 9:8), and p. 149 (Gen 40:10). Winter and Wünsche (*Tannaitischer Midrasch*, 122) quote a saying handed down from Akiba in *Mek. Exod.* 15:2: "The peoples of the world ask the Israelites, 'What is your beloved more than another beloved that you adjure us?' (Cant 5:9)." This saying shows that Akiba interpreted the Song of Solomon allegorically: the friend is God, the beloved is Israel, and the chorus of women is the Gentile nations. See Bacher, *Agada der Tannaiten* 1. 318f.; cf. p. 293. The amount of reserve that was shown concerning allegory is indicated by the tradition that Ishmael, Akiba's great rival who always stressed the literal meaning, will allow allegorical interpretation in but three passages in the Torah (*Mekilta Exodus*, Winter and Wünsche, *Tannaitischer Midrasch*, 260; cf. Bacher, *Agada der Tannaiten* 1. 247ff.).

47. *Mek. Exod.* 15:27, quoted from Winter and Wünsche, *Tannaitischer Midrasch*, 151.

a prophetic act, it would only be a sign and not a prefiguring, which is what true typology is.

By means of symbolical interpretation a deeper meaning and an intrinsic reason is sought for legal regulations and customs that outwardly seem arbitrary or curious. A number of ingenious interpretations of this kind have been preserved for us from Johanan ben Zakkai, the great disciple of Hillel who taught in Jerusalem until he fled, just before the city was captured.[48] The regulation requiring the piercing of the ear of a slave who, after completing his time of service, does not wish to be set free has the following meaning: "An unworthy person who has heard that the Israelites were to be servants of God alone (Lev. 25:55) and yet has taken a strange yoke on himself shall carry on his ear the sign of his degradation."[49] Concerning Exod 20:25 he says, "Iron, which was used for weapons of warfare and so is a reminder of divine judgment, must not be used in the construction of the altar, which signified reconciliation with God."[50] As a general principle, however, the following statement was considered valid: The laws are "regulations of the Most Holy One, and no justification should be sought for them."[51]

The interpretation of Scripture by the Tannaim is not restricted to the literal sense and is made up almost exclusively of these careful and restrained symbolical and allegorical interpretations of biblical history and the clothing of external customs with symbolical meaning. Their cosmological and theosophical speculations about the creation account and about Ezekiel 1 are intended for limited circles of the initiated.[52]

In large measure the eschatology and messianism of the scribes fits into this category. The statements of the Tannaim about eschatology revolve mostly around questions about the time of the end, the duration of the messianic kingdom, and the company of those who are destined for salvation. In contrast to the apocalyptic writings, the majority of these eschatological statements are associated more or less closely with biblical sayings. Since the haggadic method of interpretation was rather free, it is not surprising that in the time of the Tannaim statements about the end were even added to many passages of Scripture that originally were not intended to be eschatological or messianic.[53] We will have an opportunity to make a detailed comparison with NT methods in our study of

---

48. Bacher, *Agada der Tannaiten* 1. 25f.

49. According to *t. B. Qam.* 7:5 (ibid. 1.130f.). A different interpretation is given in *b. Qidd.* 22b (L. Goldschmidt, *Der Babylonische Talmud* [Berlin, 1930-36] 6. 579f.) and *Mek. Exod.* 21:6 (Winter and Wünsche, *Tannaitischer Midrasch*, 241).

50. According to *t. B. Qam.* 7:6 (Bacher, *Agada der Tannaiten* 1. 31; cf. Str-B 1. 283). For other similar interpretations see Bacher, *Agada der Tannaiten* 1. 31-36, 334ff. The etymological interpretation of the daily offering of two lambs (Num 28:3), which was debated by the schools of Shammai and Hillel, borders on allegory (ibid. 1. 19f.).

51. Johanan ben Zakkai (ibid. 1. 41, from *Pesiq.* 40a).

52. See ibid. 1. 17, 43, 135-39, 177-79, 339-48 (cosmology). Akiba specifically forbids the sharing of such matters with the unlearned.

53. Volz, *Eschatologie*, 9f., 51.

the NT. In the following survey, we will only seek to determine the extent to which typology was used as a method of interpretation in the eschatology of late Judaism.

4. THE ESCHATOLOGY

We have surveyed nearly the entire range of the thought of Palestinian Judaism. We have noted a variety of uses of Scripture, but have discovered very little typology. Now, however, in the sphere of eschatology we discover a great wealth of Scripture interpreted typologically. We see that the diversity of eschatological ideas did not originate in abstract thinking but from the contemplation of history, primarily biblical history. In the apocalyptic writings, the idea of the end in which everything will be changed clearly develops from the descriptions of the present distress that come at the conclusion of those accounts of history. It is even more impressive to observe that the messianic hope of the Tannaim has developed in a way that exactly parallels contemporary events.[54] The universal longing of mankind for the reversal of the present distress and the restoration of what has been lost has had an obvious effect on the formation of these ideas of the future.[55] The direct influence of this movement spread as a reflection of the

---

54. The messianic ideas of the Tannaim varied in intensity and form under the influence of contemporary events. The first generation of Tannaim, who died before the destruction of the second temple, show almost no interest in messianism, as far as can be ascertained from the few sayings which have been handed down to us (*Die Messianischen Vorstellungen*, 3; neither does Bacher find any messianic sayings from this period). The messianic hope was awakened by the great national disaster of A.D. 70 and, of course, was given a political cast (ibid., 4f.; Volz, *Eschatologie*, 175f., 186). Akiba must have been the spiritual leader of the revolt in A.D. 130 inasmuch as he proclaimed Bar Cochba as the Messiah, although, contrary to every messianic tradition, he was not a descendant of David nor was he distinguished for his miracles or piety (Bacher, *Agada der Tannaiten* 1. 92, 291; cf. pp. 292f., 319, 332f.; cf. ibid. 2. 557; Klausner, *Die Messianischen Vorstellungen*, 7f.). A large number of messianic sayings from the scribes of this period are evidence of an outburst of the messianic hope (passages are given in ibid., 6; cf. Bacher, *Agada der Tannaiten* 1. 94, 144ff.; Volz, *Eschatologie*, 175f.). The defeat of Bar Cochba and its terrible consequences did not extinguish the messianic hope, but merely transformed it. Messianic sayings were handed down by the disciples of Akiba and Ishmael (Klausner, *Die Messianischen Vorstellungen*, 9f.). It was emphasized frequently that the coming of the Messiah would be preceded by a period of tribulation and degeneration (ibid., 11, 40; Bacher, *Agada der Tannaiten* 2. 145, 222, 236, 382). The coming of the Messiah retreats further into the future (Klausner, *Die Messianischen Vorstellungen*, 12; cf. pp. 29f.; cf. also Bacher, *Agada der Tannaiten* 2. 187f.). Probably the fate of Bar Cochba gave rise to the idea of a warlike Messiah from the tribe of Joseph who dies in order to make way for the Son of David (ibid. 2. 390; Klausner, *Die Messianischen Vorstellungen*, 91f.).

In all these variations certain basic elements are constant: The messianic kingdom is an earthly kingdom of definite duration that precedes the final (God's) kingdom (ibid., 26; on the duration of the messianic kingdom, see *ibid.*, 27-29; Bacher, *Agada der Tannaiten* 2. 472). In that kingdom, Israel will be admired as the center of the Gentile nations (Klausner, *Die Messianischen Vorstellungen*, 104). In its land paradisaical fruitfulness will prevail (ibid., 109ff.). The Messiah will be a mighty sovereign and an ethical personality towering above all other men, nevertheless, fully human and not divine (ibid., 70-72; Volz, *Eschatologie*, 176). Besides "Messiah" and "Son of God," the only other title that occurs frequently is "Menahem ben Hezekiah" (Klausner, *Die Messianischen Vorstellungen*, 67-69; Volz, *Eschatologie*, 173ff.).

55. See n. 54.

universal hope of mankind for the return of the golden age.[56] By looking into biblical history and by listening to biblical prophecy this universal hope was often transformed in late Judaism and elevated to a typological view. Many details in these portraits of the future are based on the belief that in the last days God will restore to the human race the work that is described in the story of creation and will consummate for Israel the work he began in the time of Moses and that he caused to prosper once again under David.

The biblical story of creation is certainly being considered typologically when it is not simply a renewal of the world that is expected, but clearly a second, new creation that will surpass the first in splendor.[57] This supposition is confirmed by the statement that the second creation will also be preceded by chaos and primordial silence.[58] The original paradisaical condition of creation is used extensively as a pattern for depicting the blessed conditions in the messianic kingdom and the second aeon.[59] At this very point, however, universal ideas and aspirations have had a much stronger influence than has the biblical story of creation, for the biblical story is much more cautious in this matter. The garden of God, paradise, is not a type out of the past; it is a present reality, though, of course, it is closed to mankind. It is located in the easternmost portion of the earth, or, according to others, in heaven, or between heaven and earth, and will be opened up to those who are perfect.[60]

There are many ways in which Adam is a prototype. The destiny which he brought on himself by his fall has become the lot of all mankind.[61] Since there is no typological heightening it would be better not to designate Adam in his fallen condition as a type of present humanity that bears his likeness. The original Adam may indeed be called a type of the perfect man in the new age, since it is said about him that he will gain paradise with its fruitfulness, childbirth without pain, the tree of life and immortality, the perfect glory ($\delta\acute{o}\xi\alpha$)—i.e., greater things than Adam had.[62] To enhance this eschatological hope, Adam's

---

56. See p. 19 n. 56.

57. "And the first heaven shall depart and pass away, and a new heaven shall appear, and all the powers of the heavens shall give sevenfold light (cf. Isa 30:26)" (*1 Enoch* 91:16; cf. 72:1; *2 Apoc. Bar.* 32:6; 57:2). See Volz, *Eschatologie*, 361.

58. "Then shall the world be turned into primeval silence seven days, like as at the first beginnings; so that no man is left" (4 Ezra 7:30; cf. *Sib. Or.* 5:480ff.; *2 Apoc. Bar.* 3:7).

59. Volz, *Eschatologie*, 413f., 415f.

60. Ibid., 414. On the location of paradise see *1 Enoch* 60:23; *2 Enoch* 31:1; *1 Enoch* 32:2; 77:3; *2 Enoch* 8; *2 Apoc. Bar.* 51:11. On the reopening of paradise see Volz, *Eschatologie*, 225f., 417; cf. *2 Enoch* 8–9.

61. They, like him, are victims of sin and death, *2 Apoc. Bar.* 17:2f.; 48:42f.; 54:15; 56:5f.; 4 Ezra 3:4ff.; 4:30; 7:118.

62. 4 Ezra 7:36; a tree of life for the resurrected Adam, *Apoc. Mos.* 28:4; childbirth without pain, *2 Apoc. Bar.* 73:7; "And the righteous and elect shall have risen from the earth and ceased to be of downcast countenance. And they shall have been clothed in garments of glory" (*1 Enoch* 62:15; cf. *Apoc. Mos.* 20:1, 2 where it is said of the first man: Eve grieved after she ate, "I was bare of the righteousness with which I had been clothed . . . I have been deprived of the glory with which I was clothed." For more about the glory of the first Adam see *Adam and Eve* 12ff.; cf. Volz, *Eschatologie*, 189f.

person and the creation in general are described more gloriously than in the biblical account. *2 Enoch* says, "Adam was created by God as a second angel, great and glorious" (30:12f.). The angels are to revere him as God's image.[63] We will have many more opportunities to observe how in the typological approach the type has been reshaped in view of the eschatological antitype.

This idea of the return of the original man—whether that return be typical or literal—influenced the development of the concept of the Son of Man, which is so significant in the NT.[64] In Daniel's vision, however, when the Son of Man appears with the wild beasts, one should scarcely seek an allusion to Adam's stay with the animals in paradise.[65] It is more likely that the statement about the preexistence of the Son of Man in the figurative language of *1 Enoch* resulted from the connection between the first man and the perfect man of the last days.[66]

Our last example from primeval history is the flood, which has often been used as a type of the final judgment. As in the time before the flood, so wickedness will be rampant also before the final judgment.[67] At the end the universe will be cleansed by a general conflagration just as the earth was once cleansed by the flood.[68] The flood is "the first end."[69] Accordingly, expressions are used in the description of the flood that ordinarily serve to describe the eschatological end of the world.[70] It is true typology when it does not speak merely of a repetition of this judgment, but of this judgment in a new form.

Just as the eschatological salvation and judgment of mankind is found prefigured in primeval history, so the end of Israel's history is found prefigured in the Mosaic period, the period when the foundations were laid for the people of God. It was the apocalyptic writers primarily who made use of primeval history, and the rabbis who made use of the Mosaic period. Although Eliezer ben Hyrcanus disagrees, Joshua ben Hananiah assumes that the final deliverance will also occur in the spring.[71] This deliverance will be so glorious that the deliverance from Egypt will be forgotten.[72] Israel's stay in the wilderness, before their

---

63. *Adam and Eve* 12–13.

64. On Daniel, see Volz, *Eschatologie*, 11ff.; on the figurative language of *1 Enoch*, see ibid., 21; on 4 Ezra, see ibid., 39f.

65. Daniel 7; see Volz, *Eschatologie*, 189f.

66. *1 Enoch* 37–71; see Volz, *Eschatologie*, 190.

67. "And unrighteousness shall again be consummated on the earth . . ." (*1 Enoch* 91:6; cf. *Jub.* 23:15ff.; *Adam and Eve* 49).

68. *1 Enoch* 106:17; *Adam and Eve* 49:3; see Volz, *Eschatologie*, 319, 337.

69. *1 Enoch* 93:4; cf. 10:2.

70. *1 Enoch* 83:3f.; cf. *Jubilees* 5.

71. "In that night they were delivered and in the same night they will be delivered in the future, as it says, 'This is the same night forever.' These are the words of Rabbi Joshua (ben Hananiah). Rabbi Eliezer (ben Hyrcanus) says, 'In that night they were delivered, but in the future they will be delivered in Tishri, as it says in Psalm 81:4 . . .'" (*Mek. Exod.* 12:42, quoted in Winter and Wünsche, *Tannaitischer Midrasch*, 49; cf. Bacher, *Agada der Tannaiten* 1. 145; Volz, *Eschatologie*, 370).

72. "The sages say, 'the days of your life' means in this world only, but 'all the days of your life' includes the days of the Messiah; this means that in them also one will think of the deliverance

sin with the golden calf, was regarded as the time of the nation's first salvation and the prototype of the future salvation. This is the reason for the extensive embellishment of the pentateuchal narratives that is mentioned above. The following examples are illustrative of this. In the messianic age, according to Eliezer ben Hyrcanus, Israel will be nourished miraculously just as in the Exodus from Egypt.[73] This same scholar vividly describes the sending of the manna as follows: "Come and see how the manna came down to the Israelites. A north wind swept the wilderness clean, and rain washed the earth. The dew arose, and by the blowing of the wind, was frozen into golden tables on which the manna fell. And what did the Israelites say? If the Holy One, blessed be He, prepared manna for those who made him angry, how much more will he give a good reward to the righteous in the new age."[74]

The experience at Sinai is also developed in a special way. The interpretation has been handed down from Eliezer ben Hyrcanus that among those who assembled at the foot of Mount Sinai there were no blind, mute, deaf, lame, or feebleminded.[75] It was generally expected that the same would be true in the last days.[76] "Rabbi Eleazar from Modiim says, . . . at the time when the Torah was given to the Israelites, all the kings of the earth trembled in their palaces . . . (they) came together to Balaam the evil doer. They said to him, 'Balaam, perhaps he will do the same thing to us that he did to the human race at the time of the flood. . . .' "[77] It is appropriate, then, for Sinai to be designated in various ways as the place where God will appear for the final judgment.[78]

---

from Egypt. Then Ben Soma (Simon ben Soma, at the beginning of the second century) said, 'Someday in the future the Israelites will not remember the Exodus from Egypt, for it says (Jer 16:14f.) . . .' " (*Mek. Exod.* 13:3, quoted in Winter and Wünsche, *Tannaitischer Midrasch*, 58; cf. Bacher, *Agada der Tannaiten* 1. 428). Also Eleazar ben Azariah (ca. 90-100) according to *Mek. Exod.* 13:2, Winter and Wünsche, *Tannaitischer Midrasch*, 57; cf. Bacher, *Agada der Tannaiten* 2. 142.

73. Ibid. 1. 319, following *Cant. Rab.* 1:8.

74. *Mek. Exod.* 16:13, quoted in Winter and Wünsche, *Tannaitischer Midrasch*, 157. This same scholar taught that the manna will be preserved for the messianic age, *Mek. Exod.* 16:33, Winter and Wünsche, *Tannaitischer Midrasch*, 164. Cf. Rabbi Eleazar ben Hisma (ca. 110 according to Str-B 4. 954) in *Mek. Exod.* 16:25, Winter and Wünsche, *Tannaitischer Midrasch*, 161. *2 Apoc. Bar.* 29:8: "And it shall come to pass at that self-same time that the treasury of manna shall again descend from on high. . . ." *Sib. Or. Proem* 86f.; 5:281f.; cf. 3:749 (passing over to the common conception of the food from paradise).

75. *Mek. Exod.* 20:18. The details are based exegetically on the literal wording, e.g., "From what (do I conclude) that there were no lame persons among them? Because it says, 'They stood at the foot of the mountain (Exod 19:17).' " Winter and Wünsche, *Tannaitischer Midrasch*, 222; Str-B 1. 594.

76. See *1 Enoch* 96:3; *2 Apoc. Bar.* 73:2f.; *4 Ezra* 7:121; Str-B 1. 593f.

77. *Mek. Exod.* 18:1, quoted by Winter and Wünsche, *Tannaitischer Midrasch*, 179. Akiba's fanciful depiction of the scene at Sinai has no eschatological depth (*Mek. Exod.* 19:4, ibid., 195; cf. Bacher, *Agada der Tannaiten* 1. 321f.). For elaborations of the wilderness wandering with eschatological features, see Volz, *Eschatologie*, 360. In the second century there was a notion which shows a rounding out of the total outlook. It was the idea that these miracles stopped, as in the beginning, after the transgression (with the golden calf); cf. Str-B 1. 594.

78. *1 Enoch* 1:4-7; cf. *2 Macc* 2:8. The description of the eschatological theophany includes a number of features from the theophany at Sinai (cf. Ps 97:2-5).

It is fully in accord with this trend of thinking when Moses, the first redeemer, is compared with the second redeemer, the Messiah. Of course, this is stated explicitly only in a late text (ca. A.D. 300).[79] The hope that Moses would return as redeemer must have been alive already in NT times.[80] Therefore, this eschatological motif and other aspects of the great importance Moses had for Judaism may have contributed to the glorification of Moses' person in late Judaism.[81]

David, in a way completely different from Moses, stands in the center of the typology associated with his time. The most fully developed picture of the Messiah from the middle of the first century B.C. is found in Psalms of Solomon 17 and 18. In them the promise given to the house of David (2 Sam 7:5ff.) is clearly presented as the basis of the messianic hope.[82] If in this picture the Messiah is expected to defeat his enemies, gather his people within the ancient borders, destroy the wicked, and establish righteousness and cultic purity, then OT prophecy, the allusions to David's kingdom, and the poet's aspirations are all in harmony. Besides "Messiah," the only other title for the king of salvation that is common among the Tannaim is "Son of David."[83] This title expresses the hope that David's dynasty will be restored.[84] The Messiah is frequently portrayed as David *redivivus* (occasionally as Hezekiah *redivivus*).[85] The proverb which states that proselytes will not be received in the messianic age any more than they were in the time of David and Solomon is an example of the typological approach to David's kingdom.[86]

Finally, we are dealing with a typological interpretation of biblical history when the powers hostile to Israel—Syria and Rome—are designated by the names of the nation's biblical enemies—Edom and Amalek, and when OT passages prophesying judgment on Edom and Amalek are applied in this way to contemporary foes and their imminent destruction.[87] Joshua ben Hananiah and Eliezer ben Hyrcanus find in Exodus 17 an allusion to the battle against Amalek in the messianic age and to his exclusion from salvation.[88] It is obvious, however, that they are thinking of Rome.[89] Only when Amalek is understood as referring to Rome does Eleazar's allegorical interpretation that is referred to above take on

---

79. *Pesiq.* 49b, quoted in Str-B 1. 69; cf. pp. 69f.

80. Cf. Mark 9:4 and p. 64 n. 17.

81. Sir 45:1ff.; *As. Mos.* 11:4ff.; *2 Apoc. Bar.* 17:4; see Volz, *Eschatologie*, 194f. and W. Bacher, *Agada der Tannaiten* 1. 116, 154, 210 (Jethro compares himself with Moses as the sun compared with a lamp), 321. Moses too is censured, ibid. 1. 218, 239; cf. p. 441.

82. See *Pss. Sol.* 17:4.

83. Klausner, *Die Messianischen Vorstellungen*, 67.

84. *Mek. Exod.* 16:32, Winter and Wünsche, *Tannaitischer Midrasch*, 164.

85. Volz, *Eschatologie*, 207.

86. Klausner, *Die Messianischen Vorstellungen*, 80; Str-B 1. 929.

87. See Volz, *Eschatologie*, 280.

88. See *Mek. Exod.* 17:16, quoted in Winter and Wünsche, *Tannaitischer Midrasch*, 178.

89. Bacher, *Agada der Tannaiten* 1. 146f., 152 n. 3: The haggadic equation of Amalek with Rome is shown, e.g., in the comment in *Mek. Exod.* 17:12, ". . . this sinful kingdom makes war from the break of day until evening. . . ."

its full meaning.[90] Not Amalek, which has long been extinct, but Rome is seeking to snatch the weak souls in Israel from the sphere of God's protection to destroy them. Men who are afraid of sin will have to oppose him.[91] This danger can only be averted by fasting and prayer and by appealing to the fathers.[92] But once such types are applied exclusively to the present, the true typology is lost and so is the heightening and the prophetic impulse.

The Sabbath is interpreted as an eschatological type more than any other OT institution. It is said that the Sabbath is one-sixtieth of the world to come, עוֹלָם הַבָּא[93] (i.e., the heavenly world of spirits).[94] Psalm 92, which was sung on the Sabbath by the Levites, is destined for that world because that world is all Sabbath and rest.[95]

Two basic ideas permit the picture of the last days to develop repeatedly from history; they are the ideas of restoration and consummation. Adam will be raised again (*Apocalypse of Moses* 28), Moses and Elijah, who were translated, will return,[96] the Messiah will come as David *redivivus* (or Hezekiah or Josiah *redivivus*), paradise will be reopened.[97] The hope that fallen institutions and abandoned places would be reestablished is a pallid form of the idea of restoration.[98]

---

90. See above, pp. 29f.

91. *Mek. Exod.* 17:9, quoted in Winter and Wünsche, *Tannaitischer Midrasch*, 170.

92. See Bacher, *Agada der Tannaiten* 1. 212; cf. ibid. 2. 572. This is the case also when Judith and Baruch utilize a story out of the past to portray the relationship of their people to the contemporary oppressors.

93. *b. Ber.* 57b, A. Wünsche, *Bibliotheca Rabbinica, Eine Sammlung alter Midraschim zum erstenmal ins Deutsche übertragen* (Leipzig, 1880) 86.

94. Str-B 4. 839f.

95. *M. Tamid* 7:4, following *b. Roš Haš.* 31a by Akiba (see Str-B 4. 839); cf. *Jub.* 50:9; *Adam and Eve* 51.

The hopes that were attached to the holy places and institutions are nothing more than the universal human longing for restoration and return: In the messianic age Jerusalem will be rebuilt in fabulous glory and immensity by God himself or by the Messiah (Str-B 4. 883f.). With respect to the temple, until the year 70 "it had generally been expected that the messianic age would augment the glory of the temple as much as it would add to the beauty and splendor of Jerusalem" (ibid. 4. 884f.). After that time it was hoped that the temple would rise again in greater glory (ibid. 4. 884). The idea that there would be no temple in God's perfect city (e.g., in Rev 21:22) "would simply have been unthinkable in the old synagogues" (ibid. 4. 884).

On the continuation of sacrifices in the messianic age, the opinions of the rabbis are divided. In an earlier period, the resumption of sacrifice was expected. In the time of the Tannaim, however, the view was propounded that only thank offerings would be presented in the messianic age. No sin offering would be necessary because there would no longer be any sin (ibid. 4. 885). The detailed account in the Mishna (*Yoma*) about the Day of Atonement, the high point of the entire cult, seems to be based on the expectation that the institution would be revived (see J. Meinhold, "Joma," in Beer-Holtzmann, *Die Mischna* [Giessen, 1912ff.] *Seder II, Tractate 5*, 27).

E. Lohmeyer (*Kolosser* [*Kritisch-exegetischer Kommentar über das Neue Testament*, 1930] 43ff.) concludes that in Judaism an idea of a re-presentation of eschatological events was associated with the ceremonies on the Day of Atonement. From the few passages which he quotes, however, this can only be conjectured with great reservation. (For the principal evidence, see the passage from the *Midr. Cant.* 8:8 [131b] in Str-B 2. 19; 4. 1067f. and the few parallel passages. They do not say anything about this. Furthermore, they are no earlier than the fourth century.)

96. See J. Jeremias, "Ἠλ(ε)ίας," *TDNT* 2. 931ff.

97. See n. 99.

98. See n. 95.

Faith in the consummation is associated with the hope for restoration as the other basic theme. By his creative power and saving purpose God will complete the work he began in creation and redemption in a new creative and redemptive act that will cause the first to pale by comparison. This is true typological thinking.

These two basic ideas were not the creation of late Judaism; they were adopted from the religious ideas of the OT.[99] They were greatly expanded in late Judaism, but they were no longer rooted deeply in OT faith. The genuine typological thought has been forced far into the background by the earlier point of view that was common to all mankind. For our study of the NT, however, it is extremely important to demonstrate that these ideas were current in the environment of the

---

99. Literature on interpretation in the OT, especially typology: Principles governing the ideas of "restoration" and "new creation" in the OT are found in O. Procksch, "Wiederkehr und Wiedergeburt," in *Das Erbe Martin Luthers und die Gegenwärtige theologische Forschung* (Leipzig, 1928). For a compilation of the most important materials on the idea of the restoration of creation in the end time, see H. Gressmann, *Der Messias* (Göttingen, 1929): the restoration of paradise, pp. 149-64 and 164-81; the restoration of the Mosaic period, pp. 181-88; the return of David, pp. 232-69; the return of Josiah, pp. 334-37.

The question about the nature of this typological thinking and its significance for OT eschatology cannot be separated from the larger issue of the origin of OT eschatology, which cannot be discussed here (see W. Eichrodt, *Theology of the Old Testament* [Philadelphia, 1961-67] 1. 385ff.). We agree with Eichrodt's position (ibid. 1. 390f.). Biblical typology has much greater significance for the formation of OT eschatology than Gressmann allows. He sees only the universal ideas of restoration. "However, the notion of a recurrence of the Mosaic period and its events . . . continues to be mysterious, since history does not repeat itself. This idea can most easily be explained as a pallid mythical conception of the renewal of the paradisaical age" (Gressmann, *Messias*, 183; cf. H. Gressmann, *Der Ursprung der israelitisch-jüdischen Eschatologie* [Göttingen, 1905] 219, 193). His position is similar concerning the return of David (Gressmann, *Messias*, 278ff.). Cf. this with O. Procksch (*Die letzten Worte Davids* ([Leipzig, 1913] 124): "All attempts to trace this hope [the messianic hope of the prophets of Judah] to foreign sources that cannot be found lose their justification when its origin in David's awareness of royalty can be demonstrated. This, of course, arose not out of his own intellect, but on the basis of divine decree" (2 Sam 7:27b). Instead, the typological idea of the consummation of God's redemptive plan appears to be the heart of OT eschatology. And as faith in the creation grew out of the revelation of God's mighty intervention in history (see Eichrodt, *Theology* 2. 50ff.), so the expectation of a new creation was united with assurance about the consummation of redemptive history. It was clearly stated that this hope envisioned the complete restoration of the ancient time of salvation, and this is also in conformity with general usage in the history of religions. The typological idea of the consummation of salvation is the core; the concept of restoration provides the appropriate clothing. The universal mythological ideas associated with it are decorative embroidery. Proof for this hypothesis cannot be given here.

We will refer to the most important passages in order to provide a brief summary and in order to comment on a few elements that are crucial for the study of the NT. It is significant that the idea of the restoration of paradise appears, as we mentioned above, almost exclusively in prophecies about the return of David or the restoration of the Mosaic period or some other time of salvation in history.

The earliest prophecies of salvation are associated with the figure of David: Gen 49:8-12; Num 24:17-19 (J); in these the vision of David and of the future David *redivivus* seem to be intertwined (similar to the royal psalms, cf. Psalms 2, 72, 110). The origin of the hope for the complete renewal of David's kingdom must be sought in the accounts in 2 Samuel 7 and 23:1-7 (cf. Procksch, *Die letzten Worte Davids*, 124). Amos already prophesies the restoration of "the booth of David that is fallen," i.e. (according to KAT on this passage), the kingdom of David that is fallen (Amos 9:11f. is certainly genuine; see KAT on this passage in contrast to Gressmann, *Messias*, 233f.).

According to the prophecies of Isaiah and Micah, the Messiah will not come from the reigning

dynasty of David but directly "from the stump of Jesse" (Isa 11:1) or from Bethlehem (Mic 5:2). As Gressmann concludes (ibid., 246, 249; also see KAT on Isa 11:1) he is not thought of as David's offspring, but as David himself who will come again (Isa 11:1-9; 9:1-6; 7:13-17; and Mic 5:1-5). In Ezek 34:23f.; 37:24f.; Hos 3:5f. (according to KAT, this passage is not from Hosea); Jer 30:8f. (according to KAT, this passage is not from Jeremiah) the Messiah is explicitly called David (he appears as David's offspring in Jer 23:5f.; Zech 3:8; 6:12).

In addition to the return of David, it seems that the pious and heroic king Josiah was expected to return also (cf. Jer 30:18-21; cf. esp. Gressmann, *Messias*, 334f.). He is the prototype for the prophecy in Zech 11:4-14; 13:7-9; (11:15-17); 12:1–13:1 about the dying Messiah-king who will rise again at the consummation of redemption (O. Procksch, *Die Kleinen prophetischen Schriften nach dem Exil* [Stuttgart, 1929] 111, 113f.; cf. Gressmann, *Messias*, 334ff.).

From the beginning, the Mosaic period was viewed in prophecy as the ideal period in the life of the nation (this was true already of Elijah, cf. 1 Kings 19, esp. v 8 with Exod 24:18; 1 Kgs 19:11 with Exod 33:22; 1 Kgs 19:12 with Exod 34:6; consider Jehu's association with Elisha and with Jehonadab the son of Rechab in 2 Kgs 1:15f.; Jer 35:6f.; and Amos 5:21-26; Hos 12:9, 13; 13:4; 9:10; etc.).

Hosea's prophecy expects the relationship between the God of Sinai and the people to be completely restored by the people being led back into the wilderness (Hos 2:14-18; cf. 12:9): After God and the people have recovenanted in the wilderness, they will march again through the Valley of Achor (cf. Josh 7:24-26) into the paradisaical land, "as in the days of her youth, as at the time when she came out of the land of Egypt." The threatened exile to Assyria will signify a second Egyptian bondage (Hos 8:13; 9:3; 11:15; Ezek 20:33-38).

Specific details from the Mosaic period appear in the picture of the future in Isaiah: Yahweh comes to Mount Zion in a pillar of smoke and flaming fire, Isa 4:5 (perhaps a later addition; cf. KAT); Exod 13:21f.; 19:16, 18; 24:15ff.; 40:34ff. Assyria will be destroyed in a second Passover night, Isa 30:27-33 (see KAT on this passage).

Jer 31:31-34 looks for a "new covenant" that is not simply a renewal of the covenant of Sinai, but rather its consummation (a true typology).

Deutero-Isaiah describes the deliverance from Babylon explicitly as the antitype of the liberation from Egypt. Assurance of the new deliverance grows in one's mind as one considers God's hand in the first deliverance (cf. Isa 43:16f. and 51:9f. with the crossing of the Red Sea in Exod 14:14). The new thing that God now creates will be so glorious that the old will no longer be remembered (Isa 43:18f.); God prepares a way through the wilderness for his redeemed people (Isa 43:19; 40:3-5; 41:14-20; 48:20f.; 49:9-11; 52:12; cf. Jer 16:14f., a later allusion, see KAT on this passage). As in the first Exodus, God will lead them through the wilderness and give them water from the rock to drink (Exod 17:6; Isa 48:21; cf. 49:10). From the rock the paradisaical water will flow (cf. Gen 2:10ff.) that will transform the wilderness into a paradise (Isa 41:17-20; cf. 43:19-21). The introduction of features from paradise produces the typological heightening; they make the new appear to be a state of perfection.

The same purpose is served when the concept of the restoration of paradise is introduced into the other prophecies about the restoration of the Mosaic period (cf. Hos 2:20) and about the return of David (cf. Amos 9:13; Isa 11:6-8 [v 9 speaks of sinlessness and knowledge of God; this same combination is found in Ezek 36:24ff., note v 35]; Mic 5:10-14; Ezek 34:25ff.).

The prophecies about a new Jerusalem that are based primarily on the idea of restoration are interpreted in a similar way: Isa 52:1f.; 54:1-3 (a large family), 11-17. It is in this connection that the consummation is first compared explicitly with "the garden of the Lord" (Isa 51:3; cf. Ezek 36:35); very likely Deutero-Isaiah has made use of J. This promise of salvation is based on Abraham, from whom God made a great nation (Isa 51:2). Deutero-Isaiah, as we have just observed, has prepared for the NT use of the terms "Jerusalem," "Zion," etc., in that "chiefly through him the words 'Jerusalem,' 'Zion', 'Jacob' and 'Israel' have become figurative terms for 'people of God' " (P. Volz, *Jesaia zweite Hälfte, Kapitel 46–66* [KAT; Leipzig, 1932] 2).

But above all, Deutero-Isaiah has been privileged to give to the NT messianic figure in whom Jesus saw the best prototype of himself—the Servant of the Lord (cf. Isa 42:1-7 [1-4, 5-9 respectively, according to Volz]; 49:1-16; 50:4 [9], 11; 52:13–53:12; and possibly 61:1-3). This figure embraces the entire messianic hope of the OT in all its depth, and Isaiah was permitted to see in this figure basic and essential features which seem to be based on a typological approach.

The title leaves various relationships unresolved: "Servant of the Lord" (עֶבֶד, LXX: δοῦλος Isa 49:3, 5; or παῖς 49:6; 52:13; cf. 42:1) is used in the OT as a title of honor for the king, especially for David (cf. 2 Sam 3:18; 7:4, 8, 19ff., 25ff.; 1 Kgs 3:6; 8:24ff.; 11:13, 32; Ezek 34:23; 37:24; Pss 78:70; 89:3, 20, 39; etc; of Solomon 1 Kgs 3:7-9, 8:28ff.), for the prophets (1 Sam 3:9f.; Amos 3:7; Jer 7:25; Ezek 38:17; Zech 1:6; cf. Mal 4:4; etc.), but also for certain godly individuals (1 Kgs 8:22f.; Joel 2:29; Pss 27:9; 31:16; 34:22; 35:27; etc.).

The Servant of the Lord in Deutero-Isaiah is primarily a prophetic figure. Divine election (Isa 49:1f., 5; cf. 42:1a) has destined him to turn Israel and the nations back to God (Isa 42:1b-4, 6f.; 49:1a, 2, 5f.; 50:4; 53:1). Jeremiah may have been the pattern from which the prophetic features of the Servant of the Lord were formed. He too has been chosen for his vocation "from the womb" (Isa 49:1; cf. 42:1 with Jer 1:5; cf. also the mission to the Gentiles as in Jer 1:10). His work, like Jeremiah's, seems to be unsuccessful (Isa 49:4; 53:1; cf. Jer 6:10, 29; 9:1). By his preaching he too brings persecution on himself (Isa 50:6f.; cf. 53:7, mistreatment; 59:8f., false accusation) and ultimately death (Isa 53:8f.; with this cf. Jer 11:15, 18-23; 12:5; 15:10, 15f.; 17:14f.; 18:18, 23; 29:[14-18], 7f., 10; cf. esp. Jer 11:19: "But I was like a gentle lamb led to the slaughter," with Isa 53:7). Nevertheless, he perseveres in his task—the proclamation of the word—(Isa 50:4f.) and he knows that he will not be disgraced, because the Lord is with him (Isa 50:7-9; cf. Jer 15:19-21; 17:16; 20:11).

The emphasis is no longer on the distress associated with his vocation as a prophet, but on the anguish and deliverance of the godly in general, an emphasis that is familiar to us from the Psalms and that is reminiscent of Jeremiah's prayers. In addition to the trouble the Servant of the Lord encounters because of his calling, he, like the godly people of the Psalms who suffer, is troubled also with natural afflictions, unattractive appearance, and sickness (Isa 53:2-4; cf. Isa 49:8 with Ps 69:13; Isa 53:3 with Pss 22:6; 69:7; Isa 53:10 with Ps 22:30). He truly suffers innocently because he is the righteous one (Isa 53:9, 11). The portraits of this godly person who suffers has none of the features that usually appear in such cases—no arguing with God (cf. Jer 20:14-18; 12:1ff.; etc.) and no cry for vengeance (cf. Jer 11:20; 15:15; 17:18; 18:21-23; 29:12; and similar passages in the Psalms). The "nevertheless" to which Jeremiah (cf. Jer 15:19-21; 17:16; 20:11) and the psalmist (cf. Ps 73:23ff.; etc.) were led after a hard struggle is present here in profound faith (Isa 50:7ff.). Because he is certain that God is with him, he knows that he will triumph and that his foes will be destroyed (Isa 50:7-11). He is able to do what no prophet could do, because he is and remains righteous and because he clings tenaciously to God. He can bear vicariously the sin of the people and as "the righteous one . . . make many to be accounted righteous" (Isa 53:4ff., 11).

He resembles a priest who offers himself as a sacrifice (cf. Isa 53:4ff. with Lev 4:1-4; etc.). He also performs the office of a priest when he prays for others (Isa 53:12) and preaches the Torah (Isa 42:1-4; cf. Hos 4:6).

As the psalmist predicted in faith (Ps 73:23ff.), he is the righteous one who is actually raised from the dead and appears as king of all kings (Isa 52:15). Even as the suffering one he bears royal characteristics (cf. Isa 52:14f.); he is anointed for his vocation (Isa 61:1) and comes as a representative of God's covenant (Isa 42:6). The penitent lament of the people (Isa 53:4ff.) is reminiscent of Zech 12:10ff. Like the king referred to there, so the Servant of the Lord comes forth as a good shepherd (Isa 53:6; cf. Jer 17:16). Gressmann is probably right in supposing that the figure of Josiah as a royal martyr has influenced the development of these two images; he, too, represented God's covenant to his people in a special way (Isa 42:6; cf. 2 Kgs 23:3; see Gressmann, *Messias*, 310; also see pp. 334ff.).

Thus the name "Servant of the Lord" seems to have made it possible for this figure to combine the features of the martyr prophet, the innocent sufferer (the priest), and the martyr king to form the picture of a true mediator of salvation. When the features characteristic of previous instruments of the covenant, purged of all that is contrary to God, are transferred to this new picture, we are justified in speaking of a pneumatic typology.

A typological approach to past redemptive history has had an influence in shaping prophecy, but this is only one of the ways the historical tradition has been interpreted and applied in the OT. The historical accounts extending from the Yahwist to the Deuteronomist are more than simply copies of the sources; they interpret the tradition in the light of the present situation of God's people. This interpretation of older historical tradition occurs within the framework of the OT through the work of the Chronicler. Although he uses other sources, he primarily edits the older canonical histories

early church; for example, that it was natural for them to view the Mosaic period typologically.[100]

The biblical exegesis of Palestinian Judaism, whose basic features continued primarily in the scholarship of the Pharisees, has, therefore, preserved OT material in its eschatology and in other things that it quotes from Scripture. The fact that, as a general principle, they took seriously the literal meaning and shut themselves off from the non-Jewish world contributed substantially to this. We move much further away from the realm of the OT when we turn now to Hellenistic Judaism's interpretation of Scripture. This had become allied with Hellenism, while the scholarship of the Pharisees had arisen in reaction to it.[101]

(see Sellin, *Introduction*, 236ff. and Schürer, *History* 2/1. 340f.). The same is true of Psalms that edit historical material. In Chronicles the figure of David is given special prominence, in the Psalms (esp. in Book IV, Psalms 90–106) the Mosaic period is stressed (on the history, see Zunz, *Gottesdienstlichen Vorträge*, 37, 125; *Enc. Jud.* 4. 619; on Chronicles, see G. von Rad, "Das Geschichtsbild des chronistischen Werkes," BWANT 4 (1930) 3.

The explanations of the names of people and places that are especially common in Genesis are examples of individual interpretations in the older books of the Bible (see Zunz, *Gottesdienstlichen Vorträge*, 179). (A. Schulz ["Exegese im Alten Testament," *Zeitschrift für Semitistik* 3 (1924) 178-93] attempts to find explanatory glosses which originally were in the margin and have been incorporated into the text.)

These are a few indications that the stream of biblical exegesis began in the OT itself. It can be traced further through the versions; the LXX and the Targums are by no means simply literal translations. They are interpretations and, therefore, substantial transformations of Scripture. On the LXX, see A. Gfrörer, *Kritische Geschichte des Urchristentums* (Stuttgart, 1831) 1/2. 8-18; S. Z. Frankel, *Über den Einfluss der palästinensischen Exegese auf die alexandrinische Hermeneutik* (Leipzig, 1851) 21; E. Zeller, *Die Philosophie der Griechen in ihrer geschichtlichen Entwicklung* (Leipzig, 1881) 3/2. 254ff.; C. Siegfried, *Philo von Alexandrien* (Jena, 1875) 16-19; P. Heinisch, *Der Einfluss Philos auf die älteste christliche Exegese* (Münster, 1909) 16f. On the Targums, see Zunz, *Gottesdienstlichen Vorträge*, 67f.; F. Weber, *System der altsynagogalen palästinensischen Theologie* (Leipzig, 1880) XVIff.; P. Seidelin, "Der Ebed Jahwe und die Messiasgestalt im Jesajatargum," *ZNW* 35 (1936) 194ff.

100. See J. Jeremias, *Jesus als Weltvollender* (Göttingen, 1930) 112f.: "It is a question of ideas that were daily bread for Judaism in the time of Jesus, when the Israelites in the wilderness were represented as a prototype of the messianic community of salvation, or Moses as a prototype of the redeemer." It is necessary to point out that our study above will afford a survey of the basic ideas, but not a complete reproduction of the material. Such are easily accessible from the indexes of Strack and Billerbeck, *Kommentar*, *TDNT*, and similar works once the basic outline has been established. A glance at the passages cited shows how this interpretation of history, like the other kinds of biblical exegesis, was extremely common in the later period. At the same time, we should point out that although the assembled material has been systematized, it has not been substantially deepened.

101. K. Rengstorf, "διδάσκω," *TDNT* 2. 142. Josephus stands midway between Palestinian and Hellenistic Judaism with respect to his use of Scripture. S. Rappaport (*Agada und Exegese bei Flavius Josephus* [Frankfurt, 1930]) has collected the examples of Josephus's treatment of Scripture from his writings and has investigated their origin by comparing them with the haggadah of Rabbinic and Hellenistic Judaism. (See Rappaport's characterization of Josephus's editing and exposition of biblical history, ibid., XXVIIf.; no factors appear other than those we meet also in Hellenistic and Palestinian Judaism.) According to everything we have been able to communicate above, we cannot expect to find any typology in Josephus, since he makes no eschatological statements. See A. Schlatter, *Die Theologie des Judentums nach dem Bericht des Josephus* (Gütersloh, 1932).

Chapter Three

HELLENISTIC JUDAISM

1. PHILO

a. General Characteristics

We begin our study of biblical interpretation in Hellenistic Judaism with a consideration of Philo, the most outstanding representative of this school of thought. Philo's system is a remarkable attempt to combine Hellenistic wisdom and Israelite religion. He adopted thoughts and ideas from almost every school of Greek philosophy, especially from Plato and the Stoics.[1] While he was very open to Greek philosophy, he always considered Holy Scripture to be the source of all wisdom. When he traced Greek wisdom to the Holy Scriptures and presented his philosophy in the form of an exposition of Scripture, he was following his convictions and was not simply making a concession to his fellow Jews who were bound to tradition.[2] What has actually happened, however, is that he has subordinated the faith of the OT to Greek philosophy.[3]

For him the Septuagint is Holy Scripture.[4] He believes that it corresponds exactly with the Hebrew original because he is convinced that the translators were also inspired (*Vit. Mos.* 2.37ff.). Moreover, he frequently bases his interpretation on the very passages that have been translated incorrectly from the original.[5] It is interesting to note that his use of Scripture is almost entirely confined to the Pentateuch. He wrote three large volumes of commentary on the Pentateuch, whereas in all of his Greek writings there are only twelve quotations

---

1. L. Cohn, *Schriften der Jüdisch-Hellenistischen Literatur in deutscher Übersetzung* (Breslau, 1909-38) 1. 14.

2. E.g., Heraclides borrowed from Genesis, *Leg. All.* 1.107; Zeno drew from Moses, *Omn. Prob. Lib.* 57; the Greek legislators borrowed from Moses, *Spec. Leg.* 4.61.

3. E. Schürer, *The History of the Jewish People in the Age of Jesus Christ* (New York, n.d.) 2/3. 368.

4. Cohn, *Schriften* 1. 10; C. Siegfried, *Philo von Alexandrien als Ausleger des Alten Testaments* (Jena, 1875) 142f.

5. Siegfried, *Philo*, 142; on the text of the quotations, ibid., 161f.

from the prophets, eighteen from the historical books, and nineteen from the Psalms.[6]

Philo's method of interpretation is not uniform. The method he chooses for a particular text is determined by his aim and purpose. But this is not adequate to explain all the variations. The more subtle differences in exegetical procedure (e.g., the various kinds of etymologies) and the inconsistencies and contradictions in his system can be fully explained only in terms of different sources.[7] For this reason the various methods of interpretation are frequently taken as a starting point for isolating sources in Philo's writings.[8] For our purposes, it is not essential that we know the origin of each of Philo's expositions; nevertheless, such studies do provide us with a valuable insight. They show us that we cannot view Philo as a solitary ingenious exegete, for he is a representative of and a compiler of the exegetical tradition of the Alexandrian school of Hellenistic Judaism in the time of Jesus. Furthermore, we are not concerned about minute details in the manner in which he makes his deductions, but about the principles that guide his interpretation of Scripture. We are looking for typology, and typology is an approach that is based on principles. Therefore, with the suggestion in mind that the inconsistencies in Philo's exegesis can be explained in terms of sources, we will survey the methods of interpretation that he employs in his two large exegetical works. In view of the situation we mentioned above, we will, in this way, gain a clearer picture than we would have were we simply to give a systematic survey of Philo's method of interpretation.

b. Biblical Interpretation in Philo's Writings

i. *Philo's Exposition of the Mosaic Law.* Of Philo's three great works on the Pentateuch there is one that will introduce us to most of the exegetical procedures he used. It is a systematic exposition of the Mosaic law in which he attempts to show its content, value, and importance.[9] The book is divided into three parts: an account of creation to demonstrate that the world and the Law are in harmony (*Op. Mund.* 3), an account of the lives of the patriarchs as constituting the unwritten laws (*Decal.* 1), and an account of the laws of Moses. The first part of the work is *De Opificio Mundi* (On the Creation), which in later editions was placed incorrectly at the beginning of the allegorical commentaries. Rather than follow the text of Scripture verse by verse, he chooses appropriate narrative

---

6. L. Cohn and P. Wendland, *Philonis Alexandrini Opera* (Berlin, 1896-1930) 7. 43; cf. A. Schlatter, *Geschichte Israels von Alexander dem Grossen bis Hadrian* (Stuttgart, 3d ed. 1925) 296; Cohn, *Schriften* 1. 13.

7. A. Gfrörer, *Kritische Geschichte des Urchristentums* (Stuttgart, 1831) 1/2. 1ff.; 1/1. 77f.; Schlatter, *Geschichte Israels*, 299f.

8. E. Stein, *Die allegorische Exegese des Philo von Alexandrien* (Giessen, 1929); I. Heinemann, *Philos griechische und jüdische Bildung* (*Fest.* zum 75. jahrige Bestehen des jüdischen theologischen Seminars; Breslau, 1929); M. Adler, *Studien zu Philo von Alexandrien* (Breslau, 1929).

9. Cohn and Wendland, *Philonis Alexandrini* 1. 1-60; 4. 1-118, 269-305; 5.

selections from primeval and patriarchal history that he retells and to which he adds his interpretations. In a similar way, he selects and classifies various laws.

The largest part of *De Opificio Mundi* (1-133) is not devoted to exposition, but to thoughtful explanations of how and why everything in creation happened as it did. The sequence of the creative acts, for example, is explained by the symbolism of numbers. The special emphasis on the seventh day seems appropriate because the number seven is so important in arithmetic, geometry, astronomy, and human life. It is also important because of its etymology (*Op. Mund.* 89-128). The juxtaposition of the two accounts of creation in Genesis 1 and 2 is explained by the fact that Genesis 1 records the creation of the ideal world in the Platonic sense, while Genesis 2 records the creation of the visible and material world. The story of the Fall is explained by psychologizing. In addition, particular expressions in the biblical account that seem to be mythological are interpreted figuratively (*Op. Mund.* 157). For example, the trees of the garden are spiritual values that confront man with a choice (*Op. Mund.* 153f.), and the serpent is greed (*Op. Mund.* 157ff.). Although psychologized in this way, the historicity of the event is preserved, even though it has little typological significance that shapes future history. It simply provides an instructive example indicating the way man can be defeated repeatedly by sin (*Op. Mund.* 152, 165f., 167-69). It is clear that the explanations and interpretations of the biblical account are drawn from philosophy and not from the Bible.

According to *De Abrahamo* (On Abraham) 5, the second part of this work presents seven persons from primitive times as the ideal incarnation of the unwritten laws (νόμοι ἄγραφοι, *Decal.* 1; *Abr.* 5). "But, since it is necessary to carry out our examination of the laws in regular sequence, let us postpone consideration of particular laws, which are, so to speak, copies (εἰκόνες), and examine first those which are more general and may be called the originals (ἀρχέτυποι) of those copies" (*Abr.* 3). Here, again we do not find commentary alone, but exposition and interpretation governed by this point of view. First of all, the biblical narratives about Enosh, Enoch, and Noah are interpreted so as to make these men representatives of three virtues (*Abr.* 7-47). The procedure is based on the etymologies of their names (*Abr.* 8, 17) and on peculiarities in the translation where the Septuagint has rendered the original incorrectly (*Abr.* 9, 18f.).

This kind of exposition is carried out for each of the three patriarchs with extensive commentary. The following statement is an example of Philo's method of interpretation: "Very properly, then, Moses thus associated these three together, nominally men (λόγῳ μὲν ἀνδρῶν), but really, as I have said, virtues (ἀρεταί)—teaching (μάθησις), nature (φύσις), practice (ἄσκησις)" (*Abr.* 54). The discussion about Abraham constitutes the largest part of the book that bears his name. The books about the other two patriarchs have been lost. Philo's methodology exhibits a fair amount of consistency and can be clearly seen in *De Abrahamo*. First of all, portions of the biblical narrative are told in such a way as to accentuate the features that serve as ethical models. To this recitation of the literal meaning with its symbolical application there is added from time to time a decidedly allegorical interpretation of the narrative in order to make it refer to psychological processes.

The allegorical interpretations are clearly set apart from what has gone before by means of introductory formulas, e.g., "Here we may leave the literal exposition and begin the allegorical."[10] Because of some external similarity, the principal features and persons in the narrative are reinterpreted in these allegorical expositions to make them expressions of and factors in psychic processes that are primarily ethical in nature. Philo's interpretation of Genesis 14 is an example of this: Four of the kings signifiy our four passions—pleasure, desire, fear, and grief. The other five represent our five senses (equal in number) because they rule over us. The five are subject to the four and pay them tribute; so from our senses arise the passions of pleasure, fear, etc. Conflict arises when the tribute is no longer paid; i.e., in old age when the senses become dull. "Two fell into the wells" means that touch and taste penetrate to the interior of the body. The other three "took to flight" means they are directed outside the body. "The wise man attacked them all" means that reason rushed upon them and conquered them (*Abr.* 236-44; cf. 217-24). Etymology is used extensively for drawing inferences. For example, etymology is used to draw from the narrative about the offering of Isaac the meaning that God restores to the one who does his will the gift of perfect happiness (Isaac = laughter = joy of the understanding), which belongs to God alone (*Abr.* 200-7).

Such an interpretation needs no further proof, because "Those who can contemplate fact stripped of the body and in naked reality, those who live with the soul rather than with the body," see this deeper meaning.[11] "But the story here told is not confined to the literal and obvious explanation, but seems to have in it the elements of a further suggestion obscure to the many but recognized by those who prefer the mental to the sensible and have the power to see it" (*Abr.* 200). Moreover, this has become the traditional way of interpreting (*Abr.* 99, 217).

It is not necessary to stress the fact that foreign elements are read into Scripture not only by allegorizing but also by symbolical interpretation. The important thing is not God's dealing with Abraham, but Abraham's virtue which God rewards with the approval it deserves. This is the same kind of virtue as is found in the Stoic sages. God's transcendent majesty and intelligence are accentuated, and in this way he is removed from the events of this world. The center of attention now is man, who by absorption in his psyche has ascended to the world of mind.

---

10. *Abr.* 118, τὰ μὲν οὖν τῆς ῥητῆς ἀποδόσεως ὧδι λελέχθω· τῆς δὲ δι᾽ ὑπονοιῶν ἀρκτεον . . .; cf. *Abr.* 68, 88, 99, 200, 217, 236.

11. *Abr.* 236, οἱ ψυχῇ μᾶλλον ἢ σώματι ζῶντες.

The lives of the three patriarchs incarnate the Stoic concept of the perfect sage. As an appendix Philo adds the story of Joseph, who is the model of the statesman. "The factors which produce consummate excellence (i.e., the ideal of the Stoic sages) are three in number: learning, nature, practice. And these names (ἐπώνυμοι) are represented in three of the wise men to whom Moses gives the senior place. Since I have described the lives of these three, the life which results from teaching, the life of the self-taught and the life of practice, I will carry on the series by describing a fourth life, that of the statesman. This name again has its representation in one of the patriarchs who, as Moses shows, was trained to his calling from his earliest youth" (*Jos*. 1). In Philo's opinion the statesman is merely an adjunct to the sages, who, as citizens of the world, live according to natural law.[12]

The first part of this book follows the same arrangement as *De Abrahamo*. The events in the life of Joseph are narrated section by section. The literal meaning of the biblical account is presented first, emphasizing only those ethical points that are important for the purpose of the treatise; then the allegorical interpretation follows. In the second part, which describes the dealings between Joseph and his brothers in Egypt, allegorical interpretation is completely lacking (*Jos*. 157-270).[13]

Philo's exposition of patriarchal history contains no typological interpretation at all. Whenever the historicity of the patriarchs has not been completely destroyed by allegory, they are presented as ethical "types," or ideals, and do not fit our definition according to which a type must point to something greater in the future.

The essay *De Josepho* (On Joseph) is followed immediately by *De Decalogo* (On the Decalogue; see *Decal*. 1). The commentary on the Ten Commandments is preceded by a description of the way in which the Law was given. In the last part of the book there is an enumeration of the particular laws and regulations that fall under each of the commandments (*Decal*. 154ff.). These laws and regulations are discussed in the same order in the four books that follow, *De Specialibus Legibus* (On the Special Laws). The primary concern of these books is to justify the Mosaic laws that were offensive or ridiculous to non-Jews by demonstrating their practicality and usefulness and by indicating their deeper symbolical meaning. Here allegorical interpretation falls decidedly into the background.[14] We look in vain in these books for any typological interpretation of OT institutions or customs, because Philo had no suitable antitype.

De Vita Mosis (On the Life of Moses) is a separate book that, because of its literary character, is related to this extensive and systematic treatment of the Mosaic legislation.[15] In this book the life of Moses is idealized in the customary

---

12. Cohn, *Schriften* 1. 155; Schürer, *History* 2/3. 342.
13. See Cohn, *Schriften* 1. 155ff.
14. Cohn, *Schriften* 2. 4.
15. Schürer, *History* 2/3. 348f.; also in Cohn and Wendland, *Philonis Alexandrini* 4. 119-268.

way, but it is not reinterpreted symbolically or allegorically. Nearly all of the allegorical interpretations are found in the second part of the book (*Vit. Mos.* 2). They refer almost exclusively to the institutions that directly concern Moses, each of which "has as its objective the presentation of some philosophical idea by interpreting the legislation symbolically."[16]

ii. *Philo's Commentary on Genesis.* Philo's other major work on the Pentateuch is his large allegorical commentary on Genesis.[17] In this commentary the allegorical method of interpretation is used exclusively. Ordinarily the literal meaning is referred to simply in order to dismiss it as being impossible. Therefore, not only are individual narratives interpreted symbolically, but selected sections are interpreted allegorically, verse by verse, without any regard for the historicity of the things recorded. However much they may differ, the interpretations as a whole form a basic unity because an extensive psychological and ethical system is developed from Genesis. "The different individuals, who here make their appearance, denote the different states of soul (τρόποι ψυχῆς) which are found in man. To analyze these in their variety and their relations both to each other and to the Deity and the world of sense, and thence to deduce moral doctrines, is the special aim of this great allegorical commentary."[18]

The interpretation of particular concepts and persons in psychic and ethical categories is based on etymology and on the symbolism of terminology. Etymology is employed consistently with proper nouns, but not exclusively. Here are a few examples of the symbolism of terminology taken from the exposition of Gen 3:8b-18: "Man" is an allegorical expression for the mind, "woman" for the senses, "serpent" for pleasure, "the wild animals" for the passions (*Leg. All.* 3.49, 76, 107, 113). Once introduced, the allegorical interpretation of a particular term is adhered to throughout. The fact that these interpretations can be applied repeatedly to a variety of statements about their respective objects is proof of their usefulness. Therefore, this kind of exposition is restricted only by traditional etymology and the symbolism which results from its use, and by the letter of Scripture that is its starting point. In other respects the meditation is quite free. If, in spite of all this, the end result is not an absolute confusion, but is a unity of ethical and psychological arguments and exhortations, then it is obvious that this exegesis must, in the final analysis, be guided by some preconceived notion of what the end result will be. While freely meditating on the text, the exegete seeks the *tertia comparationis* that connect the concepts and events in the word of Scripture with their interpretation.[19] It is clear that the book as a whole does not provide a scholarly commentary or any scholarly speculation. What it does provide is edifying and admonitory expositions of the

16. Cohn, *Schriften* 1. 218f.; cf. Gfrörer, *Kritische Geschichte* 1/1. 86.
17. Cohn and Wendland, *Philonis Alexandrini* 1.61-298; vols. 2, 3.
18. Schürer, *History* 2/3. 339; cf. Cohn, *Schriften* 3. 3ff.; Gfrörer, *Kristische Geschichte* 1/1. 87ff.
19. P. Heinisch, *Der Einfluss Philos auf die älteste christliche Exegese* (Münster, 1909) 92.

Stoic kind that show some similarities with the midrashim. This is clear from
the mood of the exposition (*Leg. All.* 3.36, 47, 52, 104) as well as from the
frequent repetition of the same exhortations.[20]

Compared with the writings of Philo that we have already discussed, his other
works, including the fragments that have been preserved from his third volume
on the Pentateuch, are relatively unimportant for our study.[21]

c. Philo's Method of Interpretation

i. *Literal and Figurative Interpretation.* We will summarize the results of our
survey and give additional references to demonstrate that what we have concluded
from individual passages is universally applicable.

First, we must point out that Philo the "allegorist" is familiar with and upholds the literal meaning of the text. He calls it the "literal and obvious explanation" (ἡ ῥητὴ καὶ φανερὰ ἀπόδοσις) or he uses some other combination of
these adjectives (*Abr.* 200).[22] He retells and explains biblical history as the record
of actual events, including the principal features of primeval history and the very
details of patriarchal and Mosaic history.[23] Above all, he insists that the literal
sense of the Law must be fulfilled, quite apart from its deeper meaning (*Migr.
Abr.* 89-93; *Exsecr.* 154).[24]

To these stories and laws that he interprets in the literal sense he frequently
adds rational explanations and reasons, most often with apologetic intent. For
example, Israel heard the words of God on Sinai because the fire that was
descending was transformed into articulate sounds that the people could understand (*Decal.* 46). Philo cannot conceive of a God who speaks like a human
being.[25]

Most often a symbolical interpretation is added to the explanation of the literal
sense. This meaning is implicit already in the manner in which the literal sense
is explained, but is also utilized in the conclusions that are set forth. Symbolical
interpretations are found primarily in the second section of Philo's systematic
treatment of the Mosaic law.[26]

ii. *Allegorical Interpretation.* For Philo the allegorical meaning is the proper

---

20. Cohn, *Schriften* 3. 3f.

21. Philo's third work on the Pentateuch is a relatively brief catechetical exposition that originally
included Genesis and Exodus. In addition to numerous Greek fragments, certain sections of the
exposition of Genesis and fragments of the exposition of Exodus have been preserved in Armenian
translation (published by J. B. Aucher, *Philonis paralipomena Armena, Venetiis* [1826]) (Schürer,
History 2/3. 327ff.; cf. p. 324 n. 9).

22. See Siegfried, *Philo* 163.

23. See above, pp. 43-48; cf. Gfrörer, *Kritische Geschichte* 1/1. 85-87; Heinisch, *Einfluss*, 53.

24. See Gfrörer, *Kritische Geschichte* 1/1. 104f.; Siegfried, *Philo*, 163; Heinisch, *Einfluss*, 54.

25. For similar rationalizing explanations, see above on *De Opificio Mundi* and *De Specialibus
Legibus*; cf. Siegfried, *Philo*, 163; Heinisch, *Einfluss*, 53f.

26. See above, p. 46. Of course, our terminology does not coincide with Philo's. When he
designates something as σύμβολον, he usually understands it to be the visible expression of an
invisible truth and interprets it allegorically (*Spec. Leg.* 3.178; *Rer. Div. Her.* 120).

meaning of Scripture.[27] In many passages he excludes the literal meaning, but never the allegorical (*Jos.* 28; *Spec. Leg.* 3.178).[28] The allegorical meaning is related to the literal meaning just as the soul is related to the body (*Migr. Abr.* 93). ". . . the letter is to the oracles but as the shadow to the substance and that the higher values therein revealed (by the literal meaning) are what really truly exist" (*Conf. Ling.* 190). Accordingly, he urges those who are concerned only with the literal sense to strive for the higher meaning (*Conf. Ling.* 190; *Sobr.* 33; *Spec. Leg.* 1.213f.).[29] When he states that the allegorical meaning is the meaning intended for the initiated (μύσται), he does so primarily to accentuate its sublime significance (*Cher.* 42, 48; *Som.* 1.191).[30] Moses gave the Scripture its present form for pedagogical reasons because not everyone is able to grasp the deeper hidden truth (*Deus Imm.* 53ff.). Moses was God's interpreter and he translated God's words into human language (*Vit. Mos.* 2.188f.; *Poster. C.* 1).[31] Because Moses himself intended to give Scripture this double meaning, the two stand side by side without any contradiction (*Op. Mund.* 25; *Sacr. A. C.* 12).[32] Thus, Philo protects himself from the charge that the interpretations are his own invention (*Som.* 1.172). This is why he always begins his argumentation with the text and builds no arbitrary bridges afterward to suit the beliefs of his contemporaries.[33]

How, then, does Philo discover and defend the allegorical meaning of a passage? Frequently he introduces his allegorical interpretation by stating that what follows is said in accordance with the "laws of allegory" (κανόνες or νόμοι τῆς ἀλληγορίας, *Abr.* 68; *Spec. Leg.* 1.287; *Som.* 1.73, 102).[34] At no time, however, does he mention any of these laws explicitly. There are certain principles that he has in mind and not a specific number of hermeneutical laws, comparable to the *middoth* of the rabbis.[35] The most important of these principles is the conviction that Scripture has a deeper meaning and that this meaning can be found by searching—indeed, it must frequently be searched for. He knows that he and the philosophers, the Greek allegorists (*Poster. C.* 7),[36] and the

---

27. For the characteristics of the allegorical meaning, see Siegfried, *Philo*, 164; cf. Gfrörer, *Kritische Geschichte* 1/1. 87.
28. See Heinisch, *Einfluss*, 54f.; a different view is presented by Gfrörer, who lists passages in which Philo seems to admit only the literal meaning (*Kritische Geschichte* 1/1. 86f.) and also other passages in which he accepts only the allegorical meaning (ibid. 1/1. 95ff.).
29. Ibid. 1/1. 81f.; Heinisch, *Einfluss*, 55.
30. See Gfrörer, *Kritische Geschichte* 1/1. 99ff.; Heinisch, *Einfluss*, 56f.; and J. Döpke, *Hermeneutik der neutestamentlichen Schriftsteller* (Leipzig, 1829) 109f.
31. See Gfrörer, *Kritische Geschichte* 1/1. 94ff.
32. Heinisch, *Einfluss*, 56.
33. Gfrörer, *Kritische Geschichte* 1/1. 106f.; however, cf. Heinisch, *Einfluss*, 92.
34. See Siegfried, *Philo*, 160ff.; Heinisch, *Einfluss*, 69.
35. Stein, *Allegorische Exegese*, 49; however, cf. Siegfried, *Philo*, 164.
36. See Cohn, *Schriften*, on that passage; on the principles for the interpretation of Greek myths, see p. 19 n. 56.

allegorizing Hellenistic Jews who preceded him[37] all agree on the principle that one must interpret allegorically when the Holy Scriptures make incorrect or unworthy statements about God (these are mostly anthropomorphisms),[38] or when the literal meaning is absurd or contradictory (*Det. Pot. Ins.* 48; *Poster. C.* 49ff.; *Leg. All.* 1.105; 3.55, 236).[39] The allegorical method can also be employed when it provides a richer meaning, or whenever there is an opportunity to do so (*Decal.* 1; *Spec. Leg.* 1.327). There are many occasions and points of departure for this in Scripture. Since the very words are inspired by God, every detail in the wording and in the manner of presentation has special meaning; nothing is superfluous.[40]

None of the principles we have mentioned are heuristic rules. They state only when allegorical interpretation can or must be used; they do not indicate how the allegorical meaning is to be discovered. Positive clues and proof for the substance of the interpretations emerge from the etymologies and symbolism, which are often traditional. Siegfried and Heinisch give numerous examples of the symbolism of objects and numbers, of the etymologies of proper names, and of other etymologies that often degenerate to trivialities.[41] Tradition and consistent use of etymological and symbolical interpretation give a certain cohesiveness and continuity to Philo's exposition. Of course, these "laws" in themselves will not enable one to discover an allegorical interpretation. In general, the following principle is more helpful: The inspired Scripture must also be interpreted by inspiration. Philo claimed he had this inspiration.[42] As a result, in spite of all his serious and consistent treatment of the text, Philo's philosophy is the final and decisive factor in his exposition.

d. The Philosophical Basis for Philo's Hermeneutics

We have not been able to find any trace of a typological interpretation of Scripture in Philo. This is not accidental; it can be accounted for by the general attitude of his philosophy toward historicity. Scripture for him is not at all a record of redemptive history. Instead, he views it as a manual for a philosophy of life. Philo knows of no direct rule by God in history. Consequently, his system has

---

37. For passages in which Philo refers to his predecessors see Siegfried, *Philo*, 26f.; Heinisch, *Einfluss*, 26.

38. E.g., *Poster. C.* 1-7; *Leg. All.* 1.43f.; *Plant.* 32ff.; see Siegfried, *Philo*, 165f., 199ff.; Heinisch, *Einfluss*, p. 70 (for the use of this principle by the Greeks, see ibid., 7).

39. See ibid., 72ff.; this principle was followed by the Stoics also.

40. Siegfried, *Philo*, 168-80; Heinisch, *Einfluss*, 80-87. Siegfried cites particular applications of this principle that, of course, Philo does not hold in common with the Greeks; these are to be considered as examples and not as rules that Philo would have followed consciously or unconsciously.

41. For the symbolism of objects, see Siegfried, *Philo*, 182-90; for the symbolism of numbers, see ibid., 180ff.; Heinisch, *Einfluss*, 102ff. For the etymology of names, see Siegfried, *Philo*, 190-96; Heinisch, *Einfluss*, 109-12; for general principles, see *Cher.* 56. For other etymologies, see Siegfried, *Philo*, 173; Heinisch, *Einfluss*, 88f.

42. Gfrörer, *Kritische Geschichte* 1/1. 57f.; Heinisch, *Einfluss*, 50f.; E. Zeller, *Die Philosophie der Griechen in ihrer geschichtlichen Entwicklung* (Leipzig, 1881) 3/2. 351f.

no place for eschatology.[43] Here and now through mystical absorption the immortal soul can ascend to God and "through death attain to pure ether, that is, to blessed life or to eternal death."[44] Instead of the tension between the present and future manifestations of God's power in history that moved apocalyptic and rabbinical writings, there is the tension between the lower, visible world and the higher, invisible world.

Philo's system is permeated by the Platonic viewpoint in which the visible, perceptible world is the expression and copy of a transcendent world of ideas. In Genesis 1 Philo discovers that God first created an immaterial world which contains the ideas (ἰδέαι), the patterns (παραδείγματα) or archetypes (ἀρχέτυποι), of everything in this visible world (*Op. Mund.* 16, 29, 36, 129, 134). Nothing in this world was created without an incorporeal pattern (*Op. Mund.* 19, 130). The visible world is the image (ἀπεικόνισμα, *Op. Mund.* 16), radiance (ἀπαύγασμα, *Plant.* 50), and copy (μίμημα, *Plant.* 50) of that world. It can also be called the type (τύπος) of that world, because the world of ideas is designated as its seal (σφραγίς, *Op. Mund.* 129, 134; cf. 34) and frequently as its archetype (ἀρχέτυπος, cf. *Op. Mund.* 16, 71; *Cher.* 86; *Plant.* 50).

The true man, the intellectual man, is a copy of that world. God willed that his creature should be able to know him, so he imprinted the features of his own mind on the human mind as he breathed his own breath into him (*Det. Pot. Ins.* 86). Man was created in the image of God (κατ᾽ εἰκόνα τοῦ θεοῦ). The image (εἰκών) of God, however, is the divine Logos (λόγος, *Op. Mund.* 139; *Rer. Div. Her.* 230). As God is the pattern (παράδειγμα) and archetype (ἀρχέτυπος) for the Logos (*Leg. All.* 3.96), so the Logos is the pattern and archetype for the rational soul (λογικὴ ψυχή) in man, so that the soul of man is the third-hand copy (τρίτος τύπος) of the creator (*Rer. Div. Her.* 231). It is a genuine coinage (δόκιμον νόμισμα) that has been stamped (τυπωθέν) with God's seal (σφραγίς), whose imprint (χαρακτήρ) is the divine Logos (*Plant.* 18).

There is, then, a certain sense in which the human mind belongs to the higher world. By virtue of its origin, the human mind is able to enter that world (*Op. Mund.* 69ff.) in order to perceive the mind of God which comprehends that entire world of ideas (*Leg. All.* 3.96). On Mount Sinai Moses saw with his mind the incorporeal patterns of the furnishings for the sanctuary (*Leg. All.* 3.102; *Vit. Mos.* 2.74, 141). This ability to see indicates that he had entered the world of ideas (*Vit. Mos.* 1.158).

Philo's philosophical ideas put a new light on his hermeneutical principles, which we discussed above. For Philo, the letter of the divine oracle is like the shadow of the body, and it is the meaning conveyed by the letter that really exists (*Conf. Ling.* 190; *Migr. Abr.* 12). The earthly copies of the world of ideas are frequently called shadows (*Leg. All.* 3.102; cf. 3.96: the Logos is called God's shadow). Therefore, the quest for the allegorical meaning is, to a certain

---

43. Volz, *Eschatologie*, 59-62.
44. Ibid., 60.

degree, an attempt to advance from the visible copies to the originals. The allegorists are those men who are friends of the soul, not the body, and who are able to associate with God as with an intelligible, incorporeal being (*Deus Imm.* 53ff.; the same thing is said of Moses in *Leg. All.* 3.100ff.).

The world of the psyche also appears in Philo as a higher world, which, like the world of ideas, is the true reality behind the visible world. For this reason he says that disorder in the soul is "the original (ἀρχέτυπος) of all wars. If this be abolished, neither will those occur which still break out in imitation of it (οἱ κατὰ μίμησιν)" (*Poster. C.* 185). When the persons of the biblical narrative who live in the external world are interpreted by Philo as mental powers, then for him they are related to the literal meaning of Scripture as shadows or types (τύποι) of a psychical world that is the same as the world of ideas. In this connection, we should point out that the persons in the story of the Fall are called typical examples (δείγματα τύπων) "bidding us resort to allegorical interpretation guided in our renderings by what lies beneath the surface," i.e., to interpret it as referring to the life of the psyche (*Op. Mund.* 157). Consequently, for Philo allegorizing is the same as advancing from the visible world to the higher world of ideas, from the types (τύποι) to the prototypes (ἀρχέτυποι). Moreover, a few of his statements suggest that he views the direct literal meaning as the humble means of expression and the allegorical meaning as the corresponding higher intelligible reality—the idea, which is the only true reality. Accordingly, when interpreting Scripture he finds two realities side by side that are related to one another in a comparative way.

This kind of typology differs from biblical typology in two respects. First, the historical facts that are recorded are not the lower reality which points to the higher reality. They are the inspired literal sense or simply the inspired words. The question of the historicity of this record is not left open. Very often historicity is totally rejected by stating that God has not acted as is recorded here; he has merely inspired the written words in order to express higher truths through them. The second difference is that the direction in which one is to interpret is not the horizontal-temporal but the vertical-spatial. The higher antitypes do not belong to the last days, which will break into time at the end, but to a higher, invisible world that stands unchanging above the events of this world.

It must be kept clearly in mind that the way in which he conceives of Scripture and interprets it is intimately tied to his general theological approach. Philo's allegorizing is in harmony with a theology that does not take seriously the reality of God in history and in creation nor the historicity of revelation and, consequently, makes Scripture a collection of oracles addressed to this world from above. It is not based on the biblical view of God and the world, but on Platonism. Philo's Christian disciples have eliminated the second of these two differences in that they no longer view the allegorized oracle as being related to a world of ideas filled with Stoic concepts, but to the narratives and teachings of the NT.[45]

2. HELLENISTIC JUDAISM BEFORE PHILO

Philo is rightly considered to be a representative of a great exegetical tradition. We need to determine how much of the literature of Hellenistic Judaism that has been preserved is a part of this tradition.[46]

a. Aristobulus

Many try to find allegorical interpretation in Aristobulus, the earliest representative of Hellenistic Judaism whose writings are still available to us.[47] It is possible to appeal to Origen, who considered Aristobulus as an allegorist along with Philo.[48] But in the meager fragments that remain from Aristobulus's large book, an exposition of the Mosaic Law, there is no truly allegorical interpretation.[49] His exposition is governed by the principle that the tradition must be interpreted in a way that corresponds with reality (φυσικῶς λαμβάνειν τὰς ἐκδοχάς, 1:6). His exposition shows that he does not use this principle to justify the derivation of a higher allegorical meaning from the word of Scripture. What he wants to do is avoid a crassly materialistic (literal)[50] misunderstanding of the biblical language with its rich imagery. He tries to use Greek concepts to express what is described in the Bible in biblical terms—the realities of God, his work, and his commands. Aristobulus's principle is not dangerous unless philosophy is allowed to determine what the realities of God and his work can be. Then it is the source of all the novel interpretation of Scripture that was customary in Hellenistic Judaism and in the enlightened Christianity of the eighteenth and nineteenth centuries. The narratives are disintegrated by rationalistic explanations, the history is reduced to symbolism, and the literal account is nothing more than an allegorical expression of a universal idea.

Aristobulus believed that Greek philosophy was informed by the Bible (2:1-4), and that the biblical view of God is basically in agreement with that of philosophy

---

45. See Heinisch, *Einfluss*, 92ff.

46. Ibid., 24f.

47. Probably between 170 and 150 B.C. (Schürer, *History* 2/3. 237). On the question of genuineness, see Zeller, *Philosophie* 3/2. 257; Schürer, *History* 2/3. 241f.; Stein, *Allegorische Exegese*, 7f.

48. Origen, *Contra Celsus* 4.51.

49. There is a survey of the extant fragments and other information in Schürer, *History* 2/3. 238f. Fragments for which the exact wording has been preserved are found in Eusebius *Praep. Ev.* 8.10 and 13.12; see idem, *Hist. eccl.* 7.32.17f. We have taken our quotations from P. Riessler, *Altjüdisches Schrifttum ausserhalb der Bibel* (Augsburg, 1928) 179ff. The first is an attempt to explain the anthropomorphisms in the Bible and the other is an attempt to explain the Sabbath command.

50. On the technical meaning of this term, see Cohn, *Schriften* 4. 6 n.2.

(2:62).[51] So far as we can determine, however, this belief leads him only to the brink of rationalistic exposition; the literal meaning has not yet been destroyed by allegory.[52]

He is not giving a new interpretation, for he is only providing a correct exposition when he explains the phrase "hands of God" as a biblical expression for God's power (1:17; cf. 1:13-18) or when he interprets the statement about God's rest in Gen 2:2 as a reference to God's purpose to preserve the order of creation (2:74). The following explanation borders on rationalistic reinterpretation: "We should not understand the divine voice in terms of spoken words, but of actions," i.e., God did not speak like a man, but he produced actions that were perceived as sound (2:7ff.).[53] The division of creation into six days is intended to show the time and the position of each relative to the others (2:75f.). His justification of the Sabbath command by indicating its appropriateness is also rationalistic. He states that the hallowing of the seventh day is in keeping with the significance of the number seven in the history of the world (2:67).[54] There may be many examples in Aristobulus's work as a whole where Scripture is handled in the same way that Philo does in his systematic exposition of the Mosaic law; nevertheless, it has nothing in common with Philo's great allegorical commentary.[55]

b. The Epistle of Aristeas

The *Epistle of Aristeas* was directed to a Greek-speaking public for apologetic and propagandizing purposes.[56] Its interpretation of the dietary laws and the laws of cleanliness is closer to Philo than to Aristobulus. The general argument—that these laws were designed to protect the Jews from the influence of idolaters— is in harmony with the literal meaning (128-42). The exposition of the individual commandments, however, does not give a more profound reason for them, as does Aristobulus's exposition of the Sabbath. Alongside the ritual ordinance, which continues to be binding in the literal sense, it places a moralistic precept that has been derived by symbolical and allegorical interpretation (144ff.). For example, the command not to eat birds of prey is meant to warn against oppressing the weak while relying on one's own strength (145-49). "Only do not

---

51. Schürer, *History* 2/3. 237: Aristobulus is already "a Hellenistic philosopher in the proper sense. He is acquainted with and expressly quotes the Greek philosophers Pythagorus, Socrates, Plato, and is at home with their views as a philosopher by profession."

52. This is the opinion of Döpke, *Hermeneutik*, 115; Zeller, *Philosophie* 3/2. 264; Schürer, *History* 2/3. 240f.; and Stein, *Allegorische Exegese*, 10; however, see Siegfried, *Philo*, 24 and Heinisch, *Einfluss*, 16ff., who view Aristobulus as the first to apply to the OT the Stoic method of interpreting myths.

53. Similar to Philo, see above, p. 48.

54. Similar to Philo, see above, p. 44.

55. According to Schürer, *History* 2/3. 239; on Aristobulus and Philo, see Stein, *Allegorische Exegese*, 7-10.

56. The date of origin is very uncertain, undoubtedly before 63 B.C.; the opinion of most scholars is ca. 96 B.C. See Schürer, *History* 2/3. 308f.

fall into the opinion, which has long been refuted, that Moses gave these laws out of consideration for such animals. These holy commands have been given for the purpose of righteousness, in order to awaken godly thought and to build character" (144; 168f.). This is how such interpretations are justified.[57]

c. 4 Maccabees

4 Maccabees also considers the fulfilling of the Law to be the true philosophy.[58] This book, however, was intended for Jews, and its basic attitude toward Scripture is altogether different from the attitude of the two writings we have just discussed (cf. 4 Macc 18:1). The principle that guides the expositions sounds Stoic. It states that the godly mind is the absolute sovereign over the desires (4 Macc 1:1; 18:2). The substance of the principle is reformulated to make it an expression of the piety of Pharisaism:[59] The godly mind, i.e., the mind inspired by the faith of Pharisaism, fulfills the Law by conquering desire (4 Macc 7:18ff.). (In their "Pelagianism" the Pharisees and the Stoics are in agreement.) The validity of this guiding principle is illustrated by Scripture, which a father should read to his family (4 Macc 18:10ff.).[60] The fulfilling of the Law, even the dietary laws, which seem so irrational, is life according to the sound mind (4 Macc 5:22). This is not proven by reinterpretation and exposition of the statements, but by demonstrating that virtue and piety are promoted by fulfilling those laws. God gives many commands, but he always commands what is right for humanity (4 Macc 5:23-26). There is nothing here that can be regarded as an allegorical interpretation of the dietary laws.[61]

d. The Wisdom of Solomon

Just as Pharisaism is combined with Greek philosophy in 4 Maccabees, so the proverbial wisdom of the OT is combined with Greek philosophy in the Wisdom of Solomon.[62] Biblical history is used to illustrate and verify the basic idea that wisdom, piety, and salvation go together just as do folly, godlessness (i.e., idolatry), and ruin.[63] This school does not interpret Scripture by exegeting the bib-

---

57. Siegfried (*Philo*, 26) classifies the *Epistle of Aristeas* with Aristobulus. Heinisch (*Einfluss*, 23) is of the opinon that allegory is rather developed in the *Epistle of Aristeas*, whereas Stein (*Allegorische Exegese*, 11) finds "no true allegory, only symbolic exposition."

58. It may have been written near the end of the first century B.C. or in the first half of the first century A.D. (Schürer: first century A.D.; Sellin: before A.D. 70; Riessler: shortly before the birth of Christ).

59. See Schürer, *History* 2/3. 244.

60. See 4 Macc 2:2, 17, 19; 3:6ff.; the Maccabean youths, chaps. 7–17.

61. Heinisch, *Einfluss*, 26f. So also Siegfried, *Philo*, 20; Zeller, *Philosophie* 3/2. 277: "We do not find any ideas which would lead to speculations like those of Philo, and there is no allegorical interpretation."

62. See Schürer, *History* 2/3. 231ff.; Siegfried, *Philo*, 22f.; therefore, the book should be dated "between Jesus ben Sirach and Philo," Schürer, *History* 2/3. 234. E. Sellin (*Introduction to the Old Testament* [New York, 1923] 160) dates it in the first century B.C.

63. See Wisdom 10–12, 16–19.

lical text, but by retelling it in an appropriate fashion. In this way the wisdom and goodness of God are shown to be ruling throughout biblical history, and to this extent it is possible to speak of a symbolical interpretation.[64] The historicity, however, is always retained firmly, so that history is never viewed simply as a humble means for expressing higher ideas, and the narrative is never considered as an allegory.[65]

There are, therefore, antecedents of Philo's method of interpretation in the earlier writings of Hellenistic Judaism, but there are no true parallels to his allegorizing.[66] The material is too meager to provide a complete picture, but this does not account for the absence of any trace of typology. The only adequate explanation is that this school of Jewish thought, which is closely akin to Philo, has a rationalistic tendency.

SUMMARY: THE PLACE OF TYPOLOGY IN LATE JUDAISM

In our search for typology in the literature of Judaism in NT times, we have encountered a great variety of interpretive methods and a still greater variety of interpretations. In all this literature, Scripture is considered to be the source of all knowledge and the basis for the formation of life. It was thought that life (in the broadest sense of the term) was to be found in Scripture (John 5:39). The use of Scripture is not controlled by an interest in the theoretical, but always by present needs, and its use varies accordingly. An answer for every contemporary issue is sought in Scripture, and everything that is considered important or worthwhile is derived from it. Therefore, the results of this kind of biblical interpretation are largely determined by the expositor's own questions and ideas. This approach is never viewed as the authoritative tradition nor is it applied to Scripture in a mechanical way, not even in Philo. It is worked out in dialectical interplay between other influences and absorption in Scripture. The theology and philosophy of the interpreter is the primary factor which determines and governs the use of the principles of interpretation (literal, symbolic, typological, allegorical) and especially the use of formal elements in deriving the meaning (com-

---

64. Wisdom is often considered to be a hypostasis between God and the world.

65. Siegfried (*Philo*, 24) goes too far in his assertion that "Persons and things in sacred history are viewed as symbols of higher realities." Wisdom does state that the bronze snake was only a σύμβολον . . . σωτηρίας, and that it was God himself who helped; but this is an appropriate literal interpretation (16:5-7; cf. 16:25f.; see above, p. 18 n. 55). Heinisch (*Einfluss*, 25) finds allegory in Wis 17:21; 18:24; 14:7; 16:25-29. Stein (*Allegorische Exegese*, 12-15) finds allegory in 10:10(14); 16:6f.; 18:24. But they read too much of Philo into the passages. Commenting on the whole book, Stein says (*Allegorische Exegese*, 14f.), "Except for some details, Wisdom is far from allowing the core of the biblical narrative to be absorbed in the typical. The interpretation is symbolical; there is no allegorical reinterpretation, that is reserved for the allegorizing of Philo." Cf. Döpke, *Hermeneutik*, 118. On the use of Wisdom in the NT see Schürer, *History* 2/3. 234.

66. See Cohn, *Schriften* 1. 8: "In reality Philo is the only literary representative of a 'Jewish-Alexandrian philosophy.' We know of no other scholar who could be called his predecessor or who could be placed in the same category with him."

binations of parallel passages, etymologies, the symbolism of things and concepts, and logical conclusions).

This can be clearly seen in the interpretation of biblical history. We will give our primary attention to this because biblical history offers the most opportunities for typology. There is a considerable difference between the method of interpretation used in the Apocrypha and Pseudepigrapha and the method used by the rabbis and Philo. The former briefly present the historical material from Scripture in keeping with their own points of view and only offer the reader the results of their interpretation. The latter manifest great skill and scholarship as they derive their interpretation by means of a literal exposition of the biblical narrative. In spite of this formal difference in procedure, the interpretation of Scripture in the Pseudepigrapha and the interpretation of the rabbis is basically literal-symbolical-typological, while Philo's interpretation is basically symbolical-allegorical. Nevertheless, these hermeneutical principles allow a great deal of latitude in interpretation not only in the details, but also in the aggregate. The historical record assures the Maccabees of the certainty of God's active power in history. The apocalyptic writings view that same record as the expression of a plan of history that inspires quiet composure because the outcome of history has been determined by an eternal, unalterable decree. For the rabbis, however, this history is the symbol of the glory of Israel even in the face of the present wretchedness, and it gives ample instruction for the shaping of national and personal life in the present. Finally, for Philo this history (interpreted symbolically, of course) is the expression of his philosophy of life. Our study of Philo has indicated that allegorizing which is based on principles gives a more profound meaning to the content of Scripture, but this is even more true of typology. It is no accident that typology is used by these expositors almost exclusively in the shaping of their eschatology; it is the consequence of their general philosophy.[67]

It would scarcely have been possible for Judaism in the time of the NT to consider the biblical history of the past as the inferior pattern of something greater in the present. On the contrary, they considered the present to be wretched in every respect and looked to the past as having been much brighter; it was the time of Israel's greatness and the time when God was present with his people. The most one dared to expect was that greater things would happen in the future, in the new age (for Philo this would come in the utopian, invisible world of ideas—but we cannot discuss that now). This background clarifies what it meant in this kind of environment when Jesus and his disciples testified by word and

---

67. The cult seems to be something of an exception to this. In it a notion of a representation of the past salvation is combined with a notion of the patterning of the perfect salvation. See the enthronement psalms (47, 96–99) and W. Eichrodt, *Theology of the Old Testament* (Philadelphia, 1961-67) 1. 127f. Cf. the pillar of cloud as a symbol of God's presence—in the tabernacle, Exod 40:34-36; at the dedication of Solomon's temple, 1 Kgs 8:10f.; over the sanctuary of the end time, Isa 4:5 (this is not from Isaiah, according to KAT).

deed that "one greater than Jonah" and all the other prophets "is here," or "one greater than Solomon is here," or "one greater than the temple is here."

Thus, the final and decisive factor in the interpretation of biblical history and of Scripture in general appears to be the interpreter's relationship to God, i.e., to the Lord. This relationship makes Scripture and all it contains reasonable and enduring (John 5:37-39; 8:19). For us, Christ makes the Jewish interpretation of Scripture seem to be nothing more than a remarkable confusion of truth and error. This is an impressive symbol of the fact that the prophetic scriptures are not "a matter of one's own interpretation" (2 Pet 1:20f., *RSV*). They can only be understood correctly in the Spirit from whom they originated. If the Father of Jesus Christ is the God of the OT, then rabbinical exegesis and Philo's concept of God originate in a falsification of the core of Scripture. NT interpretation, however, is the elevation of that core. If it is the Spirit of Jesus Christ who spoke through the prophets (1 Pet 1:11), then the only appropriate exegesis is done in this Spirit (1 Cor 2:10f.). If Jesus of Nazareth is "the one who was to come," if he is the goal of all biblical history, then he is the focal point that gathers all the rays of light that issue from Scripture. Now they do not shine miraculously here and there, but give a clear, unambiguous picture that is consistent with the salvation that Christ brings.

Part II

TYPOLOGY IN THE NEW TESTAMENT

Chapter Four

THE SYNOPTIC GOSPELS AND ACTS:[1]
JESUS CHRIST

1. THE PROPHET

The only way that Jesus' contemporaries could describe the impression Jesus made on them by his person and work was by referring to persons in OT redemptive history and prophecy. In outward behavior Jesus was much more like a scribe surrounded by disciples than he was like John the Baptist,[2] and yet,

---

1. Special studies about the OT in the Synoptic Gospels: an earlier work, E. Haupt, *Die Alt-testamentlichen Zitate in den vier Evangelien* (Kolberg, 1871). The books that should be listed here are primarily those published at the turn of the century and afterward on the topic "Jesus and the OT." Of those published after the turn of the century: J. Meinhold, *Jesus und das Alte Testament* (Freiburg, 1896). He adopts the position of older liberalism in contending that Jesus did away with the OT. He does not believe that Jesus set the OT aside in order to maintain the distinction between two stages in redemptive history that were equally dependent on God's revelation of himself to the community, but in order to reveal the unchanging nature of God and demonstrate that the OT conception of God is an obsolete delusion. M. Kähler, *Jesus und das Alten Testament* (Leipzig, 1896; see above, p. 14 n. 48). E. Klostermann, *Jesu Stellung zum Alten Testament* (Kiel, 1904). J. Hänel, *Der Schriftbegriff Jesu* (Gütersloh, 1919), includes tables to show the extent to which Jesus used Scripture and to classify those usages (pp. 30-99), the text of Jesus' quotations (pp. 105-45), and a comparison of the extent to which Jesus used various individual books (pp. 191-97). He also lists the passages Jesus used, following the order of the OT books (pp. 35-44; cf. pp. 192ff.; the Apocrypha, pp. 66-68). Among more recent works on the subject "Jesus and the OT": O. Schmitz (Furche, 1933) 280ff. E. Hirsch (*Deutsche Volkstum und evangelischer Glaube* [Hamburg, 1934] 836-45) contends that one is not justified in accepting the OT as a sacred book because of Jesus' position. Jesus' outward stance toward Scripture is historically conditioned. His real position is probably expressed in Matt 5:33ff., which indicates that he rejected the basic principle underlying the OT relationship between God and men. A. Oepke (*Theologica Militans* 21 [1938]) characterizes Jesus' attitude toward cult, Law, Scripture, the God of the OT, and OT redemptive history as "an inseparable confusion of acceptance and rejection of the Old in the eschatological situation" (p. 25); i.e., in accordance with typology. J. Hempel ("Der synoptische Jesus und das Alte Testament," *ZAW* 56 [1938] 1-34) describes Jesus' attitude in terms of the basic characteristics of the way the OT was viewed by Jesus' contemporaries in Palestine and from the main tenets of OT faith. The footnotes indicate our indebtedness to J. Schniewind, who has given special attention to the essential continuity between the OT and NT in his commentaries on Mark and Matthew (NTD).

2. See K. Rengstorf, "διδάσκω," *TDNT* 2. 139, 153ff.

even those who had little in common with his spirit had to admit that he did not teach like the scribes (Mark 1:22, 27). The people summarized their impression of Jesus by saying, "He is a prophet."[3] The notion that history repeats itself is a pallid form of the typological approach. The fact that this notion was applied to Jesus is evidence of its vitality in his day; people thought that in Jesus "John the Baptist, Elijah, or one of the prophets" had returned.[4]

Both Jesus himself and the church detected a profound relationship between the things he did and the things that were done by these men of God, and they used this relationship in the form of genuine typology to describe Jesus' importance and dignity. Jesus considered it a vital part of his mission to continue and to fulfill the work of the prophets (Mark 12:1ff. par.). He preaches and works like a prophet. His every word and deed give expression to his claim that one greater than a prophet is here. Jesus knew that he would share the fate of a prophet; nevertheless, his suffering and death is something totally different from the martyrdom of a prophet. It was God who led him to this conviction and strengthened him in it. In the Gospel accounts the evangelists have emphasized Jesus' relationship to redemptive history by alluding to appropriate OT stories and by quoting suitable prophecies. In Jesus' relationship to the prophets of the Old Covenant there is a wealth of typological connections. These are indicated by direct quotations and by allusions which are often difficult to detect. We will begin with the clear passages in which Jesus is placed explicitly in a typological relationship to the OT prophets either by God or by Jesus himself.

a. The Basis

The words spoken by God at Jesus' baptism (Mark 1:11 par.) remind us of the call of the Servant of the Lord in Deutero-Isaiah.[5] When he submitted to John's baptism of repentance, Jesus set out on the path of the Servant who has come "to serve and to give his life as a ransom for many" (Mark 10:45).[6] As the Servant of the Lord he is the recipient "of the love of Him who elects."[7] For Jesus this service consists primarily in prophetic activity, as it did for the Servant of the Lord.

The story of the transfiguration (Mark 9:2-8 par.) brings us to the heart of these relationships. The dating of the episode is unusual (Mark 9:2),[8] and it emphasizes the significance of this event and its connection with the preceding story about Peter's confession and with Jesus' first announcement of his passion.

---

3. Mark 8:27 par.; cf. Mark 6:15 par. Luke; Matt 21:11; Luke 7:16, 39; Herod also, Mark 6:4.
4. Matt 16:14; cf. Mark 8:28; 6:14f.
5. Mark 1:11, . . . ὁ ἀγαπητός, ἐν σοὶ εὐδόκησα; Isa 42:1, . . . ὁ ἐκλεκτός μου, ὃν εὐδόκησεν ἡ ψυχή μου.
6. Cf. Isa 53:10ff.
7. G. Schrenk, "εὐδοκέω," 2. 740f.
8. Similar formulas for dating are found only in Mark 14:1, 12; 16:1.

The three intimate friends are witnesses of the event.[9] The high mountain (Mark 9:2) is an obvious allusion to the place where divine revelations occurred in the OT.[10] Christ is changed into the form of the heavenly Son of Man.[11] What does it signify when Moses and Elijah come to the transfigured Lord? According to the older interpretation, the Law and the Prophets were paying homage to someone greater. This, however, is not supported by the wording of the passage or by the biblical point of view.[12] The ideas that were commonly accepted at the time indicate that the disciples must have interpreted the presence of these two men as a proclamation that the new age had come.[13] This also explains Peter's mysterious remark about the erection of shelters (σκηνάς), because in the last days God will again pitch his tent among his people, just as he did in the time of Moses.[14] Moreover, the cloud that enveloped them (νεφέλη ἐπισκιάζουσα αὐτοῖς) had appeared during the wilderness wandering and at the dedication of the first temple as a sign of God's presence, and it was expected that it would reappear in the last days.[15] The high point of the event was the voice from heaven, and this confirms our interpretation. Like the word spoken by God at Jesus' baptism, it reminds us of Ps 2:7. The wording is changed to the second person and is expanded with the command "listen to him" (ἀκούετε αὐτοῦ) that is taken from Deut 18:15 where the coming of the prophet is predicted. These changes indicate that the voice is speaking to the disciples. They have confessed Jesus as the Christ, and he has announced his cross to them. Now they must see him as the "only beloved Son of God," the Messiah. They must listen to him because he is the promised prophet. In this experience the disciples share in "an imposing revelation of Jesus' relationship to redemptive history."[16] Jesus deserves a place with Moses and Elijah, but he is not like them; he is *the* prophet (Deut 18:15) and the Messiah (the Jews had already applied the Deuteronomy

---

9. Cf. Deut 19:15.

10. Cf. 2 Pet 1:18, ἁγίῳ ὄρει.

11. Cf. Dan 7:9; Rev 1:14. The clothing of the heavenly being is resplendent, Rev 3:5; 4:4; 7:9; *1 Enoch* 62:15f. On the shining of his face (Matt 17:2), cf. Rev 1:16; 4 Ezra 7:97; also Exod 34:29 (not ἔλαμψεν here, but δεδόξασται). See H. Gressmann and E. Klostermann, *Das Evangelium Matthäus* (HNT; Tübingen, 1909). Luke 9:31 says of the prophetic figures, ὀφέντες ἐν δόξῃ.

12. For a summary of earlier interpretations, see J. Jeremias, "'Ηλ(ε)ίας," *TDNT* 2. 938f.

13. We will have to try to discover what the appearance of these men meant to Jesus' disciples from the ideas that were current. It was generally held that Elijah would return as the forerunner of the Messiah and Moses would return either as the first redeemer or as another forerunner with Elijah. Harnack refers to the first of these ideas (J. Jeremias, "'Ηλ(ε)ίας," *TDNT* 2. 938); Jeremias refers to the latter idea, citing *1 Enoch* 90:31; 4 Ezra 6:26; Rev 11:3ff. and *Apoc. Pet.* 2 (ibid., 938f.), and so does E. Lohmeyer (*Das Evangelium des Markus* [MeyerK; Göttingen, 1937] 175). It is very appropriate in connection with the announcement of the passion that the two forerunners of Rev 11:3f. are afflicted persons (cf. Luke 9:30). If the coming of these men is historical, then it is unnecessary and impossible to explain every detail on the basis of some eschatological theory; the meaning is clear from the ideas that were customarily associated with Moses and Elijah at that time.

14. See below, p. 181.

15. 2 Macc 2:8; see p. 57 n. 67.

16. See K. Rengstorf, *Das Evangelium nach Lukas* (NTD; Göttingen, 1937), on this passage.

passage to the Messiah).[17] The new age has begun. What the disciples have confessed in prescient faith and contrary to public opinion has been presented to them in great splendor that surpasses all expectation. Jesus of Nazareth, who is journeying toward suffering and death, is not simply a prophet—he is the Christ of God.

The same basic elements are found in the sayings of Jesus, primarily in those which show his attitude toward John the Baptist. On the one hand, Jesus identifies himself fully with John. Matthew is correct when he summarizes the preaching of them both with the identical words (Matt 3:2; 4:17). Jesus speaks of Elijah's coming and being rejected, and in the same breath he mentions the suffering of the Son of Man (Mark 9:12f. par. Matthew).[18] Rejection of the Baptist and rejection of Jesus are put on the same plane (Mark 11:30ff. par.; Matt 11:18f. par. Luke; cf. Matt 21:32). In addition to this profound interrelationship there is typological heightening, because John is more than a prophet (Matt 11:9ff. par. Luke)—he is the one who is to prepare the way in the last days; he is Elijah come again. "Yet he who is least in the kingdom of heaven," i.e., he who sees and enters the kingdom, "is greater than he" (Matt 11:11 par. Luke; cf. Mark 2:18ff. par.). How much greater, then, is "the coming one" who brings the kingdom (Mark 1:7f. par.; the people were well aware that Jesus had greater powers than John [Mark 6:14ff. par.])? "All the prophets and the Law prophesied until John" (Matt 11:13; cf. par. Luke 16:16). An era in God's redemptive history corresponding to the former age has come to an end. Now the kingdom of God has begun. What was vaguely hinted at in the former age has come to perfect fulfillment.[19] In this comparison of Christ "the prophet" with the "Elijah who had returned," it is clear that a genuine Christian typology is

---

17. In rabbinic literature, Deut 18:15, 18 is referred to extremely seldom; it is applied to Jeremiah (Str-B 2. 626f.), but he is not considered to be a messianic figure (ibid. 1. 730). It is obvious not only in the NT (cf. John 6:14f.; 1:21; 7:40f.; Acts 7:37; cf. 3:22) but also in Josephus that in the time of Jesus the hope connected with Deut 18:15, 18 was alive. The expectation was that "the prophet" would come as the messianic redeemer (ibid. 2.479f.). (Perhaps the messianic interpretation has been suppressed in reaction to Christianity, and the word that points beyond the OT has been turned back to the OT; see below, p. 83 n. 100).

18. This is more clear in the parallel passage, Matt 17:11f.

19. Accordingly, it is not strange that no truly typological ideas were associated with John the Baptist. As a forerunner of the Christ he is almost an antitype; he is Elijah come again (Mark 9:13 par. Matthew; Matt 11:14; Luke 1:17; cf. John 1:21, 25). Nevertheless, he stands only on the threshold of the new age.

On the expectation of the return of Elijah, see Str-B 4. 779ff.; Jeremias, "Ἠλ(ε)ίας," TDNT 2. 931ff. (for the oldest passage containing the statement that is added to Mal 4:5, see Sir 48:10). There are only a few details in the description of John the Baptist that are reminiscent of Elijah: Mark 1:6 par. Matthew, καὶ ζώνην δερματίνην περὶ τὴν ὀσφὺν αὐτοῦ, which in 2 Kgs 1:8 is a characteristic of Elijah, καὶ ζώνην δερματίνην περιεζωσμένος τὴν ὀσφύν. The clothing of hair has no exact counterpart; cf. 2 Kgs 1:8; Zech 13:4. This detail is missing in Luke also; the wording of Luke 3:2 is reminiscent, perhaps consciously, of the calling of the OT prophets generally; cf. Jer 1:2; Hos 1:1; Joel 1:1 (on the account of the birth of John the Baptist, see below, p. 84 n. 103). The story of John's death (Mark 6:14-29 par. Matthew) can be compared with the hostility between Elijah and Jezebel (there are no clear allusions).

very different from the notion that the past will be repeated in a somewhat heightened form.

This difference must be kept in mind in interpreting the saying about Jonah (Matt 12:41 par. Luke; cf. Jonah 3:4-9), where the typological connection is stated explicitly. Jesus compares his own influence in Israel with the preaching of the prophet Jonah in the heathen city of Nineveh. Both are a summons to repentance in God's name, but "one greater than Jonah is here," one who is greater than a prophet. What we have said about Jesus' relationship to John the Baptist sheds light on the heightening that is indicated by the word "greater." A similar comparison that has been made by the scribes may help to clarify this. They said, "I sent a prophet to Nineveh, and he caused them to turn in repentance. And these Israelites in Jerusalem—how many prophets I have sent to them!"[20] In this saying, the heightening is only relative, like the heightening found in the idea that history repeats itself. There is nothing that goes beyond the possibilities of the old. Back of this saying of Jesus is the claim that is found in all of his preaching. It is the claim that something greater is here, something more than a continuation of the old, something that fulfills the old on a higher level. This makes it especially clear how the comparison of Christ and Jonah is related to the comparison of Christ and Solomon. "Now what kings possessed and what prophets longed for is fulfilled. Here is a summons to repentance greater than the summons of the prophets, and a joyous word greater than the word of the first son of David. Here is God's Messiah who is both king and prophet."[21] This comparison is no mere homiletical speculation. It indicates how God has ordered history and how he will view these people in the judgment. The heathen of Nineveh repented; Israel, however, has not turned, even though they have been called to repentance by one who is much greater than Jonah. This is why the people of Nineveh will condemn Israel in the judgment. The typological relationship of the saying and, consequently, its power to convince are based on the relationship between Jesus and Jonah. What gives the saying special poignancy is that it deals with heathen in the past, but with Israel in the present. This is what reveals the typological significance of the present moment: salvation and judgment are nearer now than ever before.

This is the basis on which we will discuss Jesus' relationship to the prophets. This relationship is underscored by Jesus and the evangelists in his preaching of repentance, in his proclamation of salvation, and in his attitude toward his contemporaries.

b. Jesus' Redemptive Acts

i. *His Preaching of Repentance.* The cleansing of the temple (Mark 11:15-19 par.) is a concrete example of the way Jesus' call to repentance is related to the

---

20. *Midr. Lam.*, Intro. No. 31, quoted by J. Jeremias, "'Ιωνᾶς," *TDNT* 3. 408 n. 17.
21. J. Schniewind, *Das Evangelium nach Matthäus* (NTD; Göttingen, 1937) 358.

preaching of the prophets. We are reminded of the things Jeremiah did (Jer 7:1ff.; 26:1ff.), and, as a matter of fact, Jesus had Jeremiah in mind. He borrowed the phrase "den of robbers" (σπήλαιον λῃστῶν) from Jeremiah's great sermon on repentance (Mark 11:17 par.; cf. Jer 7:11). And yet what he did must have been more significant than a mere prophetic act. The restoration of temple and cult was expected in the messianic age.[22] The prophetic word that Jesus quotes shows that he shared this expectation: "My house will be called a house of prayer for all nations" (Isa 56:7; cf. Mark 11:17). In this context Jesus intends primarily to emphasize that the temple is a house of prayer (Matthew and Luke omit "for all nations," πᾶσιν τοῖς ἔθνεσιν); nevertheless, the quotation brings to mind the new and universal worship of God that was expected in the last days (cf. Isa 2:1-4 with Matt 8:11 par. Luke). This is stated explicitly in the parallel account (John 2:17-22),[23] but even in the tradition of the Synoptic Gospels it is clear that Christ will do more than the prophets did. He will not merely cleanse the temple of abuse; he will literally replace it.[24]

On another occasion Jesus hurls Isaiah's word about hypocritical lip service (Isa 29:13) at his hearers as if it were meant for them (Mark 7:6 par. Matthew). He would not have disputed the fact that this saying was directed originally against Isaiah's contemporaries. That is not important because the saying is more applicable now than ever before. In the same discourse, Jesus, like the prophets, smashes the human ordinances and restores God's commandment, the commandment of Sinai (Mark 7:8ff. par. Matthew; cf. Mark 10:1ff. par. Matthew). Like the prophets, he exposed the hypocrisy that lay hidden behind the outward observance of the Law and demanded obedience from the whole heart (Mark 7:6f., 14ff. par.; cf. Matt 21:28ff.; 23:3).

Matthew has Jesus confront the legalism of the Pharisees with Hos 6:6, where the central concern of prophetic preaching is expressed. This is very appropriate because the Pharisees made the Law serve their self-righteousness, which was egocentric and, consequently, merciless (Matt 12:7; 9:13). Both passages in Matthew proclaim as clearly as possible that one greater than a prophet is here. Jesus joins the prophets in calling men back to the order of the Old Covenant. It is God's command which must be upheld, not some human ordinance. Obedience—total obedience—is a requirement for existence before God, but it does not give one a right to that existence (cf. Luke 17:17ff.; etc.). Jesus is also establishing something new. As the Lord of the Sabbath, he places himself above God's command (Matt 12:8) and makes union with himself a requirement for unconditional existence before God (Matt 9:12f., 6).

Jesus presents the full range of this typology once again in the Sermon on the Mount. None of these sayings are ethical guidelines; such guidelines were

---

22. See Ezekiel 40–48; *1 Enoch* 90:28f.; etc.
23. See below, p. 191.
24. See below, p. 86 on Matt 12:6; and p. 115.

already familiar to the Jews in many localities.[25] With remarkable conciseness and clarity, they have as their goal an attitude of absolute obedience, of complete conformity to the will of God (Matt 5:20; 7:21ff., 24ff. par. Luke). Consequently, they too are similar to the prophetic call to repentance. In the way he formulates his statements Jesus clearly indicates what distinguishes them from all the sayings of the prophets. The formula "but I tell you" can "scarcely be understood except as a confrontation between Moses and the Messiah. 'You have heard that it was said to the people long ago' means 'you have heard what was said in the Law, what was stated in the Ten Commandments.' In the words 'but I tell you,' one is speaking who is greater than Moses, the one who brings the law of the Messiah and who writes that law in the heart."[26] Not only does Jesus reveal the full magnitude of the divine requirement that is back of the OT law in a way that shatters all human righteousness, but he does so with a claim to such exclusive and absolute authority that the OT law itself is destroyed.[27] Moreover, Jesus does not use a phrase such as "This is what the Lord says" (כֹּה אָמַר יְהֹוָה) or "declares the Lord" (נְאֻם יְהֹוָה) to authenticate his proclamation, as the prophets do. He simply says, "but I tell you." He presents himself as a person who is able to hear God directly.[28] He who in this way inevitably brings every human being under judgment is personally involved when he proclaims the beatitudes at the beginning of the Sermon on the Mount. He is the one who enables men to fulfill the Law by the grace which is back of the entire discourse (Matt 5:17). This is the something extra that the prophets earnestly desired from the law of the Messiah (Jer 31:31ff.; Ezek 36:25ff.).

In the Sermon on the Mount, especially in the material found only in Matthew (5:17ff.), Jesus is portrayed as "the new Moses, who with his phrase 'but I tell you' introduces the law of the new divine order."[29] He is the new Moses in accordance with NT typology, and not a duplication of the old Moses, as was thought by the early Catholic church. We cannot be certain that Klostermann is correct in thinking that the sermon has been located on a mountain so as to

---

25. See Gressmann and Klostermann, *Matthäus*, on this passage; G. Kittel, *Die Probleme des palästinensischen Spätjudentums und das Urchristentum* (Stuttgart, 1926) 26.
26. Schniewind, *Matthäus*, 255.
27. It is impossible here to go into a detailed discussion of the problems of the Sermon on the Mount. We concur in principle with Schniewind's exposition in which he points out the features in each of Jesus' commands that are the basis of our typology, not only in the antitheses, but in the entire Sermon on the Mount.
   According to Gressmann and Klostermann (*Matthäus*, 42), the formula "but I tell you," which is our starting point, is a later addition in the third, fifth, and sixth antitheses, i.e., in the very statements that not only transcend the OT sayings, but set them aside. We must avoid any discussion of such literary-critical problems here. In any case, these antitheses are in keeping with Jesus' usual attitude toward the Law.
28. K. Rengstorf, "διδάσκαλος," *TDNT* 2. 156; cf. Chrysostom: τὶς γὰρ προφητῶν οὕτω ποτὲ ἐφθέγξατο; τὶς δικαίων; τὶς πατριάρχων; quoted in Gressmann and Klostermann, *Matthäus*, 42.
29. Schniewind, *Matthäus*, p. 237; Rengstorf, "διδάσκαλος," *TDNT* 2. 156.

correspond with Sinai and is, therefore, an obvious reference to this kind of typology.[30]

Jesus is indicating what his call to repentance has in common with the call of the prophets when he incorporates in his preaching the principal sayings of the prophets concerning repentance. His words, however, never conceal the fact that they are spoken by someone greater than the prophets, one who is Lord of the Sabbath and has authority on earth to forgive sins. Jesus states this clearly in the Sermon on the Mount with the phrase "but I tell you." Even when Jesus did not make this clear statement, his contemporaries who were familiar with the OT never failed to understand what he meant (Mark 3:6 par.; 2:7ff.).

ii. *His Proclamation of Salvation in Word and Action.* We are reminded continually that the typological nature of Jesus' preaching of repentance is dependent on its connection with his proclamation of salvation. This is true of both his words and his actions. It is the OT once again that reveals the significance of Jesus' preaching and actions as savior. The OT leads us from faith to faith— with respect to Jesus Christ, it leads to recognition of his glory, and with respect to his saving acts, it leads to seeing and hearing with a mind open to God's miracles. "The secret of the kingdom of God has been given" only to those who are receptive to Jesus' call to repentance (Mark 4:11 par.; cf. Matt 21:31). They *understand* (Mark 4:12 par.) that the parable of the sower describes the present kingdom (cf. Luke 17:20f.), and that God's reign has already begun, because Jesus is driving out demons (Matt 12:28 par. Luke). The OT contributes to this understanding by its prophecy and by the types that occur in its redemptive history. Those who have been influenced by the OT are the ones to whom Jesus' comprehensive statement applies: "Blessed are your eyes because they see, and your ears because they hear. For I tell you the truth, many prophets and righteous men longed to see what you see but did not see it, and to hear what you hear but did not hear it" (Matt 13:16f.).[31] Jesus is not speaking about something the prophets predicted; it is something they longed to see because the salvation they possessed was not yet complete. As we have intimated already, Jesus' use of prophecy and redemptive history is confined to the typological approach. Predictive prophecy indicates how the present salvation is related typologically to the redemptive history that preceded it.

It is from this point of view that we will survey the passages in which Jesus explains his redemptive acts by referring to OT prophecy. John the Baptist asks, "Are you the one who was to come?" Jesus answers by calling attention to his signs and his preaching (Matt 11:1ff. par. Luke). (It is significant that he ranked preaching higher than even the greatest miracle.) He quoted words from the prophecy in Isa 35:5f. in connection with his signs and he referred to the promise

---

30. Cf. Matt 5:1 and Gressmann and Klostermann, *Matthäus*, on the passage.
31. Cf. the par. Luke 10:23f. where "kings" appears rather than "righteous." Is this in consideration of the psalms of David? Cf. Luke 24:44 or cf. 11:31.

in Isa 61:1 in connection with his preaching.[32] The way these two passages coincide with his ministry should indicate to the Baptist that what the men of old longed for and predicted has come. The word of Scripture leaves no doubt about the decision that must be faced: "Blessed is the man who does not fall away on account of me" (Matt 11:6 par. Luke). According to Luke (4:18-21), Jesus quotes the promise from Isa 61:1f. in the synagogue at Nazareth for the very same reason. Jesus exercises freedom in his use of the OT and he stops just before the words "and the day of vengeance" (Isa 61:2)—words that are elaborated in the rest of that chapter.[33] The passages from Matthew (chap. 11) and Luke (chap. 4) show that Jesus does not limit himself to an arbitrarily chosen text in a wooden and superficial way. He borrows freely from various OT passages to prove that expectations found throughout the OT are fulfilled in his work. The redemption which in the past was only provisional and typical has now reached its consummation. The difference between these passages and proof from Scripture, such as is attempted in Matthew's fulfillment citations, is obvious. When seeking scriptural proof one clings with increasing determination to rather incidental external features in both the prediction and the fulfillment. Jesus points to the essential thing, the fact that the powers of sin and death have been defeated. This defeat, however, is still hidden. Jesus points to what is happening and then exhorts people not to fall away on account of him (Matthew 11). The decision that must be made concerns his person. The Scripture passage is intended to help one make this decision, but it will not enable him to predict the details of the fulfillment. What was important in Jesus' preaching of repentance was that word and action were uniquely bound to his person. This is even more true of his proclamation of salvation. The word of God that the prophets passed along was not dependent on their own persons when they promised salvation to the penitent and, in individual cases, interceded earnestly for God's forgiveness.[34] Jesus pronounces forgiveness on his own authority, and it is through fellowship with himself that he grants fellowship with God (Mark 2:15 par.; Luke 19:9).

We encounter these basic features again when the OT is used in a directly typological manner to explain Jesus' signs. The nature of Jesus' actions is disclosed when they are compared typologically with the actions of the prophets; consequently, such comparisons are similar to the characteristic of Jesus' actions and their portrayal in the Gospels that Schniewind calls "messianic secret."[35]

---

32. Cf. Isa 35:5f. with Matt 11:5: τότε ἀνοιχθήσονται ὀφθαλμοὶ τυφλῶν, καὶ ὦτα κωφῶν ἀκούσονται. τότε ἁλεῖται ὡς ἔλαφος ὁ χωλός, καὶ τρανὴ ἔσται γλῶσσα μογιλάλων (also cf. Isa 29:18f. and Isa 26:19: ἀναστήσονται οἱ νεκροί, καὶ ἐγερθήσονται . . .). Isa 61:1: πνεῦμα κυρίου ἐπ' ἐμέ, οὗ εἵνεκεν ἔχρισέν με εὐαγγελίσασθαι πτωχοῖς.
33. However, on ἀνταπόδοσις, cf. Isa 35:4.
34. E.g., Moses' intercession, Exod 32:30-35; cf. Jer 7:16; 11:14; 14:11; 15:1; etc.
35. Schniewind, *Matthäus*, 199f.

This is probably why we find only veiled allusions here and no explicit references. Therefore, we will begin by assembling all the parallels.

A number of Jesus' miracles have no parallel in the OT. These are primarily the exorcisms that are so prominent among Jesus' healings. Perhaps there is some relationship between this entire phenomenon and the fact that "the time had come."[36] Other miracles that have no connection with exorcisms and yet are not attributed to men of God in the OT are his healings of the blind (Mark 8:22ff.; 10:46ff. par.; Matt 9:27ff.), the deaf (Mark 7:32ff.), and the lame (Mark 2:1ff. par.). These infirmities are mentioned in the OT, particularly in a figurative sense (Isa 29:9f., 18; 42:18ff.; 43:8), and their eradication, in both the literal and spiritual senses, was expected to occur in the new age, i.e., in the new creation (Isa 35:5f.). The same is true of other infirmities that Jesus healed (Mark 1:30 par.; 5:25ff. par.; Luke 13:11; 14:2). There are OT parallels to his healings of lepers, his raising of the dead, and many of his nature miracles. The fact that these extraordinary miracles are the very ones that are attributed to the prophets indicates that in our search for the typological relationship, as well as in other assessments of Jesus' miracles, we must not focus on the tension between natural law and the miraculous.

In the Gospel accounts of the cleansing of lepers by Jesus (Mark 1:40-45 par.; Luke 17:11-19) there is no evidence of any reference to the two OT parallels (Num 12:10ff.; 2 Kgs 5:1ff.). This is an argument against the suggestion that Mark 1:40-45 records what originally was a ritual in which the man was simply pronounced clean, and that under the influence of the OT it was gradually transformed into a miraculous healing demonstrating that Jesus, as a second Moses (Num 12:10ff.), has conquered leprosy and so has fulfilled a messianic expectation.[37] Moreover, Jesus' general attitude toward the Law is much more in keeping with the traditional account in which the one healed is commanded to seek the prescribed pronouncement of cleanliness. A person who had actually been cleansed from leprosy must have been an impressive "testimony" for the people of Jerusalem (Mark 1:44),[38] especially since the rabbis believed God alone could heal this disease.[39]

Klostermann and others are too hasty in interpreting the other story about Jesus healing a leper (Luke 17:11-19) as a variant of this one.[40] Its only connection with 2 Kings 5 is that in both instances some demonstration of the individual's faith is required (Luke 17:14—2 Kgs 5:10-14) and that the single grateful individual, whose response is similar to Naaman's (Luke 17:15-18—2 Kgs 5:15), is a non-Israelite also. In any case, news about a person who can

---

36. Cf. Matt 12:28 par. Luke; Mark 1:24 par. Luke; Mark 5:7; Luke 10:18.

37. J. Weiss, quoted in THKNT (1928ff.) on Mark, 29. According to Leviticus 14 (LXX) καθαρίζειν can mean "pronounce clean."

38. See K. Bornhäuser, *Das Wirken des Christus durch Taten und Worte* (Gütersloh, 1921) 71.

39. Str-B 4. 751.

40. HNT, 173; contrast K. Rengstorf, *Lukas*, 182.

cleanse lepers by authoritative command and not by intercession, as the prophets did, would indicate to anyone acquainted with Scripture, even without any additional evidence, that one greater than Moses and Elijah is here.

Of the stories about Jesus raising the dead, the one about the young man from Nain (Luke 7:11-17) points clearly to OT parallels (1 Kgs 17:17ff.; cf. 2 Kgs 4:18ff.). The fact that the deceased is the "only son of a widow" cannot be considered a valid point of contact. It is a detail that is common in similar stories.[41] Besides, it has no precise analogy because the widow from Zarephath (1 Kgs 17:10) has other children,[42] and the Shunammite whose only son Elijah raised (2 Kgs 4:14ff.) is not a widow (2 Kgs 4:22). It is no accident, however, when as a sign of restoration it is stated at the end of the account in Luke (7:15), as in 1 Kings (17:22, LXX, which differs from the MT), that the person who had been raised began to speak. Nor is it an accident when the story ends with the words from 1 Kgs 17:23 (cf. 2 Kgs 4:36): "and he gave him to his mother" (καὶ ἔδωκεν αὐτὸν τῇ μητρὶ αὐτοῦ). The conclusion of the story indicates that parallels are being drawn deliberately. This is more than an assimilation of form. Those who witness the action declare, "A great prophet has appeared among us" (Luke 7:16a). In Jesus the miracle-working presence of God has been restored in the way that it once was mediated through the prophets. This signifies that the last days have begun, for "God has come to help his people" (Luke 7:16b; cf. 1:68). Jesus is "the prophet" (Deut 18:15, 18).

The story about the raising of Jairus's daughter (Mark 5:21-24, 35-43 par.) contains no reference to either of the OT stories about raising the dead. Perhaps all three narratives deal with children for the very profound reason that people of God "did not oppose death indiscriminately, but only at those times when its sway seemed senseless."[43] The other common feature is the concealment of the miracle since it was performed solely from a desire to help. In each instance, this secrecy is motivated by faith. "The prophet shuts himself in with the dead person, and Jesus drives out the crowd and remains in the dead girl's room with five witnesses."[44] If one compares these common elements and also contrasts Jesus' authoritative command (Mark 5:41) with Elijah's wrestling in prayer (1 Kgs 17:20-22), he will realize that the same Lord is acting in each instance, although now he is acting through one greater than Elijah.

The story of the miraculous feeding is reminiscent of several OT parallels.[45] The story that shows the greatest similarity in outward form is the tradition about Elijah feeding one hundred men with twenty barley loaves. The evangelist, however, has not made the slightest allusion to this. If "there are connections

---

41. For parallels to the "hellenistic type miracles of raising the dead" see HNT on this passage.
42. 1 Kgs 17:13, LXX: τέκνοις; the MT has the singular: לִבְנֵי.
43. Rengstorf, Lukas, 85; A. Schlatter, Das Evangelium des Lukas (Stuttgart, 1931) 253.
44. Lohmeyer, Markus, 108.
45. Mark 6:35-43 par.; Mark 8:1-9 par. Matthew; John 6:1-13; cf. Exod 16:4; 1 Kgs 17:8-16; 2 Kgs 4:1-7, 42-44.

with other events, either earlier or later in the divine history of the people, it is strange that this story makes no mention of the fact."[46] It was only later in the Gospel of John that these relationships were worked out in both directions.[47] As a matter of fact, our story deals primarily with the present situation; it is concerned about hunger and food. Jesus, however, may have had something more in mind. This miracle, more than any other, was a miracle he had performed by himself. Perhaps he intended this revelation of his glory to be a sign. He had often represented the new age with the metaphor of a meal. The word "desert" (ἔρημος), which is given special emphasis, is reminiscent of the time of Israel's salvation.[48] "As God once manifested himself to Israel in the desert, so now Jesus stood before them and served them food when they had none." "Thereby he manifested himself to the people as the one whom God had given them as their shepherd so that they might live by him."[49] Although "not a single detail in Mark 6:41-44 differs from the established practice of devout Jews,"[50] the account is pointing to the Last Supper,[51] and in that way it points beyond to the "great Last Supper" (cf. Luke 14:16; 22:16; Matt 22:1ff.). Consequently, the event itself becomes a type of the future.

There is a sense in which the relationships are reversed in the story of Jesus' stilling the storm (Mark 4:35-41 par.). The similarity in the descriptions of the external situations and the numerous verbal points of contact prove beyond a doubt that the evangelist had the story of Jonah in mind (Jonah 1:3ff.).[52] The

---

46. Lohmeyer, Markus, 129; cf. Rengstorf, Lukas, 104f.

47. The parallelism between Matt 14:19f. and 2 Kgs 4:44 that is advanced by Dittmar (Vetus Testamentum in Novo [Göttingen, 1903] 34) is confined to words required by the subject matter: (ἔδωκεν, A) and ἔφαγον. Only in John 6:9, which differs from the Synoptics, do we find ἄρτους κριθίνους, which obviously is from 2 Kgs 4:42; see p. 184 n. 27.

48. It seems that in the choice of locations Jesus and the evangelists had also in mind the typological significance of the moment. We must remember the role that mountains play in the stories of Moses and Elijah and in the Gospels: Moses and Elijah received God's revelation on a mountain (Exod 19:24; chaps. 33–34; 1 Kgs 19:8). Jesus goes to the mountain to pray (Mark 6:46 par. Matthew; Luke 6:12; 9:28f.; cf. John 6:15); it was on the mountain that he called the twelve (Mark 3:13 par. Luke); on the mountain he delivered his great sermon (Matt 5:1; 8:1); on the mountain the transfiguration occurred (Mark 9:2, 7 par.). It is even more obvious that the desert becomes a typological symbol: John the Baptist appears in the desert (Mark 1:3f. par.; cf. Matt 11:7 par. Luke; Luke 1:80); after his baptism Jesus is led there by the Spirit (Mark 1:12 par.); he goes there to escape from persecution (Matt 14:13; it is somewhat different in Mark 6:31; cf. John 11:54; 1 Kgs 19:3; in this case it comes after the death of Elijah who had returned, Matt 14:1-12), and the miraculous feeding also took place in the desert (Mark 6:35 par.); the warning in Matt 24:26 indicates that Jesus and the evangelists were familiar with the expectation that the messianic age would begin in the desert.

49. A. Schlatter, Der Evangelist Matthäus (Stuttgart, 1929) 233.

50. Lohmeyer, Markus, 127.

51. Cf. Mark 6:41 par.: λαβὼν (τοὺς πέντε ἄρτους) with Mark 14:22 par.: λαβὼν (ἄρτον).

52. Jonah 1:4: καὶ ἐγένετο κλύδων μέγας ἐν τῇ θαλάσσῃ καὶ τὸ πλοῖον ἐκινδύνευσεν συντριβῆναι. Mark 4:37: καὶ γίνεται λαῖλαψ μεγάλη ἀνέμου, καὶ τὰ κύματα ἐπέβαλλεν εἰς τὸ πλοῖον.

Jonah 1:5: Ἰωνᾶς δὲ . . . ἐκάθευδεν; 1:6: καὶ προσῆλθεν πρὸς αὐτόν. . . . Mark 4:38: καὶ αὐτὸς ἦν . . . καθεύδων; Matt 8:25: καὶ προσελθόντες ἤγειραν αὐτόν. . . .

evangelists were well versed in the Bible, and when they described these events, the familiar OT phrases flowed from their pens. But even if the parallels are intentional, they cannot be considered typological. The action that is the focal point in the Gospel account has no counterpart in Jonah. Jerome's interpretation cannot be forced on the NT; he says, "We find a type of this sign in Jonah. When others are in danger, he is unconcerned and sleeps. He is awakened, and the power and the bond of his suffering (is this the common element in the comparison?) deliver those who awakened him."[53] Yet, in a nontypological way, the allusions to Jonah point out that one who is truly greater than Jonah is here. Jesus does what is predicated of God in the OT—what Jonah obtained by prayer and the sacrifice of himself. According to the OT, God alone rules over wind and sea (cf. Pss 89:9; 107:29f.; thus Mark 4:41). Moreover, the story relates that Jesus walked on the water (Mark 6:48ff. par. Matthew); this too is something ascribed only to God in the OT and is stated in the poetic language of praise (Ps 77:19; Isa 43:16; Job 9:8).

On the whole, it is impossible to detect that the OT miracle stories have had any significant influence on Jesus' saving acts or on the Gospel accounts. As we have observed already, this is proof of the historical veracity of the tradition. Allusions are scarcely adequate to express the typological relationship, namely, what the stories have in common and what has been heightened. These two things are not found in the particular variety of miracles, but in the manner in which they are performed. Persons who are familiar with Scripture do not need to have these things pointed out to them; they are self-evident, particularly since this is the approach Jesus taught to his church. For the prophets and for Jesus such actions depend on one's relationship to the one Lord and on faith and prayer (cf. Mark 9:23, 29). They do not depend on such things as magic formulas that are used to summon the help of special powers. In the OT we see the man of God wrestling for an answer to his prayer; here we see one whose petition is transformed into thanksgiving for the answer (John 11:41f.). His will is so at one with the will of God that, being assured of having been heard, he has the powers of nature under his control (Mark 1:41; 5:41; 4:41; 1:27) and matter poses no limits to his actions (cf. Mark 9:23; 11:23f.; the following are relevant also: 9:35; 4:23). By virtue of his relationship to God, Jesus' saving power is unlimited, although there are limits to its use (cf. Mark 1:34; 6:5). Here we touch on another important aspect of Jesus' saving activity. Even the manner in which he

---

Jonah 1:6: Τί σὺ ῥέγχεις; ἀνάστα καὶ ἐπικαλοῦ τὸν θεόν σου, ὅπως διασώσῃ . . . καὶ μὴ ἀπολώμεθα. Mark 4:38: . . . οὐ μέλει σοι ὅτι ἀπολλύμεθα; par. Matt 8:25: σῶσον, ἀπολλύμεθα.

Jonah 1:11: καὶ κοπάσει ἡ θάλασσα ἀφ' ἡμῶν. . . . 1:15: καὶ ἔστη ἡ θάλασσα. . . . Mark 4:39: καὶ ἐκόπασεν ὁ ἄνεμος, καὶ ἐγένετο γαλήνη μεγάλη.

Jonah 1:16: καὶ ἐφοβήθησαν . . . φόβῳ μεγάλῳ τὸν κύριον. Mark 4:41: καὶ ἐφοβήθησαν φόβον μέγαν.

53. Quoted in K. Klostermann, *Das Markus Evangelium* (Tübingen, 1927).

grants miraculous aid and other redemptive gifts is compared by Jesus and the evangelists in an instructive way with the methods of the prophets.

iii. *His Manner of Using His Authority.* When bestowing or withholding his redemptive gifts, Jesus was subject to the plan of God that had been revealed in the commissioning of the prophets. The people of Nazareth were displeased because Jesus performed his miracles on behalf of strangers, i.e., primarily in Capernaum (Luke 4:23) and not for his unbelieving fellow citizens. To defend himself, Jesus refers to the sending of Elijah to the widow of Zarephath (Luke 4:25f.—1 Kgs 17:8ff.) and to the healing of Naaman the Syrian by Elisha (Luke 4:27—2 Kgs 5:1ff.). These OT examples were meant to teach them that God's grace will be shared at God's direction with those who receive it by faith. In line with the prophetic movement, this principle completely destroys not only the country's claim to its son, but also the people's claim to their Messiah. At least this is what the saying meant to Luke. "The fact that Jesus performed miracles in Capernaum and not in Nazareth signifies that salvation has turned from the Jews to the Gentiles in accordance with the actions of Elijah and Elisha."[54] When they heard this saying, the citizens of Nazareth prepared to stone him for blasphemy.[55] This is more than an expression of their anger at being refused a miracle. If we wish to confine ourselves strictly to the immediate context, then we must seek the explanation for this in Jesus' blasphemous claim to be equal with the prophets. In Luke's interpretation, the reason apparently lies in what the saying implies about Israel being rejected in favor of the Gentiles.[56]

The story of Jesus' encounter with the Canaanite woman (Matt 15:21-28; Mark 7:24-30) is reminiscent of Elijah's stay in the house of the widow of Zarephath (1 Kgs 17:8-24; cf. 2 Kgs 4:18-37), but we can detect no references to that story in the evangelist's account.[57] The suggestion is scarcely tenable that originally Mark 7:26 read, "the woman was a Phoenician widow" (ἡ δὲ γυνὴ ἦν χήρα Φοινίκισσα; cf. 1 Kgs 17:9). By making insignificant changes in the text of Mark, not only has Matthew given the story a biblical and archaic form, but he has also accentuated its basic meaning.[58] He calls the woman a Canaanite (Χαναναία, Matt 15:22; Mark 7:26 has Συροφοινίκισσα), and he designates the area as "Tyre and Sidon" (Matt 15:21; Mark 7:24 has simply "Tyre"). Both are *typological* terms for Gentiles in the OT.[59] The story is designed to show

---

54. HNT on Luke, 62.

55. See Rengstorf, *Lukas*, 56.

56. Cf. Acts 13:46, 50; 14:19; see Jeremias, "'Ηλ(ε)ίας," *TDNT* 2. 935. The words of Luke 4:25ff. are found only in Luke. Their insertion in this context may be secondary, but the principle of universalism that is expressed by them and perhaps even the words themselves are Jesus' own (cf. Matt 11:20ff.; 12:38ff.).

57. There are no clear assimilations in the text; cf. 1 Kgs 17:10: ἐπορεύθη εἰς Σαρέπτα . . . (Σιδονίας) . . . καὶ ἰδοὺ ἐκεῖ γυνὴ χήρα. . . . Mark 7:24: ἀπῆλθεν (Matthew: ἀνεχώρησεν) εἰς τὰ ὅρια (Matthew: μέρη) Τύρου (Matthew: καὶ Σιδῶνος. . . . Matt 15:22: καὶ ἰδοὺ γυνὴ Χαναναία. . . .

58. Gressmann and Klostermann, *Matthäus*, 133.

59. See Schniewind, *Matthäus*, 378.

Jesus' attitude toward the Gentiles. In spite of any appearance to the contrary, it is in agreement with what we have just presented: Jesus grants his salvation to the one who believes. It is, however, offered first to Israel and then to the Gentiles.[60] Jesus was conscious of being guided in this matter and he saw his path outlined in the prophets. The mission of the prophets concerned the covenant people first of all, although they recognized that the Gentiles were included in God's saving purpose.[61] In this same vein, Deutero-Isaiah says concerning the prophet in whom Jesus recognized himself, "It is too small a thing for you to be my servant to restore the tribes of Jacob and bring back these of Israel I have kept. I will also make you a light for the Gentiles, that you may bring my salvation to the ends of the earth" (Isa 49:6).[62] In the story we are considering, the emphasis lies on the fundamental restriction of Jesus' earthly activity to Israel, which was necessitated by the course of redemptive history. This is why it could not be compared with the story of Elijah.

Just as typology sheds light on Jesus' attitude about the Gentiles sharing in the messianic salvation, so also it elucidates the use of his miraculous power exclusively for blessing and not for punishment. The suggestion of the sons of Zebedee in Luke 9:54 that Jesus "call down fire from heaven" is formulated in a way that shows verbal dependence on Elijah's request for a similar miraculous visitation (2 Kgs 1:10, 12). Even if the explicit reference at the end of the statement—"even as Elijah did" (ὡς καὶ Ἠλίας ἐποίησεν, Luke 9:54)—is a gloss and should be stricken, the connection is still obvious.[63] This shows clearly that typology is more than a gradual heightening of different stages in redemptive history; it involves a contrasting of one stage with another. In the activity of the prophets there is a continual intermingling of salvation and miracles of punishment (Exodus 7ff.; Numbers 12; 1 Kgs 13:18ff.; 2 Kgs 2:23ff.). John the Baptist expected Jesus to perform both, but expected them to be raised to the level of perfection (Matt 3:12 par. Luke). To be sure, the Son of Man will one day visibly execute judgment on God's enemies, i.e., on all who have not received him here (Matt 25:31, 46; etc.). In the context of his present mission, however, he rejects the miracles of punishment. He does not do this only on certain occasions like that one, but because a different spirit characterizes his mission, as the early addition has correctly explained (Luke 9:55, D; cf. Mark 10:45 par. Matthew; Luke 19:10; John 3:17). The kingdom is present already; nevertheless, this is still the time of sowing and not the time of harvest (cf. Matt 13:24ff.). The OT miracles of punishment continue to show us that God is judging with forbearance (ἀνοχή). For us and for Christ, they are types of the future judgment; they are

---

60. Mark 7:27: πρῶτον, like Rom 1:16; Acts 13:46; etc. Matthew states it more pointedly to emphasize, in keeping with his basic tendency, how much Jesus strove for Israel so that there is no excuse for the unbelief of the Jews (see Schniewind, *Matthäus*, 472).

61. Cf. Isa 2:1ff. (Mic 4:1ff.); Jer 1:5; Isa 45:20-24; etc.

62. Cf. Isa 42:6; cf. Luke 2:31f.; Acts 1:8; John 8:12; and Matt 5:14.

63. Omitted from Hesychian e vg sy^sc, but included in C Koine D it; see HNT on this passage.

not, however, types of the present church age.[64] The church stands under the sign of the crucified and resurrected one. Therefore, the church is already in the new aeon, but it is not yet under the sign of the returning Son of Man.

God's call has not become easier in this age; rather, it is more serious and difficult. This is illustrated typologically in the way Jesus responds to those whom he has called. To those who want to follow him Jesus denies the request that Elijah readily granted his disciple, Elisha, when he called him[65] (cf. Luke 9:61 with 1 Kgs 19:19-21). Of course, this is no explicit reference; at most, one might imagine that the concluding simile of the plowman is indicative of a subconscious memory (cf. Luke 9:62 with 1 Kgs 19:19).[66] Though the disciples' relationship to Jesus conforms outwardly to rabbinic practice, the way in which he wins his disciples "is something unparalleled in his day, and it is not accidental that we have no similar examples."[67] Jesus is not a rabbi; one who is greater than a prophet is here.

The story of the stranger who was driving out demons (Mark 9:38-40 par. Luke), which also deals with the relationship between discipleship and the working of miracles, has an OT counterpart in Num 11:27f. Jesus, like Moses, rejects the suggestion of his zealous disciples, who, like Joshua, are unwilling that anyone outside the narrow circle of disciples be gifted with divine power. In both instances—even in the NT story—the divine power is the Spirit of God, because it is to the Spirit that Jesus attributes his power over demons (Matt 12:28; cf. Mark 3:22f.; see Num 11:29). The others prophesy by the same Spirit as Moses, but not in Moses' name. The stranger, however, drives out the demons in Jesus' name and by his Spirit. Therefore, the elements of a typology are undeniably present. Has the evangelist indicated this in any way? There are reminiscences in the wording.[68] Furthermore, the similarity is so great, even in the details, that many have suggested that Numbers 11 has influenced the shaping of this story.[69] Undoubtedly the evangelist saw the connection. Jesus is not merely an instrument of the Spirit, as the prophets were; he is the Lord of the Spirit. His followers receive the Spirit and all other redemptive gifts through him.[70]

---

64. See p. 197 n. 81.

65. ἐπορεύθη ὀπίσω, 1 Kgs 19:21, LXX.

66. On the "looking back" cf. the story of Lot's wife in Gen 19:17, 26 (referred to in Luke 17:31f.).

67. Rengstorf, "διδάσκαλος," TDNT 2. 153ff. The quotation is from p. 156 n. 49.

68. Mark 9:39: ὁ δὲ Ἰησοῦς εἶπεν, Μὴ κωλύετε αὐτόν. Num 11:28: καὶ . . . Ἰησοῦς (Joshua) . . . εἶπεν . . . κώλυσον αὐτούς.

69. Cf. Hauck, Markus (THKNT; Leipzig, 1931) 115.

70. On the other hand, there is no typological connection between the actions of the disciples in the story of Jesus' blessing the children in Mark 10:13 par. and the actions of Gehazi when confronted by the Shunammite woman who was seeking Elisha's help in 2 Kgs 4:27. The fact that Jesus, like the prophet, helps the poor, the children, and the women, while the servant wants to avoid such annoyances, is too general and too trivial a basis to connect these two events. Furthermore, Gehazi is a servant, not a disciple.

In both content and method Jesus' saving activity is an antitype of the activity of the prophets, and the effect that his activity has on the people is the antitype of the effect of the work of the prophets. Some people are willing to be built into the church of God; others, however, are hardened and rebel against God and those whom he sends. Both responses occur in fulfillment of typology. Jesus' destiny is shaped in the same way. Jesus saw these connections clearly and he related his path of suffering and his exaltation typologically to the experiences of the prophets. First, we will indicate the typological relationships of Jesus' suffering, and then, in conclusion, we will discuss the place of the church in typology because the other kinds of typology that concern Jesus' person flow into the church.

c. Jesus' Death

The evangelists stress the fact that Jesus was not surprised when his mission ended in suffering and death. He deliberately took this on himself as being God's will and was confident that he would subsequently be exalted. Jesus' three announcements of his passion disclose the way in which he taught his disciples after they confessed that he was the Christ. "He then began to teach them that the Son of Man must suffer many things and . . . be killed and after three days rise again" (Mark 8:31).[71] This is no human prediction; it is a proclamation of God's will for the Son of Man. "This δεῖ (must) under which His suffering, death and resurrection, and according to Lk. His ascension, stand, belongs to the mysterious divine work of judgment and salvation in the last time."[72] The divine purpose is revealed in Scripture so that the suffering, death, and resurrection of Christ are a fulfillment of prophecy. This insight is emphasized by the evangelists and by the entire NT and it can be traced to Jesus himself (Luke 24:25ff., 44ff.). Of the eight passages in which Mark refers explicitly to OT prophecy,[73] six (all from the mouth of Jesus) refer to Christ's suffering and death.[74] Only two, however, contain actual quotations (Mark 12:10f. par. = Ps 118:22f.; Mark 14:27 par. Matthew = Zech 13:7); the other four merely refer to Scripture in general (Mark 9:12, 13 [John the Baptist!]; 14:21 par., 49 par. Matthew). Luke adds to the number of references and, with the exception of two (Luke 4:17-21; 7:27 par. Matthew; [21:22]), all refer to Jesus' death in Jerusalem

---

71. καὶ ἤρξατο διδάσκειν αὐτοὺς ὅτι δεῖ τὸν υἱὸν τοῦ ἀνθρώπου πολλὰ παθεῖν καὶ . . . ἀποκτανθῆναι καὶ μετὰ τρεῖς ἡμέρας ἀναστῆναι, Mark 8:31; 9:31; 10:32-34 par.; cf. Luke 17:25; 24:6f., 26, 46f.

72. W. Grundmann, "δεῖ," *TDNT* 2. 24.

73. Other explicit references in the Synoptic Gospels to Scripture passages: (1) References to the Law: Mark 7:10 par. Matthew; 10:4-8 par. Matthew; 10:19 par.; 11:17 par.; 12:29-33 par.; Matt 5:17, 21, 27, 31, 33, 38, 43; 7:12; 9:13; 12:7; 12:5 (cf. Matt 4:4, 6, 7, 10 par. Luke; Luke 2:22, 23, 24, 27, 39). (2) Teaching based on an interpretation of Scripture: Mark 12:19-27 par. (resurrection); 12:36f. par. (Son of David). (3) References to OT history: Mark 2:25f. par. (12:1-9 par.); (Matt 11:13 par. Luke); Matt 12:39-42 par. Luke; 23:35-40; Luke 4:25-27; etc.

74. The other two are Mark 1:2f. par.; 7:6 par. Matthew.

(cf. Luke 18:31; 24:25ff. [32], 44ff.), but only Luke 22:37 (= Isa 53:12) contains a quotation. In Matthew the proof from Scripture is regularly worked out in the fulfillment citations, but no quotation is adduced for Jesus' death.[75] Although numerous general references give the impression that all of Scripture ("Moses, the Prophets, and the Psalms," Luke 24:44) is full of the prophecy that the Messiah must experience a violent death, actually these are the only passages that are referred to explicitly (Mark 12:10f. par. = Ps 118:22f.; Mark 14:27 par. Matthew = Zech 13:7; Luke 22:37 = Isa 53:12).[76] Are we to assume that for apologetic and dogmatic purposes Jesus and the evangelists postulated something that did not exist at the time, but appeared later in the form of a proof from Scripture that was compiled slowly and with great effort?[77] The typological view of Jesus' death, which was the view of Jesus and the evangelists, points to a different solution.

Jesus perceives that even what was stated about the hardening effect of the prophetic message is fulfilled typologically through his activity. This is certainly true of his saying about the hardening of the people in which he quotes Isa 6:9f., regardless of the way the various traditions of the saying are evaluated. One tradition is found in Mark (4:11f.) and Luke (8:10) and another in Matthew (13:13ff.). According to Mark, Jesus proclaims his message of salvation in a veiled form so that (ἵνα, 4:12) those who are not willing to hear his call to repentance may be hardened; according to Matthew he does so because (ὅτι, 13:13) the people are already hardened, just as Isaiah (6:9f.) prophesied. Matthew places the word of Isaiah in the mouth of Jesus as a kind of fulfillment citation so that he designates the hardening of the people as the fulfillment of that prediction. Mark, however, has preserved what is clearly the more original form of the introduction. In it Jesus simply alludes—although unmistakably—to the word of the prophet indicating that what was said in that passage, as well as in many other places in the prophets (cf. Jer 5:21; Ezek 12:2; Deut 29:3), is now fulfilled typologically. The original context is not important.

His enemies are not the only ones whom Jesus accuses of blindness and obstinacy; he accuses his disciples as well (Mark 8:18 [eliminated from Matt 16:9]; cf. Mark 6:52). This is why he uses prophetic words that apply to the covenant

---

75. References in Matthew to the fulfillment of Scripture (not counting parallel passages): 2:5f.; 13:14f.; 21:16; (24:15; 23:39). The fulfillment citations: 1:22f.; 2:15, 17f., 23; 4:14-16; 8:17; 12:17-21 (13:14f.); 13:35; 21:4f.; 26:56; 27:9f. (35). Of these the following fulfillment quotations refer to Jesus' suffering: 26:56 (without any passage being quoted); 27:35 = Ps 22:18 (a later expansion); (8:17 = Isa 53:4, applied in an obvious way to the healing of diseases).

76. In John a number of additional passages dealing with this topic are cited explicitly (see below, pp. 179ff.).

77. K. Weidel, "Studien über den Einfluss des Weissagungsweises auf Die evangelische Geschichte," *TSK* 83 (1910) 87: "The proof from prophecy, strictly speaking, . . . seeks to demonstrate that this or that saying from the OT, was fulfilled in a specific event in the life of Jesus." This is a very superficial and mechanical conception of scriptural proof. Weidel explains all of Jesus' references to the "fulfillment" of Scripture as creations of the church, because they would only be meaningful when such proof from Scripture was being carried on (ibid., 88-107).

people of the OT (cf. Mark 8:18 with Jer 5:21; Ezek 12:2). Jesus dies not only by and for the sin of the people, but also for the sin of his disciples.

The hardening of the people is fulfilled with strange inevitability in Jesus' ministry; in the same way, the destiny of the prophets must also be fulfilled in him. This is clearly stated in the parable of the wicked tenants (Mark 12:1-12 par.). Just as this people has persecuted and killed the prophets (δοῦλοι θεοῦ),[78] so they will kill the beloved Son (υἱὸς ἀγαπητός), the Messiah, in the most disgraceful way (Mark 12:8).[79] This is how they make their stubborn rebellion against God complete, and the Old Covenant is broken once and for all. The vineyard, God's salvation, will be taken from the tenants and given to others, not to another earthly people, not to humanity in general, but to the people of the New Covenant.[80] The saying about the stone that is rejected and later becomes the cornerstone is added to provide a reference to prophecy. Jesus uses it to connect the announcement of his exaltation more clearly than ever with the announcement of his death (Mark 12:10f. par. = Ps 118:22f.). Undoubtedly this saying signifies that by God's miraculous action the rejected stone will become the main support of the building. There is no indication of how this will happen (cf. Acts 4:11), nor of the significance of the building (cf. 1 Pet 2:4f.), nor of the judgment resulting from the rejection of the stone (Luke 20:18 has been added to the passage; cf. Matt 21:43; 1 Pet 2:7f.). The OT applies the metaphors of the building and the vineyard to the people of God in various ways, so that what is implied in the conclusion of the parable of the vineyard may resonate here also. The fact that both of these metaphors are applied to the people of God in the OT (cf. Isa 5:1ff.; 28:16) may explain why Jesus juxtaposes them here. In accordance with the exegesis of his day, he may have understood the passage from the Psalms to be directly Messianic. This is certainly in harmony with the original meaning of the primary OT passage (Isa 28:16).[81]

The basic idea of the parable of the vineyard reappears in Jesus' pronouncements of woe on the Pharisees (Matt 23:29-39; cf. par. Luke 11:47-51; 13:34f.). Jesus rebuked the Jews by saying that when they erect monuments on the graves of the prophets (Matt 23:29) and complain hypocritically about the way their fathers treated the prophets (Matt 23:30), they themselves testify they are sons of the murderers of the prophets. "Fill up, then, the measure of the sin of your

---

78. On the use of this term in the OT, see above, p. 40, under "Servant of the Lord"; the term is applied to the prophets in Amos 3:7; Jer 7:25; 25:4.

79. See Mark 1:11; on υἱός (θεοῦ) as a title for the Messiah in Judaism and the Gospels, see P. Feine, *Theologie des Neuen Testaments* (Leipzig, 7th ed. 1936) 47ff.

80. In no way is this parable an allegory that has been adapted to the way things actually happened (e.g., Matt 21:39 nor even Mark 12:8), as has been suggested as an objection to its being attributed to Jesus. It may be "loaded down with artificiality and inappropriate figures" (Lohmeyer, *Markus*, 249), but none of Jesus' parables simply portrays "a bit of agricultural life" (ibid., 247; cf. Schniewind, *Matthäus*, 146).

81. Ps 118:22f. was applied by the rabbis (1) to Abraham, (2) to David, (3) also to the Messiah (Str-B 1. 875f.). KAT on Isa 28:16: "The old application to the Messiah is most natural."

forefathers!" (Matt 23:32). There is one prophet left, the Christ, and the present generation will kill him. The persecution of the prophets, the death of Jesus, and also the persecution of the disciples, who are endowed with the Spirit, are all viewed together once again in a saying that resembles a stereotyped expression: "Therefore I am sending you prophets and wise men and teachers. Some of them you will kill and crucify; others you will flog in your synagogues and pursue from town to town. And so upon you will come all the righteous blood that has been shed on earth from the blood of righteous Abel (Genesis 4) to the blood of Zechariah" (2 Chr 24:20ff.: the last book in the Palestinian canon![82] Matt 23:34f.). This encompasses the history of God and fallen mankind that spans the entire OT and that comes now to its ultimate fulfillment in the cross and resurrection of Christ. Since all of this will be fulfilled in "this generation," the judgment will also be fulfilled on this generation typologically (see Matt 23:36). "This generation" is the present generation of Israel and is representative of the whole nation, who, in their opposition to God, are representative of humanity.[83]

Everything will happen primarily in and through Jerusalem, which represents Israel (cf. Isa 40:1f.).[84] Viewing all of these relationships typologically, Christ expected to die in Jerusalem (Matt 23:37-39 par. Luke; Luke 13:33; cf. 9:31, 51, 53; 18:31; Matt 16:21). Therefore, the destruction of old Zion and of the first temple is the ultimate typological fulfillment of the devastation that was announced by the prophets (Matt 23:38f. alluding to Jer 22:5; 12:7). The church of Christ, however, sees this as a sign that God "has taken his vineyard from the tenants" and as an omen of the judgment that will come on "this generation."[85]

The judgment will occur when "the sign of the Son of Man" (Matt 24:30) appears, when the risen and exalted Christ returns visibly. This is what is meant by the saying about the sign of Jonah.[86] When the Jews demanded that Jesus give them an unambiguous sign from God, he told them about this sign: "As Jonah was a sign to the Ninevites, so also will the Son of Man be to this generation" (Luke 11:30). Another version of the saying that is found in Matthew explains this. As Jonah was buried in the belly of the fish for three days and three nights (Jonah 2:1 = Matt 12:40a), so the Son of Man will spend three days and three nights inside the earth, in Sheol, the place of the dead (Matt 12:40).

---

82. Also according to *b. B. Bat.* 14b (L. Goldschmidt, *Der Babylonischen Talmud* [Berlin, 1930-36] 8. 55); Matt 23:35 suggests that this was already true in NT times. Scarcely ever is noncanonical material quoted in the NT with the same emphasis as canonical (see G. Schrenk, "γραφή," *TDNT* 1. 756), but no fixed limits to the canon can be detected as yet.

83. Schniewind, *Matthäus*, 230.

84. See KAT on the passage.

85. In this larger context, Jesus' saying in Nazareth (Matt 13:57 par.), which seems to be no more than a proverb, takes on a more profound significance. It is the main point of the story in which the evangelists have obviously summarized the result of Jesus' ministry in Galilee (in Mark and Matthew it comes at the end, in Luke at the beginning).

86. Matt 12:38-40 par. Luke 11:29f.; cf. Matt 16:1-4 par. Mark 8:11-13 (in Matt 16:4, Mark 8:12 has been expanded from Q).

This typological comparison was undoubtedly handed down in the exegesis of the synagogue that described the deliverance of Jonah as deliverance "out of the belly of Sheol."[87] The sign of Jonah is the coming of someone who has virtually or actually passed through death. What was demanded was a sign that would convince the unbeliever (a sign from heaven, σημεῖον ἐκ τοῦ οὐρανοῦ, Matt 16:1). There is but one sign of the Son of Man and it is not his preaching about his resurrection, but his coming again for judgment (cf. Matt 24:30).[88] This must be the meaning of the shorter version of the saying in Luke also. Jesus' preaching of repentance cannot be the sign because it is not the kind of "sign" (σημεῖον) that is meant by the word; furthermore, the sign was to come in the future ("will be given," δοθήσεται, Luke 11:29).[89] The psychological question whether the citizens of Nineveh knew what had happened to Jonah (the Bible does not mention that they had been told) so that they could have viewed him as one who, in some sense, had risen from the dead is foreign to the NT idea of Scripture; besides, the legend seems to assume that they did know.[90] Even if the tradition in Luke is closer to the original version,[91] one may still wonder whether this typology, together with passages like Isa 53:10; 52:13, supplied the words Jesus used for the hope of his resurrection in his announcement of the passion. The phrase "after three days" (μετὰ τρεῖς ἡμέρας), which was not fulfilled precisely (Mark 8:31; 9:31; 10:34; cf. Matt 12:40: "three days and three nights"), simply means "after a brief period of time." It is surprising to find that only Matthew (16:21; 17:23; 20:19) and Luke (9:22; 18:33) have changed it to "on the third day" (τῇ τρίτῃ ἡμέρᾳ), in harmony with the early Christian kerygma (1 Cor 15:4).

Every aspect of Jesus' prediction of his passion—his suffering, death, and resurrection—have their scriptural basis in the typology of the prophets. This typology was brought to Jesus' attention by the voice from heaven at his baptism; consequently, Jesus was aware of the way he would die from the very beginning.[92] The story of the escape to Egypt is intended to disclose this fundamental feature already in the story of the Christ child. Along with other motifs, the

---

87. J. Jeremias, "Ἰωνᾶς," *TDNT* 3. 409 n. 27.

88. In the present context with the words that follow about Jesus' preaching of repentance, however, the former may also be included (cf. Luke 16:30f.). Jesus' return under the veil of faith, which occurred in his postresurrection appearances to his disciples, and his visible return are often intertwined in Jesus' preaching.

89. Ibid. 3. 408ff.

90. Ibid. 3. 409 n. 26.

91. The shorter form of the saying in Luke 11:30 could have arisen from the omission of the statement about the three days and three nights that was not fulfilled precisely (Schniewind, *Matthäus*, 357), but it is more likely that it is the original form and that Matt 12:40 is an appropriate explanation (T. Zahn, *Das Evangelium des Matthäus* [Kommentar zum Neuen Testament; Leipzig, 1903ff.] 473; Gressmann and Klostermann, *Matthäus*, on this passage; Jeremias, "Ἰωνᾶς," *TDNT* 3. 409f.).

92. Cf. Mark 1:11 with the calling of the Servant of the Lord in Isa 42:1; see above, p. 62.

memory of Moses may have influenced its formation.[93] The typology of the prophet does not provide any scriptural basis for the goal that lay beyond Jesus' death—his exaltation at the right hand of God, which Luke places also explicitly under the necessity (δεῖ) of the redemptive decree (Luke 24:26; Acts 3:21). What it does provide is a forceful means of expression. The phrase, "he was taken up into heaven" (ἀνελήμφθη εἰς τὸν οὐρανόν),[94] which describes the ascension, appears to have been taken from the account of Elijah's translation.[95] There are no contacts with the haggadah about Moses' assumption other than the similarities demanded by the subject matter,[96] nor is there any real typological connection between the ascension of Christ and the traditions about the assumptions of the prophets. Moreover, that is scarcely what the evangelists wish to suggest. Christ's exaltation to the right hand of God (cf. Acts 2:33; etc.), his being lifted from all earthly limitations into unrestricted community with God's power (Matt 28:18, 20), cannot be compared with the assumption of OT saints that simply obviated their death and burial. The evangelists do not present the story of the ascension in order to tell a miracle story. This is obvious when their accounts are compared with the Jewish elaborations of the stories about assumptions in the OT. They want to proclaim as an article of faith that Christ has been exalted as Lord. The story of the assumption of Elijah (2 Kgs 2:1, 11ff.) may have provided a vehicle for expressing this conviction. Other details in the story may be associated with the expectation of the coming of the Son of Man (cf. Acts 1:11b: clouds). The significance of the ascension itself is most likely prefigured in the prophecy of Ps 110:1. Here again we come into contact with other kinds of typology. We cannot fully master the typological basis for the divine necessity which stands over the death of Jesus until we have also surveyed these other kinds of typology that concern Christ.

2. THE SON OF DAVID AND LORD

Because Jesus' activity surpassed the functions of a prophet, the people began to ask, "Could this be the Son of David?" (Matt 12:23; cf. John 7:42). The

---

93. Cf. Matt 2:20 with Moses' escape to Midian in Exod 4:19f.: ἄπελθε . . . τεθνήκασιν γὰρ πάντες οἱ ζητοῦντές σου τὴν ψυχήν. ἀναλαβὼν δὲ Μωυσῆς τὴν γυναῖκα καὶ τὰ παιδία. . . . For other common motifs see Gressmann and Klostermann, *Matthäus*, on this passage.

94. Mark 16:19; Acts 1:2, 22 (11: ἀναλημφθείς); Luke 24:51 Hesychian, Koine: ἀνεφέρετο εἰς τὸν οὐρανόν.

95. 2 Kgs 2:11: καὶ ἀνελήμφθη Ἠλίου ἐν συσσεισμῷ, ὡς εἰς τὸν οὐρανόν; v 12: καὶ Ἐλισαῖε ἑώρα; cf. Acts 1:11: ὁ Ἰησοῦς ὁ ἀναλημφθεὶς ἀφ' ὑμῶν εἰς τὸν οὐρανὸν . . .; Mark 16:19: ἀνελήμφθη εἰς τὸν οὐρανὸν καὶ ἐκάθισεν ἐκ δεξιῶν τοῦ θεοῦ (cf. Psalm 110).

96. The haggadah about the assumption of Moses, recorded by Josephus (*Ant.* 4.8.48 §§320-26), contains similar features: It took place ἐν τῷ ὄρει τῷ Ἀραβεῖ καλουμένῳ . . . Ἰεριχοῦντος ἀντικρύ, and it happened "while he still embraced Eleazar and Joshua and spoke with them, when a cloud suddenly stood over him, he was removed from their sight into a valley below" (ἀφανίζεται κατά τινος φάραγγος) (cf. Str-B 1. 753). Zech 14:4 expects Yahweh to be revealed on the Mount of Olives in the new age (cf. Acts 1:12; Luke 24:50 is somewhat different).

anticipation of the coming of the Son of David was the predominant messianic hope of the people and the teachers.[97]

Although this messianic title was very familiar to the rabbis, it is seldom found in the Gospels. It occurs most frequently in Matthew.[98] The title is not used by Jesus or his disciples (Matt 21:9 is the only possible exception), but only by the people (Matt 12:23; 21:9, 15), especially by those who were seeking help from the Messiah (cf. Mark 10:47 par.; Matt 9:27; 15:22) and by the evangelists (Matt 1:1). This is characteristic of the way all of the ideas related to this theme are used with reference to Jesus.

The application of this title to Jesus indicates that the people in their curiosity and hope transferred the expectation of the Son of David to Jesus. It is frequently reported that people fell prostrate before Jesus. Perhaps they did this to show honor to the messianic king (Luke 5:12; 17:16).[99] The Sanhedrin rejected Jesus' messianic claim after they used the concept of the Son of David to test it. They also suspected him of being a political messianic king, and this is why they put him on the cross. With the question about taxes (Mark 12:13-17 par.), they were attempting to bring this messianic king into conflict with Caesar. This is the only way to make sense of Pilate's question (Mark 15:2 par.), which is the same in all the traditions, of the behavior of the soldiers when they mocked him (Mark 15:18; cf. Luke 23:11), and of the inscription over his cross (Mark 15:26 par.). The Sanhedrin is not content simply to get rid of Jesus; they want to hang him on the cursed tree, for whoever dies on the cursed tree cannot be God's Messiah.

Jesus took a definite stand regarding the messianic role that was attributed to him from both good and bad motives and had developed from the earliest messianic expectations in the OT (Mark 12:35-37 par.). Appealing to Ps 110:1 (Mark 12:36 par.) he explains that though the Messiah will come from David's line— that is not contested—he is greater than a son of David. "David himself calls him 'Lord.' How then can he be his son?" (Mark 12:37). The Messiah, therefore, must not simply rank relatively higher than David; he must be fundamentally higher. The term "Lord" (κύριος) makes him equal with God. The way in which this is deduced from Ps 110:1 is culturally conditioned; it presupposes that the psalm comes from David and points to the Messiah.[100] Nevertheless, the content of Jesus' statement is very important for our investigation. He places the Christ

---

97. See p. 32 n. 54.

98. See Feine, *Theologie*, 70.

99. See Rengstorf, *Lukas*, on these passages.

100. On contemporary interpretations of Psalm 110, the OT passage most frequently quoted in the NT, see Str-B 4. 452-65: In the time of Jesus this psalm was most likely interpreted messianically (also in the LXX), but in rabbinical studies of Scripture one does not come across the slightest trace of a messianic understanding of Psalm 110 until the second half of the third century (ibid., 452). The psalm was applied to Abraham (ibid., 453ff.), to Hezekiah (ibid., 456), and to David (ibid.; on the later messianic interpretation see ibid., 457ff.). There are good reasons for supposing that Rabbi Ishmael (active A.D. 100-135) "exclusively from tendencies hostile to Christianity" abandoned the traditional messianic interpretation of the Psalms and substituted the application to Abraham (ibid., 459f.).

in typological relationship not only to David, but also to the Son of David of messianic expectation. In principle, then, the prophecies that are messianic in the narrower sense are also illuminated by typology. Accordingly, Jesus compared himself with David and Solomon and viewed his own career as a typological fulfillment of the promises concerning the Son of David.

The saying "one greater than Jonah is here" gives clear expression to prophet typology. Jesus places it side by side with the saying that expresses Son of David typology, "one greater than Solomon is here" (Matt 12:42 par. Luke). He is greater than the first son of David, who did not measure up to the messianic promise that was made to the house of David (2 Sam 7:11ff.). Jesus adds this saying to the story of the visit of the Queen of Sheba to Solomon in the height of his glory (1 Kgs 10:1ff.), and directs it to Israel as a call to repentance. "The Gentile queen came from the ends of the earth, as a great many nations will come in the messianic age; she came to hear the wisdom of the first son of David . . .; Israel, however, does not listen to him who reveals the wisdom of God."[101]

The Gospel of Matthew puts much emphasis on the fact that Jesus descended from David. In obedience to Christ, Matthew asserts, even in the heading and in the genealogy of Jesus (Matt 1:2-17), that Jesus is more than a mere son of David. To be sure, Jesus is "legally a son in David's line"[102] even without the virgin birth (Matt 1:18ff.) and apart from the genealogy that is interrupted by it (Matt 1:16). But the conclusion of the genealogy (Matt 1:16), which is certainly not a later alteration, and the fact that the genealogy is traced back beyond David to Abraham (see the heading in Matt 1:1 also) show that Jesus is more than a mere son of David; he is the descendant of Abraham in whom all the promises are fulfilled.[103]

Just as there is a typological relationship between Jesus and the Son of David, so there is also between Jesus and David. Consequently, Jesus is related typo-

---

101. Schniewind, *Matthäus*, 358.

102. Ibid., 211.

103. In Matthew and Luke the OT is used to throw light on the virgin birth. Matthew, in keeping with his method of scriptural proof, designates the virgin birth as a fulfillment of Isa 7:14 (Matt 1:22, which is certainly in agreement with the original meaning of the passage; cf. KAT on the passage; the rabbis apply it to Hezekiah for polemical reasons, Str-B 1. 75). The birth narrative in Luke, which is also colored by the OT without any explicit quotations, places the story of the birth of John the Baptist parallel to the births of men of God in the OT (see below), so that the circumstances around the birth of Christ appear as "the greatest heightening of what the OT relates about the births of Isaac, Samson, and Samuel, and what the first chapter of Luke, in conformity with such examples, tells about the birth of John" (HNT on Luke, 14). (On ἐπισκιάζω, see above on Mark 9:7.) Therefore, the virgin birth is not to be interpreted as implying "physical" sonship to God in keeping with Hellenistic ideas. It must be explained in terms of the OT idea of God's shaping of history in creative power (cf. Rengstorf, *Lukas*, 20). On the story of the birth of John the Baptist note the following allusions: cf. Luke 1:7 with Gen 18:11; 1:13 with Gen 17:19; 1:18 with Gen 15:8; 18:11f.; 17:17; Luke 1:37 with Gen 18:14; and 1:41, 44 with Gen 25:22, LXX; Luke 1:15 with Judg 13:4f. (Samson); 1:31 with Judg 13:3; 1:80 with Judg 13:24f.; Luke 1:15 with (1 Sam 1:11); 1:46-55 with 1 Sam 2:1-10; 1:69 with 1 Sam 2:10; 1:80; 2:40, 52 with 1 Sam 2:26 (Samuel).

logically to the Messiah who comes as David *redivivus*. This is implied in Jesus'
appeal to David in the conflict that arose concerning the disciples' picking of
grain on the Sabbath (Mark 2:23-28 par.), as reflection on the exegesis of the
passage will show. Without allowing himself to be drawn into a casuistic debate
concerning the exposition of the Sabbath command, Jesus defends the conduct
of his disciples "even while taking for granted that they have broken the law."[104]
In the arguments he advances from Scripture (Mark 2:25f. par.—1 Sam 21:1-6;
Matt 12:5; cf. Num 28:9f.), Jesus cites two instances in which persons violated
the regulations of the OT law (with the first of these cf. Lev 24:9) without being
censured by Scripture. What does the conduct of Jesus' disciples have in common
with these exceptional cases that allows him to claim the same prerogatives?
What David did at Nob (1 Sam 21:2-7), the first example to which Jesus refers,
is necessitated by his extraordinary need ("were hungry and in need," χρείαν
ἔσχεν καὶ ἐπείνασεν, Mark 2:25). This is also the way in which the scribes
attempted to justify the action of the righteous king.[105] David has been banished
and is fleeing from Saul, because God had chosen him to be king. He needed
what he received from Ahimelech[106]—the bread (and the sword)—in order to
keep alive.

In addition to its emphasis on David's special need, Jesus' account of the
story differs from the OT by stressing that David took the consecrated bread (in
1 Sam 21:6 he received it from the priest) and that he had companions to whom
he gave some of it. These changes were probably due to the tradition of the
synagogue—that tradition also placed the event on a Sabbath[107]—and to Jesus'
reason for referring to the event. He does not compare the conduct of his disciples
with what David did; rather, he compares himself and his disciples with David
and his companions. Because Jesus permits and defends what his disciples have
done, he makes himself responsible for their violation of the Law just as David
was for his companions.

Two explanations that have become widely accepted do not adequately take
into account the emphasis on the special need and the comparison of Jesus with
David. (1) Jesus wanted to prove "that there are stipulations of the Law that may
be broken in certain circumstances without penalty."[108] (2) Jesus did not under-
mine the Law by casuistry as the scribes did;[109] he reestablished the divine

---

104. Zahn, *Matthäus*, 448. Cf. Str-B 1. 616: "Picking grain, though it was permitted according
to Deut 23:25, was viewed as part of the work of harvest and as such was prohibited (for references
see ibid. 1. 617f.). Under certain circumstances what Jesus' disciples did could have been punished
with death by stoning" (for references see ibid. 1. 618). Accordingly, this is not a case of breaking
an OT command, but of violating rabbinical casuistics. (On this see *Mishnah*, Seder II, Tractate 1;
in German: Beer Schabbath in *Ausgewählte Mischnatractate* 5 [Tübingen, 1908] 10-36; a history
of the Sabbath is included there also.)

105. Str-B 1. 618, on Matt 12:3.

106. Mark says Abiathar, but that is an error.

107. J. Jeremias, *Jesus als Weltvollender* (Gütersloh, 1930) 80.

108. Klostermann, *Markus*, 35; cf. Lohmeyer, *Markus*, 65.

109. See below, n. 112.

command when it was threatened with perversion by the scribes. At the same time, however, he set it aside with "the new command" in accordance with his words "but I tell you." The first of these, but not the second, gives expression to another interpretation that is based on Mark 2:27 and Matt 12:7: In this event the Pharisees should see "how much their manner of interpreting the Law differs from the meaning of the Bible and from the will of God. God is not more concerned about the Sabbath or the consecrated bread than he is about man, and he does not make these things the means of our worship for their own sakes."[110]

Jesus' attitude toward the Law, in which he goes beyond the prophetic standard, and the lengthy comparison of Jesus and David are explained when we observe that Christ-David typology is the background of the saying and the general presupposition that supports it. If David, who is a type of the righteous king, may even (on the Sabbath) take sacred bread (Lev 24:5-9) and give it to his hungry companions without being reproved, then certainly he who is "greater than Solomon" may permit his hungry disciples to pick grain on the Sabbath.[111] By associating with him who "has no place to lay his head" (Matt 8:20) they have become involved in a similar situation of need (Mark 10:38ff.). Moreover, they have become the people of the New Covenant, who, because of their commitment to the "law of Christ," are free from the ordinances of the Old Covenant.

This interpretation of the saying is in harmony with Jesus' other statements. In giving a general summary of his position, Jesus does not stop with the universal principle in Mark 2:27, which was also advocated by the scribes.[112] He gave it a new meaning by adding a statement that must be interpreted messianically:[113] "The Son of Man is Lord even of the Sabbath" (Mark 2:28 par.). The typological basis is stated explicitly in a second example that is quoted only by Matthew. If the temple service of the priests takes precedence over the Sabbath (Num 28:9),[114] then what is done in the service of Jesus will be even more acceptable because "one greater than the temple is here" (Matt 12:6). Jesus' work is more important than the worship of God in the temple because Jesus takes the place of the temple.[115] The absence of an appropriate quotation to

---

110. Schlatter, *Lukas*, 188f.; cf. Zahn, *Matthäus*, 449; Hauck, *Markus* (THKNT) 39f.

111. According to Rengstorf, *Lukas*, 68f.; cf. Jeremias, *Jesus*, 80; Schniewind, *Matthäus*, 61f., 350.

112. Cf. *Mek. Exod.* 31:13, "Rabbi Simeon ben Menasiah (ca. 180) said: Look, it says in Exod 31:14, 'Observe the Sabbath, because it is holy to you' (= for your benefit), i.e., the Sabbath is intrusted to you and not you to the Sabbath" (quoted in Str-B 2. 5). (Nearly the same thing is found in *2 Apoc. Bar.* 14:18, ". . . he (man) was not made for the sake of the world, but the world was made for his sake.") "However, this principle is not valid in all situations. It merely indicates that the Sabbath might only be profaned to save a person's life" (Str-B 2. 5).

113. So Klostermann, *Markus*; Schniewind, *Matthäus*; Rengstorf, *Lukas*; and Lohmeyer, *Markus*, on this passage.

114. Also according to rabbinical interpretation, see Str-B 1. 620.

115. See below, pp. 115f. and 191f.

reveal the typology underlying the first argument may have been a consequence of the messianic secret.[116]

Just as Jesus elucidated his vocation by applying David typology directly to it, so he also viewed his destiny and his preaching of redemption as a (typological) fulfillment of the predictions about the Son of David and arranged them accordingly. All four evangelists report that Jesus so ordered his last entrance to Jerusalem that those who were able to see might perceive that the promise in Zech 9:9 was being fulfilled (Mark 11:2 par.).[117] Shortly before this, by healing the blind man from Jericho who addressed him as the Son of David, Jesus publicly acknowledged this role. According to Mark, this was the first time that he did (10:47, 49 par.). This may explain the cry that arose (Mark 11:9f. par. = Ps 118:25f.) from the crowd of disciples who suspected what was happening. It was not unusual for people to sing this very common festival psalm, so that the casual observer would not have known it was a proclamation of his messiahship.[118] The interpretation that the resurrected one gave his disciples of his entire life, including this incident (see John 12:16) and concerning its scriptural basis, may have superimposed the splendor of Easter on the account of the triumphal entry by reshaping it and adding details. Apparently Matthew added the second animal in order that Zech 9:9 might be fulfilled more precisely.[119] In the light of history, we dare to assert that Jesus was content to fulfill the distinctive features in the prophecy. The other details are common motifs and are not taken especially from royal typology. The spreading of clothing on the road (Mark 11:8 par.) and on the colt (Luke 19:35) is associated with the honoring of kings in the OT (2 Kgs 9:13; cf. 1 Kgs 1:33ff.).

The triumphal entry reminds us of two passages of Scripture that indicate the king is heading toward suffering and death. From Psalm 118, which is part of the Passover Hallel (Psalms 113–118), Jesus derives the saying about the stone that is rejected (Mark 12:10 par.), and from the second half of the book of Zechariah (Deutero-Zechariah) he draws the prophecy concerning his death that he announced on the road to Gethsemane (Mark 14:27 par. Matthew =

---

116. Cf. Zahn, *Matthäus*, 450, "If the first example (v 3) lacks an appropriate application, which by analogy with Matt 12:41 should have read, 'One greater than David is here,' and which must have been especially obvious to the Son of David, then it must be because Jesus did not want to contribute anything to the spread of any slogan whereby he was proclaimed to be the Messiah; cf. Matt 9:27-31."

117. Cf. Str-B 1. 842: Nowhere in the Pseudepigrapha is there any reference to Zech 9:9; on the other hand, in the rabbinical literature it is rather common to apply the passage to the Messiah (for examples see ibid. 1. 842ff.). Cf. *b. Sanh.* 98a: "Rabbi Alexandrai (ca. 270) said: Rabbi Jehoshua ben Levi (ca. 250) contrasted Dan 7:13 . . . and Zech 9:9. . . . If the Israelites are deserving (are worthy of it), he will come with the clouds of heaven; if they are not deserving (he will come) poor and riding on a donkey" (quoted in ibid. 1. 843).

118. Schniewind, *Matthäus*, 139; cf. Str-B 1. 845.

119. Matt 21:7 is from Mark 11:7 par. Luke, influenced by Zech 9:9 = Matt 21:5, which differs from both the LXX and the MT.

Zech 13:7): "I will strike the shepherd, and the sheep will be scattered."[120] Besides, Jesus seems to have recognized immediately that his being anointed at Bethany (Mark 14:3-9 par. Matthew; John 12:1-8) was the symbolic anointing of a king (cf. Mark 14:7, 9) as well as an anointing in preparation for his death (cf. Mark 14:8).

The prophecy in Zechariah about the death of the shepherd falls within the scope of royal typology, because "shepherd" in this passage is a figurative title for the king that is common in the OT. "The good shepherd . . . means a good king who leads the people of God; because shepherd and king are closely related concepts in prophecy."[121] God permits the violent death of the shepherd, which results in the scattering of the flock of which only a third will be preserved as a purified remnant.[122] If the prophet had King Josiah in mind as the model of the good shepherd and Jehoiakim as the model of the bad king,[123] then the origin of the prophecy in typology is clearly stated. This, of course, is the typology of the OT, not the NT. The figurative form of the prophecy made it possible for Jesus to place it directly on the level of the NT and to apply it, not to an earthly king and to Israel, which is what the prophet had in mind, but to himself and his disciples who are the new Israel. The basic ideas of the prophecy and of Jesus' concept of his kingship are in agreement: the prophet is not the only one who must suffer; the good king who will establish God's justice and truth among his people must suffer also. In Zech 12:8, 10, the shepherd who was slain reappears to his people. Accordingly, this prophecy expands the range of royal typology to include the resurrection (cf. Mark 14:28). What Zechariah says about the impression that the reappearance of the shepherd makes on the people is similar to the description of the dismay of the nations when the Son of Man returns (Matt 24:30; cf. Zech 12:12-14; Rev 1:7).[124]

The concept of the shepherd gives royal typology its full range and depth. Jesus uses this concept in teaching and preaching about his mission as savior. He has compassion on the people because they are like a flock that is scattered and fainting without a shepherd.[125] He knows he is sent to the lost sheep of Israel (Matt 15:24 [10:6]; cf. Ezek 34:10). As early as in the nativity story in Matthew, it is stated that he is of the Son of David from Bethlehem who will feed the people of God (Matt 2:6 = Mic 5:2; cf. Matt 1:21).[126] We have a clear

---

120. Also cf. Mark 14:24 with Zech 9:11.

121. Mic 5:3; Jer 23:1; Ezek 34:2ff.; cf. 1 Sam 16:11; 2 Sam 7:8. O. Procksch, *Die kleinen prophetischen Schriften nach dem Exil* (Stuttgart, 1929) 109.

122. Zech 13:8f.; Zech 13:7-9, the prophecy about the downfall of the shepherd, should be put with 11:4-14 (ibid., 108).

123. Ibid., 111; cf. H. Gressmann, *Der Messias* (Göttingen, 1929) 334ff.

124. John 19:37 = Zech 12:10 is superficial scriptural proof.

125. Mark 6:34; Matt 9:36; cf. Ezek 34:5: καὶ διεσπάρη τὰ πρόβατά μου διὰ τὸ μὴ εἶναι ποιμένας; cf. Num 27:17; 1 Kgs 22:17.

126. The story of the nativity is simply filled with ideas about his being the son of David, but the virgin birth is found there also (see above, n. 103; John implies that the first, the external sign, is unimportant as compared with the latter, the incarnation of the Logos, 7:41f.; cf. 6:42; 7:27).

reminder of Ezekiel's prophecy in the saying "The Son of Man came to seek and to save what was lost."[127] For one who is familiar with Scripture, this allusion indicates that God himself has come in Christ to save his people and to gather them and lead them because the prophecy in Ezekiel promises that God himself will take charge of his flock instead of the shepherds who failed (Ezek 34:11ff.). In the parables about the Good Shepherd, Jesus describes the way in which he fulfills this mission (Matt 18:12-14; cf. Luke 15:4-7). He does not see his kingship as consisting in his ruling and judging, but in his "serving and giving his life as a ransom for many" (Mark 10:42ff. par. Matthew). This is how he builds his kingdom (βασιλεία), which is also the kingdom of God (βασιλεία τοῦ θεοῦ), in the proper sense of the word. This is what the concept of the shepherd-king means when it is incorporated into the title "Son of Man." In Luke 19:10 what was predicted about the good shepherd is stated concerning the Son of Man. When he returns, the Son of Man[128] as royal judge (Matt 25:34) will separate the people as a shepherd divides the sheep from the goats (Matt 25:32), and so he will carry out the judgment which, according to Ezek 34:17, God himself will perform for his flock.[129]

It is natural that the statements about Jesus' subsequent glory usually and quite properly come from the prophecies belonging to royal typology. Jesus used the words of Psalm 110 to inform his judges of his imminent exaltation, "You will see the Son of Man sitting at the right hand of the Mighty One" (Mark 14:62 par.—Ps 110:1). This Son of Man is truly the Son of David and Lord.[130]

But the earthly Jesus already possesses this honor. God himself has shown him the typological significance of the Son of David promise. The use of Ps 2:7 in the voice from heaven at Jesus' baptism and at the transfiguration can be interpreted this way (Mark 1:11 par.; 9:7 par.). Jewish exegesis applies this psalm to earthly kings and to the earthly Messiah ben David.[131] When God uses this title to address Jesus, however, the phrase "Son of God" describes a much closer relationship to God than the OT or late Judaism would consider proper for an earthly king (2 Sam 7:14; Ps 89:27f.) or a Messiah ben David.[132] It signifies much more than it does in apocalypticism when it is applied to the heavenly Son of Man.[133] When asked by the high priest whether he was the "Son of the Blessed One," i.e., the Messiah ben David, Jesus answered, "I am" (ἐγώ εἰμι)—

---

127. Luke 19:10: ἦλθεν . . . ὁ υἱὸς τοῦ ἀνθρώπου ζητῆσαι καὶ σῶσαι τὸ ἀπολωλός. Ezek 34:16 says this about God as the good shepherd, τὸ ἀπολωλὸς ζητήσω (cf. Ezek 34:11, 15; cf. 34:23 where David *redivivus* is God's mediator).

128. See above on Matt 24:30 and Zech 12:12ff.

129. There is no verbal correspondence in Matt 25:32; cf. Ezek 34:17: ἐγὼ διακρινῶ ἀνὰ μέσον προβάτου καὶ προβάτου, κριῶν καὶ τραγῶν.

130. See above on Mark 12:35ff.

131. Str-B 3. 673ff.; cf. pp. 19f.

132. Ibid. 3. 15f., 19.

133. Ibid. 3. 17.

words that are applied to God in the OT (Mark 14:62; cf. Exod 3:14; Isa 43:10; 52:6f.).[134]

Accordingly, Son of David typology provides support for Jesus' call to repentance, direction for his work as savior, and illumination for the end of his mission in suffering, death, resurrection, and subsequent glory. The OT prophecy rises above what is strictly a type and in varying degrees it approaches the level of the NT. It is impossible to fully ascertain how much Jesus sensed the degree to which the individual prophecies still fall short of the NT fulfillment. The important thing is that he viewed the entire Son of David expectation as basically typological. Moreover, it is significant that the only prophecies he has quoted directly are actually very close to the New Covenant, while he simply alludes to the others. The emphasis always is on what is intrinsic and essential, never on fortuitous externals. Once again, comparison with the methodology of the evangelists will specially accentuate this quality.

Son of David typology, even more emphatically than prophet typology, leads us to still another kind—the typology of the Son of Man.

3. THE SON OF MAN

Jesus appropriated the expectations of "the prophet" and "the Son of David," but he did not apply these messianic titles to himself. He called himself exclusively by the title "the Son of Man." According to what we have been able to learn from late Jewish eschatology about the Son of Man,[135] it is clear that the NT associates many ideas with this title in which other typological connections are concealed. This is especially true of connections with creation typology, a kind of typology that we have not yet discussed. Therefore, we will attempt first to set forth the ideas that are inherent in this title in the NT.

a. The Content and Origin of the Concept "Son of Man" in the New Testament

A survey of the passages in which this title occurs shows that some very definite ideas were associated with it in the NT. "The Son of Man" (ὁ υἱὸς τοῦ ἀνθρώπου) is used as a title for Jesus about seventy times in the Synoptics (divided equally among the three evangelists) and twelve times in John. It is always found on the lips of Jesus as a title for himself. In the rest of the NT, with the exception of Acts 7:56, it occurs only in quotations from the OT.[136] Of the fourteen passages in Mark (most have parallels) that contain the title, two speak of the Son of Man's authority on earth (Mark 2:10 par., 28 par.). All of the others speak of his having to suffer, die, and rise again (Mark 8:31 [par.]; 9:9, 12 par. Matthew;

---

134. Schniewind, *Matthäus*, 159.
135. See above, p. 34.
136. 1 Cor 15:27 and Heb 2:6f.—Psalm 8; Rev 1:13ff.; 14:14–Dan 7:13; see p. 134 n. 32.

9:31 par.; 10:33 par.; 10:45 par. Matthew; 14:21a par., 21b [par.], 41 par.
Matthew) or of his future glory and coming again (Mark 8:38 [par.]; 13:26 par.;
14:62 par.). With the exception of the first two, these passages all come after
Peter's confession (Mark 8:27ff.). The same pattern is found in the passages that
Matthew and Luke have in common, and in the passages that belong to the
special material of each.[137] Even the passages in John, whose wording is stamped
with the character of that Gospel, conform to this pattern.[138] Consequently, most
of the statements about the Son of Man are divided into two very distinct groups
of ideas that seem diametrically opposed to each other. The sayings about the
hidden authority of the Son of Man on earth seem to be the nucleus for the other
statements that do not presuppose any such concise and pregnant concept, even
if we take into consideration the way the traditions are related to one another.[139]
Philologically the title simply means "human being,"[140] but it always has a
messianic flavor when applied to Jesus. These sayings create the impression that
the title "Son of Man" connotes a definite messianic idea that was not formulated
by Jesus, but was shaped and revealed by God's redemptive decree and would
be fulfilled by Jesus. We will try to discover the source of the NT sayings about
the Son of Man. (This is not the place to discuss the common roots of this

---

137. "Son of Man" in the Synoptics, except for Mark (and par.): (a) In the category of Jesus'
announcements of his suffering: passages common to Matthew and Luke: Matt 12:40 (cf. Luke 11:30,
borders on *b*). From Matthew's special material: Matt 26:2. From Luke's special material; Luke 22:48
(cf. Mark 14:41 par. Matthew and Luke, which is slightly earlier); 24:7 (a reference to Jesus'
announcement of his passion). (b) In the category of eschatological ideas: passages common to
Matthew and Luke: Matt 24:27, 37, 39, 44 (12:40; see above, *a*). From Matthew's special material:
Matt 10:23; 13:41; 16:27, 28; 19:28; 24:30a; 25:31. From Luke's special material: Luke 12:8 (cf.
Matt 10:32, obviously a secondary omission); 17:22; 18:8; 21:36. (c) Sayings about the earthly
ministry of the Son of Man: passages common to Matthew and Luke: Matt 8:20; 11:19; 12:32 (they
emphasize the veiling of his glory in his human form). From Matthew's special material: Matt 13:37
(in comparison with par., the following has been added: The Son of Man, who now sows the seed,
will later send his angels to gather the harvest [Matt 13:41]; 16:13 (compared with the par., the
following has been added in Matt 16:16: The Son of Man is "the Son of the living God"). From
Luke's special material: Luke 19:10 (cf. 9:56 Koine al lat sy^c; Matt 18:11 Koine D) appears to be
parallel in substance to Mark 10:45 par. Matthew, which is omitted from Luke.
   "Son of Man" in the Gospel of John: (a) Jesus' announcement of his passion is represented in
John in the special emphasis that is placed on the goal of his suffering and death, i.e., on his
resurrection and subsequent glory, by the phrases: "The Son of Man must be lifted up" and "The
Son of Man will be glorified" (ὑψόω includes crucifixion [John 12:33] and ascension to the Father
[cf. John 12:32; cf. Acts 2:33; 5:31], so also does δοξάζω; for the crucifixion, see John 12:23 [his
"hour" has come, then v 24 follows immediately (the kernel of wheat); v 27 is followed by δοξάζω
again in v 28]; cf. 13:31f.; 14:13; 16:14. The ascension is very clear in 17:4f.). The lifting up of
the Son of Man: John 3:14 and 12:24 (δεῖ); 8:28; cf. 6:62 (ascend). Glorification of the Son of Man:
John 12:23; 13:31. (b) Passages about the earthly ministry of the Son of Man: John 1:51; 3:13 (his
glory which is visible only to faith, or to him alone); 6:27, 53; 12:34b; 5:25 (the judgment is
transferred to him—that is always true for John—because he is the Son of Man; here without an
article); the close connection with the statements in *a* is obvious: 3:13—3:14; 6:27—6:53—6:62.
   138. See n. 137.
   139. See n. 137.
   140. Cf. its use 90 times to address Ezekiel; Ps 8:5; Matt 9:8; see H. Cremer, *Biblico-Theological Lexicon of New Testament Greek* (Edinburgh, 1872) 589-91.

concept in the history of religions.) As we might have expected, typological interpretation played a role in their genesis.

In seeking the source of these sayings, it is necessary first of all to consider the statements about the future glory of the Son of Man. Time and again they contain allusions to Dan 7:13. The Daniel saying is reproduced word for word in key passages like Mark 13:26; 14:62 without any indication that it is a quotation.[141] The fact that the title has its origin in Daniel, which Josephus considers Israel's favorite book in NT times,[142] will explain how the title could be used without any interpretation and yet be understood in a messianic sense. In the context of Dan 7:13, the Son of Man is not someone whose coming is to be expected in the future. Analogous to the animals that symbolize the world empires (Dan 7:2ff.), the Son of Man is a visionary symbol for the saints of the Most High (Dan 7:22) to whom the kingdom (βασιλεία) and authority (ἐξουσία) will be given after the world empires have been judged (Dan 7:14-22, 27). Most likely Pseudo-Daniel did not create the figure of the Son of Man as a symbol in his allegorical vision. Presumably, he appropriated it along with the entire allegory whose meaning is not confined to the stated interpretation.[143] Perhaps originally, and certainly before it was used in the NT, the Son of Man was not a symbol, but was an actual eschatological person who had messianic functions. He is portrayed as such a person in shining splendor in the figurative language of 1 Enoch (37–71) and also in 4 Ezra, but in a less colorful way similar to the hope of an earthly Messiah. Moreover, in the apocalyptic visions, the line separating metaphor and real expectation is fluid—for all language concerning the things that will come after the end is metaphorical in some sense. (In the NT, this interrelationship between the Son of Man and the "people of the Most High" became a meaningful way of expressing a true reality.)

Jesus adopted the saying about the future coming of the Son of Man (Dan 7:13) as a suitable way to express his own hope for the future, but he also reshaped it and enlarged it in a remarkable way. Dan 7:13 is the only possible source for his frequently repeated statement about the imminent "coming" of the Son of Man (ἔρχεσθαι, ἐλθεῖν, Matt 10:23; 25:31; Luke 18:8), which is always described as his coming in the last days to bring God's sovereignty and as his

---

141. Dan 7:13 is rendered rather freely from the LXX. The ὡς, which is connected with the vision, is dropped in the quotation (and ἤρχετο is changed to ἐρχόμενον). The placing of the article before the two words υἱός and ἄνθρωπος makes no significant difference. Instead of ἐπὶ τῶν νεφελῶν τοῦ οὐρανοῦ as in Matt 24:30 = Dan 7:13, LXX, Mark 13:26 par. Luke has ἐν νεφέλαις (Luke νεφέλῃ) (see G. Dalman, The Words of Jesus Considered in the Light of Post-biblical Jewish Writings and the Aramaic Language (Edinburgh, 1909) 241f.

142. A. Schlatter, Einleitung in die Bibel (Stuttgart, 5th ed. 1901) 263; Josephus Ant. 10.11.7 §§266-81.

143. P. Volz, Die Eschatologie der jüdischen Gemeinde im neutestamentlichen Zeitalter (Tübingen, 2d ed. 1934) 189f.; Gressmann, Messias, 345f.; W. Bousset, Die Religion des Judentums im späthellenistischen Zeitalter (Tübingen, 3d ed. 1903) 253. On the origin of the figure of a Son of Man in the history of religions, see J. Jeremias, "Ἀδάμ," TDNT. 1. 142; W. Bousset, Religion, 346ff.

coming "on the clouds of heaven" (Mark 13:26; 14:26; cf. Acts 1:11). It goes beyond Daniel 7, however, when his coming is described as his appearing "with great power and glory" (μετὰ δυνάμεως πολλῆς καὶ δόξης, Mark 13:26 par.) or "in his Father's glory with the holy angels" (ἐν τῇ δόξῃ τοῦ πατρὸς αὐτοῦ μετὰ τῶν ἀγγέλων τῶν ἁγίων, Mark 8:38 par.; Matt 25:31; cf. Matt 13:41; 24:31) or "in his kingdom" (ἐν τῇ βασιλείᾳ αὐτοῦ, Matt 16:28 which differs from Mark and Luke). In these descriptions the Son of Man is already surrounded by and endowed with the things that Dan 7:14 says will be given him when he comes. The coming of the Son of Man has obviously been assimilated to the OT description of the eschatological revelation of Yahweh.[144] The reference to the day of the Son of Man (Luke 17:24 [Matthew παρουσία]; cf. v 22; also v 26) is an allusion to the OT expectation of the "day of the Lord."[145] The picture of Dan 7:9 of the "Ancient of Days" sitting on his throne and pronouncing judgment is completely in harmony with the OT expectation.[146] Both things are said about the Son of Man in the NT: He sits at God's right hand (Mark 14:62 par.—Ps 110:1) on his glorious throne (Matt 19:28; 25:31) and pronounces judgment (Matt 25:31ff.; cf. 16:27; 13:41). It is especially these passages from Matthew that prepare the way for the combination that is found in the Apocalypse. Phrases taken from the description of the theophany in Ezekiel's vision (1:26ff.; cf. 8:2) and from the description of the "Ancient of Days" in Daniel (7:9ff.) are used to describe the Son of Man who sits on the throne.[147] What the key passages in the Synoptics indicate is obvious here. This Son of Man is a divine being (Matt 16:13, 17); he is God himself appearing in human form.[148]

In *1 Enoch* the Son of Man has the role of world judge, just as Jesus does.[149]

---

144. Cf. Pss 96:13; 98:9. For ἐν δόξῃ see Isa 60:1f.; Hab 3:3f. In Dan 7:10 the angels attend the appearing of the "Ancient of Days." Cf. Deut 33:2, LXX; Zech 14:5.

145. Amos 5:18; Zeph 1:7, 14ff.; 2:2; Joel 1:15; 2:31 and many other places.

146. It is on earth that the ruler and judge will sit on his throne; cf. Exod 18:13; 2 Sam 19:8; 1 Kgs 1:13; 2:12; 8:20 (and so does the universal ruler, as the antitype, called "king" in Matt 25:34). However, God as sovereign and judge of the world sits on his throne in heaven; cf. Ps 9:4; Sir 1:8; 1 Kgs 22:19; Ezek 28:2; Ps 47:7ff.

147. For a comparison of Rev 1:12ff. with Ezek 1:26ff. and Daniel 7 see W. Bousset, *Apokalypse* (MeyerK), 194ff.; cf. idem, *Die Religion des Judentums im späthellen istischen Zeitalter* (Tübingen, 3d ed. 1926); W. Bousset, *Apokalypse*, 194: "It is significant that the Son of Man comes with the majesty that in Daniel is characteristic of God himself, the Ancient of Days, the judge of the world. Also cf. Rev 1:17f.; 2:8; and especially 22:12f.—in *1 Enoch* 46:1 these predicates have not been transferred; this seems to be a phenomenon unique to the NT."

148. In Ezek 1:26 the theophany is described as ὁμοίωμα ὡς εἶδος ἀνθρώπου; and 8:2, ὁμοίωμα ἀνδρός; cf. Rev 1:13: ὅμοιον υἱὸν ἀνθρώπου.

149. Cf. *1 Enoch* 61:8ff.: "The Lord of Spirits placed the Elect One on the throne of glory" (cf. 62:2; in the NT it is in much more active terms) ". . . he shall judge . . . the holy . . . he will summon all the host of the heavens, all the holy ones above, and the host of God . . . all the angels of power" (cf. Mark 13:27, although it is very different). Most of these passages are very reminiscent of features the NT has used to reshape the vision of Daniel. They are the very passages which prove that the NT is not literarily dependent on the apocalypses, at least not any of them that we are acquainted with (see n. 147).

There is one other basic feature that is prominent in the key NT passages that distinguishes the NT portrait of the Son of Man and world judge from the apocalyptic picture and from what the OT says about God as judge. The Son of Man does not simply judge those who stand before him; he also identifies with them. The Son of Man will acknowledge everyone who acknowledges Jesus (Mark 8:38 par.; Luke 12:8 [this is the original as compared with the par. in Matthew]). The world judge speaks of "the least of his brothers" (Matt 25:31, 40, 45). He gathers his own around him (cf. Mark 13:27) as a shepherd gathers his flock (Matt 25:31ff.) and allows them to share his sovereignty (cf. Matt 19:28).[150] The Son of Man in the NT is not only nearer God than the Son of Man of apocalyptic writings, but is also nearer man.[151] He is our brother, as his name declares,[152] but he is not just an ordinary man; he is *the* man. The NT emphasizes that it was not by necessity but by willing condescension that he became man (cf. Heb 2:6-8 with Ps 8:4-6), and it classifies him as the second Adam.[153]

Our study of the first category of ideas shows that insofar as any literary dependence can be detected, these statements about the Son of Man originate exclusively in the OT,[154] principally in Daniel 7 and in the descriptions of God's (eschatological) coming. Concerning the nature of the Son of Man, they state that he is God come in human form, and that he is man in God's image, the second Adam. The relationship that we have suggested here between Adam-Christ typology and the person of the Son of Man will have to be considered later in our study of NT typology.

Many of the sayings about the earthly ministry of the Son of Man do not belong in the category dealing with Jesus' announcement of his passion. These may have come from the sources of the concept of the Son of Man that we have considered here. Certainly the sayings about his authority (ἐξουσία) belong to the ideas that are associated with Daniel 7. The phrases with which the resurrected one speaks of his ἐξουσία in Matt 28:18 are largely borrowed from Dan 7:14.[155] Would not, then, the ἐξουσία to forgive sins (Mark 2:10 par.) also imply the authority of the divine world judge, which is present here in Jesus? It is not an ordinary man who is Lord of the Sabbath; it is the Son of Man and Messiah (Mark 2:28 par.).[156] However, because this fulness of divine authority is veiled in lowly human form (cf. Matt 12:32 par. Luke), this claim of the Son of Man leads to offense and to the cross (cf. Mark 2:7; 3:6). Perhaps the phrase

---

150. Cf. Dan 7:14, 27; cf. Matt 5:5. On the judgment, cf. John 5:27.

151. See n. 149.

152. Cf. Cremer, *Theological Lexicon*, 589-91.

153. Cf. 1 Cor 15:20-22 (second Adam), v 27 = Ps 8:6 (the psalm of the Son of Man [8:4] interpreted messianically); 15:45, 47; see below on this passage.

154. See n. 149.

155. Dan 7:14, LXX: καὶ ἐδόθη αὐτῷ ἐξουσία καὶ τιμὴ βασιλική, καὶ πάντα τὰ ἔθνη τῆς γῆς . . .; cf. Hag 1:13 (God speaks): ἐγώ εἰμι μεθ' ὑμῶν, λέγει κύριος . . .; Matt 28:28: ἐδόθη μοι πᾶσα ἐξουσία . . .; v 20: ἐγὼ μεθ' ὑμῶν εἰμι. . . .

156. See above on the passage.

"the Son of Man came . . ." (Mark 10:45 par. Matthew; Luke 19:10; Matt 11:19 par. Luke; cf. Luke 9:56; Matt 18:11) includes the promise of his coming again. In both instances someone "comes" with ἐξουσία over life and death: the one for salvation, the other for condemnation. In both instances—at least for the evangelists—it is somehow a coming "from heaven." In both instances, according to John, it is a coming in glory (δόξα; cf. John 1:14) and is accompanied by angels (cf. John 1:51). In both instances the time (καιρός) has come for the kingdom to begin. In the future it will be accompanied by glory, but for now it is under the cross (Dan 7:22—Mark 1:15—Luke 21:8; cf. Mark 1:15b; 10:45; Matt 12:32).

Here we find some connections with the ideas centering around Jesus' announcement of his passion, and typology will help to explain them.[157] The Son of Man must suffer, die, and rise again. The fact that he is a divine being and yet appears in lowly human form is what actually leads to his suffering.[158] The necessity (δεῖ), however, is not reached by empirical deduction; it is decreed by God and revealed in Scripture.[159]

This raises two interrelated questions. In what sense can the concept of Messiah that is revealed in Jesus' announcement of his passion be called God's revealed plan of redemption, and how is the person of the Son of Man related to that concept?

Jesus and the evangelists found a scriptural basis for their conviction that the Messiah had to be rejected by his people and had to pass through suffering and death on his way to glory. From our study thus far it would be natural to suppose that with the aid of typology they found this basis in an idea that occurs throughout the OT, the idea of the prophet, king, and, as the whole passion narrative indicates,[160] righteous man. In the pursuit of his calling he suffers, dies, and rises again for God's sake. It would be natural to suppose that they found this basis also in the prophecy about the Servant of the Lord, in which the ideas of prophet, priest, and righteous man were united in a preliminary way.[161] If Judaism was already familiar with the idea of a Messiah who would suffer and die, in some such sense as this, and had already given a messianic interpretation to the martyr prophet, the psalms about the innocent sufferer, and Isaiah 53 (which seems unlikely),[162] then this supposition would be easier to understand. It must not be taken for granted.

---

157. See above, pp. 77f.
158. See above.
159. See above, p. 77.
160. See below, pp. 100-6.
161. See above, pp. 40f.
162. On the interpretation of Isaiah 53 in Judaism, see Str-B 1. 481ff.; J. Jeremias, "Erlöser und Erlösung im Spätjudentum und Urchristentum," *Deutsche Theologie* (1929) 118ff.; P. Seidelin, "Der Ebed Jahwe und die Messiasgestalt im Jesajatargum," *ZNW* 35 (1936) 194-231. (They do not apply the passage to a suffering Messiah. "My servant" is a messianic title, but no features of the suffering servant are connected with it.) On Psalms 22 and 69, see Jeremias, *Jesus*, 115; on the martyr prophet, see ibid., 113; for further details, see n. 164.

The concept of Messiah that is found in Jesus' announcement of his passion may well be based on this association of ideas. The subject of this concept appears now to be the figure of the Son of Man taken from apocalyptic prophecy. In Daniel 7 there is only passing reference, if any, to the thought of suffering that precedes glory. The Son of Man, who is weak compared with the ravenous beasts who precede him, is the representative of the saints of the Most High who must suffer in subjection to the world powers until the end.[163] The observation that the figure of the Son of Man has taken on characteristics of the Servant of the Lord in later apocalyptic writings takes us one step further.[164] The sufferings of the Servant of the Lord, however, are features that cannot be transferred, so the Son of Man continues to be a person associated with glory, and there is little to indicate any idea that suffering will precede his glorification. Therefore, when Jesus adopted the title "Son of Man" in announcing his passion, he did not appropriate for himself a messianic concept that had already been formulated.

From the beginning Jesus ordered his steps in accordance with the prophecy about the Servant of the Lord, and yet he consistently referred to himself simply as the Son of Man. Is it not likely that he was the one who fully developed this combination of which there is only the faintest suggestion in apocalyptic writings? The Son of Man has come to do the work of the Servant of the Lord,[165] and the risen and exalted Servant of the Lord[166] will come again as the Son of Man (Mark 14:62b par.). Is it not even more likely that in the NT the three typological themes—prophet, king, and righteous man—which are the background for the figure of the Servant of the Lord, would flow into the saying "The Son of Man must suffer . . ."? We were able to clearly demonstrate this transition in shepherd-king typology.[167]

---

163. G. Dalman, *Words*, 241f., 264f.

164. Cf. *1 Enoch* 46:4 with Isa 52:15; *1 Enoch* 48:4 with Isa 42:6; 49:6; *1 Enoch* 62:2a; cf. *1 Enoch* 46:3 with Isa 42:1; cf. 61:1; 11:2. Jeremias assumes that the sayings about the hiddenness of the Son of Man suggest that he must pass through suffering (*Jesus*, 110). Moreover, 4 Ezra 7:28 should be translated, "After 400 years my servant (not "son") the Christ dies," in order then to reappear as the glorified Son of Man (ibid., 111; additional references are given there). R. Otto (*The Kingdom of God and the Son of Man* [London, 1938] 246) has a very different opinion: The synthesis that Jesus made of the Christ and the suffering servant in the person of the Son of Man, "of which no one had thought or could think, was not only unprecedented; it must have seemed blasphemous."

The question as to the extent to which Judaism was familiar with the idea of a suffering and dying Messiah and whether Judaism united it with the person of the Son of Man cannot be discussed here. The strongest evidence against the supposition that the idea of a suffering and dying and rising Messiah would have been familiar to some wider circles is the stubborn resistance to these ideas that is reported uniformly by the NT (cf. Matt 16:22 and many other passages). This is the opinion of Strack and Billerbeck (Str-B 2. 274ff.), who have collected all evidence of the idea of the "suffering and dying Messiah in the synagogue." (J. Jeremias [*Jerusalem zur Zeit Jesu* 2. 108] believes that the idea of the suffering Messiah belonged to the esoteric traditions of the rabbis.)

165. Mark 10:45 par. Matthew; the Son of Man is the subject of this saying, which is reminiscent of Isa 53:10ff.

166. Isa 52:13-15; cf. Acts 2:33; 5:31; in John 3:14b; 12:32, 34 it is stated explicitly that the Son of Man will be lifted up; substantially the same thing is already found in Mark 14:62 par. = Ps 110:1.

167. See above, pp. 88f.

When Jesus combined the figure of the Servant of the Lord and the ideas that are in it and behind it with the figure of the Son of Man, he did not combine elements that are essentially incompatible; and when he introduced the title "Son of Man" as a title for the Messiah in the announcement of his passion, he did not fill an external shell with alien content. Instead, he developed the nucleus that was contained in that shadowy figure, who comes at the conclusion of OT prophecy, into the person we described above when we considered the saying about his glorification. This is not only appropriate for the Son of Man ruling as world judge, but also for the necessity found in the announcement of Jesus' passion. There is no metaphysical necessity for this.[168] It is necessary because all that the OT said and prophesied about the men of God and the messengers of God converges in him, and the OT view of God's relationship to the world comes to a focus in him. The man who is completely God's man and who in his mission deals with mankind must endure the affliction that comes to all men of God. Because he truly overcomes that affliction as no one had ever done before, he becomes what is predicted of the Servant of the Lord (Isa 53:5, 10ff.)—"the righteous servant who will justify many." He does so as *the* man, the second Adam, who redeems everyone.

We turn now to an investigation of the way Christ is related in typology to Adam and to the righteous one and how this relationship is connected with the idea of the Son of Man. This will give us additional clues for the hypothesis concerning the typological substratum of the Son of Man sayings that is suggested by the foregoing discussion.

b. The Second Adam

Adam-Christ typology seems to be back of the genealogy of Jesus in Luke 3:23-38.[169] In contrast to Matt 1:2-16, this genealogy traces Jesus' ancestry back beyond Abraham to Adam. When Luke received it, the genealogy may already have had its present form, which embraces eleven times seven generations (world weeks) and corresponds to one of the expectations of apocalypticism (4 Ezra 14:11f.).[170] But it was "extremely important to Luke that the genealogy he adopted show that Jesus the son of Abraham and the son of David was also the son of Adam who fulfills the destiny of the sons of Adam. This is in harmony with the universalism of the third Gospel."[171] Moreover, as Paul's disciple, Luke was familiar with the concept of the second Adam.[172] The result is as follows:

---

168. Cf. Lohmeyer, *Markus*, 166: The sufferings of the Son of Man "are no longer the expression of the incomprehensible relationship between God and his people as they are in the figure of the Servant of the Lord. Instead of this, they are integral to the meaning and being of the Son of Man. The law of his suffering follows from the law of his being and since this law is from God, he suffers because he is God's kind of person, and he is God's kind of person because he suffers." Also on p. 5: "The point of the sufferings of the Servant of the Lord is that he bore them for our sakes. There is nothing comparable."

169. HNT on Luke, 57; Rengstorf, *Lukas*, 50; Jeremias, "Ἀδάμ," *TDNT* 1. 141.

170. Rengstorf, *Lukas*, 49; however, see HNT on Luke, 57.

171. Rengstorf, *Lukas*, 50.

172. Cf. Luke 23:43 where paradise is mentioned.

'Ιησοῦς . . . ὢν υἱὸς . . . τοῦ 'Αδάμ = בֶּן אָדָם (Heb.) = בַּר אֱנָשָׁא (Aram.) = υἱὸς ἀνθρώπου (LXX) ("Jesus . . . was the son . . . of Adam, that is, the Son of Man"). This is the way the Gospels indicate the connection between the Son of Man concept and Adam typology. Luke places the story of Jesus' temptation immediately after his genealogy so that the words "Adam, the son of God" ('Αδὰμ τοῦ θεοῦ) stand between the two pericopes, indicating that he found Adam-Christ typology in both.

Luke was not the first one to introduce this typology into the Gospels. It is found also in Mark's version of the temptation (1:12f.), which is strangely different from Matthew and Luke. The story of Jesus' temptation, at least in its basic features, is connected with the narrative of Adam's fall (Genesis 3). Christ was tempted by Satan as Adam was (in late Judaism it was customary to attribute Adam's temptation to Satan).[173] The first man fell in the temptation, and in his fall he drew all men after him. Christ, however, overcame the temptation. Here, then, one has broken the domination of the invincible power that separates man from salvation. This power is lamented by the author of 4 Ezra (5:116ff.) because he had no knowledge of Christ's coming. The NT, however, perceives the fact that redemption has begun inasmuch as a man has overcome temptation (Rom 5:18; Heb 4:15; 2:17f.). Because he overcame, he, as "the author of their salvation" (Heb 2:10), is able to lead everyone who follows him out of slavery to sin and death (cf. Heb 2:14ff.).

Typology is really present and it will not escape the notice of anyone familiar with the ideas about Adam's fall that were prevalent in Judaism. The evangelist himself seems to allude to them purposely. This is the only adequate explanation for the statement in Mark 1:13b. Does this remark about the wild animals simply portray the reality of Jesus' dangerous isolation in the desert, and does the statement about the angels attending him only indicate that God was there to protect him or that the hungry one was fed? This is no mere description of the external form of the event without any reference to its meaning, any more than the description of John the Baptist is in Mark 1:4, 6. These are the very features that Jewish tradition used to embellish the account of Adam's stay in paradise. This connection seems to indicate that "as Adam was once honoured by the beasts in Paradise according to the Midrash,[174] so Christ is with the wild beasts after overcoming temptation. He thus ushers in the paradisaical state of the last days when there will be peace between man and beast (Is. 11:6-8; 65:25).[175] As Adam in Paradise enjoyed angel's food according to the Midrash,[176] so the angels give heavenly food to the new man. Jesus reopens the Paradise closed to the first man."[177] Whether the evangelist had all these details in mind will have to

---

173. See above, pp. 33f.
174. *Apocalypse of Moses* 16.
175. Str-B 3. 254; 4. 892, 964f.
176. *Adam and Eve* 4.
177. Jeremias, "'Αδάμ," *TDNT* 1. 141.

remain an open question, but anyone hearing this story who had become acquainted with OT history in this form through the synagogue, as the early Christians had, could not understand these phrases in any other sense or derive any other meaning from them.

The typology has been removed from the version of this story that is preserved in Matthew (4:1-11 par. Luke). If Mark was alluding to some more detailed account with which he was acquainted, it could not have been this form.[178] The omission of the phrase "he was with the wild animals" is significant, and cannot be dismissed as the mere omission of a descriptive comment (as, e.g., in Mark 4:38—Matt 8:25).

The way the story of Jesus' temptation has been developed in Matthew and Luke has obviously been influenced by the idea that the Mosaic period will be restored. Jesus' fasting for forty days[179] in the desert and the angels' attending him afterward, i.e., bringing him food (cf. Acts 6:2), are features characteristic of this version and are reminiscent of the OT stories about Moses (Exod 34:28; Deut 9:9, 18) and Elijah (1 Kgs 19:5, 8) fasting in the desert. Only in the case of Elijah, however, is anything mentioned about angels attending him. Satan's demand for a sign is in accord with the expectation that in the messianic age the miracles of the Mosaic period would reoccur, especially the miraculous feeding (John 6:14f.).[180] Finally, against the background of these ideas, it is no accident "that Jesus' words in Matt 4:4, 7, and 10 are all from Deuteronomy.[181] They are from passages which describe the way God tested Israel in the desert and where it is explicitly stated, 'As a man disciplines his son, so the Lord your God disciplines you' (Deut 8:5).[182] Israel is God's firstborn son (Exod 4:22; Hos 11:1); the Messiah, however, is a son with whom God is well pleased (Matt 3:17)." Here the place of Adam-Christ typology is taken by the relationship of Israel, i.e., the OT saints, to Christ: "As Israel was tested in the desert, so also was the only Son, the Messiah."[183]

From this typology we derive the following interpretation: Jesus exhibits the obedience (cf. Heb 5:8) which Israel should have learned (cf. Deut 8:2f.; Jer 31:32); therefore, he is the firstborn of the new people of God.

As a matter of fact, this is the way the words must be interpreted regardless of their origin: The testing is truly messianic ("If you are the Son of God . . . ,"

---

178. Schniewind, *Matthäus*, 47.

179. Matthew adds "and forty nights," καὶ τεσσάρακοντα νύκτας, as in Exod 34:28.

180. See above, pp. 34f.

181. Matt 4:4 = Deut 8:3b; Matt 4:7 = Deut 6:16, "This saying occurs also in Ps 95:7ff.; 1 Cor 10:9, 13; Heb 3:8f.; the stimulus in each instance is the story of Israel's wandering in the desert"; Matt 4:10 = Deut 6:13.

182. πειράζειν; in the OT this word means: to put their obedience on trial.

183. Schniewind, *Matthäus*, 228; also Gressmann and Klostermann, *Matthäus*, 27; however, see G. Kittel, "ἔρημος," *TDNT* 2. 658. (Obviously, the connection must not be based on the superficial similarity: 40 days—40 years [Deut 8:2]. That all the other references to the desert wandering approach it from the point of view of the consummation or of obedience does not exclude the matter of testing, but includes it.)

εἰ υἱὸς εἶ τοῦ θεοῦ . . .); it corresponds to the view of the Messiah in the synagogue.[184] In Jesus' answers, however, there is no mention of "what the dignity or the task of the Messiah would be"; "rather the language of the answers is the language of Jesus' 'piety,' a direct relationship to God corresponding to the relationship that all men should have to God."[185] In his temptation Jesus proves to be God's man; he succeeded where Adam, Israel, and all "righteous persons" failed. He will not rule as a superman; he will be a Messiah who is like his brothers in every respect, "yet without sin" (Heb 4:15), i.e., he will continue to belong completely to God. To the very end, the path of the Messiah leads through testing and temptation to the cross (the voice of the tempter is still heard in the word of mocking in Mark 15:32). Because he continues to be the righteous one, he makes many righteous.

The typological relationship of Jesus to Adam in Mark's version of the story of Jesus' temptation is replaced in Matthew and Luke by his relationship to the "righteous one."[186] Christ is clearly the antitype of the tempted and suffering man of God (cf. Luke 3:38).

c. The Righteous Sufferer

In order to gain a complete picture in terms of the goal we have set for ourselves, we will first examine the story of Jesus' passion to collect all the OT quotations and allusions that are related to Jesus' suffering.

The betrayal by Judas is sketched against a background of Scripture passages which announce that the righteous one is forsaken and betrayed by his own friends (Jer 11:19; 12:6; 20:10; Ps 55:12ff.; Job 16:20). The announcement that the betrayer is one "who is eating with me . . ." (Mark 14:18) is an allusion to Ps 41:9. In John (13:18) the passage is quoted as having been "fulfilled." According to Acts 1:17-20 the death of the betrayer[187] is seen as the fulfillment of the curse which the righteous one utters against his companion who lies in ambush against him (Acts 1:20 = Ps 69:25).[188] The shaping of the parallel narrative in Matthew (27:3-10) has been influenced by the passage from Zechariah (11:12f.) that is quoted in the fulfillment citation. The description of Jesus' death is reminiscent of the account of the death of the traitor of Ahitophel (2 Sam 17:23: ἀπῆλθεν . . . ἀπήγξατο).[189]

---

184. See p. 32 n. 54.

185. Schniewind, *Matthäus*, 229.

186. The remarkable saying in *T. Naph.* 8:4 that is reminiscent of the story of Jesus' temptation is also about "the righteous man": "If you work that which is good, my children, both men and angels shall bless you . . . the devil shall flee from you, and the wild beasts shall fear you, and the Lord shall love you, and the angels shall cleave to you." (It is a common Jewish idea that God tests the righteous in order to exalt them [Str-B 1. 135].)

187. See *Angelos* 4. 52ff. for other parallels from the haggadah.

188. Cf. Wis 4:17, 19.

189. However, Klostermann (*Markus*, on Mark 14:51f.) is scarcely correct when he says, "The incident in Mark 14:51 (the young man who fled) originated in the scriptural proof" or "was presented in the light of the prophecy" (i.e., Amos 2:16).

In Gethsemane Jesus experiences the ultimate separation from God of which the Psalms speak only by way of anticipation.[190] Compare Mark 14:34 (par. Matt), "My soul is overwhelmed with sorrow" (περίλυπός ἐστιν ἡ ψυχή μου), with Pss 42:5, 11; 43:5: "Why are you downcast, O my soul?" (ἵνα τί περίλυπος εἶ, ἡ ψυχή; cf. Jonah 4:9). In Matt 26:36 Jesus commands his disciples to stay behind while he sets out to struggle for ultimate obedience. This is clearly an allusion to Abraham's command to his servants when he set out to offer his sacrifice.[191] (Here it is Jesus, not God, who is compared with Abraham in contrast to both earlier and later allegories.) The wording of Jesus' prayer in Mark 14:36 (different from Matthew and Luke) reminds us of the word with which Job humbles himself under God's omnipotence (Job 42:2, LXX: "everything is possible for you, and nothing is impossible," πάντα δύνασαι, ἀδυνατεῖ δέ σοι οὐθέν—Mark 14:36: "Abba, Father, everything is possible for you," ἄββα ὁ πατήρ, πάντα δυνατά σοι); this statement is too general, however, to guarantee any connection.

False witnesses, like the ones who appear at Jesus' trial before the Sanhedrin (Mark 14:56 par. Matthew; not in Luke or John), became part of the picture of the innocent sufferer as early as Ps 27:12.[192] The silence of Jesus when he is questioned and accused by his judge[193] is the kind of conduct that is prophesied about the Servant of the Lord in Isa 53:7. When describing the mocking after the trial before the Sanhedrin[194] and the abuse by Pilate's soldiers,[195] the narrator may have had Isa 50:6 in mind: "I offered my back to those who beat me, my cheeks to those who pulled out my beard; I did not hide my face from mocking and spitting."

There are allusions to OT sayings also in the portrayal of the events around the cross. Ps 69:21 may have helped to shape the saying about Jesus being offered a drink in Matt 27:34 (cf. Mark 15:23), and it certainly has done so in Mark 15:36 (par. Matthew; cf. Luke 23:36); in John 19:28f. there is an explicit reference to the fulfillment of Scripture, although there is no actual quotation.[196] The dividing of the righteous man's clothing among his executioners conforms to the tradition, and so does the offer of a narcotic drink (Mark 15:23). This particular detail is emphasized because in it the lowliness of the Son of Man is

---

190. On the prophecy announced by Jesus on the way to Gethsemane, see above, pp. 87f.

191. Matt 26:36 has καθίσατε αὐτοῦ compared with Mark 14:32: καθίσατε ὧδε through the influence of Gen 22:5, LXX: καθίσατε αὐτοῦ.

192. See Schniewind, Matthäus, 183.

193. Mark 14:60f. par. Matthew; omitted in Luke and John before Pilate (Mark 15:4f.); more emphatic in Matt 27:12, 14; cf. John 19:9f.; omitted in Luke; also at his arrest in Mark and John.

194. Mark 14:65 par. Matthew; cf. Luke 22:63f.; omitted in John; cf. John 19:2.

196. Ps 69:21 (68:22, LXX): ἔδωκαν εἰς τὸ βρῶμά μου χολὴν καὶ εἰς τὴν δίψαν μου ἐπότισαν με ὄξος. Mark 15:23: ἐδίδουν . . . ἐσμυρισμένον οἶνον. Matt 27:34: ἔδωκαν . . . οἶνον μετὰ χολῆς μεμιγμένον. Matt 27:48 (par. Mark): λαβὼν σπόγγον πλήσας τε ὄξους καὶ . . . ἐπότισεν αὐτόν. John 19:28f.: διψῶ . . . σπόγγον οὖν μεστὸν τοῦ ὄξους ὑσσώπῳ περιθέντες. Luke 23:36: obviously it is just assumed without any connection.

fulfilled in accordance with Ps 22:18. There are allusions to this passage in Mark 15:24 and Luke 23:34; in Matt 27:35 the allusions are clearer, and in John 19:24 the passage is quoted explicitly. The description of the mocking of the crucified one is dependent on Ps 22:7; the correspondence is very close in Mark 15:29 and Matt 27:39, but the form is somewhat different in Luke 23:35.[197] The sneering words "He trusts in God. Let God rescue him now if he wants him," which are recorded only in Matthew (27:43a), are a reproduction of Ps 22:8. Even though this is not indicated in the text, the evangelist may see the disgrace prophesied of the Servant of the Lord in Isa 53:12 fulfilled in the fact that Jesus was crucified between two criminals. Jesus' prediction in Luke 22:37 and the addition to Mark 15:28 (Θ λ φ it), which can certainly be traced to Luke, refer explicitly to the fulfillment of the Isaiah passage. In observing that Jesus' friends stood at a distance from the cross, Luke recalls that the righteous sufferer was not spared the experience of separation from his closest friends.[198]

Jesus' words from the cross are the most profound expression of what the evangelists want to indicate by the way they tell the story. When he cries out that he has been forsaken by God, it is a cry that bursts forth from the ultimate depths of the distress through which the Son of Man has to pass (Mark 15:34 par. Matthew = Ps 22:1). In its place, Luke 23:46 (= Ps 31:5) has preserved the words of the final cry Jesus uttered just before he died; these words are reported also in Mark 15:37 and Matt 27:50. "It is a quotation from a psalm that Jesus may have said often as an evening prayer."[199] It is very important for the interpretation of Jesus' death that his last two prayers "are taken from two psalms that deal with the suffering of saints who were rescued when they were at the point of death and who became heralds of salvation."[200] Jesus faced death consciously and deliberately as being the destiny of the Messiah that had been ordained by God's redemptive decree and would, therefore, issue in victory. This is emphasized appropriately in John 19:30.[201] In the two other sayings from the cross, which are preserved only in Luke, Jesus demonstrates that he is the Servant of the Lord, who intercedes for sinners even on the cross.[202]

---

197. Ps 22:7 (21:8, LXX): πάντες οἱ θεωροῦντές με ἐξεμυκτήρισάν με, ἐλάλησαν ἐν χείλεσιν, ἐκίνησαν κεφαλήν.

198. Luke 23:49: εἱστήκεισαν δὲ πάντες οἱ γνωστοὶ αὐτῷ ἀπὸ μακρόθεν. Ps 38:11 (37:12, LXX): καὶ οἱ ἔγγιστά μου ἀπὸ μακρόθεν ἔστησαν (cf. Ps 88:8 [87:9, LXX], γνωστούς).

199. J. Jeremias, "Das Gebetsleben Jesu," ZNW 25 (1926) 136; Str-B 2. 269.

200. Jeremias, "Gebetsleben," 139.

201. See Bornhäuser, Wirken des Christus, 219-22.

202. Isa 53:12: He "made intercession for the transgressors" (Hebrew; translated differently by P. Volz, Jesaia: "He has taken the place of sinners"; cf. 53:6); omitted in Luke 23:34a (+ א * Koine C pl; lat, sy^cp; - BD*WΘ pc; a sy^s sa; the omission in these important manuscripts would be explained if it were a matter of an ancient interpolation which might have originated in an agraphon; see HNT on this passage; however, see also Rengstorf, Lukas, on this passage). Cf. Luke 23:43 with Isa 53:11: "After the suffering of his soul, he will see the light and be satisfied with the knowledge of the Lord. My Servant has brought righteousness to the many because he himself bore their sins" (translated from P. Volz, Jesaia, on this passage).

The early Christian kerygma sees God's plan fulfilled also in Jesus' burial (1 Cor 15:4). The Lord of life is laid in a grave, just as every human being is. Thus Isa 53:9 may be back of the detailed description of his interment.[203]

Finally, the words of the resurrected one may be an allusion to the praise of the righteous man who has been delivered from death (Matt 28:10; cf. Ps 22:22).[204]

For the most part, the OT passages in which Jesus and the evangelists found the scriptural basis for his suffering deal either with the righteous sufferer or with the Servant of the Lord. The most prominent in the first category are the passages from Psalms 22 and 69.[205] While there are more scriptural references in Matthew and John than in Mark, these Psalms are used somewhat less in Luke.[206]

Did the evangelists interpret these statements about the righteous sufferer that are taken from the Psalms as direct prophecies or in some typological way? We cannot ask them this pointed question. Their only concern is that these statements from the Psalms were fulfilled in Jesus' experience; they are not interested in what the poet had in mind originally. The way in which the OT passages are introduced suggests that theirs is a typological approach which looks for similarity in essentials, not simply for the fulfillment of external features. There are no explicit statements that prophecy has been fulfilled, such as we might have expected, especially from Matthew;[207] the passages are simply alluded to. The distress of the saint that is portrayed by the psalmist is fulfilled in Jesus.

These psalms were not chosen arbitrarily. Their selection is justified by the

---

203. Isa 53:9 (Hebrew): "He was assigned a grave with the wicked and with the rich in his death." Cf. Volz (ibid.) who conjectures: "He was assigned his grave with the wicked; he was buried with the rich."

On John 19:36f.: The two Scripture passages that John adds to the description of the removal of Christ from the cross contain authentic Johannine thought.

204. Ps 22:22 (21:23, LXX): διηγήσομαι τὸ ὄνομά σου τοῖς ἀδελφοῖς μου; cf. Heb 2:11f. Cf. Luke 24:39; John 20:29, 25 with Ps 22:16 (21:17, LXX): ὤρυξαν χεῖράς μου καὶ πόδας.

205. Ps 22:1—Mark 15:34 par. Matthew; omitted in Luke, John; v 7—Mark 15:29 par. Matthew; Luke 23:35; omitted in John; v 18—Mark 15:24 par. Matthew, Luke, John; v 8—Matthew 27:43a; v 22—Matt 28:10 (an allusion); v 16—Luke 24:39; cf. John 20:20, 25, 27; v 15—John 19:28 (is there an allusion in the διψῶν?); Ps 69:21—Mark 15:36; Matt 27:34, 48 (stronger); Luke 23:36 (scarcely detectable); John 19:28-30; (v 25—Acts 1:16ff.); v 4—John 15:25; v 9—John 2:17; Ps 31:5—Luke 23:46; Ps 38:11 (LXX)—Luke 23:49; Ps 41:9—Mark 14:18; John 13:18; omitted in Matthew, Luke; Ps 42:5 (= 42:11; 43:5)—Mark 14:34 par. Matthew; (Ps 16:10—Acts 2:25-28; 13:34-37; on the resurrection); (Ps 18:4f.—Acts 2:24).

All these psalms (except Psalm 18, which is a royal song) deal with the tempted, suffering, and persecuted godly person; as do the following passages: Gen 22:5—Matt 26:36; Gen 22:6—John 19:17: Jesus is compared with Abraham (if in Rom 8:32 Paul had Gen 22:16 in mind, then Jesus would be compared with Isaac and God with Abraham; this must be understood in terms of the double line that pervades all Pauline Christology: God sent, Rom 8:3, and Christ became man, Phil 2:7, . . . God gave, Rom 8:32, and Christ gave himself for us, Gal 2:20; Rom 5:6-8); Gen 37:20 (about Joseph)—Mark 12:7; Gen 40:3ff.—Mark 15:27 par. (cf. Matt 28:10 with Gen 45:4; 50:19; see p. 192 n. 70); Job 42:2—Mark 14:36.

206. Cf. Matt 27:34, 43a, 48; John 19:24, 28, 34; 15:25; 2:17; and see Luke 22:34b, 35, 36. Cf. Rengstorf, *Lukas*, 253.

207. The only exception is in John 19:24, 28; cf. Matt 27:29 Δ Θ λ φ it.

original meaning. It is no ordinary person who is speaking in Psalm 22; it is the champion of a cause who is also the spokesman for a group of saints. In his victory he extols the triumph of his cause, which, in reality, is Israel's cause, and the cause of God's kingdom and of his righteousness.[208] The details in the description of the suffering the psalmist sees coming on him (Ps 22:16-18) take on their proper meaning only if this is the description of one who is crucified or, at least, one who is condemned.[209] The Septuagint, Symmachus, and Aquila may even have interpreted Psalm 22 (and Psalm 69) messianically.[210]

Therefore, it is quite apparent that in his anguish on the cross Jesus prayed in the words of this psalm (Mark 15:34 par. Matt = Ps 22:1). The saying is certainly original, for it was an offense to the church. It has been suppressed in Luke and John; in Mark 15:34 D it var, par. Matthew, it has been softened by the change in translation from ἐγκατέλιπες (LXX) to ὠνείδισας.[211] The church's use of this and similar psalms to portray Jesus' passion can certainly be traced to this dominical saying.

In the Synoptics, this psalm first appears in the story of Jesus' passion. The passages about the suffering Servant of the Lord accompany the sayings and actions of Jesus from the outset, beginning with the voice from heaven at his baptism (Mark 1:11 par.—Isa 42:1).[212] This is emphasized appropriately by the fulfillment citations in Matt 12:17-21 (= Isa 42:1-4) and Matt 8:17 (= Isa 53:12). He associated with the poor, the forlorn, and the outcasts (Matt 12:20; 9:12; 11:19) and did not appear in public (Matt 12:19; 10:27). "It is for this very reason that he is the Servant of the Lord who brings justice to many (Mark 10:45), even to the Gentiles (Matt 12:18, 21; 8:10-12; etc.), i.e., he brings God's

---

208. G. Kittel, *Die Psalmen* (KAT; Leipzig, 1922) 89.

209. Ibid., 87; Bornhäuser, *Wirken des Christus*, 208ff.; but cf. A. Weiser, *The Psalms* (OTL; Philadelphia, 1962) 224.

210. Bornhäuser (*Wirken des Christus*, 215, 220; accepted by Jeremias, "Gebetsleben," 139) wants to infer this from the titles in the LXX. This does not seem to be adequate proof, although in principle the possibility cannot be ruled out.

211. See Klostermann, *Markus*, on this passage; on the original form of the cry see Jeremias, "Gebetsleben," 130 n. 8.

212. Passages about the suffering Servant of the Lord (see W. Dittmar, *Vetus Testamentum in Novo* [Göttingen, 1903] on Isaiah 53): Mark 9:12—Isa 53:3, "We esteemed him not," perhaps also: "suffer much," cf. Isa 53:2-4 (cf. Otto, *Kingdom*, 249-51); Mark 10:45 par. Matthew—Isa 53:11f.: "many" (רַבִּים 3 times; cf. ibid., 210), also Mark 14:24 par. Matthew (Luke and 1 Cor 11:24: ὑπὲρ ὑμῶν): ὑπὲρ πολλῶν (the Servant of the Lord is also "a covenant for the people," Isa 42:6); (Matt 8:17—Isa 53:4, quoted explicitly and applied to Jesus' miracle); Mark 14:61 par. Matthew; Mark 15:5 par. Matthew; Luke 23:9—Isa 53:7 (silence); Mark 14:65 par.; Mark 15:16f. par. Matthew; cf. Mark 10:34—Isa 50:6 (mocking and flogging); Luke 22:37 (cf. Mark 15:27 par.)—Isa 53:12 (transgressor); Luke 23:34, and 42f.—Isa 53:11f. (intercession for the transgressors); Mark 15:45ff. par.—Isa 53:9 (burial); (Acts 3:13—Isa 52:13; 53:11); (Acts 8:32f.—Isa 53:7f. quoted explicitly). See also Jeremias ("Erloser und Erlosung im Spätjudentum und Urchristentum," *Deutsche Theologie* [1929] 118): "From the beginning of Jesus' ministry until the cross, Isaiah 53 remains the only key there is to his consciousness of sovereignty and the only key there is for understanding his good news."

command and his triumphant salvation (Matt 5:13-48)."[213] In conformity with the prophecy about the Servant of the Lord, Jesus' ministry was meant first for Israel, and then also for the Gentiles (Isa 49:6; 42:6).[214]

Above all, the prophecy about the Servant of the Lord gives clarity and certainty to Jesus' and the church's belief concerning the necessity and the meaning of Jesus' suffering and death by showing that both are ordained by God's redemptive decree. This is indicated by the similarities in the wording of Mark 9:12 (cf. Isa 53:3) and Mark 10:45; 14:24 (cf. Isa 53:11f.), which can be traced to Jesus himself.[215] Like the church (cf. Acts 3:13—Isa 52:13; 53:11, παῖς), Jesus may have found the promise of his resurrection in the portrait of the Servant of the Lord.

What all of Scripture declares about the prophets, the kings, and the righteous and what it prophesies about their future antitypes are brought together in the prophecy about the Servant of the Lord: The Christ must suffer, die, and rise again. If Jesus was certain of this in himself and taught it to his disciples (cf. Mark 8:31; 9:31, διδάσκειν), then he was not blindly following the authority of the literal meaning of some passage or oracle—ordinarily we would only find some allusions even in the case of passages about the Servant of the Lord. Jesus is proclaiming what perceptive eyes (Luke 24:45) find in all of Scripture (Luke 24:27, 44). His suffering and death were not necessary because of anything inherent in the idea of a redeemer, but because of the relationship between God and man that is revealed in Scripture.[216]

The necessity of Jesus' suffering and death has been inferred from Isaiah 53, and that same passage discloses the meaning of his suffering and death with the words "for many" (ὑπὲρ or ἀντὶ πολλῶν) that are reminiscent of the key passages, Mark 10:45; 14:24 par. Matthew (cf. Isa 53:11f.). Once again, everything is brought together that the OT and late Judaism expected in terms of the suffering and death of the prophets, the kings, and the righteous.[217] Jesus' suffering, death, and resurrection on behalf of "many," i.e., on behalf of all, accomplished what the self-surrender of all the martyrs of the Old Covenant could not do—the creation of a new people that has been sanctified by God and that will live forever. Consequently, this cannot be comprehended in the idea of

---

213. Schniewind, *Matthäus*, 353.

214. See above, pp. 74f.

215. See n. 212.

216. See Otto, *Kingdom*, 251: "Mere blind oracular necessity existed for him as little as did the blind authority of the letter of Scripture. The necessity of the suffering of the Son of Man was not forced upon him by an oracle. It followed by inner logic when he saw himself as the eschatological redeemer and saviour, in the light of Isaiah's ancient redeemer who was most inwardly akin to him, and in the light of his fate" (hence, not as in p. 78 n. 77, or Klostermann, *Markus*, on Mark 14:49).

217. Numerous examples of the widespread view that "the righteous, the godly, the prophets, and the fathers" have to give their lives vicariously for the people are given in Str-B 2. 279ff. (in keeping with the general Jewish viewpoint it is not applied to the Messiah); see Otto, *Kingdom*, 253f.; Schniewind, *Markus*, on Mark 10:45.

substitution, but only by faith and in the unique mystery of the person of Jesus Christ. It is suggested by the typological relationship of Christ to Adam and to the righteous sufferer.

Thus we have found significant confirmation for our hypothesis concerning the typological background for Jesus' announcement of his passion and for the Son of Man who bore that suffering.

The full meaning that the NT finds for Jesus Christ in his typological relationship to the OT can be appreciated only when we consider how Christ was viewed by his church, the ones for whom his ministry, as well as his suffering, death, and resurrection, were intended.

Chapter Five

THE SYNOPTIC GOSPELS AND ACTS: THE CHURCH OF JESUS CHRIST

1. THE CALLING OF THE TWELVE NEW TRIBES

Some persons have questioned whether Jesus ever intended to establish a church. The typological approach demonstrates that the idea of a church—a community of God existing in this world and nourished by God's forgiving grace and promise—is inseparably bound to the idea of the Christ. The prophets were sent on behalf of the covenant people. King and people belong to one another like shepherd and flock. The Son of Man is the representative of the "saints of the Most High."

Jesus himself affirmed this aspect of his place in typology. The Pauline proclamation concerning the new people of God and the true Israel created by Christ can be traced to Jesus[1] just as certainly as he is the one who called the twelve.[2]

Jesus' concept of the old people of God, Israel according to the flesh, is the same as that of the prophets. In God's plan of redemption Israel was the first to be called to God's kingdom. For this reason Jesus first gathers the lost sheep of the house of Israel into God's flock (as is emphasized by Matthew in particular, 15:24; cf. 10:5f.). In fulfillment of God's promise, he cares for the natural descendants of Abraham (Luke 13:16; 19:9; also 1:55, 73; Acts 3:25f.).[3] But he is doing what the prophets did and he frequently uses their very words to proclaim that not everyone from Israel will attain salvation and that many Gentiles will enter the kingdom with Abraham, Isaac, and Jacob (Matt 8:10-12 par. Luke; cf. Luke 4:25ff.;[4] 14:21ff. par. Matthew). John the Baptist also rejected any claim to salvation that is based on natural descent from Abraham, for he said,

---

1. See below, pp. 140-51.
2. It can scarcely be contested that Jesus formed a band of twelve men (see K. Rengstorf, "δώδεκα," *TDNT* 2. 325f.). According to 1 Cor 15:4f., this is part of the earliest kerygma. The church struggled with the scandalous fact that one of the twelve betrayed Jesus.
3. However, cf. Acts 7:5, 17; and see below, p. 121.
4. See above, p. 74.

"Out of these stones God can raise up children for Abraham" (Matt 3:9 par. Luke). This suggests what is really the decisive factor.

The flock that Jesus gathers from Israel is not the nucleus of the people of the Old Covenant; it is a new people who are not related to the old people by natural descent, but are related to them in redemptive history and in a typological way. This is expressed most clearly in the call of the twelve, where it is stated, "He appointed twelve that they might be with him and that he might send them out to preach" (καὶ ἐποίησεν δώδεκα ἵνα ὦσιν μετ᾽ αὐτοῦ, καὶ ἵνα ἀποστέλλῃ αὐτοὺς κηρύσσειν, Mark 3:14; cf. Luke 6:13; Matt 10:1). The number twelve is clearly an allusion to the twelve tribes of Israel. As early as in chaps. 30 and 31 of Jeremiah, it was believed that the twelve tribes would arise again in the new age.[5] Jesus creates[6] the new people of God in that he, like God, calls[7] from the crowd the twelve who follow him in continuous fellowship and he sends them forth to gather the twelve tribes. They are the representatives of and the active nucleus for the formation of the twelve new tribes.[8]

This interpretation is confirmed in the NT. What Jesus says to Peter in Matt 16:18 applies to all the twelve. Their names are on the foundation stones of the walls of the new Jerusalem, the perfect church, whose twelve gates bear the names of the twelve tribes of Israel. Therefore, the new Jerusalem represents the twelve new tribes, the new Israel (Rev 21:12-14; cf. Eph 2:20). The church acknowledges that the appointment of the twelve was not to be repeated in redemptive history when they filled the place that Judas had abandoned, but not the place left vacant by the death of James the son of Zebedee (Acts 1:15ff.; 12:1ff).

The church, like Jesus, gathers the twelve tribes from Israel first of all.[9] They share Christ's kingly reign because they announce the kingdom and usher it in, just as he did (Mark 6:12f. par.; cf. Luke 10:17ff.); for one person it means salvation, for another it means condemnation. Afterward, the church will share in the manifestation of his glory. This is certainly how the obscure saying in

---

5. G. von Rad, "Ἰσραήλ," *TDNT* 3. 358; cf. Acts 26:7; Jas 1:1; Rev 7:4; 12:1; 21:12ff.; see below on this passage.

6. ἐποίησεν; the same word is used in Gen 1:1, LXX: it is not a restoration, but a new creation.

7. προσκαλεῖσθαι; the same word is used of God in Acts 2:39 = Isa 57:19.

8. K. Schmidt, "ἐκκλησία," *TDNT* 3. 520; J. Schniewind, *Das Evangelium nach Matthäus* (NTD I) 65; E. Lohmeyer (*Das Evangelium des Markus* [Göttingen, 1937] 74) refers to the symbolic meaning of the place: "As once God called Moses and Israel to himself on Mount Sinai (cf. Mark 3:13). . . ."

K. Rengstorf states that by his call of the twelve Jesus is announcing his claim on Israel and is declaring that this claim is on the whole people ("δώδεκα," *TDNT* 2. 326; cf. *Barn.* 8:3); therefore, the twelve will judge the twelve tribes (Matt 19:28; "δώδεκα," *TDNT* 2. 327). Adequate consideration has not been given here to the fact that the twelve are not simply apostles, but are primarily the foundation of the new people of God.

9. What is commanded in Matt 10:5f. is what actually happened according to Mark 6:7ff.; Acts 2ff.

Matt 19:28 (par. Luke 22:28-30) should be interpreted.[10] When the Son of Man appears, the kingdom (βασιλεία) will be given to the new people of God (Matt 19:28) as it was given to the "saints of the Most High" in Dan 7:27.

When metaphors used for Israel in the OT are applied to Jesus' disciples, it is an allusion to the fact that they, as the new people of God, are related typologically to the old people of God. The metaphor of a plantation is used frequently in the OT to portray God's care and patience, his testings and judgment of his church. He plants and cultivates (Isa 5:1f.; Jer 2:21; Ps 80:8ff.), but he also looks for fruit (Isa 5:2-4; Jer 2:21) and destroys what is unproductive (Isa 5:5; cf. Ps 80:12ff.). In the Gospels this metaphor is changed in a significant way. God's plantation, his kingdom, is even more clearly distinguished from the people that are entrusted with its management (Mark 12:1ff. par.; cf. Isa 5:1ff.). The people to whom it is now entrusted will produce the fruit (Matt 21:41) because they are a new people. The metaphor of producing fruit and seeking fruit, which illustrates God's testing, training, and rejection, is applied to individuals and not to the new people of God as a whole.[11] To be sure, even this new eternal people of the kingdom that springs up from God's Word is still inseparably mixed with pseudo-Christians, as the parables of the sowers indicate (Matthew 13; Mark 4).

We have already discussed the metaphor of a flock.[12] Jesus went about on this earth as the good shepherd who gathers the lost sheep (Mark 6:34; Matt 9:36; 15:24; cf. [10:6]; 18:12 par. Luke). When the shepherd dies, the flock, the people of the king, is scattered (Mark 14:27 par. Matthew—Zech 13:7 is applied to the twelve). When the Son of Man returns he will sort his flock and gather the sheep to himself (Matt 25:31ff.). Until that time the church exists in the world as the little flock (Luke 12:32; cf. Isa 41:14; Dan 7:27), like sheep among wolves (Matt 10:16).[13] This metaphor sets forth three stages in the life of the church: first, under the earthly Christ; second, under the resurrected and exalted one; and third, under the returning one. Rather than having a typological relationship of its own, this metaphor gives expression to one.

The designation of the disciples as brothers and sisters is another of these metaphors (Mark 3:33-35 par.; cf. Matt 25:40; 28:10; John 20:17). "In Judaism, too, ἀδελφός means a co-religionist, who historically is identical with a compatriot. Yet, the latter as such is also called רֵעַ = πλησίον, and in Rabbinic

---

10. See A. Schlatter, *Erläuterungen zum Neuen Testament* (Stuttgart, 1928); Schniewind, *Matthäus*; H. Gressmann and E. Klostermann, *Das Evangelium Matthäus* (HNT; Tübingen, 1909) on this passage: κρίνειν = "rule" as in 1 Sam 8:5; *Pss. Sol.* 17:28; cf. Matt 5:5; Luke 12:32; Rev 3:21; 20:6; 21:12ff.; however, cf. Rengstorf, "δώδεκα," *TDNT* 2. 321-28.

11. Luke 13:6-9; Matt 7:16-20 par. Luke (cf. Jdt 12); Matt 12:33; 5:13; cf. Matt 3:16 par. Luke (cf. Isa 10:33); see below, pp. 193f.; cf. Revelation 2-3.

12. See above, pp. 88f.

13. Cf. the rabbinical saying that is quoted by J. Jeremias, "ἀρνίον," *TDNT* 1. 340: "There is something great about the sheep (Israel) that can persist among 70 wolves (the nations)." Cf. John 10:1ff. For the OT passages, see above, pp. 88f.; also cf. Pss 77:20; 78:52; 74:1; 79:13; 95:7; 100:3.

writings this is sometimes explicitly distinguished from אָח = ἀδελφός."[14] When Jesus designates as his brothers and sisters those who believe in him and in that way do the will of God—something that happens only at climactic points in the gospel—he is appointing the new people of God who experience the forgiveness of sins.[15] The resurrected one uses the term brother to welcome back those who had denied and forsaken him (Matt 28:10; John 20:17). The church is the band that the resurrected one has gathered around him and that lives by the forgiveness of sins. In the church one is not lost because he is a sinner, but only because he does not repent (cf. Peter and Judas).

In these typological metaphors, it is clear that the church was established when Jesus called the disciples, particularly the twelve; nevertheless, in the work of redemption the founding of the new redemptive people was completed only by Jesus' death and exaltation. When Jesus dies, God's vineyard is taken once for all from the tenants and given to a new people (Mark 12:9f. par.; cf. Matt 21:43). Only when Jesus dies is the Old Covenant finally abolished and the New Covenant established. This is what Jesus is announcing when he institutes the Lord's Supper.

2. THE PEOPLE OF THE NEW COVENANT AND THE MEANS OF THEIR REDEMPTION ARE ESTABLISHED IN THE INSTITUTION OF THE LORD'S SUPPER[16]

Both the relationship of the Last Supper to the Passover Feast and the saying about the cup are reminiscent of the founding of the former people of God through the deliverance from Egypt and the covenant on Sinai.

The Lord's Supper was instituted in the setting of a Passover meal, at least in the opinion of the writers of the Synoptic Gospels.[17] In Luke, Jesus' last meal with his disciples is explicitly called the Passover meal (πάσχα, Luke 22:15), and the way it begins is described in conformity with Jewish custom.[18] Moreover,

---

14. H. von Soden, "ἀδελφός," *TDNT* 1. 145; cf. Str-B 1. 276.

15. Cf. Isa 33:24 with: Mark 2:14ff. par.; Matt 11:19 par. Luke; Luke 15:1f.; 19:1ff.

16. In our study of the typology of the Last Supper we will begin with the accounts that are available, noting what scholarship has discovered about the original form, and we will disregard any features that have no typological significance.

17. According to Mark 14:12, the preparation of the meal took place τῇ πρώτῃ ἡμέρᾳ τῶν ἀζύμων, ὅτε τὸ πάσχα ἔθυον. The first designation of time is vague and is more clearly defined by the second (as in Mark 1:32, 35). Accordingly, the meal took place on the night following the slaughter of the Passover lambs that occurred on the afternoon of the 14th of Nisan (cf. Mark 14:17). This is true also in Matt 26:17; but not in John (see below, pp. 189f.).

18. J. Jeremias (*Die Abendmahlsworte Jesu* [Göttingen, 1935] 62; cf. p. 40). [The English translation, *The Eucharistic Words of Jesus* (New York, 1955) is from the 2d German edition concerning which Jeremias says, "This new edition is in very many respects a new book." It is impossible to correlate Goppelt's references with this translation.] Rengstorf (*Das Evangelium nach Lukas* [NTD] on this passage) and J. Behm ("κλάω," *TDNT* 3. 731f.) consider the description of the beginning of the celebration in Luke 22:15-22 to be an early independent tradition.

many of the features in the institution of the Lord's Supper that are common to all the traditions remind us of the celebration of the Jewish Passover.[19] It is quite likely that this connection with the Passover was not invented by the church, but can be traced to Jesus himself.[20] However that may be, we will begin with the accounts in the Synoptics and, by comparing the Last Supper with the Jewish Passover, will seek to set forth the typological relationship between the two.

Many of the external features of Jesus' ceremony and the ceremony of the early church can be traced to the Jewish Passover and be explained by it. The Last Supper took place at night (Mark 14:17 par. Matthew; John 13:30; 1 Cor 11:23), and that is also when it was celebrated in the early church (cf. Acts 12:12; 20:7f.; cf. Luke 24:29f.). This does not conform to the normal meal times, but it is in accord with the regulations for the Passover (Exod 12:8).[21] For the church, the night of the Passover became "the night when the Lord was betrayed" (1 Cor 11:23).

Moreover, the combining of the elements of bread[22] and wine[23] with interpretive sayings that draw their content from redemptive history[24] is prefigured in the Passover meal. The only difference, other than in content, is that Jesus did not add his interpretation to the Passover haggadah, which came at the conclusion of the preliminary dish. He added it to the grace before and after the main part of the meal, which immediately followed the preliminary dish. He probably wanted to connect his new interpretation with the distribution of the elements.[25] Moreover, the interpretation of the food itself as a divine gift is new to the Passover meal.[26] The participation, therefore, is something essentially new in the Christian celebration.

If the passing of a cup was already customary in the Passover, perhaps in keeping with a more ancient practice,[27] then the drinking from a cup cannot be interpreted, as Schniewind does, as a family custom and, consequently, as a reference to the family of God (*familia dei*).[28]

By virtue of its relationship to the Passover meal the Lord's Supper was viewed from the beginning as a recurring ceremony,[29] even if the command to

---

19. Jeremias, *Abendmahlsworte*, 14-26; cf. p. 40; and in dependence on him, J. Behm, "κλάω," *TDNT* 3. 734.

20. On the basis of Jeremias's careful study, J. Behm ("κλάω," *TDNT* 3. 732) says, "In all probability the Last Supper was the Passover."

21. *Jub.* 49:1, 12; *Mek. Exod.* 12:6; cf. J. Jeremias, *Abendmahlsworte*, 16f.

22. Ibid., 27-30.

23. Ibid., 21ff.

24. Ibid., 22-26.

25. Ibid., 26, 86; cf. p. 75.

26. The red wine signifying blood was a familiar figure (ibid., 76). The temporal food signifying divine gifts is prefigured in a rich figurative language (ibid., 87ff.) and in the feeding of Israel in the wilderness, which is also referred to in the NT (ibid., 90). But the idea is new to the Passover meal.

27. Ibid., 32f.

28. Schniewind, *Matthäus*, 173.

29. Behm, "κλάω," *TDNT* 3. 737, 735.

repeat it was not originally a part of the words of institution.[30] The command "Do this in remembrance of me" may be similar to phrases used in the institution of meals commemorating the dead. "The Lord's Supper is for Paul a feast of remembrance (1 C. 11:24 f.), not, however, in the sense of the antique memorial meal for the dead, which was designed to foster the memory of loved ones now deceased, but in the sense of the Jewish passover, which was designed to proclaim as a present reality the saving acts of God on which the faith of those participating was founded. . . . In virtue of the fact that it is thus imbedded in history and strictly related to the historical Jesus and the unique historical event of His death, Paul's view of the Lord's Supper is distinguished from the mythological ideas linked with sacred feasts in Hellenistic syncretism."[31]

Therefore, the relationship of the Christian celebration to the Jewish Passover Feast in the OT is a safeguard not only for the understanding of external features, but also for the correct interpretation of its ultimate essence.[32] The profound significance of what Jesus did in instituting the Lord's Supper is fully apparent when one remembers that the first Passover occurred at the time of the deliverance from Egypt and the establishment of the first covenant.

It is very difficult to conceive of Judas as the antitype of Pharaoh as Schöffel would like to do.[33] Pharaoh did not share in the meal as Judas did, nor was he a member of the nation as Judas was. The fact that he wants to hinder God's redemptive purpose and then actually helps to fulfill it is even more true of the Sanhedrin. Consequently, the NT nowhere suggests this connection.

The saying about the cup certainly has a typological relationship. Whether the Pauline form[34] (τοῦτο τὸ ποτήριον ἡ καινὴ διαθήκη ἐστὶν ἐν τῷ ἐμῷ αἵματι, 1 Cor 11:25) or the Markan form[35] (τοῦτό ἐστιν τὸ αἷμά μου τῆς διαθήκης, Mark 14:24) is considered more original, the content is the same.[36] It is the sealing of a covenant (διαθήκη) with blood, i.e., by the sacrifice of a life. As Paul makes clear by adding the word "new" (καινή) and Matthew with the insertion of "for the forgiveness of sins" (cf. Jer 31:34b), the saying refers to the New Covenant that is prophesied in Jer 31:31-34.

What other relationships there are to the first Passover and to the making of the first covenant cannot be fully comprehended. It is unclear whether the blood of the Passover lamb is referred to, or the "blood of the covenant" that was used in the sprinkling of blood at Sinai. The phrase "blood of the covenant" (αἷμα τῆς διαθήκης) is in verbal agreement with Exod 24:8 (LXX: cf. Zech 9:11). As a matter of fact, Hebrews (9:20; 10:29) takes "the blood of the covenant in the

---

30. Jeremias, *Abendmahlsworte*, 58; Schniewind, *Matthäus*, 175; Rengstorf, *Lukas*, 225.
31. J. Behm, "κλάω," *TDNT* 3. 739.
32. Cf. 1 Cor. 10:1ff.; see below, pp. 144f.
33. S. Schöffel, "Offenbarung Gottes im hl. Abendmahl," *Luthertum* (1937) 362.
34. J. Behm, "διαθήκη," *TDNT* 2. 133.
35. Jeremias, *Abendmahlsworte*, 59f.
36. Behm, "κλάω," *TDNT* 3. 736.

Sinai event as a prototype of Jesus' blood of the covenant and in so doing is thinking of the Lord's Supper."[37] This leads to the following interpretation: As the old divine order at Sinai was sealed with blood—for this is clearly what sprinkling with blood meant originally (Heb 9:18ff.)—so the new order is established with the blood of Jesus, i.e., by the sacrifice of his life.[38] Jesus' contemporaries, however, did not interpret that sprinkling of blood as a sealing of the covenant, but as a sacrifice for the sin of the people by which they were cleansed so they could be received into the covenant.[39] If we assume that this is the idea also in the NT, it will lead us to this interpretation: Jesus' blood is the blood of the covenant because his atoning death prepares mankind to be received into God's covenant.[40]

This phrase, however, may be an integral part of Passover typology. According to the Targum on Zech 9:11 and *Mek. Exod.* 12:6[41] the blood of the Passover lamb that was slaughtered at the Exodus from Egypt was also called blood of the covenant. Both commentaries apply Zech 9:11 to the deliverance from Egypt. They consider the blood of the Passover lamb as the covenant blood that brought about Israel's release from the "waterless pit" (Egypt). The frequent quotation of Deutero-Zechariah in the passion narrative suggests that it may have been used in a mediating way, the way it was customarily interpreted in the Synagogue. According to 1 Cor 5:7 the designation of Jesus as the Passover lamb was already familiar to the church. Nevertheless, it is scarcely conceivable that this is what the Pauline form of the saying about the cup refers to. If Jesus was thinking about the blood of the Passover lambs, then the following would be the background for his saying: "As God spared his people in Egypt because of the covenant blood and demonstrated his forgiveness by sparing them, so he once more will spare and forgive—because of the covenant blood that Jesus offers."[42] The concept of atonement and substitution that Jeremias believes was connected with the blood of the first Passover lamb[43] would have been present in this phrase already, and not simply when the words "which is poured out for many" (τὸ ἐκχυννόμενον ὑπὲρ πολλῶν, Isa 53:12) are added in Mark (14:24).

Apart from the fact that it is necessary to appeal to rabbinic interpretation to account for its transmission, the difficulty with relating the saying about the cup to the Passover lamb is that it does not provide an adequate reason for calling Jesus' blood the blood of the *covenant*. The rabbis defend the designation of the blood of the Passover lambs as blood of the covenant by referring to the covenant made with Abraham in Gen 15:18 and to the covenant promise given him that

---

37. Jeremias, *Abendmahlsworte*, 79.
38. J. Behm, "αἷμα," *TDNT* 1. 174; Schniewind, *Matthäus*, 252.
39. Jeremias, *Abendmahlsworte*, 79f.
40. Ibid., 80.
41. Ibid., 80f.
42. Ibid., 82.
43. Ibid., 81—the evidence is not very convincing.

his descendants would be delivered from Egypt (Gen 15:14).[44] It is not, however, because Jesus' blood fulfills a promise made within the framework of an existing covenant that it is called covenant blood, but because a new covenant is being established by it. This is why Rengstorf dares to make a statement that carries this matter a step further: "As once in Egypt God made his covenant with his people provisionally through the blood of the Passover lambs (Exod 24:8; Zech 9:11), so now by Jesus' dying, by his sacrifice in death—'for the forgiveness of sin' is an appropriate and more precise definition found in Matt 26:28—God establishes his eternal 'new covenant' with his people, who show that they are his people by fulfilling his will (Jer 31:31f.)."[45] The relationship between the blood of the Passover lambs and the blood of the covenant that is assumed here is not found in the biblical text nor in contemporary interpretations of it.[46]

As a matter of fact, the saying about the cup suggests both ideas. Jesus' blood, i.e., his death, like the blood of the Passover lambs, signifies sparing, deliverance, and redemption from death, slavery, and the wrath of God. At the same time, like the covenant blood at Sinai, it signifies reconciliation with God and the establishment of a new covenant, a new divine order. Now, as then, these two are inseparable and pulsate together in the words of institution, but, of course, without this clear conceptual definition of terms.

Now, as then, a people of God is formed through the covenant blood, which is also the blood of redemption. Jesus offers his covenant blood to the twelve, who represent the newly created nation of twelve tribes. Therefore, the Lord's Supper may be regarded as "a ceremony by which the church is established."[47] Here the new people of God is given in its basic form, although, like the New Covenant, it becomes a reality only through Christ's death and resurrection (here too it is the night before the deliverance is accomplished).

The typological difference inherent in all these typological relationships is obvious. There it was the blood of animals sacrificed according to God's command; here the self-sacrifice of the Son of God. There it was an earthly people; here the eternal "saints of the Most High." The Passover re-presents an event in redemptive history; in the Lord's Supper one is present who is himself "a covenant for the people."

The typology expressed in the Lord's Supper shows that the New Covenant people is related typologically to the Old Covenant people and to all its redemptive gifts. Because Christ gave himself to the church as covenant blood, cult and temple worship are abolished (cf. Hebrews). The church has not negated the ritual of the Old Covenant by reinterpretation as Philo has done; rather, the shadowy prototypes (cf. Heb 8:5; 10:1; Col 2:16f.) fall away in the presence of

---

44. *Mek. Exod.* 12:6; quoted by Jeremias, *Abendmahlsworte*, 80f.
45. Rengstorf, *Lukas*, 225.
46. Cf. especially the Targum on Zech 9:11 together with *Lev. Rab.* 19 on Lev 15:25 in Jeremias, *Abendmahlsworte*, 80f.
47. Schmidt, "ἐκκλησία," *TDNT* 3. 521; cf. Behm, "αἷμα," *TDNT* 1. 174f.

the boundless gift of Christ. Just as the means of salvation under the Old Covenant have merely typological significance for the church, so do the redemptive history and the commemorative feasts of the Old Covenant people. No longer does the church celebrate the Passover; it celebrates the Lord's Supper instead. The church does not hallow the Lord's Day by remembering the deliverance from Egypt (cf. Deut 5:15), but by proclaiming Christ's cross and resurrection; they do not hallow it by praising miracles of God performed for Israel, but by praising the mighty acts of God that have occurred among them. The history and the institutions of the Old Covenant are significant only as divinely ordained types that testify to the glory and the nature of the salvation that has been given to the church.

This is in agreement with what the Gospels and Acts indicate about the attitude of Jesus and the early church toward cult and temple. Temple worship, including the sacrifices, was revered as an ordinance of the Old Covenant.[48] Like the prophets, Jesus opposed the misuse of the temple[49] and proclaimed its ruin (Mark 13:1ff., 14 par.).[50] But his proclamation of the temple's ruin does not signify merely a chastisement in the form of a temporary withdrawal of a gift of grace, but the final replacement of the temple with something greater.[51] Here too, Jesus' death totally shatters the Old Covenant. The curtain separating the Most Holy Place from the Holy Place, a separation which was characteristic of the whole OT cult and temple order (Heb 9:2ff.), is torn in two (Matt 27:51 par. Luke).[52] Christ's blood establishes and guarantees the new divine order; no longer is there any need for another sin offering.[53]

Jesus' attitude toward the temple is carried on by the church. The confession of the Palestinian church in all its religious observances is the dominical saying, "One greater than the temple is here" (Matt 12:6; cf. 17:24).[54] For them Christ represents God's gracious presence far more than the temple does. How the church came to this realization and how this became known to the Jews is indicated in the story about Stephen (Acts 6–7). Stephen is charged with blasphemy (Acts 6:11); he is accused of saying that Jesus will destroy the Holy Place (the temple) and change the entire cultic law attributed to Moses (Acts 6:14).[55]

---

48. G. Schrenk, "ἱερόν," *TDNT* 3. 242ff. If it is frequently stressed that Jesus taught in the temple and important self-declarations (Mark 11:27 par.; 12:35 par.; cf. John) were transferred there, then it is in order to declare that "Christ does His work on the basis of and in fulfillment of the previous divine history" (p. 243). Jesus honors the temple as a divine institution (pp. 242f.) and so did the early church (p. 246).

49. Mark 11:11ff. par.; on the offerings cf. Matt 9:13; 12:7 = Hos 6:6.

50. Schrenk, "ἱερόν," *TDNT* 3. 238f.

51. Mark 14:57f. par. Matthew; cf. 15:29 par. Matthew, which is interpreted correctly by John 2:18-22 (cf. 1:14b; 4:21-24); also cf. Matt 12:6; Rev 21:22. On the "something greater," see above, pp. 65-68.

52. See Schrenk, "ἱερόν," *TDNT* 3. 245f. on Matt 27:5.

53. See Behm, "αἷμα," *TDNT* 1. 174; cf. p. 173.

54. See n. 48; cf. Matt 17:24-27; and especially: "Then the sons are exempt," 17:26.

55. τὰ ἔθη ἃ παρέδωκεν ἡμῖν Μωϋσῆς. H. Preisker, "ἔθος," *TDNT* 2. 373.

The reason this accusation is "false" (Acts 6:13) is not that it reports Stephen's words incorrectly, but that it falsely attributes to him the intention to blaspheme. Consequently, in his defense he does not uphold the truthfulness of his assertion, but he, like the prophets, simply exposes the error of their accusation. For this reason Stephen's defense contains no typology in its discussion of the temple.[56]

The attitude of Jesus and the church toward the temple incorporates the basic elements that are developed by Paul, and, on this particular point, especially by the Epistle to the Hebrews. The important feature that is given special emphasis by John is already present here: in his own person Christ takes the place of temple and sacrifice and every other OT means of salvation. He is not simply the mediator of God's New Covenant; he is the incarnation of it. His place in typology becomes clear only when we realize there is no typology that by-passes Christ; he is the antitype of the entire OT.

Finally, the institution of the Lord's Supper proclaims that the situation in which the church passes through history is not yet the consummation. The Last Supper is itself another prophecy in type, a type that points to the joyous banquet in the future that Christ will celebrate with his disciples in the kingdom of God (Luke 22:15-18; Mark 14:25; Matt 26:29; 1 Cor 11:26).[57] Therefore, each Lord's Supper celebrated by the church points to the consummation (Rev 21:2ff.).

The institution of the Lord's Supper is an important summary of all OT typology in the NT. The comprehensive concept in which this is all summarized is found here also: it is the New Covenant.[58] Jesus is the Christ, the mediator, and the incarnation of the New Covenant. His church is the people of the New Covenant.

The basic formation of this people, which began with the calling of the twelve, reaches a preliminary conclusion on Pentecost.

3. THE CHURCH OF PENTECOST

Through the Pentecost event Jesus' church becomes the people of God that the prophets had envisioned with God's word and will written on their hearts (Jer

---

56. Stephen advances two arguments primarily: Acts 7:44-50 is an account of the origin of the temple. The temple is only a copy of the tabernacle, which was made according to the heavenly pattern. It was not even built at God's command as the tabernacle was, but at David's request. Its erection was a gracious concession by God. Moreover, it was done in Solomon's time (here the train of thought merges with the second argument); therefore, only after a long period of redemptive history. What this means is clearly stated in Acts 7:43f.: God's saving activity and revelation are not bound to the temple, or to Jerusalem, or to the Holy Land. Wherever God reveals himself, that becomes γῆ ἁγία (7:33; cf. 6:13). Cf. Stephen (Acts 6:13) with Jeremiah (Jer 26:11).

57. Jeremias, *Abendmahlsworte*, 61ff.

58. Behm, "διαθήκη," *TDNT* 2. 134, "The fact that the expression καινὴ διαθήκη occurs only once on the lips of Jesus, though at a decisive point, is no more argument against its central signficance than is its infrequent occurrence in the OT apocrypha. In the light of this saying of Jesus we can easily see how Paul and the author of Heb. gave to the concept of the διαθήκη a central position in their theological understanding of history."

31:33f.) by the Spirit of God (Ezek 36:27ff.). The early church was aware of this, and the record in Acts shows that Luke was aware of it too. It was the opinion of late Judaism that the spirit of prophecy had been extinguished. Peter's sermon on Pentecost views the general outpouring[59] of that spirit as a sign that the new age has begun (Acts 2:17, 20f. from Joel 2:28-32; cf. Acts 1:4) and that the consummation is near (Acts 2:19f.). In the gospel that is proclaimed throughout the book of Acts, the third article of the creed is juxtaposed to the second. With the evidence of the cross and resurrection and under the forgiving grace of its exalted Lord, the church goes forth in the power of the Spirit to meet the Son of Man who is coming again (cf. Acts 1:1-11).

The miracle of tongues is the first manifestation of the Spirit on Pentecost (Acts 2:4-13). It seems that it is intended to be a divine sign indicating the special significance of the Pentecost event for the establishment of the new people of God, and it seems that it was understood this way by the church as well.

The miracle of tongues reminds us of the haggadic elaboration of the giving of the Law on Sinai, which was widely circulated and was, therefore, known also by the church: "Every word which came from the mouth of the Almighty (in the giving of the Law) was divided into seventy tongues" (= languages, so that each nation heard the divine commands in its own language).[60] Though he does not explain how it happened, Luke certainly intends to report that a miraculous manner of speaking was produced by the Spirit.[61] It was heard by the listeners as speech in their own native languages, just as in the haggadah concerning God's voice at Sinai (Acts 2:6, 8, 11). That Luke and the tradition he used were acquainted with the Sinai haggadah is clear from the story about Jesus sending out the seventy disciples (Luke 10:1ff.) because it refers to this same idea of seventy nations in the world. It has often been supposed that the tradition concerning tongues was developed from the first experience of glossolalia through the influence of this haggadah (as, e.g., in Acts 10:46; 19:6).[62] Luke, however, distinguished this "speaking in other tongues" from the speaking in tongues that frequently accompanied the initial receiving of the Spirit.[63] The unique feature about the speaking in tongues on Pentecost is that it was understood by the hearers. This distinguishes it from the speaking in tongues that can be interpreted

---

59. Cf. Acts 2:1, πάντες; 2:17, πᾶσα σάρξ.

60. Quoted from Str-B 2. 604f.; cf. the way Philo develops the Sinai legislation in *Decal.* 32ff. (miraculous voices and miraculous hearing), 46ff. (voices out of the fire). On the concept of the 70 nations of the world, see J. Jeremias, "ἀρήν," *TDNT* 1. 340.

61. The miracle of tongues on Pentecost did not consist in the disciples' speaking in various languages previously unknown to them (J. Behm, "γλῶσσα," *TDNT* 1. 724f.), but in their ecstatic proclamation in a new miraculous language (Meyer, *Apostelgeschichte* [9th ed.] 86; cf. Mark 16:17).

62. Behm, "γλῶσσα," *TDNT* 1. 724f.; however, see Str-B 2. 604.

63. λαλεῖν γλώσσαις, Acts 10:46; 19:7; the thing that is being stressed in 10:47; 11:15, 17 as common in the experience of the Gentile captain and in the experience on Pentecost is the receiving of the Spirit, not its effects.

only by specially gifted persons (1 Cor 14:2ff., 23). We are not justified in dismissing this feature as something fabricated for the sake of analogy, because the action of the Spirit is not a religio-psychological phenomenon that would be limited to specific forms of manifestation. Nevertheless, the Sinai haggadah may be the reason for the strong emphasis on and the development of this feature, which now endangers the clarity and unity of the section.[64] In any case, it is certain that the tradition of the church perceived the relationship to that OT type (no clear distinction was made between the haggadah and the text of the OT).

What is the significance of this relationship of the speaking in tongues on Pentecost and, therefore, the Pentecost experience itself to the proclamation of the Law on Sinai? First of all, the account of the tongues is meant to say that the gospel—"the wonders of God" (Acts 2:11) that are praised are the things that happened to Christ—applies to all nations, just as is stated about the Law in the elaboration of the Sinai story. But it means more than this. No longer is God's will merely perceived outwardly (only so that men might be without excuse, Rom 1:20; cf. 2:12ff.); it is miraculously imprinted on their hearts by God's Spirit. The New Covenant is here. Certainly these ideas were not strange to Luke, who was a disciple of Paul (2 Cor 3:3ff.).[65]

The new age in which God will gather his people from the nations of the world has already begun. There are many allusions in Acts to promises concerning that gathering. Even in Acts 1:8b, a verse containing the outline of the entire book, there are allusions to the saying from Isa 49:6 that is quoted in Acts 13:47. The introduction to the speech that explains the Pentecost event is patterned after Isa 2:2.[66] Acts 2:39 = Joel 2:32; undoubtedly Isa 57:19 referred originally to the Jews of the diaspora.) In the reception of the eunuch (Acts 8:26ff.), Isa 56:3-7 and Ps 68:31 are fulfilled, although, of course, that fact is not stated. Many interpret the saying about the famine that was coming over the world (Acts 11:28) as originally having been meant figuratively, like Amos 8:11f. Now "David's fallen tent," i.e., David's kingdom, is being reestablished so that all nations may seek the Lord (Acts 15:16f. = Amos 9:11, LXX; cf. Isa 45:22; Acts 28:26-28). The new nation is the new humanity.

In the miracle of tongues at Pentecost the church could see a direct reference to the new humanity. Just as it is a reference to the new nation in the framework

---

64. See the details in E. Preuschen, *Die Apostelgeschichte* (HNT; Tübingen, 1912) on Acts 13.

65. Just as the establishment of the people of the Old Covenant began with the Passover and was completed at the revelation at Sinai, so also the establishment of the people of the New Covenant was completed with the outpouring of the Spirit. This interpretation of Pentecost was suggested by the rabbinical interpretation of the Passover: In NT times it was already associated with the Passover as a concluding festival (Str-B 2. 597). Perhaps this was the beginning of the new interpretation which considered the feast to be a celebration in memory of the giving of the Law on Sinai, an interpretation that cannot be attested until the second century (ibid. 2. 601), and that preserves another reference to the connection with the miracle of languages that is mentioned above.

66. In Acts 2:17, the saying that is quoted from Joel 3:1ff. (LXX), καὶ ἔσται μετὰ ταῦτα, has been changed to agree with Isa 2:2 (LXX: ἔσται ἐν ταῖς ἐσχάταις ἡμέραις).

of Mosaic period typology, so in connection with primeval age typology it is a sign and a pledge of the new humanity. This will be a people with one language (Gal 3:28, etc.) just as was true in primeval times before humanity was divided by the sin of wanting to be like God (Gen 11:1ff.). Since this expectation was already present in the world around the church,[67] it is obvious that the NT had also seen this connection, even though no direct indication of it can be detected in the text.[68]

Throughout the early church's history there are repeated allusions to the fact that the church is related typologically to the first people of God—to what is reported about them and predicted about them. Whether Luke saw a typological connection or simply utilized the familiar wording of parallel narratives will have to remain an open question.

Accordingly, the allusion to Deut 15:4 in Acts 4:34 may indicate that what the Law was trying to accomplish by its commands and promises of blessing has come to pass in the church. The statement is made in Deut 15:4 that "There shall not be any needy persons among you" (οὐκ ἔσται ἐν σοὶ ἐνδεής, LXX), and Acts 4:34 says, "There were no needy persons among them" (οὐδὲ γὰρ ἐνδεής τις ἦν ἐν αὐτοῖς).

Ananias's lie (Acts 5:1ff.), like Achan's theft (Josh 7:1ff.), was an embezzlement of things dedicated to God. In both instances the word ἐνοσφίσατο is used, which occurs only one other time in the NT (Titus 2:10).[69]

The account of Peter's suggestion that seven almoners be appointed (Acts 6:3f.) is patterned after the OT story in which a similar suggestion was made by Jethro (Exod 18:17-23).[70] This is, of course, not a case of genuine typology, but it is another indication that the new church of God is related typologically to the old, especially to the people of the Mosaic period.

Just as the description of Peter's advice to the church has been influenced by the account of Moses' life, so in a similar way the commissioning of Paul is

---

67. See, e.g., *T. Judah* 25:1ff.: "And after these things shall Isaac and Jacob arise unto life . . . and ye shall be the people of the Lord, and have one tongue; and there shall be no spirit of deceit. . . ." And earlier in the *Testament of Judah* 24 (in the Armenian version; the Greek version obviously has been edited by Christians): "And the heavens shall be opened unto him and the blessing of the Holy Father shall be poured down upon him. And he will pour down upon us the spirit of grace . . . ye shall walk in His commandments first and last." The rabbis did not associate any expectations for the new age with Gen 11:1; see Str-B 1. 7 = 2. 633.

68. In Acts, of course, the dominant typology is the typology of the Mosaic period and Israel, but there is also creation typology; see below on Acts 3:21 and above on Luke 3:23ff.

69. Acts 5:2f.: καὶ ἐνοσφίσατο ἀπὸ τῆς τιμῆς. Josh 7:1: καὶ ἐνοσφίσαντο ἀπὸ τοῦ ἀναθέματος.

70. Even the beginning of the speech is surprisingly similar: Acts 6:2: οὐκ ἀρεστόν ἐστιν— Exod 18:17: οὐκ ὀρθῶς σὺ ποιεῖς. Cf. Exod 18:19f. with Acts 6:4: Moses' proper task, on the one hand, is to bring the concerns of the people before God and, on the other hand, to make God's will known to the people. The proposals agree in wording: Acts 6:3: ἐπισκέψατε δέ . . . ἄνδρας ἐξ ὑμῶν . . . οὓς καταστήσομεν ἐπί. . . . Exod 18:21: σκέψαι ἀπὸ παντὸς τοῦ λαοῦ ἄνδρας . . . οὓς καταστήσομεν ἐπί. . . .

reminiscent of Jeremiah's call.[71] Like that prophet, Paul was chosen by God from among the people[72] and was sent out (Acts 26:17f.—Jer 1:7) to complete the work of the Servant of the Lord on behalf of the Gentiles.[73] Therefore, he, like the men of God in the Old Covenant, is inspired with courage for his mission (Acts 18:9f.).[74]

We must interject here that Paul himself recognized his relationship to Jeremiah. He knew that he, like Jeremiah, had been "set apart from birth." This was true not simply in the way that all believers are set apart by being Christians (Rom 8:29), but because he had been set apart for his special office (Gal 1:15f.—Jer 1:5; cf. Isa 49:1). He deliberately chose his words to correspond with those passages. "Those who have pointed to an inner relationship between these two men are undoubtedly correct. Both were men who stood under the compulsion of the divine imperative (cf. Jer 20:7ff. with 1 Cor 9:16), whose entire lives were devoted to service in the matters intrusted to them and who, as the obverse side of their relationship to God, had to go through a sea of suffering inflicted on them by men."[75] With both of them God's power proved mighty in human weakness (2 Cor 12:9f.). When faced by his enemies, Paul, like Jeremiah, appealed to the God who knows and tests the hearts (1 Thess 2:4—Jer 11:20). In the midst of suffering and struggle Paul, like the men of God of the Old Covenant, longed to die, although Paul, of course, longed to die in order to be with Christ (cf. Phil 1:23 with 1 Kgs 19:4 [Elijah]; cf. Jer 9:2). It should not be surprising if the apostle who endured much suffering as he brought the light of Christ to the Gentiles (Isa 49:6—Acts 13:47) reminds us of the Servant of the Lord, not only in the way he expresses his consciousness of divine calling (Gal 1:15f.—Isa 49:1), but also in the way he reflects on his own labors (Phil 2:16—Isa 49:4).[76]

Accordingly, the witness of Acts about the beginnings of the church places the church of Pentecost and the important features of its history in a number of typological relationships to the people of God in the Old Covenant and to their labors.

It is significant that in the early church's witness to Christ as it is recorded in Acts, typology is found throughout in a way that argues for its being original. We will compile the significant material in an appendix, separate from the witness

---

71. Acts 9:15—Jer 1:10, LXX. Apparently βασιλεῖς has been added in imitation of Jer 1:10, LXX (cf. H. Wendt, *Apostelgeschichte* (MeyerK), on this passage).

72. Acts 26:17f.: ἐξαιρούμενός σε—Jer 1:8: ἐξαιρεῖσθαί σε.

73. Cf. Acts 26:18 with Isa 42:7 (v 16); Acts 13:47 with Isa 49:6.

74. Cf. Jer 1:18; also Exod 3:12; Josh 1:5, 9. There is no adequate support in the text for Dornseiff's ("Lukas der Schriftsteller," *ZNW* 35 [1936] 139, 141) supposition that Acts 9:4f. is dependent on 1 Sam 24:9ff.; 26:13ff. (Saul is related to King Saul, and Christ to David) and that Acts 10 is dependent on Numbers 22 (Peter is related to Balaam).

75. G. Dehn, *Gesetz oder Evangelium, Eine Einführung in den Galaterbrief* (Berlin, 1934) 45.

76. See below, p. 151.

to Christ in the Gospels. In our study of the Gospels we have already considered the material from Acts that was directly related to it.

APPENDIX I: TYPOLOGY IN THE EARLY CHURCH'S WITNESS TO CHRIST AS RECORDED IN ACTS

In the record of the missionary preaching of the apostles in Acts, the apostles' eyewitness testimony concerning the mighty acts of God (Acts 1:21f.; 2:32; 3:15; [4:33]; 5:32; 10:41; 13:31) is always accompanied by a word of Scripture that sheds light on the new age. From the very beginning, the apostolic witness of the NT was linked to the prophetic witness of the OT in order to evoke faith through the witness of the Spirit (Acts 2:33; 5:32).

By using the OT in this way, the church has preserved the typological approach that it learned from Jesus and has not degraded Scripture, as Judaism did, by making it an inspired collection of proof texts and predictions. In Stephen's defense, what Jesus said about the prophets being types of his own ministry and suffering[77] (Acts 7:51f.; cf. Mark 12:1ff.; Matt 23:31) is reshaped into a finished typology by giving it a special application to Moses (Acts 7:17-43).[78] Moses called himself a type of the future deliverer (Acts 7:37; cf. 3:22 = Deut 18:15)—Stephen's speech perceives the typology underlying the prophecy. The Mosaic period was a model of the new age. In it the promises made to Abraham were fulfilled. Abraham's descendants became a great nation (Acts 7:17b) and this nation was redeemed (Acts 7:7; cf. 7:34ff.) and received the promised land (Acts 7:5, 7).[79] At the time determined by God in prophecy and promise, Moses, the mediator of that redemption, was born (Acts 7:20; cf. 7:17).[80] His childhood was attended by many manifestations of God's grace. Therefore, he became a man "powerful in speech and action" ($\delta\upsilon\nu\alpha\tau\grave{o}\varsigma$ $\grave{\epsilon}\nu$ $\lambda o\gamma o\tilde{\iota}\varsigma$ $\kappa\alpha\grave{\iota}$ $\check{\epsilon}\rho\gamma o\iota\varsigma$, Acts 7:22; the same thing is said in Luke 24:19 about Jesus, the prophet). Moses was rejected by his people; God, however, not only gave him the honor that his fellow countrymen refused him (Acts 7:27), but gave him a far greater honor, the honor of being a deliverer ($\lambda\upsilon\tau\rho\omega\tau\acute{\eta}\varsigma$). The testimony of the apostles declares the same things about Jesus and even uses the same words.[81] Moses' actions, like the actions of Jesus (Acts 2:22) and the apostles (Acts 4:30; 5:12),

---

77. See above, pp. 79f.

78. It is remarkable that typology appears even in that part of the speech that applies to Stephen's time. See n. 56.

79. This interpretation, which in a strange way supplements the usual understanding of the promise to Abraham, takes into account those features of the OT that characterize it as an independent, self-contained book; cf. Josh 21:43ff.; 23:14.

80. $\grave{\epsilon}\nu$ $\tilde{\wp}$ $\kappa\alpha\iota\rho\tilde{\wp}$ in Acts 7:20 is certainly not meant simply as "a general indication of time" (G. Delling, "$\kappa\alpha\iota\rho\acute{o}\varsigma$," *TDNT* 3. 461), but in a very significant sense (see ibid., 459ff.).

81. Acts 7:35: $\grave{o}\nu$ $\mathring{\eta}\rho\nu\acute{\eta}\sigma\alpha\nu\tau o$ . . . $\tauo\tilde{\upsilon}\tau o\nu$ $\grave{o}$ $\theta\epsilon\grave{o}\varsigma$ $\kappa\alpha\grave{\iota}$ $\check{\alpha}\rho\chi o\nu\tau\alpha$ $\kappa\alpha\grave{\iota}$ $\lambda\upsilon\tau\rho\omega\tau\grave{\eta}\nu$ $\grave{\alpha}\pi\acute{\epsilon}\sigma\tau\alpha\lambda\kappa\epsilon\nu$. Acts 3:13-15 of Jesus: $\grave{o}\nu$ $\grave{\upsilon}\mu\epsilon\tilde{\iota}\varsigma$ $\mu\grave{\epsilon}\nu$ . . . $\mathring{\eta}\rho\nu\acute{\eta}\sigma\alpha\sigma\theta\epsilon$ . . . $\tau\grave{o}\nu$ $\delta\grave{\epsilon}$ $\grave{\alpha}\rho\chi\eta\gamma\grave{o}\nu$ $\tau\tilde{\eta}\varsigma$ $\zeta\omega\tilde{\eta}\varsigma$. Cf. 5:31: $\tauo\tilde{\upsilon}\tau o\nu$ $\grave{o}$ $\theta\epsilon\grave{o}\varsigma$ $\grave{\alpha}\rho\chi\eta\gamma\grave{o}\nu$ $\kappa\alpha\grave{\iota}$ $\sigma\omega\tau\tilde{\eta}\rho\alpha$ $\H\upsilon\psi\omega\sigma\epsilon\nu$, the same forceful constructions are used; cf. 2:23.

were accompanied by wonders and miraculous signs (τέρατα καὶ σημεῖα, Acts 7:36). In the congregation Moses spoke living words (λογία ζῶντα) that God had given him—words that were valid and life-giving.[82] This description of Moses leads to the following conclusion: By crucifying Jesus the present generation has completed what their fathers did to Moses, the prototype of the redeemer, and to all the prophets who predicted the coming of Christ (Acts 7:51f.).

The typology that is the basis of the prophecies about the Son of David has been perceived and is taken into consideration in the exposition. The connection between Jesus and David is presented similarly to the way it is done in Matthew's genealogy (Acts 13:17-23; Matt 1:2ff.).[83] First of all, redemptive history is delineated briefly from the time the patriarchs were chosen until David. Then, in contrast to David, in whom that history reaches a provisional conclusion, Christ, the promised shoot, is presented as the one who completes redemptive history (cf. Acts 13:23; Matt 1:21). Consequently, the message that the promised redemption has come is first directed to "the children of Abraham" (Acts 13:26).

Because of Christ's relationship to David, Ps 16:10 is interpreted as a prophecy of Christ's resurrection (Acts 13:35-37; 2:25-28). In Jewish exegesis the passage was not usually applied to the Messiah, but to the godly man. It was not interpreted as referring to his preservation from death, which is what it meant originally, but to his deliverance out of death.[84] As a matter of fact, in v 11 of this psalm, praise of the true life which is based on fellowship with God (Ps 16:11) moves directly to resurrection faith, like that which breaks through in Psalm 73. Moreover, we can regard it as a prediction in type concerning Christ, because this lofty statement about very intimate fellowship with God is only truly fulfilled in Christ, and through him it is fulfilled in those who are his own. Of course, this is our way of viewing history, and we must not falsely attribute our view to the development of the argument in Acts (2:29-31). Nevertheless, it is remarkable that the following interpretation is drawn from the literal sense by means of a series of typological ideas and concepts from redemptive history. Looking on the surface, David is speaking about himself in the psalm. He remained in the grave, however, and his statements have not been fulfilled in his own experience (Acts 2:29). He is a prophet, and with these words he must be pointing beyond himself to the "shoot from his stump" that was promised to him (Acts 2:30f.; cf. 2 Sam 7:12f.). His words have found their real fulfillment in Christ Jesus (Acts 2:32; this conclusion is reached because of the present

---

82. Acts 7:38; cf. 5:20: ῥήματα τῆς ζωῆς ταύτης; cf. 1 Pet 1:23; John 6:68; and Acts 7:39: ὑπήκοοι—6:7. Certainly this does not refer only to the Law (Wendt, *Apostelgeschichte*, 145; cf. Rom 7:10, 12; Gal 3:12), but also to the promise given on Sinai (T. Zahn, *Die Apostelgeschichte des Lucas* [Kommentar zum Neuen Testament; Leipzig, 1918-21] 1. 254).

83. See above.

84. Str-B 2. 18.

reality of redemption). Here are the beginnings of typological exegesis in a culturally conditioned form.

It is necessary to keep this way of thinking in mind when interpreting the concept of restoration (ἀποκατάστασις, Acts 3:21), which is a fundamental concept in typology and occurs in Acts right in the missionary preaching that bears witness to Christ. Christ Jesus "must remain in heaven until the time comes for God to restore everything as he promised long ago through his holy prophets" (Acts 3:21). The last part of the verse indicates that the words "the time for God to restore everything" do not refer to a time prior to the parousia when all customary relationships will be restored,[85] but to the new age that will begin with the parousia of Christ, who is now hidden in heaven. It is not certain what it is that will be restored, and, therefore, what this really means is not clear. According to Oepke two ideas are intertwined.[86] He indicates this by a double translation that is grammatically possible: "The restitution of all that of which God has previously spoken through his holy prophets" = "The establishment (restitution is imprecise) of all that which God. . . ." A renewal of creation is promised in prophecy, but this is not a literal restoration of the universe, or cosmos, as in Stoic doctrine.[87] As we have seen consistently, Acts is more interested in the restoration of the Mosaic period and Israel than in the restoration of creation. The restoration of Israel's relationships is the primary concern of prophecy. Ultimately, this word,[88] which is used to express the idea of restoration common to the thinking of all mankind, has been reshaped by the relative clause modifying it in accordance with the biblical concept of typology. Perhaps this word refers to prophecies like Deut 18:15 and to the widespread expectation that the Mosaic period would return (cf. Acts 3:22; 7:37). For Acts, however, Jesus, and especially the coming Son of Man, is not simply a Moses *redivivus*; he is the antitype of Moses.[89] This is what the resurrected one had in mind when the disciples asked, "Are you . . . going to restore the kingdom to Israel?" (. . . ἀποκαθιστάνεις τὴν βασιλείαν τῷ Ἰσραήλ, Acts 1:6), because he answered them in the affirmative, but rejected any human speculation about the time or season.[90] Moreover, the NT does not speak of the return of primitive man, but of the return of Adam (cf. 1 Cor 15:44ff.). It does not speak of the return of the golden age, but of the perfecting of creation (καινός, Rev 21:1ff.). There is very profound meaning in this imprecise language that is reshaping the old terminology in its struggle to find adequate expression. The former relationship between God and man will not be restored, nor will the things that were signif-

---

85. As in the addition to Mal 3:23: ἀποκατασήσει (הֵשִׁיב). In the NT this is applied to John the Baptist in Mark 9:12 par.; cf. 6:15 par.; Matt 11:10, 14; John 1:21; see Oepke, "ἀποκαθίστημι," *TDNT* 1. 389.

86. Ibid., 390.

87. Ibid., 390.

88. This is the only occurrence of the term in the LXX or NT; ibid., 391, 389.

89. See above on Acts 7.

90. Oepke, "ἀποκαθίστημι," *TDNT* 1. 389.

icantly affected by that relationship—the situation of the first man, the Mosaic period, etc. What will be restored is the promise contained in those things, certain aspects of which have been indicated by prophecy. "In Christ God gives back to Israel the entire promise (as found in these relationships and expressed in prophecy)."[91]

This restoration is not promised for the present time, but is proclaimed as being imminent, and as occurring at the time when God sends Jesus Christ (Acts 3:20), who "must remain in heaven" until then (Acts 3:21). The same strange feature that we encountered in the disciples' question (Acts 1:6) and in Stephen's defense ("Jesus will destroy this place," Acts 6:14) characterizes Jesus' preaching when he says, "The kingdom of God is near." Whoever receives this word senses that the kingdom is already here, that David's kingdom has already been rebuilt (cf. Acts 15:16 with Amos 9:11), and that the temple has already been replaced by one who is greater than the temple.[92]

This same emphasis is found in the verses that follow the statement about the future restoration (Acts 3:22ff.). These verses are not intended to provide examples of the restoration;[93] they form the conclusion of Peter's speech and stress how important the present moment is for ultimate participation in redemption. But this in itself indicates that the restoration has now begun. There is no longer any need to wait for the "sending of Christ"; it has already happened (cf. ὅπως ἂν . . . ἀποστείλη in Acts 3:20 with ἀπέστειλεν in 3:26). The prophecy is not quoted merely to show us that the fulfillment is near, but to declare that the restoration has already occurred. If it is necessary now to listen to the prophet about whom Moses spoke ("a prophet like me . . . ," Deut 18:15), then he must be here already (Acts 3:22f.). These are the days about which all the prophets spoke (Acts 3:24). Now the covenant with Abraham is fulfilled (Acts 3:25f.). Now the Servant of the Lord (παῖς, Acts 3:26) will bring about repentance and faith, so that the Son of Man will find faith in his day and be able to grant salvation.[94] Whoever hears this call to repentance will receive more than the one who submits to the call of the Baptist. The typological fulfillment, the restoration, has already come with Christ, and with Christ it is still awaited. The first is an integral part of the NT.

The early church, then, preserved the typological approach that Jesus taught them and so shaped it that it illuminated their pathway and their preaching of salvation. We will find the same thing in the other groups of NT Scriptures. We have added another appendix here dealing with typology in the Epistle of James because, in this respect as in many others, the Epistle of James is closest to the Scriptures that originated in the Palestinian church, especially to Matthew.

---

91. Schlatter, *Erläuterungen*, on this passage.
92. See above on Acts 6:14.
93. γάρ occurs in 3:22 only in Koine pm.
94. Cf. Mal 3:22f.: ἀποστέλλω ὑμῖν Ἠλίαν . . . πρὶν ἐλθεῖν ἡμέραν κυρίου . . . , ὃς ἀποκαταστήσει καρδίαν ἀνθρώπου πρὸς τὸν πλησίον.

APPENDIX II: TYPOLOGY IN THE EPISTLE OF JAMES

Little typology can be expected in James because in it the preaching of salvation, in which typology is embedded, has been displaced almost entirely by proverbial parenesis calling for repentance. This is why it is so surprising and so much more important for a proper understanding of the epistle to observe that the typology of the twelve tribes appears in the salutation (Jas 1:1).

James wants to address the "twelve tribes scattered among the nations" (ταῖς δώδεκα φυλαῖς ταῖς ἐν τῇ διασπορᾷ). By the time of Jesus the twelve tribes had long disappeared from history; however, the expectation was alive that these tribes would reappear in the new age.[95] Jews are not the only ones who can be designated as the twelve tribes, because the term is especially applicable to the true Israel that is waiting for God's salvation (as in Acts 26:7). If this is always the Israel that James has in mind, as Schlatter points out, then he is thinking primarily of the twelve tribes that have recently arisen in Jesus' twelve disciples—of the Israel for whom Christ has come already. Of course, he may have been thinking of the remnant of the circumcised that were saved. The twelve tribes are "scattered among the nations." That is not meant in a geographical sense, at least not exclusively so, but in accordance with redemptive history, as in 1 Pet 1:1, because the people are still scattered among the nations of the world far from their eternal homeland (Phil 3:20; Heb 13:14; Matt 24:31). When James calls himself "a servant of God" (θεοῦ . . . δοῦλος), in this salutation, he wants to be included in the succession of men of God who called Israel back to God.[96] In distinction from them, however, he also speaks as a "servant of the Lord Jesus Christ," as a servant of the exalted Lord of the new people of God. Just as James is "a servant of God and of the Lord Jesus Christ," so the twelve tribes whom he addresses are not only the Israel of God, but also the people of Christ. Whoever considers himself to be a part of the true Israel realizes that what follows applies to him.

Therefore, it is really clear that the pareneses which follow are a part of the stream of Christian preaching that begins with the Sermon on the Mount, not only because of its radical ethics, but also because it assumes that salvation has come and that it has an eschatological character, though this is not stated.[97] This last point is especially important for typology, and, as we noted, James is aware not only that the end is near—which is determinative of our behavior (Jas 1:12; 2:12; 5:3, 7-11)—but also that the consummation has come—which was decisive for the early Christian point of view. Through the new birth, Christians are "a kind of firstfruits of all he created" (ἀπαρχήν τινα τῶν αὐτοῦ κτισμάτων,

---

95. Von Rad, "Ἰσραήλ," *TDNT* 3. 357f. See above.

96. Cf. Amos 3:7; Jer 7:25; Dan 9:11; Mark 12:2ff.; not only the "godly," Isa 42:19, LXX; 1 Pet 2:16.

97. A. Schlatter (*Die Theologie der Apostel* [Stuttgart, 1922] 87ff.) and Preisker (*TBl* 13 [1934] 230ff.) have demonstrated this in detail.

Jas 1:18); they are already rich through faith (Jas 2:5; cf. Matt 5:3; Luke 6:20; Rev 2:9); they can consider temptation to be pure joy (πᾶσαν χαράν, Jas 1:2; cf. Matt 5:10ff.; Rom 5:3ff.; 1 Pet 4:13); they should be perfect (τέλειοι) in every respect (Jas 1:4, 25; 3:2). The kind of perfection Jesus had in mind (Matt 5:48) can only be attained at the time of the consummation when the τέλος has come.

In the course of his discussion, James repeatedly presents OT personalities as types. In connection with Abraham, he points out that, although righteousness is conferred to faith according to Gen 15:6, a part of that faith is the confirmation by works as recorded in Gen 22:1ff. He says the same thing about Rahab (Jas 2:25). As indicated in the OT and emphasized by late Judaism,[98] it is taken for granted that Rahab's faith in the God of Israel (see Heb 11:31) moved her to the action that resulted in her salvation.[99] Moreover, James compares the suffering church with the prophets (Jas 5:10; cf. Matt 5:12). The church should consider Job in particular because in the end God rewarded his patient endurance (Jas 5:11). From Elijah they should learn the power of prayer (Jas 5:17f.). But since James is looking primarily at the psychic processes and not at God's redemptive gifts,[100] there is none of the heightening in redemptive history such as is found in Matt 11:11 and that is essential for typology. For James, as for Judaism and also for *1 Clement*, those OT personalities are excellent examples to follow, but they are not types pointing to a future consummation.[101]

When James makes his selection of OT legal regulations, when he describes the "royal law" of love (Jas 2:8) and ignores the whole cultic and ceremonial law,[102] he is following Jesus once again and is treating these things in the light of the consummation. His independent attitude toward Scripture "is not disobedience to God; it is the mark of the 'perfect man,' the one who in full obedience does the perfect will of God."[103]

Consequently, our interpretation of the salutation is justified by the general character of this epistle: it locates the epistle in NT typology and, therefore, in the NT itself.

---

98. Str-B 1. 20.

99. For later "typological" interpretation see *1 Clem.* 12:7; Justin *Dialogues* 3; Irenaeus *Adv. haer.* 4.20.12.

100. See Schlatter, *Theologie*, 94f.

101. Even the creation story, to which there are many allusions in Jas 3:7-9, is not treated typologically (similar to 1 Cor 11:7f.; 1 Tim 2:13); however, cf. Jas 1:17.

102. Schlatter, *Theologie*, 91f.

103. Ibid., 96.

Chapter Six

THE PAULINE EPISTLES

1. TYPOLOGY AND PAUL'S USE OF SCRIPTURE

The way Paul uses Scripture is different from the way it is used in the Gospels, just as his epistles differ from the Gospels in their general character.[1] It was Paul who first called the Scriptures "the Old Testament" (ἡ παλαιὰ διαθήκη, 2 Cor 3:14).[2] His basic view of the OT is that its content corresponds to the gospel, and that its task is to present the gospel to the church. Christ is the affirmation of all God's promises (2 Cor 1:20). The story and the meaning of Christ's life are in harmony with Scripture (1 Cor 15:3f.), and the gospel of justification was announced beforehand in Scripture (Rom 1:2; 3:21; cf. 10:5ff.). Therefore, Scripture can and will help the church understand the salvation it has received: "For everything that was written in the past was written to teach us" (Rom 15:4; see 4:23f.; 2 Tim 3:16; cf. 1 Cor 9:9f.). This is especially true of biblical history, which must be interpreted typologically: "These things happened to them as examples (τυπικῶς, "as types") and were written down as warnings for us, on whom the fulfillment of the ages has come" (1 Cor 10:11; cf. Rom 4:23f.). "The prophetic writings . . . make known" the mystery of God, the Gospel of Christ, which was "hidden for long ages past, but now revealed . . . by the command of the eternal God so that all nations might believe and obey him" (Rom 16:25f.).[3]

---

1. We can only refer to that aspect of Paul's use of Scripture that has immediate significance for typology. For all other matters (the nature of the text from which Paul quotes, his method of quoting, etc.), see O. Michel, *Paulus und seine Bibel* (Gütersloh, 1929) and the bibliography there (see "Die Geschichte der Forschung," 1-7). The most important earlier studies are: on the text: E. Kautzsch, *De Veteris Testamenti locis a Paulo apostolo allegatis* (Leipzig, 1869); H. Vollmer, *Die alttestamentlichen Zitate bei Paulus* (Leipzig, 1895) (pp. 1-9 provide a survey of earlier research); C. Clemen, *Die Auffassung des Alten Testaments bei Paulus* (Tübingen, 3d ed. 1932), and H. Lietzmann, *An die Galater* (HNT; Tübingen, 1923), Excursus on Gal 4:31; A. Harnack, "Das Alten Testament in den paulinischen Briefen und in den paulinischen Gemeinden" (SPAW, 1928).

2. See n. 4.

3. This is certainly from Paul even if it was not in Romans originally. See P. Feine, *Einleitung in das Neue Testament* (8th ed. rev. by J. Behm; Leipzig, 1936). Translator's note: This position is reversed in the 14th ed. rev. by W. Kümmel (ET: Nashville, 1966) 222f.

The witness of Scripture is hidden from the synagogue (2 Cor 3:13-15). It will not be revealed by a better hermeneutic, but only through knowledge of Christ. The "veil" is taken away "when anyone turns to the Lord" (2 Cor 3:16).[4] There is a dialectical interplay in this because Christ opens the meaning of Scripture, and Scripture reveals the significance of Christ. This movement results in confrontation with Christ. It was only after Damascus that Paul no longer viewed Scripture primarily as law, but as a witness to the redemptive history that leads to Christ (Phil 3:4ff.; 2 Cor 4:6; 5:16ff.). By the Spirit who is the Lord (2 Cor 3:17), Scripture causes to shine forth, in instance after instance, the glory and the essence of the salvation that will be given to the church in the last days. In arranging our material, we must keep this interplay in mind, and we must also remember that Paul's interpretation of Scripture is essentially unsystematic.

These preliminary remarks indicate that Paul too considers Scripture to be typological in principle, in that it bears witness to the consummation of redemption and is based on it. But typology is not prominent in his epistles because they contain the doctrine of redemption primarily and include little redemptive history. In the Gospels, the framework for the typology is supplied by the proof from Scripture that is linked to the life of Christ. The framework in Paul's epistles is the proof from Scripture that supports his doctrine. For the purposes of our study, it will generally be unnecessary to deal extensively with this particular use of Scripture.[5] The typology that is present is there for the sake of his

---

4. Paul states this in 2 Cor 3:13-17 in a haggadic exposition of Exod 34:29-35. He explains that Moses veiled his face (Exod 34:33, 35) to conceal the fading of the radiance (2 Cor 3:13). The same veil remains over the words of the book when it is read (2 Cor 3:14) and on the hearts of the hearers (2 Cor 3:15). By ἡ παλαιὰ διαθήκη, which first occurs here (the next occurrence is in Melito of Sardis according to Eusebius *Hist. eccl.* 4.26.14, quoted by H. Windisch, *2. Korinther* [MeyerK; Göttingen, 9th ed., 1924] 121), Paul means the written documents of the old divine order (primarily the Pentateuch), as the parallel in 2 Cor 3:15a (Μωϋσῆς) shows. This veil is not taken away in the synagogue because only in Christ is it set aside, or, based on analogy (see 2 Cor 3:11, 13), because it (the OT) is set aside by Christ (2 Cor 3:14b). Paul's thought is clear: To the Jews the true meaning of the OT, its significance, and its provisional nature are hidden. It is only revealed to one who turns to the Lord, i.e., who turns to Christ and his Spirit (2 Cor 3:16). The Spirit sets "free"—even with respect to the OT—because the Spirit binds one to Christ; for "the Lord is the Spirit" (2 Cor 3:17; cf. 1 Cor 3:21-23, etc.). The Spirit sets one free from the OT insofar as it is the letter (γράμμα, see 2 Cor 3:6) that kills and enslaves, a precept that approaches a person from without; this is what it always is for Jews. Paul is indicating this characteristic of the OT when he cites it as Μωϋσῆς (2 Cor 3:14f.—ἡ παλαιὰ διαθήκη is essentially the same as Μωϋσῆς) or ὁ νόμος (Gal 4:21). Following Jesus' example, Paul drew the redemptive history and the divine plan of redemption from the OT, and the νόμος plays a very subordinate role in them.

5. Explicit Scripture references are found in Paul only in Romans 1 and 2 Corinthians, Galatians, and Ephesians. For a compilation of these references, see O. Michel, *Paulus*, 12f. This includes only sporadic references to Christ: Rom 9:33 (10:11) = Isa 28:16; 8:14; Rom 15:3 = Ps 69:9; Rom 15:12 = Isa 11:10; 1 Cor 15:25 = Ps 110:1; 1 Cor 15:27 = Ps 8:6; Eph 4:8 = Ps 68:18. Most of the prophecies quoted are statements or prophecies about Israel that are transferred to the church: Rom 9:25f.; 1 Cor 5:13; 14:21; 2 Cor 6:16ff.; 8:15; Gal 4:27; in Romans 9–11 Israel's destiny is placed under God's decree. Legal regulations are referred to in various ways: Rom 7:7; 10:5; 12:19; 13:9; 1 Cor 9:9; 2 Cor 13:1; Gal 5:14; 3:10, 12f. Most of the passages support Paul's

doctrine and is, therefore, more thoroughly undergirded exegetically and is presented in greater detail. The Gospels simply compare events and persons, frequently only by means of hints and allusions. In this matter, as in the metaphors and parables, Paul suffers by comparison with the distinct clarity of the typology in the Synoptics.

The epistles deal with the church's relationship to him who is the object of its faith rather than with Christ's coming to the church. Consequently, the typology is more concerned with the church than with the person of Christ—with the "body," not the "head." It is significant that the only typological relationship Paul uses to illuminate the meaning of Christ's coming into the world is Adam-Christ typology. Within the framework of church typology, Christ is compared also with the OT means of salvation. There is scarcely any hint of Christ's relationship to Moses, or to the prophet, or to the Son of David. Only in comparing Christ with Adam is the world-encompassing and time-fulfilling significance of Christ revealed.[6]

2. CHRIST THE SECOND ADAM WHO BRINGS THE NEW CREATION

a. Christ the Antitype of Adam

The relationship of Christ as the antitype of Adam is far-reaching in its significance for redemption. This relationship received its definitive treatment in Rom 5:12-21. According to Rom 5:14 Adam is "a pattern of the one to come" (τύπος τοῦ μέλλοντος), i.e., a type of the future Adam, a type of Christ. The correspondence between Adam and Christ is pointed out in Rom 5:12, 18f.; the difference between them is indicated in vv 15-17. In each instance the single act of one man has a consequence that affects the entire human race. The same phrases are used for both: "one man" (εἷς ἄνθρωπος, v 19), "the result of one" (δι᾽ ἑνὸς, παραπτώματος, or δικαιώματος, respectively, v 18), and "for all men" (εἰς πάντας ἀνθρώπους εἰς, κατάκριμα, or δικαίωσιν ζωῆς, v 18). The correspondence in content is even more profound. In their acts and in the effect they have on others, Adam and Christ are related to one another as a photographic negative to its positive print or as a mold to the plastic shaped by it. "As the mold determines the shape of the casting, so from Adam's power over the human race comes Christ's mission and work, his death and his resurrection."[7] The destructive power of Adam, which was considered an established fact by late Judaism,[8] is not merely something that helps to demonstrate the

---

doctrine about the relationship between God and man—the rupture of that relationship and the attainment of salvation—but he does not find this set forth in the OT in the same way that 1 Clement does. He only finds it alluded to as a base line of prophecy leading to Christ (see below on Romans 4 and Galatians 3).

6. P. Althaus, *Der Brief an die Römer* (NTD II) 205.
7. A. Schlatter, *Gottes Gerechtigkeit; Ein Kommentar zum Römerbrief* (Stuttgart, 1935) 189.
8. J. Jeremias, "᾽Αδάμ," *TDNT* 1. 142f.

saving power of Christ. That destructive power is the distress that cries out for Christ's saving power and it is the promise that points to that power within the framework of God's eternal plan of redemption. "By calling Adam a type of Christ, Paul indicates why he makes no mention either of Adam's original righteousness or of God's promise to him. Adam is himself the promise of Christ."[9] For Paul, Adam is not simply an illustrative figure. He views Adam through Christ as a true type in redemptive history, as a prophetic personality placed in Scripture by God. This is the only way he can draw certain conclusions from the relationship of Adam to Christ as conclusions that are founded on a typology.[10]

Therefore, the typological correlation is based on the divinely ordained power of type and antitype in relationship to one another in redemptive history, and this correlation has a contrasting and canceling effect for mankind (Paul's view of Sinai typology is similar).[11] In addition to this, Paul emphasizes the typological heightening which rounds out the full development of a typology when he says, "But the gift is not like the trespass" (Rom 5:15). The grace of the one man Christ, in which God's grace appeared, has the power to become effective for all in far greater measure than does the fall of the one (v 15). While condemnation was unleashed by one trespass, grace followed many trespasses (v 16).[12]

In this masterful view of human history, Moses and Israel's Law are only a chapter of minor importance. The Law was unable to stem or divert the stream of corruption that flowed from Adam. It helped instead to intensify the sinfulness that had originated with Adam (Rom 7:7ff.), and in this way it helped to prepare for the conquest of sin by grace; for sin had increased to full measure, but grace was mightier (Rom 5:20). "Also those generations who sinned and died before the Law was given" (who, therefore, did not sin against the Law) merely demonstrate "that the human race must wait for the One who will put an end to what was started by the first man" (Rom 5:13).[13] Therefore, with respect to their effect upon humanity, Adam and Sinai (which has been alluded to here) are not types of the coming one because of the partial *already* of their relationship to God, but through the *not yet*, which has also been appointed by God (cf. Gal 3:22; Rom 11:32ff.). In his forbearance (ἀνοχή, Rom 3:26) God performs his comprehensive judgment in Adam in order to abolish that judgment in Christ by his much more powerful grace.

b. Christianity as a New Creation

Through Christ, the second Adam, those who believe in him are freed from the association with corruption that began with the first Adam and they are created

---

9. A. Schlatter, *Gottes Gerechtigkeit*, 189 and 184.
10. See 1 Corinthians 15; see below on this passage.
11. See below.
12. "Paul conceived of the life of Jesus in concrete terms, just as he conceived of the things related in Genesis 3 concretely" (Schlatter, *Gottes Gerechtigkeit*, 191).
13. Ibid., 168.

anew in the image of the second Adam. Then, on the basis of Adam-Christ typology, they themselves, as new creatures, are related typologically to the old creation.

This is the background for the discussion that follows Romans 5 in chaps. 6–8. One whole section, Rom 6:1-14, describes the way we were freed from our relationship with Adam and were placed into relationship with Christ. In baptism Christians have died with Christ (6:4f., 8f.) and so have died to sin (vv 6, 11). Their old self (παλαιὸς ἄνθρωπος) has been crucified with Christ (v 6), and now they live with Christ in a new life (ἐν καινότητι ζωῆς, vv 4f., 8ff.). Moreover, in vv 14-23 the continual enslavement of the old self to sin, which leads to dissolution in death, is contrasted repeatedly with the life of righteousness, which leads to eternal life (cf. v 23; 5:12, 21).

This background is even more evident in Rom 7:7-12, where the fallen condition of man, as a result of his relationship to Adam, is described in accordance with Genesis 3. Both passages state that lust received its stimulus through the commandment (Rom 7:8, 11—Gen 3:1f.). In both instances sin is viewed as a personal force—it deceives men (ἠπάτησεν, Rom 7:11—Gen 3:13, LXX).[14] The consequence of sin is death (Rom 7:11—Gen 3:19; cf. vv 3f.). Of course, Romans is dealing with the sinning of a sinner and not the fall of an innocent person, as Schlatter points out while emphasizing the difference.[15] But the same basic features also characterize our sinning. As a matter of fact, we too sin "by breaking a command as did Adam" (ἁμαρτήσαντας ἐπὶ τῷ ὁμοιώματι τῆς παραβάσεως 'Αδάμ, Rom 5:12b, 14b).[16] This is what Paul is indicating by his deliberate dependence on Genesis 3.[17] The relationship of Christ to the first Adam becomes typological only when Christ, as the firstfruit of the new creation, steps into the center and forms new creatures.[18] This is the background for Romans 8 and many other passages.

The illumination of hearts through the knowledge of Christ is just as much God's creative act as was the creation of light in the beginning.[19] Whoever is in Christ (ἐν Χριστῷ) is a new creation (καινὴ κτίσις, 2 Cor 5:17; cf. Gal 6:15).

---

14. Gen 3:1ff.: the serpent; Rom 7:9: "sin sprang to life"; 7:11: "sin deceived me."

15. Schlatter, *Gottes Gerechtigkeit*, 239.

16. P. Althaus, *Römer*, 220.

17. Paul has not connected his comparison of the church with Eve in 2 Cor 11:3 (cf. Eph 5:31f.) in any recognizable way with Adam-Christ typology. In the first passage there is no typological parallelism (Adam-Eve: Christ-church; see A. Schlatter, *Paulus der Bote Jesu* [Stuttgart, 1934] 629); Paul simply refers in a comparative way to the cunning deception of Satan that now threatens the church through false apostles who are servants of Satan (2 Cor 11:14f.). What is stated in Gen 2:24 (=Eph 5:31; cf. 1 Cor 6:16) about Adam and Eve concerning the relationship of husband and wife is applied allegorically to the perfection of the relationship between Christ and the church in Eph 5:31f. (see J. Jeremias, *Jesus als Weltvollender* [Gütersloh, 1930] 23). Rom 16:20: "The God of peace will soon crush Satan under your feet," is probably an allusion to the Protevangelium in Gen 3:15 (there is no similarity in wording): The church is Eve's offspring to whom God gives victory over the adversary (see Schlatter, *Gottes Gerechtigkeit*, 184).

18. See above, pp. 33f.

19. 2 Cor 4:6 quotes Gen 1:3; cf. Isa 9:2.

There is an obvious allusion to Gen 1:26f. in Col 3:10 (cf. Eph 4:24) where Christians are admonished, "And have put on the new self, which is being renewed in knowledge in the image of its creator."[20] Since Paul does not hesitate to speak of man in his unrenewed condition as bearing the divine image of the first Adam (1 Cor 11:7; cf. 1 Tim 2:13f.), it is clear that he is not thinking of the restoration of man to the condition in which he was created, but of a new creation that will come about through Christ and be lived through Christ. Christ is the image of God (εἰκὼν τοῦ θεοῦ, Col 1:15; 2 Cor 4:4). Because he is the second Adam, those who belong to him will be conformed to his image (εἰκών) (2 Cor 3:18; Rom 8:29; cf. 1 Cor 15:49) and in this way they, like Adam, will "be created in the image" of their creator. (These are God's new redemptive acts that fulfill the old; it is typology, not history repeating itself.)

The similar expression, "to put on Christ" (Gal 3:27; Rom 13:14), appears to be merely another way of stating the same thing. The fact that ἐνδύω (to put on) is used in the Septuagint as a metaphor for the appropriation of spiritual and ethical powers is not adequate to explain these passages.[21] From what we have said about Adam-Christ typology we may conclude that Christ, as the new man, makes those who are clothed with him into new men.[22]

According to Gal 3:27f., "to put on Christ" is the same as "to be in Christ" (ἐν Χριστῷ εἶναι). Moreover, according to 2 Cor 5:15, 17, "to have died with Christ and to live with him," "to be a new creation," and "to be in Christ" all mean the same thing. The concept of being in Christ (ἐν Χριστῷ), which appears in the relationship of the new creation to the first creation, is also found in Adam typology. "As in Adam (ἐν Ἀδάμ) all die, so in Christ (ἐν Χριστῷ) all will be made alive" (1 Cor 15:22; cf. Rom 5:12, 18f.; the use of διά is appropriate). The idea contained in this familiar Pauline formula is in harmony with the idea expressed by Adam-Christ typology; consequently, that formula must be interpreted by it. "The first and the second Adams are progenitors of two races of men. Each implies a whole world, an order of life or death. Each includes his adherents in and under himself."[23]

Paul described and used the metaphor of the new creation and its relationship to the first creation in various ways. His expositions, however, do not contain a genuine typology with reference to the biblical account of creation. There is no clear dividing line here, particularly since the Pauline reflection allows the clarity

---

20. . . . τὸν νέον τὸν ἀνακαινούμενον εἰς ἐπίγνωσιν (cf. 2 Cor 5:16f.) κατ᾽ εἰκόνα τοῦ κτίσαντος; cf. Eph. 4:24: τὸν καινὸν ἄνθρωπον τὸν κατὰ θεὸν κτισθέντα.

21. See Str-B 2. 301; A. Oepke, "ἐνδύω," TDNT 2. 319 (it is used this way in the NT also, ibid., 320).

22. Ibid. 2. 320. To illustrate this point, we may point out that the oriental gnostic myth identified the heavenly image of the original man with his clothing and described redemption as a clothing of those returning home once again with the heavenly clothing (according to A. Oepke, Der Brief des Paulus an die Galater [THKNT; Leipzig, 1937] 69).

23. A. Oepke, "ἐν," TDNT 2. 542.

of the individual relationships to be lost in configurations of ideas. Therefore, from this genre of ideas we will present only one other element that is important for typology.

In Paul's description of the church as a new creation, we can see the openness to the final consummation that is characteristic of NT antitypes. The fundamental transfer of individuals from their relationship to Adam into their relationship to Christ is accomplished in baptism. Baptism signifies a real dying and rising again to a new life in a new world order.[24] Those who have been created anew belong to a world in which the racial, sexual, and social distinctions of this world have been set aside (Gal 3:28; 1 Cor 12:13; Col 3:11; cf. Eph 2:15). They live in a new organism, the body of Christ (σῶμα Χριστοῦ, 1 Cor 12:27).[25] The Law of Moses and the regulations of this world are now behind them (Gal 2:19; 3:25-28; 4:3f.; Rom 7:1-6; Col 2:14ff.). This new situation, however, is a present reality only in the witness of the Spirit and in faith. As such it is the basis for the shaping of life and the basis of hope for the future. In all these statements the following things stand directly in juxtaposition, mutually qualifying one another: the proclamation of the present spiritual reality that has resulted from Christ's redemptive acts and promise, the summons to an appropriate form of life, and the announcement that this spiritual reality will become visible in the future at the revelation of Christ.[26] What is believed, lived, and hoped for, however, is always a unity—a new man (καινὸς ἄνθρωπος, Eph 2:15) and a new world—because the new aeon has begun with Christ. Therefore, the one who is in Christ is created anew in spirit (πνεῦμα) and in faith (πίστις), and this re-creation in the present is not only a pledge that the person's own perfection will be a visible reality, but also that the entire creation, which has been subjected to futility with Adam, will be renewed (Rom 8:19-22).

This witness of the Spirit to faith must be combined with the witness of Christ and of Scripture. The witness of Christ and of Scripture is united here in the typology. Adam-Christ typology assures us not only that the new man is a reality which is presently hidden, but also that in the future the new man will appear in bodily form (1 Cor 15:20-22, 44-49). Christ was truly raised as "the firstfruits

---

24. Rom 6:1ff.: baptism is associated directly with Adam-Christ typology; Gal 3:27: baptism is equivalent in meaning with "putting on Christ" and "being in Christ"; Col 2:11f.: baptism is the true circumcision; according to Gal 6:15 baptism is the new creation; see below on John 7:23; cf. Titus 3:5, παλιγγενεσία.

25. Cf. Col 1:15-20: Christ is "the firstborn over all creation," and as "the firstborn from among the dead" he is "the head of the body."

26. Cf. Rom 6:1-14; 2 Cor 5:14-17; 6:1ff.; Gal 5:25; Phil 3:10ff.; Col 3:1-3: (1) You have died with Christ and have been raised with him: Col 2:12f.; 3:1; Eph 2:5f.; 2 Cor 5:17; Rom 6:5-8, 13; (2) therefore, count yourselves dead to sin and alive to God in Christ: Rom 6:8, 11; Gal 5:25; Col 3:1f.; (3) "When Christ, who is your life, appears, then you also will appear with him in glory": Col 3:4; 1:18; Rom 6:8; 8:11; Phil 3:10f.

of those who have fallen asleep."[27] As the second Adam he will draw after him in resurrection all who are his (1 Cor 15:20-22).[28]

Adam-Christ typology demonstrates that the reality of the resurrection is an absolutely indispensable part of redemptive history. It also demonstrates the indispensability of the bodily nature of that resurrection (1 Cor 15:44-49). "If there is a natural body, there is also a spiritual body" (1 Cor 15:44b). This is not an argument based on the logic of metaphysics;[29] it is a thesis that will be substantiated by what follows. The proof is found in what is written (γέγραπται, 1 Cor 15:45a) about the first Adam and in the certainty about the nature of Christ, the second Adam (1 Cor 15:45-47). According to Gen 2:7 (Paul paraphrases the passage in the manner of the Targums) the first man, i.e., Adam, was a "living being" (ψυχὴ ζῶσα); the last Adam is "a life-giving spirit" (πνεῦμα ζῳοποιοῦν, 1 Cor 15:45; cf. 6:16f.; cf. John 20:22; 7:38f.). This is not an inference that Paul makes, but something he perceives to be a typological fulfillment with respect to Christ. Paul rejects the kind of speculation about an ideal original man that is found in Philo[30] with a remark that he inserts into the course of his argument (1 Cor 15:46). He accepts the order revealed by Scripture and redemptive history.[31] Paul asserts that, according to Gen 2:7, the first man is from the earth, whereas the second man is from heaven; he is the Son of Man who assumed our flesh when he came from heaven (cf. Rom 8:3), and he will come again in a transfigured, heavenly body (cf. Phil 3:20).[32] The first Adam, like the second, imprints his likeness on those under his headship. (1 Cor 15:48). Consequently, just as we have borne the likeness of the man taken from earth by virtue of our connection with the first Adam, so by virtue of our being united with Christ, the second Adam, we will bear the likeness of the heavenly man (1 Cor 15:49; cf. Phil 3:21). The visible reality of the new creation, like the reality that is apprehended by faith, will arise in his likeness.[33] Here it is absolutely clear that the new creation is not a repetition of the first, nor is it simply

---

27. ἀπαρχὴ τῶν κεκοιμημένων, 1 Cor 15:20b; cf. Col 1:18.

28. Cf. 1 Thess 4:14; Rom 6:5, 8; 8:23 (τὴν ἀπαρχὴν τοῦ πνεύματος ἔχοντες), 11; Phil 3:10f.; Col 3:3.

29. J. Weiss, 1. Korinther (MeyerK; Göttingen, 9th ed., 1870), on this passage.

30. See above, p. 44.

31. 1 Cor. 15:46; concerning Jeremias's comments ("'Αδάμ," TDNT 1. 143) we should note that Paul applies Gen 1:26 to contemporary man (cf. 1 Cor 11:7); when Paul designates Christ as εἰκὼν τοῦ θεοῦ (therefore, not at all as "primeval man in God's image") in Col 1:15, the most that he could have borrowed from Philo's concept is the terminology.

32. Paul may have been acquainted with this messianic title (Psalm 8 is interpreted messianically in 1 Cor 15:27) but it would not have been comprehensible to Gentile Christians. Therefore, Paul substitutes ὁ ἄνθρωπος, which is the equivalent both philologically and in substance. Cf. Rom 5:15; 1 Cor 15:21; Eph 5:31f. (see n. 17); 1 Tim 2:5 (according to Jeremias, "'Αδάμ," TDNT 1. 143).

33. See above on Col 2:10; 1:5.

a reversal of the Fall; it is a perfect, i.e., a typological, renewing of creation.[34]

While contrasting Adam and Christ, Paul develops a powerful and comprehensive view of human history. The first creation is renewed in a new creation that is now hidden, but will become visible in the future. The first creation has its existence in Christ, and, as "the firstborn from among the dead," he is "the head of the body, the church" (Col 1:15-20). Between these two there is apostasy, rebellion, and destruction as well as obedience, reconciliation, and salvation (cf. Col 1:20, 13f.; Rom 5:12ff.)—first and second Adam. In John the former is more prominent; in Paul the latter.

Paul does not merely speculate about the relationship of Adam to Christ or use it as a means of illustration. He regards it as a way of using Scripture for the illumination and confirmation of faith; it is genuine typology. These important relationships have not been developed from general speculation about man as originally created or about redemption. They are revealed in the presence of the glory of Jesus Christ to the man who studies Scripture and in whom a divine miracle has caused the light of the new creation to shine (2 Cor 4:6). Although these relationships will not satisfy gnostic curiosity, when they are accompanied by the witness of the Spirit (cf. Rom 8:23, 11) they give the church assurance concerning the nature and the reality of the new creation. Consequently, the church is able to believe in the new creation as something that is now hidden, that is experienced in moral struggle, and whose future coming is expected.

To support his doctrine, Paul interprets Scripture typologically rather than allegorically or symbolically as do Philo and Origen. Therefore, he does not regard the new creation as a matter of gnosis, but of faith; it is not a ready-made concept of redemption or a fortuitous mystical experience (the Spirit is never a natural ability), but a spiritual reality in redemptive history.

The church as the new creation is related typologically to the first creation, and this relationship is interwoven inextricably with the implications of Adam-Christ typology, which demonstrates that Christ is the reality in redemptive history that comprehends the new creation. In this too he is the antitype. Of course, the typological relationship between Christ and the form of the first creation that is revealed in Scripture is not as simple as the relationship between Christ and the provisional salvation that Scripture proclaims. Here it is not primarily a matter of perfecting something that was deficient, but of eliminating

---

34. It is clear that for Paul the difference between the original Adam and fallen Adam is not so much in the transformation of his physical nature as in a change in his relationship to God. Accordingly, the fall of the first Adam and the subsequent sinning by all is not set aside by any natural process, but by the obedience of the second Adam and by reconciliation (cf. Col 1:18-20). In the immediate background of it all is God, who always working personally through his word brings about judgment and salvation, death and life. A discussion of all the other questions involved in the relationship of Adam and Christ, of the first and second creations, would involve a discussion of Pauline theology in its entirety.

the contrast between Adam and Christ. What is being contrasted, then, is the accomplishments and the consequences of the mediators of the first and second creations and not the mediators themselves. There is only one mediator—God through Christ.

In unfolding these relationships, Paul paid careful attention to Scripture. This is obvious also in his typological use of the history of the patriarchs and the history of Israel because it conforms to what we have stated above.

3. THE CHURCH AS THE "CHILDREN OF ABRAHAM" AND AS THE "SPIRITUAL ISRAEL"

In the time that elapsed between the first and second Adams, God, in his forbearance (ἀνοχή), not only tolerated sinful humanity, but also initiated the work of redemption that led to Christ. So far as his human nature is concerned, Christ descended from Israel, the community whose characteristic mark is circumcision, and God's redemptive work reached its climax and goal in this nation (cf. Rom 9:5). God's redemptive work began with the calling of the patriarchs (Rom 9:5a), and it reached the provisional form that points to Christ and his church in the great institutions of the Mosaic period (Rom 9:4). In spite of Israel's unfaithfulness, God's redemptive purpose stands (Rom 3:2ff.).

a. The Children of Abraham

For Paul, God's redemptive work that leads ultimately to the salvation of the human race through Christ begins with Abraham. Paul, like Jesus, views Abraham as the father of Christianity in accordance with God's redemptive plan revealed in Scripture. What was proclaimed authoritatively by Jesus, and to some extent by John the Baptist, was undergirded exegetically by Paul and developed in his discussion of questions that had recently arisen concerning law and gospel, natural Israel and the Israel of God.

Once again Paul's conviction that Christ is the savior of the world is the starting point and the focus of his argument. His discussions of Abraham's righteousness and of Abraham's children presuppose the reality of the cross. They are based on the fact that Christ "was delivered over to death for our sins and was raised to life for our justification" (Rom 4:25; cf. Gal 3:13) and on the logical consequence of this, that no one can fulfill the Law (Gal 3:10-12; Rom 4:13-15). When he places Abraham in the light of Christ, a radiance shining from the OT redemptive event falls on the path of the church. OT history is delivered immediately from Jewish distortions and is revealed in its most profound and original sense.

On the basis of these presuppositions, Paul demonstrates that those who believe in Christ are children of Abraham because of the similarity of their relationships to God in God's redemptive plan. Christians are children of Abraham because they attain righteousness by faith alone, just as he did (Gal 3:6f.). This is developed in greater detail and supported exegetically in Romans 4.

The faith that was credited as righteousness is the same in both instances. In spite of absolute human impossibility and every appearance to the contrary (Rom 4:18f.), Abraham believed, solely on the basis of God's word (v. 20), that God would create life out of his dead body (vv. 17b, 18). Christians believe that God raised Christ from the dead (v. 24b). Abraham's faith was based on the word which promised physical descendants to one who was dead (v 18 = Gen 15:5). Christian faith rests on the message about the crucified and resurrected one (cf. Rom 4:24f.). Typological heightening is indicated here.

It is this faith alone, without its being regarded as some kind of work or being combined with any works, that is credited as righteousness to both Abraham and the Christian (Rom 4:3-8). This crediting (ἐλογίσθη, Gen 15:6) must not be understood as the obligation to give credit for something earned, but as a gracious crediting, in logic a "synthetic proposition" (Rom 4:4). This crediting of righteousness flows from the free grace of God that takes no account of human achievement. Grace is also the reason why sin is not credited in Ps 32:1f. (Rom 4:6-8). In each instance it is a wicked man who is justified (Rom 4:5). This transitional remark is not intended to suggest that Abraham had faith that the wicked would be justified, although making the dead live and justifying the ungodly are certainly the same divine action (cf. Gal 3:11f.). Finally, this justification is not bound to circumcision: Abraham was justified before he was circumcised (Genesis 15 and 17; Rom 4:10). Circumcision did not establish his position before God or change it; it only sealed it (Rom 4:11).

According to Genesis 15, Abraham's faith, which in form and content is essentially the same as Christian faith, was credited to him as righteousness by grace alone, without regard for works and independent of circumcision (Rom 4:9-11). Accordingly, Abraham is a type of those who are justified by faith alone (independent of works and circumcision, of law and birth). This comparison becomes typology because the relationship was ordained by God (Rom 4:11f., 23; Gal 3:8) and was mediated through Christ (Gal 3:17). The typological heightening flows automatically from Christ's office as mediator.

God arranged Abraham's relationship to him, especially the sequence of justification and circumcision (Rom 4:11b, 12), in such a way that he became a type of his descendants who would be justified in the same manner. This is how God willed to fulfill his promise that "All nations will be blessed through you" (Gal 3:8).[35] Through him, i.e., if they believe as he did, they will be "blessed along with Abraham, the man of faith" (Gal 3:9; cf. Rom 4:14ff.). The way in

---

35. "Judging from the ἐν σοί, Paul intends to quote Gen 12:3 or 28:14; however, consciously or unconsciously he inserts the ambiguous phrase πάντα τὰ ἔθνη from Gen 18:18; 22:18; 26:4, which is more appropriate for his argument" (A. Oepke, *Der Brief des Paulus an die Galater* [THKNT; Leipzig, 1937] 54).

which Abraham became righteous is recorded in Scripture for the benefit of Christians (Rom 4:23).

The position as descendants of Abraham is mediated to Christians by Christ. Paul uses what is clearly an artificial interpretation of the promise to guarantee this when he says that the promise was made to Abraham and "to his seed" (τῷ σπέρματι αὐτοῦ). The singular of this collective noun points to a single individual, i.e., Christ (Gal 3:16). Therefore, Christ and those who are in Christ are the only heirs of the promise to Abraham.

The typological heightening is obvious to Paul, although, in keeping with the trend of the discussion, it has not been given any special emphasis. This heightening is found in the fact that Christ himself, as the firstfruit of the new creation, constitutes this seed. The typological heightening in the matter of faith is also immediately clear. There faith rests on the saying that promises descendants to the one who was dead; here faith is based on the testimony that was given to the incarnate Word itself by the death and resurrection of Christ. There faith is concerned with the restoration of natural vigor and continuation of life in the first creation; here it is concerned with the new creation that begins with Christ.

Abraham, therefore, is a type of all Christians who are justified by faith alone. He is not, however, a type in the secular sense, i.e., an ideal prototype of a certain genre. He is a type in the NT sense—a divinely appointed prototype in redemptive history of those in whom his relationship to God is fulfilled on a higher plane through Christ. Christ's church is the seed which God promised Abraham. In the Bible, the terms—"father" and "children" (seed)—which describe a natural relationship defined by blood and by law become expressions for the interrelationship of type and antitype in redemptive history. In his relationship to God, Abraham is, in the fullest sense of the word, a type of all Christians in their relationship to God; consequently, the promise of innumerable descendants that was made to Abraham is fulfilled in the gathering of the church. The fundamental OT promise, "All peoples on earth will be blessed through you" (Gen 12:3), is fulfilled in and through the church.

This relationship between Abraham and the church that has been justified in Christ must still be safeguarded against the claims of Abraham's natural descendants and the intervention of the Law.

Paul comments on the last point in his discussions in Galatians 3 and Romans 4. The arrangement that controls Abraham's relationship to God, the Abrahamic covenant, can neither be altered nor annulled by the covenant at Sinai.[36] If the promise of blessing to Abraham's descendants were bound to the Law, it would be worthless because wrath and curse come through the Law, not blessing (Rom 4:13-16; cf. Gal 3:10-14). Therefore, nothing from the Law can be added

---

36. When Paul speaks of the "law," which was added later (Gal 3:18f.), he is not thinking only of the revelation of God's commands, but also of the status of this law according to the Sinaitic order: its fulfillment is a requirement for existence before God.

to the covenant with Abraham. It is even more certain that the covenant with Abraham can never be abolished by the Law. Just as a human contract that has become valid cannot subsequently be annulled or amended, neither can the covenant (διαθήκη) which God gave Abraham be annulled, nor can God's promise be destroyed by the Law that was given 430 years later (Gal 3:15, 17). Although the prophets announced the breakup of the covenant of Sinai (Jer 31:31ff.), the Abrahamic covenant (we may speak of such a covenant in the same sense that Paul does)[37] will not end with the breakup of the Law because it is not dependent on the Law (Gal 3:18; cf. v 14; Rom 4:13). It bypasses the Law and moves directly to its fulfillment in the New Covenant.

This is expressed with polemical acuity in the typological interpretation of the relationship of Ishmael and Isaac, which in some respects passes over into allegory (Gal 4:21-31). This interpretation adopts a definite stance toward the claims of the natural descendants of Abraham. Hagar the slave (Genesis 16; 21:9ff.), whose naturally born children (Gal 4:23a) are also slaves (Gal 4:22; cf. v 25b), is a type of the covenant of Sinai. The children of that covenant, i.e., those who are subject to it, are slaves too (Gal 4:25). The relationship in redemptive history between Hagar and the covenant of Sinai is presented in a rather complicated way. In v 25a (the text of which is very problematic) this relationship is developed by means of etymology in keeping with the allegorical method.

Sarah, on the other hand, points to the New Covenant. The free woman gives birth to free children, but not in the ordinary way, for they are born "as the result of a promise" (Gal 4:22f.). Sarah is a type of "the Jerusalem that is above" (Gal 4:26), which is a phrase borrowed from apocalyptic language to designate the totality of the Christian church.[38] According to the promise in Isa 54:1, this new Jerusalem is like a barren woman who is miraculously blessed with many children. These children, who, like Isaac, are born because of and for the sake of God's promise, are the Christians (Gal 4:28).[39]

Paul specifies that the story of these two women, which he interprets in this manner, was told as an allegory (ἀλληγορούμενα,[40] Gal 4:24) and, therefore, must be interpreted allegorically. But only certain features of his exposition come close to being allegorical interpretation as we conceive of it. His exposition is entirely confined to a typological comparison of the historical facts. Moreover,

---

37. See Gal 3:17; of course, in this metaphor the word means "testament" in the sense of a "last will and testament"; Rom 9:4: διαθῆκαι; cf. Eph 2:12. In an analogous way, Paul speaks of the covenant of Sinai, Gal 4:24, and the New Covenant, 2 Cor 3:6; cf. Rom 11:27; Gal 4:24; 1 Cor 11:25.

38. See Str-B 3. 573f.; e.g., 2 Apoc. Bar. 4:1ff.; cf. Rev 21:2.

39. See Str-B 3. 574. The metaphor "she is our mother" occurs as early as Isa 50:1; Jer 50:12; Hos 4:5.

40. The verb occurs nowhere else in the NT; the substantive ἀλληγορία does not occur at all (see F. Büchsel, "ἀλληγορέω," TDNT 1. 260). According to Büchsel (ibid., 263) allegorical interpretation is found in Paul in 1 Cor 5:6-8; 9:8-10; 10:1-11; Gal 4:21-31. In the last two passages this has to be greatly qualified; see above on these passages.

the connection between them is mostly constructed from relationships in redemptive history. In only one instance is allegorical etymology employed (Gal
4:25a). The inclusion of the quotation in which these ideas are combined (Gal
4:27) is not an example of the rabbinic practice of arbitrarily combining parallel
passages; it is in accord with the original meaning of the passage. Actually,
Hagar-Ishmael, Sinai, and Israel according to the flesh are closely associated
because all "that which is born of the flesh is flesh" (John 3:6, *KJV*) and is
subject to "the law of sin and death" (Rom 8:2). Only the new birth, which is
a divine miracle, provides freedom. Therefore, when this interpretation is described as being taken allegorically (ἀλληγορούμενα), it simply means that this
is an instance in which the interpretation goes beyond the literal meaning. The
interpretation is not allegorical, in the proper sense of the word; rather, it is
typological throughout.[41]

The thought that Paul adds is based on genuine typology. As Isaac was
persecuted by Ishmael (the rabbis found this implied in the מְצַחֵק in Gen 21:9),[42]
so now the true children of Abraham are oppressed by the natural children (Gal
4:29). God's judgment on Israel can also be deduced from the story about Hagar
(Gal 4:30—Gen 21:10, 12).[43]

Once again we encounter the difficult question whether Paul no longer considers the covenant of Sinai as part of the positive preparation for redemption.
This question leads us to the topic we will consider next. Not only is the church
the true children of Abraham; it is also the Israel of God. In summary, however,
we maintain that this entire section deals essentially with the development of a
single typological relationship: the relationship of Abraham, who was justified
by faith, as "father" of those who are justified by faith in Christ. This is a
fundamental concern for Paul, and the scriptural evidence for it leads us to the
most extensive typology found in the NT.

b. The Israel of God

For Paul, the church is not only the new humanity and the promised children
of Abraham; it is also the true Israel. The church is the Israel of God (Gal 6:16;
cf Rom 9:6; Eph 2:12); the Jews are only Israel according to the flesh ('Ισραὴλ
κατὰ σάρκα, 1 Cor 10:18). Paul is affirming this same thing when he designates
the church as the people (λαός) in the fullest sense of the word. In the Septuagint
the use of this word is carefully restricted to Israel.[44] Paul uses the word exclu-

---

41. See p. 4 n. 12.
42. Str-B 3. 575.
43. In Rom 9:6-13 Paul refutes the claim of the natural children of Abraham in the very same
way by referring to the course of patriarchal history. Here, however, he sketches the longitudinal
section that the prophets saw between true and false Israel, not the typological cross section between
the old and the new Israel that divides the ages. The same thing applies to his whole discussion of
the position of advantage that Israel according to the flesh has had in redemptive history in Romans
9–11, and it applies also to his reference to the time of Elijah in Rom 11:3-5.
44. H. Strathmann, "λαός," *TDNT* 4. 34f.

sively in quotations from the OT and is aware of the profound meaning it acquired in the Septuagint.[45] Consequently, it is very significant that he transfers this title to the church along with certain Scripture passages that were intended for the OT people of God. The calling of the Gentiles fulfills the prophecy that originally promised the readoption of Israel: "I will say to those called 'Not my people,' 'You are my people' " (Hos 2:23—Rom 9:25f.; cf. 1 Pet 2:10). Christ fulfilled the cleansing promised in Ezek 37:23 (cf. Titus 2:14) and made his church "a people that are God's very own," which is what Israel became through the covenant of Sinai.[46] Though it may not be as obvious, the same thing is implied when the church is called the ἐκκλησία. This word is used in the Septuagint to translate the Hebrew word קָהָל especially when it is used to designate Israel as the church of God.[47] The same thing is suggested when metaphors used in the OT for Israel are applied to the church—a plantation (1 Cor 3:6-9; cf. 9:7), a flock (1 Cor 9:7), and a building (1 Cor 3:10ff.).[48] The church of Christ is the true circumcision, i.e., they are the people of God who are distinguished by God's own sign (Phil 3:3; cf. Col 2:11; the Jews call only themselves the circumcision, Eph 2:11). This circumcision, however, is no longer a circumcision in the flesh; it is the new creation in baptism. Consequently, the church is no longer a nation (ἔθνος) chosen from the multitude of nations (ἔθνη) to be a people (λαός); it is the band of those who have died and have been raised with Christ.[49] They are the new humanity by whom all the racial, social, and sexual distinctions of this world have been renounced in faith (Gal 3:28; 1 Cor 12:13; Col 3:11).

The church of Christ is not the true Israel by reason of blood relationship or submission to the covenant of Sinai. The church does not consist of Jews and converts to Judaism. It is the newly created humanity and the children of Abraham who have been miraculously called into existence. From creation typology and Abraham typology we have already refuted those claims which natural Israel bases on the divine plan of redemption.

Paul approaches the matter in a positive way when he establishes the church's position as the true Israel on the church's relationship in redemptive history to the first people of God because this is a relationship that was ordained by God and was mediated by Christ. The Israelites, like Abraham, are "our forefathers" (1 Cor 10:1).[50] All that happened to them occurred "as examples" (τυπικῶς)

---

45. See Rom 15:10, "Rejoice, O Gentiles (ἔθνη), with his people (λαός)"; Rom 10:21; 11:1; cf. 1 Cor 10:7.

46. Titus 2:14: λαὸν περιούσιον = Exod 19:5, LXX; cf. 1 Pet 2:9; 1 Cor 14:21 (—Isa 28:11f.); 2 Cor 6:16 (—Ezek 37:27); see Strathmann, "λαός," TDNT 4. 54f.

47. See H. Lietzmann, An die Korinther I, II (HNT; Tübingen, 1923) 4; K. Schmidt, "ἐκκλησία," TDNT 3. 530f.

48. See below; also see above, p. 109.

49. Gal 2:19; 6:14; Rom 6:3ff.; 2 Cor 5:14f.; Eph 2:5f.; Phil 3:10; Col 3:1ff.; cf. 2 Tim 2:11f.; Titus 3:5.

50. See below.

and it was "written down as warnings for us, on whom the fulfillment of the ages has come" (1 Cor 10:11). Israel's salvation in its perfected form now belongs to the people of Christ (cf. Rom 9:4f.; Eph 2:12, 19). Consequently, there is a typological relationship between the people of God in the Old and New Testaments that reveals to the NT people of God the nature of their salvation. Paul developed this relationship in numerous comparisons of the many redemptive gifts that they have in common.

In connection with the typologies of Adam and Abraham, Paul has already touched on the significance of the covenant of Sinai, the divine order which stands at the beginning of the history of the first Israel.[51] It seems more a part of God's action through Adam than through Abraham. When Paul compares the function of the New Covenant with the function of the Old (2 Cor 3:4-18), he is speaking of this relationship once again.

In making the transition to this topic (2 Cor 3:1ff.), Paul uses expressions to describe the salvation of the church in Corinth that occur in the OT promise (Jer 31:33; Ezek 11:19; 36:26) and that delineate the gracious gifts of the New Covenant. The church is a band of persons who have been called by Christ through the agency of the apostle in the Holy Spirit (2 Cor 3:3). They are Paul's letter of recommendation (2 Cor 3:1), the certification of his apostleship (2 Cor 3:2). This letter is not written with ink, but with the Holy Spirit. It is not written on tablets of stone (Exod 31:18; here there is a clear allusion to what follows), but on tablets of human hearts (καρδίαν σαρκίνην, Ezek 11:19; 36:26).[52] The apostle has these passages of Scripture in mind as he proceeds with his discussion. They are the basis for understanding the comparison he makes between a covenant of the letter (διαθήκη γράμματος) and a covenant of the Spirit (διαθήκη πνεύματος, 2 Cor 3:6). They are also the basis for understanding the exposition that follows, because the old divine order required that the Law which was written on stone tablets be fulfilled, i.e., the letter (γράμμα, 2 Cor 3:7; cf. v 3). The Law is an external command standing over against the individual who cannot fulfill it (Jer 31:32; Rom 7:7ff.). For this reason the Law can only result in condemnation (2 Cor 3:9a) and death (2 Cor 3:6b; cf. Rom 7:9f.). In the new divine order, the behavior that is appropriate to that order is controlled in every respect by the Spirit (πνεῦμα), who lays hold of the individual with inner power (cf. Ezek 11:19; 36:26f.; Jer 31:33). The new order does not, therefore, lead to condemnation, but to justification (see 2 Cor 3:9b; Rom 5:5; 8:1ff.); not to death, but to life (cf. 2 Cor 3:6b; Rom 8:11; etc.). Consequently, these two orders have completely opposite effects on mankind.

To properly evaluate Paul's statements about the typological nature of the covenant of Sinai, it is necessary to observe that the two primary passages (Gal 4:21ff. and 2 Corinthians 3) are not complete systematic expositions; they merely

---

51. See above, pp. 130, 138-40.
52. On this contrast, see Jer 31:32f.

contain a number of statements that have been forged into a polemic against Judaism. Paul is thinking primarily of the Law. It is not, however, the content of the Law that he has in mind, but the place of the Law in mankind's relationship to God and its effect on mankind. In this connection he views the Abrahamic covenant as the positive prototype of the Christian's relationship to God and the order of Sinai as the completion of God's action that began in Adam (cf. Gal 3:21f.; Rom 11:32).[53] As for the content of the Law revealed at Sinai, the New Covenant does not signify merely the abolishment of the commands; it indicates also the positive fulfillment of all the substance of the Law (Rom 3:19ff.; νόμον ἱστάνομεν, 3:31; 8:4; etc.). Paul certainly included the covenant of Sinai in God's gracious ordinance—the covenants (διαθῆκαι) that were a part of Israel's advantage (Rom 9:4)—so that he was thinking of the Law not only as a negative preparation for the gospel, but also as signifying the reception of Israel as God's own people.[54] Moreover, glory (δόξα), which is a characteristic of a divine order, attends the ministry of this covenant (2 Cor 3:7a).[55]

Both covenants are concerned with service in a divine order (διάκονοι διαθήκης) that bestows glory (δόξα) on its functionaries. The typological relationship between the two covenants makes it possible for Paul to draw inferences about the glory of the NT office from statements about the glory of Moses. The glory of the new must be infinitely greater in accordance with the infinitely superior quality of the New Covenant because it is not based on the letter, but on the Spirit (2 Cor 3:7f.); it does not result in condemnation, but in righteousness (2 Cor 3:9f.); it is not transitory, but abiding (2 Cor 3:11). When compared with the glory of the NT office, the OT office has no glory at all (2 Cor 3:10). Paul develops this even further by showing that at that time only one person, Moses, reflected the glory he had seen, but that now all participate, not just the apostles. Moreover, he indicates that this glory does not end; rather, it is always increasing (2 Cor 3:18).[56] When illuminated by typology the NT office leads to the discovery of the universal priesthood, although it is not given any special emphasis in this context. "He who is least in the kingdom of heaven is greater than he" (Matt 11:11). This glory, however, is not yet visible; it is only a possession believed in and hoped for, and for this very reason it is a possession that must be based on Scripture (2 Cor 4:7ff., esp. v 17; 3:18b; Phil 3:21). The NT antitype is open to the ultimate fulfillment.

The testimony of Scripture with reference to Christ's office is that something

---

53. See above on Rom 5:20f.

54. See above; see below, pp. 176f.

55. Cf. Exod 34:30; the details are obtained by a midrashlike expansion of the passage. The observation that the Israelites could not look at the radiance goes beyond Exod 34:30, 35a. The idea occurs also in Philo *Vit. Mos.* 2.70. However, cf. 1 Cor 11:7.

56. The phrase ἀνακεκαλυμμένῳ προσώπῳ is certainly a reference to Moses, even if the antithetical δέ has in view primarily the situation of Israel that is described in vv 14f. Moreover, Jewish apocalypticism had already used features from Exodus 34 in describing the eschatological glorification (cf. *2 Apocalypse of Baruch* 51; *1 Enoch* 38:4; [Dan 12:3]).

infinitely greater is here. This is true also with reference to Christ's gifts—the symbols of grace, the sacraments. Nevertheless, even the shadow is an aid in perceiving the nature of that something greater, because the same Lord is back of them both. The Christian church is the true circumcision (Phil 3:3). Paul does not simply assert, as the prophets did, that circumcision done in the flesh has no value without circumcision of the heart, without the surrender that corresponds to the sign (1 Cor 7:19; Rom 2:25-28; cf. Jer 4:4; 9:25; Ezek 16:30). He is announcing the true circumcision for which those prophets longed. This is not merely an external symbol of membership in the people of God and of one's obligation to be obedient (Gal 5:3; Rom 4:11; Eph 2:11). This is the new creation by which we are incorporated into God's people, the new humanity, and by which we are made new people (Col 2:11; Gal 6:15; Eph 2:11, 15) who serve God in Spirit and in truth (Gal 5:6; Phil 3:3). This circumcision which Christ performs (Col 2:11) is accomplished in baptism (Col 2:12). It is the bathing in water for which the prophets longed and which would purify the hearts and renew them in the Holy Spirit (Ezek 36:25f.). The idea that the church must have a substitute for circumcision is not a conclusion drawn from the OT. It has happened the other way around: the new creation that Christ brought about in baptism makes circumcision a shadow of the future reality (cf. Col 2:16f.). What the prophets longed for is fully present. The old has passed away, including circumcision, and the fulfillment has begun.

Here no contrast is being made between an OT system of redemption and a NT one; rather, in instance after instance the symbol of a past redemption is seen in the light of the symbol of the present redemption. This is why Paul can also compare baptism with other symbols of the Old Covenant in order to warn the church not to be misled by the Hellenistic mystery religions and suppose that the sacraments guarantee blessedness independent of morality simply for completing the initiation ritual and for eating some of the heavenly food.[57] The God of the Old and New Covenants, who through his word deals personally with mankind in grace and in judgment, in forgiveness and in wrath, is contrasted with the Hellenistic concept of powers that radiate from the divine ground of the universe. The living God does not tolerate any neutralizing or materializing of his grace by making it into a divine power that can be controlled at will. This is the background for the discussion that follows.

When Paul calls the Israel of the wilderness wandering "our forefathers" in a spiritual sense, he is alluding to the typological relationship. They received the symbols of grace that correspond to the Christian sacraments. "They were all baptized into Moses in the cloud and in the sea" (1 Cor 10:2). In 1 Cor 10:1 Paul states that the Israelites were under the cloud. This is not a reference to the pillar of cloud that went before them pointing the way (Exod 13:21), but to the

---

57. See Lietzmann, *Korinther*, 46f., 51.

saving and sheltering protection of the clouds (Exod 14:20).[58] This immersion under the clouds (Exod 14:20) is connected with the crossing of the sea (Exod 14:22; this is the traditional sequence) as a single, nonrecurring redemptive event that corresponds to Christian baptism.[59] The point of comparison that Paul was thinking of may not have been simply that they were enveloped in moisture or covered with water.[60] It may have been the fundamental significance that the deliverance at the Red Sea had for Israel's salvation (Exod 19:4ff.; 20:2).[61] Because the Mosaic covenant and the Mosaic Law, which is a part of that covenant, are rooted in this event (Exod 19:4ff.; 20:2), what happened to the Israelites is described as being "baptized into Moses" (1 Cor 10:2), a formula that is analogous to "being baptized into Christ" (εἰς Χριστὸν βαπτίζεσθαι) because of a correspondence in essence and not merely in form.

In a similar way, Paul finds a prototype of the Lord's Supper (1 Cor 10:3f.) in Israel's feeding on the manna (Exod 16:4, 14-18) and drinking from the rock (Exod 17:6; cf. Num 20:7-13). These gracious gifts that preserved Israel alive in the wilderness were already interpreted in the OT as πνευματικά, i.e., spiritual, supernatural, or heavenly gifts.[62] This is an interpretation that was widespread in late Judaism. These things were expected to reappear in the last days.[63] It was already common for the church to associate the manna with the bread of the Lord's Supper;[64] all that needed clarification was that to which the water pointed. In order to make the provision of water conform to the feeding with manna and, therefore, to the Lord's Supper, Paul either adopted from the midrash[65] the idea about the rock that followed Israel or he constructed it according to rabbinic analogies (1 Cor 10:4).

The rock is related to Christ also in John (7:37f.),[66] but no exact parallels can be found in Jewish literature.[67] The historicity of the rock is destroyed by Philo's allegorical interpretation in which he relates the rock to wisdom and the Logos.[68] The interpretation that Billerbeck finds in *Mekilta Exodus* is certainly closer to the thinking of Paul.[69] *Mek. Exod.* 17:6 says, "Wherever Israel may

---

58. J. Weiss, *1. Korinther*, 250; however, cf. Lietzmann, *Korinther*, 45.

59. So Paul is not thinking, as the midrash is, of a regular recurrence of the event (see *Tg. Yer. 1* on Exod 13:20ff., quoted in Str-B 3. 405; also cf. Ps 105:39; J. Weiss, *1. Korinther*, 250, finds the source of Paul's idea in Ps 105:39).

60. Lietzmann, *Korinther*, 45.

61. This significance reechoes throughout the OT (A. Oepke, "ἀποκαλύπτω," *TDNT* 3. 572).

62. Ps 78:24ff.; Wis 16:20: ἀγγέλων τροφήν, . . . ἄρτον ἀπ' οὐρανοῦ; cf. John 6:31f.

63. See above, pp. 34f.

64. Cf. above on Mark 6:34ff. and on John 6; cf. Rev 2:17.

65. *Tg. Onq.* Num 21:19, quoted in Lietzmann, *Korinther*, 45; omitted by Strack and Billerbeck.

66. See below.

67. See Str-B 3. 408; cf. J. Jeremias, "Golgotha und der heilige Felsen," *Angelos* 2. 124: "Since no appropriate correlation of Miriam's well with the Messiah has been found in rabbinical literature or in Philo, we must assume that Paul's saying is developed from Jesus' saying about himself at the Feast of Tabernacles in John 7:37f."

68. Commenting on Deut 8:15 in *Leg. All.* 2.21; cf. *Det. Pot. Ins.* 31.

69. Str-B 3. 408.

turn, God will go with her in order to provide water for his people." In some
respect, therefore, God is the rock that goes with them. Paul's statement is so
brief that it cannot be understood precisely. Perhaps it points to Christ as the
mediator of that OT redemptive event (1 Cor 8:6), or the statement may see the
rock as a type referring to Christ, just as John does. An allegorical reinterpretation of the rock (= Christ) is not in keeping with the context, which contains
a number of types from redemptive history, but no allegorical figures.

Paul indicated these typological parallels to the Christian means of grace in
order to prepare for the following argument (1 Cor 10:5ff.): Although they all
(πάντες is used five times in 1 Cor 10:1-4) had received the same redemptive
gifts, the majority of them were rejected—they "were scattered over the desert."[70] Only Caleb and Joshua reached the promised land (Num 14:30). This
brings a warning to the church not to fall by sinning as those people did.[71] God's
dealing with Israel should discourage the church from participating in sacrificial
meals where idolatry is clearly involved (1 Cor 10:7—Exod 32:6), from sexual
immorality (1 Cor 10:8; cf. Num 25:1, 9), from tempting God (1 Cor 10:9—
Num 21:5f.), and from murmuring against him (1 Cor 10:10—Num 14:2, 36).

All "these things happened to them as examples (τυπικῶς) and were written
down as warnings for us, on whom the fulfillment of the ages has come" (1 Cor
10:11; cf. v 6). Here τύπος does not mean example in the ordinary sense of the
word, as it does several other times in Paul (1 Thess 1:7; 2 Thess 3:9; Phil 3:17;
cf. 1 Tim 4:12; Titus 2:7; 1 Pet 5:3). It refers to the fact that future events are
represented in redemptive history. By his dealings with the first people of God,
the forefathers (1 Cor 10:1), God reveals to the people of God who are living
at "the fulfillment of the ages" what they may expect from him. This is why
these events have been recorded (1 Cor 10:11). Here all the elements are present
that are recognized to be essential in a NT typology. In both type and antitype
we are dealing with events that refer to the relationship between man and God.
The types occurred in the redemptive period that serves as an example; the
antitypes occur in the last days. This automatically produces the typological
heightening that is not given any special emphasis. The type has been ordained
by God to point to the future antitype. This, of course, does not mean that it
points to the specific circumstances in Corinth, for what Paul says to the church
of Christ "as it is in Corinth" applies to the church (ἐκκλησία) as a whole.[72]

Like the other means of grace in the Old Covenant, the temple too is set aside
by the fulfillment that has been given to the church. In the Gospels the resurrected
Christ is referred to as the new and true temple.[73] Paul described the church

---

70. According to Num 14:29; cf. vv 16, 23, 30; (cf. Heb 3:17). κατεστρώθησαν is from Jdt
7:14; 2 Macc 5:26.

71. ἐπιθυμητὰς κακῶν in 1 Cor 10:6 is surely meant in a general sense without any reference
to specific events, e.g., Num 11:3, 34.

72. Schmidt, "ἐκκλησία," TDNT 3. 506.

73. See above, pp. 115f.

(1 Cor 3:10-17; 2 Cor 6:16; Eph 2:20-22),[74] and even individual Christians (1 Cor 6:19), as a temple of God. The basic idea is the same in each instance: in Christ and through Christ, God lives among us by his Spirit. Paul uses this typological comparison, which he often makes into a metaphor, to indicate the nature and structure of the church (1 Cor 3:10-17; Eph 2:20-22) and he warns against defiling or injuring this sanctuary (2 Cor 6:16b-18; 1 Cor 3:16f.; cf. 6:19).

The comparison Paul makes by means of a mosaic of Scripture sayings in 2 Cor 6:16b-18 can best be described as typology. "We are the temple of the living God" (2 Cor 6:16a) because to us God has fulfilled his promise: "I will live and walk among them, and will be their God, and they will be my people."[75] The words "I will live . . . among them" (ἐνοικήσω ἐν αὐτοῖς) must not be understood to mean God's dwelling in individuals, as is clear from the accompanying phrase "walk among them" (ἐμπεριπατήσω), for then it would not be the church that is called God's temple, but the individual, as in 1 Cor 6:19.[76] These words must be understood to mean God's dwelling in his people as in a temple, just like the statements about God's tenting among his own that occur in the passages that are the background for this concept. This, of course, happens through the Spirit (πνεῦμα) who permeates everything. In no other way can one make sense of the statement that God's temple would be defiled by the image of an idol,[77] and, therefore, the church must not make any agreement with the unbelievers who are given over to an impure life (2 Cor 6:16a, 17). The church must keep itself away from this defiling company in order to continue to be what it has become in Christ—God's temple, God's people, and God's children.[78] There is no explicit statement here that the church's relationship to the temple is found in Christ, but this is taken for granted by Paul, as is clear from the other two passages where he deals with temple typology.

According to 1 Cor 3:10-17 Christ was the foundation that Paul laid for the construction of the church in Corinth, because there is no other foundation on which this structure could stand (v 11). In the building of this temple, Paul is only a laborer, God is the builder (vv 5f.). The building belongs to God (v 16), and he will examine it to determine what is really a part of it and what is merely the inferior work of men (vv 12-15). This building is holy because it is God's temple in which his Spirit lives (this is the only place where Paul gives the

---

74. Cf. Matt 16:18; 1 Pet 2:4ff.; Rev 3:12.

75. Lev 26:11: "I will put my dwelling place among you." וְנָתַתִּי מִשְׁכָּנִי בְּתוֹכְכֶם (LXX has διαθήκην); v 12: καὶ ἐμπεριπατήσω ἐν ὑμῖν καὶ ἔσομαι ὑμῶν θεός, καὶ ὑμεῖς ἔσεσθέ μου λαός. Cf. Ezek 37:27: καὶ ἔσται ἡ κατασκήνωσίς μου ἐν αὐτοῖς.

76. Lietzmann, *Korinther*, 129; J. Weiss, *1. Korinther*, 216.

77. Cf. 2 Kgs 21:7; 23:6; Dan 9:27.

78. 2 Cor 6:16, 17b, 18; υἱοὶ θεοῦ is used of the church as in Hos 1:10; Jer 31:9; Isa 43:6 (υἱοὶ καὶ θυγατέρες).

metaphor this typological connection), and God will judge anyone who attempts to destroy it (vv 16f.).

The apostles are not described as workmen in the other metaphor (Eph 2:20-22), but as stones in the building. Because of their unique place in redemptive history they are the foundation stones, the lowest layer on which the others are laid (Eph 2:20; cf. Matt 16:18). Christ now is the cornerstone, i.e., the stone that upholds the dome of the building and without which it would collapse (Eph 2:20).[79] He holds the entire building together and he makes it grow so as "to become a holy temple in the Lord" (Eph 2:21), "to become a dwelling in which God lives by his Spirit" (Eph 2:22). Paul wants to express such a wealth of ideas that in both these passages he goes beyond the temple typology, which underlies the discussion, to the more general metaphor of a building whose individual features no longer correspond to the temple of the Old Covenant.

All this typological replacement of the redemptive gifts of the first covenant people rests in Christ. He himself is God's redemptive gift that replaces all other means of redemption and all other redemptive gifts. The New Covenant exists in him (1 Cor 11:25) and so does the new creation that takes the place of circumcision. He is the spiritual rock who gives water to his own people by giving himself to them (1 Cor 10:16f.). His presence makes the church God's temple, and, finally, he himself is the sacrifice which the new church offers.

"God presented him as a sacrifice of atonement" (ἱλαστήριον), i.e., primarily as a means of universal expiation (Rom 3:25).[80] But to any reader familiar with the Septuagint the term ἱλαστήριον when qualified with the words "in his blood" (ἐν τῷ αὐτοῦ αἵματι) is reminiscent of Leviticus 16. The Septuagint uses ἱλαστήριον (in addition to the more general meaning) as a technical term for the "atonement cover" (כַּפֹּרֶת) of the ark of the covenant (Exod 25:17-22), which is a symbol of God living in his sanctuary and present with his people.[81] On the great Day of Atonement, the sin of the people was atoned for by sprinkling the blood of the sin offering on the כַּפֹּרֶת (Lev 16:14, 16, 21).[82] The events of the Day of Atonement were "a tremendous consummation of the concept of atonement that dominated the whole sacrificial law."[83] Now, however, in the larger context of the passage, Paul contrasts the new salvation to the situation under God's Law and under his wrath (νυνὶ δέ, Rom 3:21) as well as under his forbearance (ἀνοχή, Rom 3:25b, 26). This salvation, he contends, is the fulfillment of what was prophesied by the Law and the prophets (Rom 3:21). When

---

79. See above on Mark 12:10f.
80. BAG (2d ed. rev. by F. Gingrich and W. Danker, 1979) 375. H. Leitzmann, *Einführung in die Textsgeschichte der Paulusbriefe an die Römer* (HNT; 1928) 49.
81. Schlatter, *Gottes Gerechtigkeit*, 146; see J. Herrmann, "ἱλαστήριον," *TDNT* 3. 318.
82. See W. Eichrodt, *Theology of the Old Testament* (Philadelphia, 1961-67) 1. 130; Herrmann, "ἱλαστήριον," *TDNT* 3. 318f.
83. Eichrodt, *Theology* 1. 130.

he designates Christ as the ἱλαστήριον, surely he is referring to that central institution in the Old Covenant that served as the atonement between God and the people. "Paul obviously assumes that the church to which he writes is acquainted with the Mosaic Law, 7:1a. Hence it is natural that he should depict Jesus in this context as a higher כַּפֹּרֶת which is efficacious through faith rather than through purely external observance (Rom 2:28, 29; 2 Cor 3:6), which sprinkled, not with the blood of animals, but with His own blood, and which is exposed to public view rather than concealed in the inaccessible Holy of Holies."[84] How many of these typological points of comparison Paul had in mind may continue to be an open question; however, it is clear that he did not compare Christ typologically with any ordinary means of atonement but with the principal OT institution.

While the greatness and the importance of the NT redemptive gifts are illuminated here by the OT types, a comparison of Christ's death with the slaughter of the Passover lambs (1 Cor 5:6-8) reminds the church of the responsibility which issues from this sacrifice. The typology is intertwined with a parabolic and allegorical interpretation of leaven similar to what can be found in Philo.[85] Just as after the Passover there was to be no leaven among the old people of God, so no old leaven—malice and wickedness—is to be found in the church, but only bread without leaven—sincerity and truth (1 Cor 5:8; cf. Exod 12:18-20; 13:4ff.). The church resembles the people celebrating the Passover, because Christ their Passover lamb has been sacrificed (1 Cor 5:7b; cf. Exod 12:21). It appears to have been common in the church to relate Christ to the Passover lamb. In making this comparison Paul may have been adding the following idea: Like the sacrifice of a Passover lamb, but in an incomparably higher sense, Christ's death signifies a change that brings salvation, deliverance from death, release from slavery, the beginning of something new, a new age. Not only the brevity of the statement but also the nature of NT typology, which always bases its ideas on what is new, prevents us from drawing more conclusions about the meaning of the cross from the Passover lamb or from the OT place of atonement than those that lie directly in the comparison. The entire exposition is on the borderline between parable and typology.

Though no comparison is made with any one specific OT sacrifice, it is stated in Eph 5:2 that Christ offered himself to God for us (i.e., in our behalf) as a sacrifice that was acceptable to God, and by this he has proven his love for us.[86] This sacrifice was offered for the people, but not by the people. Christ's death was a sacrifice on our behalf that was acceptable to God because, as is strongly

---

84. F. Büchsel, "ἱλαστήριον," *TDNT* 3. 321; cf. Schlatter, *Gottes Gerechtigkeit*, 146; however, cf. Lietzmann, *Römer*, 49f.

85. H. Windisch, "ζύμη," *TDNT* 2. 904; cf. 1 Cor 5:6 with Gal 5:9; Mark 8:15 par. Matthew; Matt 13:33 par. Luke.

86. See A. Stumpff, "εὐωδία," *TDNT* 2. 809.

emphasized in the Gospels, he gave his own life completely to God for our sakes and in full obedience. Nothing more is implied by the words, especially not the idea of vicarious atonement, which, in the strict sense of the word, is not found in the OT idea of sacrifice.[87]

Because it is fully sufficient, Christ's sacrifice of himself is the only expiatory sacrifice that the new people of God have. But for that very reason, it fulfills what the OT sacrificial law required of the people of God: "Therefore, I urge you, brothers, in view of God's mercy, to offer your bodies as living sacrifices, holy and pleasing to God—which is your spiritual worship" (Rom 12:1). The church's sacrifice does not produce God's mercy; it is based on it (διὰ τῶν οἰκτιρμῶν). "It will not do to offer a piece of property, one must offer himself. It will no longer be sufficient to kill an animal, one must be available to God while he lives."[88] In this act the cultic command to offer the life is combined with the prophetic requirement to offer the heart (Rom 3:31; 8:3f.). Where this is not merely commanded, but is realized by God's mercy, the new aeon has come (Christians are already living in this new aeon and, therefore, must not be conformed to the old one). It is not certain whether Paul associates the concept of priestly service with worship (λατρεία).[89] Even if the idea is not found in this term, it is an appropriate one. Since all service and obedience in the church is a manifestation of this complete surrender, even the individual acts of service can be called a sacrifice or a priestly service. Paul can even call the financial contribution made to him by the church at Philippi a fragrant offering, an acceptable sacrifice, pleasing to God[90] (Phil 4:18), because he is not thinking of the material gift, but of what can be credited to their account (Phil 4:17).[91]

By bending the concept slightly, Paul, in Rom 15:16, calls his apostolic service "a priestly duty of proclaiming the gospel" (ἱερουργεῖν τὸ εὐαγγέλιον). His service is priestly because he is in charge of a sanctuary (i.e., the gospel), but especially because his goal and achievement is the presentation of the Gentiles as a sacrifice sanctified by the Spirit and, therefore, acceptable to God (Rom 15:16b). The nations become a sacrifice that is sanctified by the Spirit, when, on the basis of the apostolic preaching in the Holy Spirit and by forgiving grace, they fulfill Rom 12:1. He alone is a sacrifice sanctified by the Spirit who, acting also as priest, offers himself. Perhaps Paul includes in this phrase (ἱερουργεῖν, priestly service) the idea that he has dedicated his whole person

---

87. Eichrodt, *Theology* 1. 165.

88. Althaus, *Römer*, on this passage; cf. J. Behm, "θύω," *TDNT* 3. 184f.

89. Cf. Heb 9:6; out of 9 occurrences in the LXX, only one refers to priestly service, and there it is a synonym for λειτουργία; see H. Strathmann, "λατρεία," *TDNT* 4. 61.

90. θεῷ is to be added analogous to the two preceding expressions.

91. Cf. Phil 2:30: The service of the Philippians to Paul is called λειτουργία; cf. Rom 15:27; 2 Cor 9:12; perhaps it is some kind of priestly service; see H. Strathmann, "λειτουργία," *TDNT* 4. 221 (LXX) and p. 227.

to the gospel;[92] he sacrificed himself for it in toil and labor, in danger and persecution, so that he too is both priest and sacrifice.[93]

In Phil 2:17f. (cf. 2 Tim 4:6) this facet of the apostle's priestly service, of which there are still some hints here, appears clearly alongside that which was mentioned first: "But even if I am poured out as a drink offering while I as a priest offer your faith as a sacrifice to God, I will rejoice."[94] The preaching of the gospel moves the Gentiles to offer themselves to God in faith (Rom 12:1). While Paul as priest prepares the sacrifice, his own life is poured out as a drink offering, like those which often accompanied the ritual of sacrifice. He is not thinking simply of his martyrdom, whether that be near or distant (2 Tim 4:6), because when he performed the service entrusted to him, he was fulfilling Rom 12:1 in himself. The typological significance of this service as a sacrifice becomes very clear when one remembers that Paul views the beginning and the completion of this service as a dying with Christ (Rom 6:3-5; etc.; Phil 3:10; 2 Cor 4:10ff.; cf. Col 1:24). When we consider these relationships, we are not surprised by what Paul says just prior to this central passage in which he describes his apostolic service as a priestly offering of himself (Phil 2:17). Consciously or unconsciously, when he says "I did not . . . labor for nothing" (Phil 2:16— Isa 49:4), he speaks of his labor for the Gentiles (cf. Isa 49:6) in words from the Servant poem in which he found his own consciousness of mission expressed. Consequently, his statements about the priestly service of sacrifice in the church are not merely a metaphor or a parable; they rest on a profound typological foundation (Gal 1:15—Isa 49:1).[95]

4. TYPOLOGY AND THE HEART OF PAUL'S THEOLOGY

In this way typology proves to be a method of interpretation that is suited to Paul's primary concern and a method that is developed from that concern. Paul employs typology to proclaim the universal significance of Christ's redemption and the permanence of his church. That church depends on Christ alone. It is a new people of God, a new humanity, which is distinct from the Jews and no longer needs their shadowy means of redemption because it possesses the reality. There is another concern, however, that this one must not be permitted to crowd out; it is the church's place in redemptive history. The church's relationship to the historical Christ and to God's revelation in the Old Covenant must not be

---

92. So in 4 Macc 11:23ff. ἱερουγεῖν τὸν νόμον is used of the martyr priest Eleazar (G. Schrenk, "ἱερουγέω," *TDNT* 3. 252).

93. Lietzmann, following Lohmeyer, wants to find the idea of Rom 15:16 as the background for 2 Cor 2:14 also (see Lietzmann, *Korinther*, on this passage). But it contains only a figurative expression without any direct connection with the idea of sacrifice: the knowledge of God in Christ spreads everywhere like a fragrance. Of course, the dividing line between what is metaphorical and what is based on typology is fluid here, as it is in many other passages.

94. Translated from Goppelt's rendition of the passage.

95. See above, p. 120.

replaced by a nonhistorical, syncretistic myth. Typology demonstrates not only the nature of the new in comparison with the old, but it also shows that the new is founded directly and solely on redemptive history. Paul, of course, undergirds the typology exegetically and works it out in theological reflection. He does not regard typology as a systematic exposition of Scripture, but as a spiritual approach that gives the church basic guidance from Scripture here and now on concrete questions of faith and practice.

APPENDIX I: 1 PETER

The purpose of 1 Peter is summarized in the prayer with which the epistle closes: "The God of all grace, who called you to his eternal glory in Christ, after you have suffered a little while, will himself restore you and make you strong, firm and steadfast" (5:10). Peter views the church as being on the march, like Israel in the wilderness. Deliverance from slavery lies behind them (1:18); it was their call from darkness into light (2:10, 25). Through Christ's blood they have been sanctified as God's people (1:2; 2:9) and as a holy priesthood (2:5). The promised land lies before them. They are still scattered and living away from home (1:1), and they live by faith, not by sight (1:8). Christ's cross and resurrection and the future revelation of his glory (see 1:3, 5, etc.) are the two poles which give rise to the tension that supports, pervades, and inspires the church. All that the church possesses rests upon them. The purpose of the epistle is to assure the church that they possess this redemption and to admonish them to appropriate behavior so that they will not fall because of temptation and tribulation, but will reach the goal (cf. 5:12).

Typology is used abundantly and is an excellent means of assuring the church of their salvation. The basic statement about the OT is found in 1:10f. In it a point of view is expressed that is distinctively typological. The common basis of the Old and New Testaments is emphasized. The witness of the prophets and the preaching of the apostles spring from the same spirit of Christ (1:10, 12) and in substance they point to the same fact of redemption. "The sufferings of Christ and the glories that would follow" are the heart of prophecy (1:11), and they are the substance of the apostolic preaching that sustains the church (1:12).[96]

---

96. What is stated in Isa 40:6f. about God's word in the OT applies to the word proclaimed by the church (1 Pet 1:24f.). Here the κύριος of OT sayings is Christ, as is often true in the NT (1 Pet 3:14 = Isa 8:12; cf. 1 Pet 2:3—Ps 34:8).

1 Peter finds the prophecy that foretold the sufferings of Christ and the glories that would follow principally in Isaiah 53. The author uses phrases from this prophecy to describe the sufferings of Christ (1 Pet 2:22-25; see the parallels in W. Dittmar, *Vetus Testamentum in Novo* [Göttingen, 1903] 258f.). The comparison of Jesus with a lamb (1 Pet 1:19) may have been inspired by Isa 53:7 (cf. the formula which comes a little earlier in 1:18—Isa 52:3); it is simply a comparison (for possible typological relationships see below on John 1:29) which Peter uses to say that Jesus' death was very effective because "when he offered his blood, Jesus acted as a lamb suitable for sacrifice" (A. Schlatter, *Petrus und Paulus nach dem Ersten Petrusbrief* [Stuttgart, 1937] 82). There is no idea here of substituting the offering of Christ for an OT sacrifice.

The prophets, however, could only look at and long for the salvation that has been given to the church (1:10f.; cf. Matt 13:16f. par. Luke). Christ has died and risen again and has given us new birth. Of course, we do not see that new existence yet, but we have a living hope (1 Pet 1:3ff.). Hope is strongly emphasized in 1 Peter as characteristic of NT salvation, and it is hope that distinguishes NT salvation from salvation in the OT. The OT was waiting for salvation to be actualized. The NT awaits the revelation and fulfillment of a salvation that can be seen only by faith. The redemptive work of Christ in his death and resurrection does not consist in making visible an idea that is true, whether visible or not, and the hiddenness of Christian salvation is not the same as the invisibility of the Platonic world of ideas. Accordingly, in 1 Peter and in the NT as a whole, OT salvation, OT redemptive history, and the blessings of the OT salvation are not placed in a direct relationship to Christian salvation, as prophecy is, but are related to it typologically.

The typological material that is appropriate for the purpose of the epistle is not Christ's life and work, but the church's salvation in relationship to him.[97] We found no complete and systematic interpretation of Scripture in Paul's writings, and it is even less likely that we will find one here. Occasionally, in a particular context, there are indications that the author was familiar with the way the church is related typologically to Israel and the Mosaic period, and even to the patriarchs and primeval history. We will begin with the first of these and then deal with the material as we come to it following the order in which these things are discussed in the epistle so as not to distort the ideas through an improper systematization.

According to 1 Pet 2:4-10 the church is at one and the same time a spiritual temple, a holy priesthood, and a true people of God. They are given this challenge: "As you come to him, the living Stone . . . you also, like living stones, are being built into a spiritual house" (οἶκος πνευματικός, 2:4f.). The phrase "a spiritual house," which is defined as a holy priesthood (2:5), refers to the temple, just as it does in the parallel passage, Eph 2:21f. This idea is the reason why the church is called the house of God (οἶκος τοῦ θεοῦ) in 1 Pet 4:17. The wording of this passage, "It is time for judgment to begin at the house of God," is obviously based on Ezek 9:6 (cf. Jer 25:29). In Ezekiel those who are to bring judgment on Jerusalem are charged, "Begin at my sanctuary," i.e., the temple.

This temple, in contrast to the old, is spiritual; it is "a house formed by the Spirit and resembling the Spirit."[98] Christ's cross and resurrection are the reason for the end of the old temple of God and the establishment of the new. According to 1 Pet 2:4 this building is founded on Christ, "the living Stone—rejected by men but chosen by God and precious to him." Jesus had already used this metaphor to announce his cross and the glory that would follow (Mark 12:10f.

---

97. See n. 96.
98. Schlatter, *Petrus und Paulus*, 94.

par. = Ps 118:22f.). In 1 Pet 2:6-8 three OT passages about "the stone" are quoted to prove and to describe more clearly how through Christ the new begins and the old is destroyed.[99] Although the details are taken metaphorically, the basic typological idea is preserved—the way this building is related to the OT sanctuary. The church of the crucified and resurrected one is now the place where God is present (1 Cor 14:25), and this is where he is worshiped in spirit and in truth and is revered through true sacrifice (1 Pet 2:5b).

It is union with Christ that brings this to pass not only within Christendom, but also through it, and, to be sure, through all of its members. This same church, which is built on Christ into a spiritual temple, is also a holy priesthood (1 Pet 2:5).[100] The mark of the genuine priesthood is holiness.[101] The church is holy not because it has been sprinkled with the blood of animals (cf. Exod 29:29f.), but because of the blood of Christ (1 Pet 1:2, 15-21). This may be what the author had in mind, but he is expressing the typological heightening when he describes the sacrifices of this priesthood as "spiritual sacrifices (πνευματικὰς θυσίας) acceptable to God through Jesus Christ" (2:5b). Their sacrifices are not physical acts that are carried out in obedience to the letter. They are a Spirit-inspired surrender to all kinds of service. This service is acceptable only through Jesus Christ because he covers the sin that defiles all human activity. Therefore, the new priesthood and the new sacrifices exist in him alone. What in the OT was shadowy and inadequate and was the concern of a select few belongs in the NT to the whole people of God, who are chosen from both Jews and Greeks (2:10). In Christ they can all approach God as priests and bring true sacrifices to him.

The argument does not proceed from the old. It does not begin by asking how the temple, priesthood, and sacrifice are replaced. The new is the focus of attention, and the old serves to make the glory and the nature of the new shine forth. So one relationship shades into the other. In the church's relationship to God and in its worship, everything is fulfilled that was ever said about the temple, the thank offerings, and the priesthood—and also what has been said about the mission and the dignity of Israel. Consequently, these things have become types.

The terms used in key passages to describe Israel's position (Exod 19:5f.; Isa 43:20) are transferred to the church (1 Pet 2:9). When he established the Old Covenant at Sinai, God declared that Israel was "his treasured possession" (λαὸς περιούσιος, Exod 19:5, LXX; cf. λαὸς εἰς περιποίησιν, 1 Pet 2:9), "a royal priesthood" and "a holy nation" (βασίλειον ἱεράτευμα, ἔθνος ἅγιον, Exod 19:6 and 1 Pet 2:9). The other distinguished titles that are used here are

---

99. 1 Pet 2:6 = Isa 28:16; 1 Pet 2:7 = Ps 118:22; 1 Pet 2:8 = Isa 8:14f. (Isa 28:16; 8:14f. are quoted also in Rom 9:33 in this same form, which differs from the LXX).

100. This is certain because οἶκος πνευματικός and εἰς ἱεράτευμα are related grammatically: R. Knopf, *1. Petrus* (MeyerK; Göttingen, 7th ed., 1912), 90: "destined for"; Schlatter, *Gottes Gerechtigkeit*, 95: the house is destined to be a priesthood.

101. Ibid.

found in Isa 43:20f. In a context referring to their election at Sinai (Isa 43:16ff.) Israel is addressed as "my chosen generation, my people, whom I made my very own to declare my goodness" (τὸ γένος μου τὸ ἐκλεκτόν, λαόν μου, ὃν περιεποιησάμην τὰς ἀρετάς μου διηγεῖσθαι). The author's choice of these key OT passages makes it clear that he is not simply employing figurative expressions that were familiar in the church; rather, he is conscious that there is a typological connection between the church and the people that was formed at Sinai under the Old Covenant. Now a new people of God has been adopted as had been promised for the new age (1 Pet 2:10 borrowing from Hos 1:6, 9; 2:1, 23, passages that referred originally to Israel).

Numerous other allusions that reinforce one another prove that the author was thinking of these types. As once Israel was chosen at Sinai to be "my treasured possession out of all nations" (λαὸς περιούσιος ἀπὸ πάντων τῶν ἐθνῶν, Exod 19:5), so the Christians are the elect strangers in the world (ἐκλεκτοὶ παρεπίδημοι, 1 Pet 1:1) who have been selected out of all the nations. Like their forefathers, who were taken from their natural family ties (Heb 11:9, 13; cf. Gen 17:8; Exod 6:4; Ps 105:11) through God's call, and like Israel in Egypt and in the wilderness (Acts 7:6; 13:17),[102] they too are "aliens and strangers" (πάροικοι καὶ ἐπίδημοι) among the nations of this world (1 Pet 1:1, 17; 2:11).[103] Of course, it is impossible to prove that the author saw the typological relationship that is implicit in this familiar formula.

The same is true of the admonition "Gird up your loins" (1 Pet 1:13, *KJV*). This phrase is used widely in the OT (2 Kgs 4:29; 9:1; Job 38:3; 40:7; Jer 1:17; Prov 31:17) and was very common in early Christianity (Luke 12:35; Eph 6:14).[104] It reminds us of the command ordering the strangers in Egypt to be ready to depart suddenly (Exod 12:11).[105]

Christians are "strangers . . . chosen . . . for sprinkling with the blood of Christ" (εἰς . . . ῥαντισμὸν αἵματος Ἰησοῦ Χριστοῦ, 1 Pet 1:2). To be sure, these terms are not used in the few OT passages in which the sprinkling of persons with blood is mentioned, and, consequently, not even in the passages that deal with the institution of the covenant at Sinai (Exod 24:8; cf. Exod 29:20f.; Lev 14:14). Nevertheless, Hebrews is stating what had already been indicated by the saying about the cup at the Last Supper: The early church considered the blood of Christ through which the New Covenant was established to be sprinkled blood (Heb 12:24) and compared it with the sprinkled blood through which the Old Covenant was established (Heb 9:20-22).[106]

---

102. Cf. Exod 22:21 (= 23:9; Lev 19:33f.; Deut 10:19); Deut 26:5; Ps 105:23; Isa 52:4.

103. Passages like Acts 13:17; cf. 7:6; Heb 11:9, 13 show that this relationship was familiar to the early church. The transfer of this meaning was already prepared for in the OT; cf. Lev 25:23 and Ps 39:12; the wording of 1 Pet 2:11 is dependent on the last passage.

104. Also Pol. *Phil.* 2:1.

105. See Schlatter, *Petrus und Paulus*, 67.

106. See F. Hauck, *Die katholischen Briefe* (NTD III) 167.

In this context we should point out that the saying "It was not with perishable things such as silver and gold that you were redeemed" (οὐ φθαρτοῖς ἀργυρίῳ ἢ χρυσίῳ ἐλυτρώθητε, 1 Pet 1:18) is dependent on a passage dealing with the liberation of God's people from bondage in Egypt and Assyria (παροικῆσαι is used there also).[107]

1 Peter uses a type from primeval history to illustrate the way in which baptism separates the church from the world. Like the saying of Jesus in Matt 24:37-39 (cf. Luke 17:26ff.), 1 Pet 3:20f. compares this age, which is hastening to the end (1 Pet 4:7) and in which the judgment will begin (4:17), with the time of the first world judgment. At that time only eight people from the whole human race were saved (3:20; cf. Gen 6:18; 7:7), so now only a few from this blind generation, which is sunk in worldliness, will permit themselves to be saved (cf. 1 Pet 1:14f.; 2:9f.; 4:3f.). Our passage, however, relates the flood directly to baptism, not to the final judgment as Jesus and late Judaism do.[108]

What one sees as the points of comparison depends on the way he interprets the words "through water, and this water symbolizes" (δι' ὕδατος. ὃ . . . ἀντίτυπον . . .). They can be translated as follows: "the ark in which a few . . . were saved by water, which now as an antitype saves you too in baptism."[109] Then it would have to be interpreted as asserting that the water of the flood is a means of salvation just as the water of baptism is (διά is understood instrumentally). "The water which brought death to the others was the means of salvation for the few because it caused the ark to float and separated those who were in it from those who were destroyed by the flood."[110] These two arguments, which can be used to justify viewing the water of the flood as a means of salvation, are not satisfying. Furthermore, 1 Pet 3:21 ascribes this meaning to the act of baptism, not to the water.[111]

For this reason the phrase "through water" (δι' ὕδατος) is often understood locally.[112] The elaborations of the midrash are frequently the basis of the NT view of OT history, and, according to the midrash, Noah did not enter the ark until the water came up to his knees.[113] "Going through the water into the ark (εἰς ἥν) Noah and his family were saved."[114] The idea would be similar to the one we observed already in 1 Cor 10:1f. Then in order to be consistent, the relative pronoun ὅ (1 Pet 3:21) would not refer to ὕδωρ but to the entire process

---

107. Isa 52:3: οὐ μετὰ ἀργυρίου λυτρωθήσεσθε . . .; v 4: Εἰς Αἴγυπτον . . . παροικῆσαι ἐκεῖ.

108. See above.

109. ὅ = ὕδωρ; taking ἀντίτυπος as an adjective and βάπτισμα as in apposition, HNT; T. Zahn, 1. Petrus; Schlatter, Petrus und Paulus, on this passage; and BAG, 132.

110. Schlatter, Petrus und Paulus, 141; cf. T. Zahn, 1. Petrus, 115f.

111. Cf. 1 Pet 3:21b, ἀπόθεσις and ἐπερώτημα.

112. H. Windisch, Die katholischen Briefe (HNT; 1911); R. Knopf, 1. Petrus; Hauck, Die katholischen Briefe, on this passage.

113. Midr. Gen. Rab. on Gen 7:7, A. Wünsche, Der Midrasch Bereschit Rabba (Bibliotheca Rabbinica; Leipzig, 1880) 139.

114. R. Knopf, 1. Petrus, 155.

that was described (διεσώθησαν δι᾽ ὕδατος, they were saved through water) and would be translated: "As the antitype of this, baptism now saves you."[115]

As was true in 1 Cor 10:1f., it is not simply the external event that is being compared. Passing through the water of baptism is symbolic of passing through a water of judgment. According to the NT and for Paul especially, baptism saves in that it judges the old man, and, therefore, the final judgment is fulfilled in it proleptically. It is impossible to prove whether or not the author had something like this in mind, but if he did, this is a case of true typology (the consummation is already present in Christ). 1 Peter is familiar with the idea of the Christian's suffering and dying with Christ and with the idea that this suffering is a kind of judgment.[116]

In this context ἀντίτυπος(ν) can only mean "as an antitype," and the term in itself does not indicate that either of the things compared is superior to the other, as is the case in Heb 9:24.[117] It is significant, however, that this term which denotes typology occurs in 1 Peter, a very short epistle, but one containing a wealth of typology.

Finally, a remarkable passage shows that, in addition to being familiar with the typologies of Israel and of the primeval period, this epistle was also familiar with the church's relationship to the patriarchs. An admonition to women in the church is supported by a reference to the behavior of "holy women . . . who put their hope in God," especially Sarah (1 Pet 3:5f.). The persons admonished were placed in relationship to those women in redemptive history. They are called "children of Sarah" analogous to the way that the church is called "children of Abraham" (also cf. 1 Cor 10:1). "The relationship to Sarah is stressed because the women of the church are being instructed about behavior that is proper for women."[118] Those women are holy because they belong to the people who are chosen by God, to a holy nation (ἔθνος ἅγιον).[119] This leads us to the second factor that distinguishes this reference to an OT example from Jewish parallels. What is being emphasized is not moral conduct per se, but a trait that is fitting for the faith of a people "who put their hope in God."[120] This is how typology elucidates the reference to an OT personality for ethical exhortation (compared with Judaism, the OT is seldom used this way in the NT). The women of the OT have this significance not because they are OT personalities, but by virtue of their being members of the typical redemptive people. Therefore, their

---

115. Hauck, *Die katholischen Briefe*, on this passage; cf. Knopf, *1. Petrus*, 156.

116. Cf. 1 Pet 3:21b, δι᾽ ἀναστάσεως; 4:13, 17f.; etc.

117. The opposite is asserted in HNT on 1 Peter, p. 70: as in Heb 9:24, ἀντίτυπος = "a poor copy"; but this is contrary to the general attitude of 1 Peter. T. Zahn, *1. Petrus*, 116 n. 78: ἀντίτυπος = "a higher type."

118. Schlatter, *Petrus und Paulus*, 127f.

119. Cf. Knopf, *1. Petrus*, 126.

120. Accordingly it does not contradict the Pauline doctrine that persons become sons of Abraham on the basis of faith alone, if here the ethical conduct which is the consequence of this faith (in 1 Peter "hope" is often used instead of "believe") is mentioned as an attribute.

ethical behavior is not in itself exemplary for the church, but it is exemplary as a characteristic that is appropriate for the faith that God's people have; it is an essential element in their relationship to God.

Even this brief reference to the patriarchal age proves that 1 Peter interprets the OT in a truly typological manner. Within the brief scope of 1 Peter there is a comprehensive typological approach that seems to combine the influence of the early church and the influence of Paul, as is true in other aspects of the epistle as well.

APPENDIX II: 2 PETER AND JUDE

There is a statement in 2 Pet 1:19-21 about the importance of OT prophecy that is significantly different from the statement in 1 Pet 1:10-12. "The word of the prophets" is a "light shining in a dark place" pointing the church to the future consummation. Therefore, Christ's church differs from the church of the OT only in that they have a guarantee of the absolute fulfillment of that prophecy in Christ's advent, in the glory that the apostles saw and to which they bore witness, and so they hold on to that prophecy with much greater joy (2 Pet 1:16-19a). We must remember, of course, that the passage in 1 Peter mentions the fulfillment of prophecy in order to encourage thanksgiving for the salvation that has been given to the church, while 2 Peter is defending the Christian's eschatological hope against gnostic attack (cf. 2 Pet 1:16; 3:4). Nevertheless, in 2 Peter there is an obvious loss of an awareness that salvation is a present reality.

Motivated by this primary objective, 2 Peter applies all OT types to the future. In response to the objection that "everything goes on as it has since the beginning of creation" (2 Pet 3:4), he points to the flood (3:5f.) as a type of the future destruction of the world by a deluge of fire, which, according to prophetic promise, will be followed by "a new heaven and a new earth" (3:13 = Isa 65:17; 66:22).[121]

With obvious literary dependence on Jude, 2 Peter 2 is combating a gnostic, libertine false doctrine. It gave the church strength and serenity to know that this internal distress that was caused by false teachers was part of God's plan of redemption because it was revealed by the prophets and the apostles. This is stated explicitly in Jude (vv 17f.; cf. v 14). 2 Peter shows sensitivity for this concern by placing the attack on false teaching in the mouth of the apostle Peter and by drawing explicit parallels between this phenomena in the church and similar experiences of the people of God in the OT. In 2 Pet 2:1 the author attributes the following statement to Peter (cf. 2 Pet 1:1): "But there were also false prophets among the people, just as there will be false teachers among you." Of course, the reason for comparing old false prophets and new false teachers

---

121. See above, p. 34, and Matt 24:37-41 par. Luke; Luke 17:28f.; 1 Pet 3:20: characteristically referring to the present.

is not that this forms an ingenious parallel, but that the author sees the former as the types and the latter as the fulfillment—fulfillment in a typological sense.[122]

In Jude 11 and 2 Pet 2:15 Balaam appears as a prototype of the personality and conduct of the false teacher.[123] According to Num 31:16 Balaam had advocated tempting Israel to idolatry and fornication (cf. Num 25:1).[124] Legend has made an actual case of bribery out of Balak's attempt to bribe Balaam into action (Num 22:6f., 17; 24:13).[125] Therefore, Balaam comes to be the "type" of anyone who, because of greed, seduces others to idolatry and licentious conduct, as is the case of the false teachers that are being combated.[126] In Jude 11 Cain and Korah are designated as prototypes along with Balaam. How Jude viewed Cain as a prototype will have to be deduced not only from Genesis 4 but also from the way his person is developed in late Jewish writings.[127] What is being compared in the case of Korah is clear. He rebelled against the divinely ordained order and leadership of the community.

The illumination brought by typology shows the church not only that the coming of false teachers is part of God's will, but also that the condemnation of the false teachers is sure (οὐαὶ αὐτοῖς, Jude 11; 2 Pet 2:14ff.). The latter is pointed out more emphatically with a series of OT examples in 2 Pet 2:3-9 and Jude 5-7. Jude recalls the punishment of the Israelites in the wilderness who refused to believe God and obey him (Num 14:26-38), the banishment of the disobedient angels (Gen 6:1ff.) that is recorded in 1 Enoch 12:4–13:1, and the destruction of Sodom (Gen 19:4-25). In chronological order 2 Peter cites the fall of the angels, the destruction of the generation of the flood with the rescue of Noah, the ruin of Sodom, and the protection of Lot. Both epistles cite these examples as warnings that point to the future. 2 Pet 2:6 refers to Sodom as "an example of what is going to happen to the ungodly" (ὑπόδειγμα μελλόντων ἀσεβεῖν), and Jude 7 says, "They serve as an example" (πρόκεινται δεῖγμα). These examples are compared directly with the ungodliness of the false teachers. In the example of the Israelites in the wilderness, the deliverance which preceded their fall is emphasized as the primary point of comparison (Jude 5).[128] The example of the fallen angels and the example of Sodom are not really typologies; they are used symbolically as analogies. Finally, the main reason 2 Peter uses

---

122. Knopf, *1. Petrus*, 287.
123. See Num 22–24; 25:1-3; 31:16; Neh 13:2.
124. Cf. Str-B 3. 793 and Rev 2:14f.
125. Cf Str-B 3. 771; e.g., Philo *Vit. Mos.* 1.268.
126. Whether the resistance to the angel in Num 22:22f. was interpreted as contempt for angelic beings (cf. 2 Pet 2:10; Jude 8) must remain an open question (see Windisch, *Die katholischen Briefe*, on this passage).
127. See R. Knopf, *Judas* (MeyerK; Göttingen, 7th ed. 1912), 230. The Epistle of Jude provides explicit proof of what we have assumed in many passages: Early Christianity was familiar with the noncanonical traditions of late Judaism. The apocalyptic literature is referred to here: *1 Enoch* is quoted in Jude 14f. Cf. Jude 9, which refers to the legend about Michael that is from the *Assumption of Moses*; cf. Jude 6 with *1 Enoch* 12:4–13:1.
128. So also 1 Cor 10:1ff.; Heb 3:7ff.

the last two examples (2:5-7) is simply to derive the principle stated in 2:9.

The typology in these two epistles is not fully developed, primarily in that it is not applied to Christ with appropriate heightening. In Jude this may be due to the brevity of the exposition, and in 2 Peter it may be the result of the loss of a consciousness of redemptive history.[129]

---

129. These discussions of the false teachers correspond with what is stated in 2 Timothy (3:8f. draws a comparison with the Egyptian magicians Jannes and Jambres [*Tg. Ps.-J.* Exod 7:11]; 2 Tim 2:19a [= Num 16:5] and 2:19b [cf. Num 16:26] contain allusions to the things that happened to Korah) and in the letters to the seven churches in Revelation (2:14f. mentions Balaam again; 2:20 speaks of Jezebel as temptress to idolatry). Here the typological basis for the warnings concerning the false teachers, false prophets, and false messiahs in the prophecies in the Synoptic Gospels and Revelation is obvious. Except for the apocalyptic mode of expression, 2 Peter 2 is parallel to them.

Chapter Seven

THE EPISTLE TO THE HEBREWS

1. THE USE OF SCRIPTURE AND TYPOLOGY IN HEBREWS

Of all the NT writings the Epistle to the Hebrews draws most extensively from the OT for the development and support of its exposition. There are many allusions to the OT, and the author's own message is clothed in the language of the OT. Nowhere else in the NT is there such a concentration of biblical passages that are compiled explicitly and systematically as scriptural proof or such an abundance of biblical statements that are exegeted.[1] In no other book are so many OT terms applied directly to Christ or to other aspects of NT salvation.[2]

The expositions are bound to contemporary thought forms and especially to contemporary exegetical methods. There is much that is reminiscent of Philo,[3] but unless a person is fascinated by superficial matters of form, he will discover fundamental differences in the way individual Scripture passages are interpreted. With the present historical reality of redemption as its starting point, Hebrews holds to the historicity of Scripture and is committed in principle to the literal

---

1. The only possible parallels are a few examples in the Synoptic Gospels: Mark 12:26f., 36f. par.; a few missionary sermons in Acts; and above all a series of passages in Paul: Rom 3:10ff.; chaps. 4, 9–11; 1 Cor 9:9f.; 10:1ff.; 11:7ff.; 2 Cor 3:4ff.; 6:16ff.; Gal 3:6ff.; 4:21ff. See G. Schrenk, "γραφή," *TDNT* 1. 759f.

2. Of the royal psalms, not only are Psalms 2 and 110 applied directly to Christ, but Psalm 45 also (45:6f. = Heb 1:8f.); of the psalms that dealt originally with the righteous, not only are Psalm 8 (8:4-6 = Heb 2:6ff.; cf. 1 Cor 15:27) and Psalm 22 (22:22 = Heb 2:12) applied to Christ, but also Psalm 40 (40:6-8 = Heb 10:5-10: an exceptionally bold transfer). This increase in the number of passages that are interpreted as directly messianic is so much more striking when the transfer is made directly and with a marked reinterpretation of the historical meaning. This is true also of the transfer to Christ of OT statements about the Lord (κύριος) = Yahweh: Ps 102:25-27 = Heb 1:10-12; Deut 32:43, LXX = Heb 1:6b. This transfer is common in the rest of the NT also.

3. On the various views about the relationship of Hebrews to Philo, see J. Holtzmann, *Lehrbuch der Neutestamentlichen Theologie* (Tübingen, 2d ed. 1911) 2. 329 n. 3; B. Weiss, *Biblische Theologie des Neuen Testaments* (Berlin, 5th ed. 1888) 460 n. 3. On hermeneutical points of contact, see C. Siegfried, *Philo von Alexandrien* (Jena, 1875) 323f.; Holtzmann, *Lehrbuch*, 330f.; P. Feine, *Theologie des Neuen Testaments* (Leipzig, 7th ed. 1936) 394ff.

sense of Scripture.[4] Therefore, the meanings which Hebrews directly attributes to the OT message can largely be defended in the light of the modern historical interpretation of Scripture as typological interpretation.[5] The historical significance is handled in a variety of ways by Hebrews, as is done in the proofs from prophecy in Acts.[6] Generally, however, Hebrews has applied passages such as 2 Sam 7:14 (Heb 1:5); Ps 45:6f. (Heb 1:8f.); Ps 22:22 (Heb 2:12); Ps 40:6-8 (Heb 10:5-7) to Christ as though they were direct references to him. We cannot judge Hebrews by our standards of logic because it has been developed on the basis of a different way of thinking.[7]

Though it might be possible to justify such things on the basis of certain considerations that the author had in mind, it is much more important to observe that the entire train of thought in Hebrews views Scripture fundamentally as redemptive history and uses typology to make it applicable to the present. The individual expositions appear to be simply a way of expressing the typological approach. It is very clear that typology is not so much a method of exegesis as it is a spiritual approach that is the background for, and is independent of, the formal treatment.

This use of the OT in a comprehensive typological manner is justified by the primary concern of the epistle. In Christ the fulfillment ($\tau\epsilon\lambda\epsilon\acute{\iota}\omega\sigma\iota\varsigma$) has come, and this calls for uncompromising commitment. The Law, the regulations of the Old Covenant, could not achieve its goal of perfection (Heb 7:11, 19), namely, cleansing from sin (9:9, 14; 10:1f.) and fellowship with God (7:19). Jesus, however, as the perfect high priest (2:10; 5:9; 7:28) is establishing a church composed of perfect persons (10:14; 12:2; cf. 11:40).

Scripture contains God's provisional message of salvation that now, at the end

---

4. W. Beyschlag, *Neutestamentliche Theologie* (Halle, 2d ed. 1895) 2. 296: "He does not allegorize like Philo or Origen, i.e., he does not use clever and arbitrary methods to reinterpret the data of the OT as meaning something strangely different because of some purely formal similarity. Instead, he interprets typologically, i.e., he finds the NT truth in those OT facts which are really a prelude, a seed or embryo of that NT truth in sayings and phenomena whose meaning is not exhausted in the present reality, but actually comes to fulfillment only in Christ." Similarly, Weiss, *Biblische Theologie*, 433; A. Schlatter, *Die Theologie der Apostel* (Stuttgart, 2d ed. 1922) 462ff.; Feine, *Theologie*, 394ff.; finally, G. Wuttke is excellent (*Melchisedech der Preisterkönig von Salem* (Giessen, 1927) 6ff.: "Accordingly, the use of Scripture in Hebrews is typological, not allegorical. The contrast cannot be emphasized too strongly. Hebrews has allegory in only a very few passages . . .: 3:6; 10:20; and perhaps the metaphor in 12:22" (p. 7). "In 7:2b, 3 we find a use of Scripture that is totally different from the author's customary manner" (p. 8). Wuttke considers these verses to be "a rhetorical embellishment adopted by the author." "By all indications it originated in a Philonic atmosphere" (p. 11). Also A. Tholuck (*Kommentar zum Brief an die Hebräer* [Hamburg, 1836]), F. Bleek (*Der Brief an die Hebräer* [Berlin, 1828-40]), and Riggenbach (*Der Brief an die Hebräer* [Leipzig, 1922]) have detailed discussions of the use of Scripture in Hebrews.

Our real question has not been considered here. We are not asking how much of what is put into words in Hebrews can be called typological interpretation on the basis of our historical concept of Scripture, but to what extent the author himself saw typological connections.

5. Tholuck, *Hebräer*; Bleek, *Hebräer*; and Riggenbach, *Hebräer*. See n. 4.

6. See above, pp. 122f.

7. See above, 103f.

of this age, has reached its ultimate fulfillment. "In the past God spoke to our forefathers at many times and in various ways, but in these last days he has spoken to us by his Son" (Heb 1:1f.). And so the completeness of Christ is compared with Scripture, with the very inadequacy of the salvation of the fathers, and with the prophecy of better things to come; it gives the church assurance that the fulfillment has begun, and God's dealings with the fathers become an exhortation to the church to accept this perfect salvation.

The latter function is served by the exhortations at the beginning of the epistle (chaps. 1–6) and at the end (10:19ff.; cf. chaps. 12–13) that, like 1 Cor 10:6ff., are based on Mosaic period typology. The first is developed in the description of Christ as the true high priest that forms the core of the epistle. This description is another example of Mosaic period typology. The OT priesthood and cult that Christ fulfills and abolishes are not described in terms of the institution in Jerusalem but in accordance with the regulations in the Pentateuch. Aaron is the high priest that the author has in mind (Heb 5:4) and the cult is not located at the temple in Jerusalem, but at its prototype, the tabernacle (σκηνή, 8:3-5; 9:1ff.; cf. ἔξω τῆς παρεμβολῆς, 13:11).[8] It is the original form of the OT cult, the redemptive order of the Old Covenant, and not some human perversion of it, that is shown to be totally inadequate when compared with the new.

First of all, we will consider the description of Christ as the true high priest that forms the core of the epistle.

2. JESUS, THE TRUE HIGH PRIEST

The picture of Christ as high priest that is presented here, utilizing the OT cultic order typologically, is a comprehensive means of describing his work and importance. This picture includes his humiliation and exaltation and the redemptive significance of his suffering before God and for the church. The comparison of Christ with the OT order is another clear indication that the consummation has begun. Of the many NT titles for Christ, the only one with a meaning that is equally comprehensive is the title "Son of Man." It too includes humiliation and exaltation, the meaning and redemptive significance of Jesus' mission. It is not surprising that the first portrayal of Christ as high priest (Heb 2:8b-18) is introduced by quotations from Psalms that are interpreted messianically of the Son of Man in the NT[9] (Ps 8:4-6 = Heb 2:6-8a): the Son of Man (υἱὸς ἀνθρώπου), who is exalted above all the angels and to whom all is placed in subjection, must

---

8. "By using this same method, the synagogue reaches its conclusion as to what its religion should be and should accomplish. The rabbis, Josephus, and Philo determine what the Jewish cult should be simply from the requirements of the Law without inquiring whether it should still be practiced that way" (Schlatter, *Theologie der Apostel*, 474).

9. See above on 1 Cor 15:27.

be made lower than the angels "for a little while" (*RSV*). In this way Jesus is shown to be a true high priest (Heb 2:8-18; esp. v 17).[10]

We will try to unfold the concept of Christ as high priest without introducing any systematization that would do violence to the sequence of thought in Hebrews, which is a loose arrangement of haggadic expositions. In this way we will demonstrate how this typology illuminates Jesus' office, his work, and the meaning of his death in particular.

Aaron is an example of the fact that one must be called by God to be truly a high priest (Heb 5:4). It is clear that Jesus was appointed to this office by God because the saying in Ps 110:4 applies to him: "You are a priest forever, in the order of Melchizedek" (Heb 5:5f.).[11] Jesus would hardly have assumed the office for himself. He pleaded with God to deliver him from this service because it would involve his suffering and death (5:7f.).[12]

When this saying is applied to Jesus' call, it implies that his high priesthood is superior to the high priesthood of the OT; in fact, it abolishes that high priesthood (chap. 7). Jesus is a high priest in the order of Melchizedek (Ps 110:4), not in the order of Aaron (Heb 7:11). The nature of Melchizedek's priesthood, especially its superiority to the Levitical priesthood, is ascertained from Gen 14:17-20 (Heb 7:1-10). By means of a hermeneutical principle that Philo used frequently,[13] the immortality of that priestly king is deduced from Ps 110:4 and from the silence in Genesis concerning his ancestry and death (Heb 7:3). In this respect Melchizedek is "like the Son of God" (ἀφωμοιωμένος δὲ τῷ υἱῷ τοῦ θεοῦ, Heb 7:3; cf. v 15). This is all that is stated about Melchizedek's relationship to Jesus. Though many have considered Melchizedek as a type of Christ, these statements are scarcely sufficient grounds for doing so (there is no connection between Jesus and Melchizedek in redemptive history) or for considering him as the incarnation of Christ as the Gnostics did. Hebrews is content with the relationship of Melchizedek to Christ that is assured by Ps 110:4 and the silence of the narrative in Genesis. Jesus is a high priest like Melchizedek. Therefore, what Scripture says about Melchizedek is even more applicable to Christ, especially his superiority to Levi (Heb 7:4-10).

When Abraham met Melchizedek, there is a sense in which Levi was still in his body (Heb 7:10). Consequently, the priests from the tribe of Levi share the same position relative to that high priest as their ancestor did. It is obvious that Melchizedek is Abraham's superior because he received the tenth from Abraham and blessed him (7:4-9).

Jesus' call to be a high priest like Melchizedek does not merely show his

---

10. The sayings in the royal psalms and those concerning the righteous man were also transferred to the high priest (see n. 2).

11. This quotation from Psalm 110 is the beginning as well as the pivotal point in the description of Christ as high priest in Hebrews (Heb. 5:10; 6:20; 7:3, 11, 15, 17, 21, 24, 28; 10:1, 12, 14. See W. Dittmar, *Vetus Testamentum in Novo* (Göttingen, 1903) 243f.

12. See H. Strathmann, *Der Brief an die Hebräer* (NTD III), on this passage.

13. See Siegfried, *Philo*, 179 and Str-B 3. 693-95.

superiority to the OT priesthood; it signifies the abrogation of that priesthood (Heb 7:11-22 [and 28]). If the Aaronic priesthood had achieved the perfection that is the objective of the divine order, it would not have been necessary to establish another priesthood (7:11, 15-19). Jesus has been called to a different priesthood which is not connected with the Aaronic order. This is obvious because he descended from Judah, not from Levi, and according to the Mosaic Law he is not entitled to any priestly function (7:13f.). The saying that is applied to Jesus at his installation cancels what was decreed about Levi in the Mosaic Law (7:18, 28; cf. 4:7; Galatians 3), particularly because this saying was confirmed by God with an oath (Heb 7:20-22), whereas the other was not.[14] The abrogation of the priesthood signifies the abrogation of the whole Law (7:12), i.e., the abolishing of the entire Old Covenant (διαθήκη). In keeping with his more exalted position as high priest, Jesus has also "become the guarantee of a better covenant" (7:22). This is clearly a comprehensive view of redemptive history.

Finally, Christ's high priesthood is distinct from and superior to the Levitical priesthood because, in accordance with Ps 110:4, his priesthood, like Melchizedek's, is everlasting.[15] It was necessary for one Levitical priest to follow the other (7:23-25).

Ultimately, these complicated exegetical discussions are used to develop a typology (cf. 7:1-10), but this is not simply a way of stating the facts. It indicates that the OT includes more than types. The OT is a prophecy and as such it refers directly to the fulfillment and, therefore, points beyond itself.

The same basic elements are found in the description of Jesus' ministry as high priest. The high priest's task is to reconcile a sinful people to God through the sacrificial blood. Hebrews presents an excellent outline of the ministry and sacrifices of the OT priest in conformity with the regulations for the great Day of Atonement, which is the most distinctive summary of the OT cult.[16] In order

---

14. ὤμοσεν; the quotation is from Ps 110:4 (109:4, LXX).

15. See above on Genesis 14.

16. The high priest goes once a year in the Most Holy Place (Heb 9:7 ἅπαξ τοῦ ἐνιαυτοῦ; 9:25 κατ' ἐνιαυτόν = 10:1, 3; in accordance with Lev 16:34, cf. v 2), but not without the blood of the sin offering (Heb 9:7, 12; αἷμα τράγων καὶ μόσχων, 9:13, and 10:4: αἷμα ταύρων καὶ τράγων in accordance with Lev 16:2f.; μόσχος in Leviticus 16 is the regular term for the bull used for the sin offering [16:3, 6, 11, 14f.; 18:27]. τράγος is found in Leviticus 16 only in Aquila [16:8] and in a few minuscules [16:5, 7, 15]; the older MSS have χίμαρος instead. Cf. Heb 9:19 concerning the covenantal sacrifice at Sinai: Lev 8:14 [μόσχος], 18 [κριός]). Then after he has made atonement for himself (cf. Heb 5:3; 7:27 [here it was daily, of course] in accordance with Lev 16:6, 11-14, 17, 24, 33; the same is true of the sacrifice at Sinai in Lev 9:7), he can complete the atoning sacrifice for the people (Heb 5:3; 7:27 following Lev 16:7-10, 15, 24, 30, 33). Atonement was made for the sanctuary also (Lev 16:16, 20, 33; cf. Heb 9:23, which probably should be taken in a more general sense here than 9:21. There is no OT passage that corresponds exactly with 9:21. It is probably a combination of Exodus 40 [the dedication of the tabernacle] and Leviticus 8 [the consecration of the priests] as in Josephus *Ant.* 3.8.6 §206. See T. Zahn, *Hebräer* [Kommentar zum Neuen Testament; Leipzig, 1903ff.] 278). For an account of the Day of Atonement with an analysis of Leviticus 16 see in Beer-Holtzmann: *Mishnah, Seder II, Tractate 5*, 1-27.

to be able to truly intercede for the people, the priest must be able to sympathize with their weaknesses (5:1f.; cf. 2:17f.). Moreover, in order to come into God's presence, he must be holy and pure (5:3; 7:27). The Levitical high priest is able to be sympathetic because he is human (7:28). He can attain holiness and purity only by making daily sacrifices for himself before he presents the sacrifices for the people (5:3; 7:27). Christ is the perfect high priest. He has become "like his brothers in every way" (2:17). From Ps 22:22 and Isa 8:18 the conclusion is drawn that he is not ashamed to call us his brothers (Heb 2:12f.). He "has been tempted in every way, just as we are"—therefore, he can sympathize with us fully and intercede for us (2:17f.; 4:15f.)—"yet he was without sin" (4:15). Because he is holy and pure, he does not need to bring any sacrifice for his own sin before he can approach God on our behalf; indeed, he is always in God's presence (7:26f.). Once again the correspondence and the superiority are obvious.

In what sanctuary does Christ approach God on our behalf? The Levitical high priest goes through the Holy Place into the Most Holy Place (once a year) with the blood that has been sacrificed for his sins and the sins of the people (9:1-9 from Lev 16:2, 14; cf. Heb 9:25). The arrangement of this sanctuary is proof that as long as the first tabernacle (i.e., the Holy Place in distinction from the Most Holy Place; usually this term signifies the tabernacle as being the first sanctuary in point of time) stands, the way into the Holy Place is still not open (9:8). The earthly sanctuary is served by the Levitical priesthood (8:3f.). Christ does not need that sanctuary. He has gone in through the curtain (to the Most Holy Place), i.e., through his body (10:20) because he obediently offered himself in his suffering and death (5:7-9). He has passed through heaven bringing his own blood (4:14; 7:26) before God's throne in the Most Holy Place and has sat down at the right hand of God to intercede for us forever (4:16; 9:11f., 24; 8:1f.; 10:12; 7:25f.). Jesus performs his priestly service in heaven (8:1; cf. 9:11, 23f.) where the archetype (=τύπος) is found. Moses constructed the earthly tabernacle as its copy and shadow, according to Exod 25:40 (Heb 8:2, 5). Such an exalted priestly ministry is in keeping with the fact that Jesus has become the mediator of a superior covenant (8:6), the new covenant promised in Jer 31:31-34 (=Heb 8:8-12). Just as the installation of another priesthood (7:11ff.) indicates that the first is inadequate, so the announcement of a new covenant shows that the old is obsolete and aging (8:13). Here OT prophecy has already made the institutions of the covenant of Sinai into types of the means of redemption in a new divine order.

Does the *horizontal* typology of redemptive history in Hebrews intersect a *vertical* typology like Philo's?[17] We cannot accept the assertion of Holtzmann who says that "the entire world view of Hebrews moves within the metaphysical antithesis that was prevalent in Alexandrian philosophy between idea and phe-

---

17. Holtzmann, *Lehrbuch* 2. 332. It is true that the terms τύπος (σκιά, ὑπόδειγμα) are used in a sense different from Rom 5:14; 1 Cor 10:11.

nomenon, eternal and finite, celestial and cosmic, prototype and antitype."[18] The contrasting of upper and lower worlds is found in Hebrews only in the concept of the heavenly sanctuary (and the heavenly Jerusalem, 12:22;[19] the same analogy applies to it). This idea, which can be traced to Exod 25:40, is not unique in Philo; it was already widespread in Judaism at an early date.[20] Besides, Hebrews does not introduce this idea as a self-evident metaphysical fact, but bases it on Exod 25:40, which is scarcely more than is done in Acts 7:44; Gal 4:26 (Heb 12:22); and other similar passages, particularly in Revelation (e.g., 15:5). There is no metaphysical speculation in this concept. It has been welcomed as a means for rounding out the picture of Christ as high priest and simply as a practical way of expressing Christ's work as our representative at God's right hand. The church has been assured of this fact ever since Jesus quoted Ps 110:1 (Mark 12:36; 14:62), the psalm about the high priest. The major point of comparison is not an earthly sanctuary versus a heavenly one, but the priestly service of the Old Covenant in the past and the priestly service of the New Covenant in the present.

The statement made here to express the superiority of the heavenly compared with the earthly has, in reality, nothing in common with the Platonic depreciation of the visible material world in contrast to the invisible world of ideas—a concept that is totally foreign to the Bible. For Hebrews, and for the entire NT, "heavenly" signifies a more direct contact with God, consequently not earthly and temporal, but abiding and invisible, like God is, not comprehensible through the intellect, but only by faith. It is not because it belongs to a better part of this world that Christ's heavenly service as priest is more exalted than the Levitical service (Heb 4:14; 7:26), but because it is nearer God. Thus Hebrews places this concept completely within the typology of redemptive history. As we have seen, Hebrews does not deduce the existence of a higher world from Christ's service as priest at the heavenly sanctuary; what it infers is the existence of a new divine order in history. The author does not use this to exhort his readers to immerse themselves in mysticism and strive to rise to that higher world, as Philo does; he makes it the basis of faith in the reality of the fulfillment and the basis of hope that the fulfillment will come in the future (13:14).[21]

It is very significant that in Hebrews, where it would most likely be found, there is no vertical typology like Philo's. NT typology is an expression of a nonmystical view of history and the world that is based in faith and hope on the appearing and coming of Christ and that neither glorifies nor destroys history. This view does not separate redemption and eschatology in a mystical dualism, but is certain that salvation is a reality now and that it is coming in the future.

18. Ibid. 2. 331f.
19. See below on the passage.
20. See Str-B 3. 700ff.
21. Phil 3:20a would be much more conceivable in Philo; 3:20b prevents any speculation here also.

What prevents the dissolution of redemptive history into metaphysical ideas is the fact that this typology, which reaches a climax in the heavenly priestly ministry, finds its primary focus in the absolute reality of the cross as a unique historical event. The interpretation of the cross in Hebrews also brings together the typological approaches to the Old Covenant and to its redemptive order. Here again the divine necessity for Christ's death issues from the typology. Jesus' death proves the permanent validity of the central principle of the old cult— "Without the shedding of blood there is no forgiveness" (Heb 9:22; cf. Lev 17:11). The high priest enters the Most Holy Place to atone for his sins and for the sins of the people, but not without blood (Heb 9:7; cf. 5:1; 8:3; from Leviticus 16); Christ, as the crucified one, has gone into God's presence with his own blood (Heb 9:12; chaps. 11, 14). When the first covenant was established, it was necessary that the people be atoned for through the sprinkling of blood (9:13-20, 22)[22] because a covenant or will (διαθήκη) does not take effect until the death of the one who made it (9:15, 16, 18). It was also necessary for Moses to consecrate the earthly sanctuary for its intended purpose through the sprinkling of blood (9:21).[23] A much superior sacrifice is required for the purification of the heavenly sanctuary (9:23).[24]

Just as the typological correlation demonstrates the necessity of Christ's death, so the typological heightening indicates the importance of his death in that it fulfills the meaning of the old and, for this reason, abolishes it. All of this is expressed in the statement that if "the blood of goats and bulls[25] and the ashes of a heifer[26] sprinkled on those who are ceremonially unclean sanctify them so that they are ceremonially clean, how much more, then, will the blood of Christ, who through the eternal Spirit offered himself unblemished to God, cleanse our consciences from acts that lead to death, so that we may serve the living God" (9:13f.). The superiority of the new is clearly stated, but so is the failure of the old. If the sacrifice of animals had been able to take away sins (10:4) and to clear the conscience (9:9), it would not have been repeated continually (10:2; cf. 10:1-4). This statement is not a universal truth; it is a truth supported typologically by the certainty that Christ's sacrifice was effective and, therefore, was not repeated. This idea is emphasized in 9:25-28 and 10:10ff. and in the rationale given for 10:1-4.

An appeal is made to prophecy also to confirm the fact that the old is inadequate and is only a type of the perfect. The ineffectiveness of animal sacrifices

---

22. Cf. Exod 24:4-6; the details do not correspond exactly with the OT tradition; see Michel, *An die Hebräer* (MeyerK; 7th ed. 1936) 122f.

23. See n. 16.

24. The dedication (ἐγκαινίζεσθαι) of the sanctuary through the sprinkling of blood when the covenant was made (Heb 9:21) was a cleansing (καθαρίζεσθαι, Heb 9:22) and was repeated in the cleansing of the tabernacle on the Day of Atonement (Lev 16:16); consequently, Heb 9:21 and 9:23f. can be included in this idea.

25. See n. 16.

26. Num 19:9, 17; for further details, see Michel, *Hebräer*, 115.

is not surprising. According to Ps 40:6-8 (= Heb 10:5-7) God does not desire the animal sacrifices required by the Mosaic Law. What he wants is loving obedience (Heb 10:8f.). The words of the psalm are boldly interpreted as an expression of Christ's purpose in his incarnation (10:5). In accordance with this word that was written about him "in the scroll" (10:7), Christ rejected the old system of sacrifice in order to do the true will of God (10:9b). The will of God that Christ fulfills is the sanctification of humanity by the obedient offering of his own body (10:10; cf. 4:7f.; 9:14).

According to Hebrews, the priestly and prophetic concepts of sacrifice from the OT are united in Christ's crucifixion. On the one hand, it continues to be true that without the shedding of blood there is no forgiveness—the sinful life can only be redeemed by another life (9:22). On the other hand, true sacrifice, true dedication of life, is not the presentation of the blood of some other living being; it is the dedication of one's own heart (10:5-10).[27]

In his death on the cross Christ has presented the perfect sacrifice. He was able to accomplish once and for all the perfection that none of the sacrifices of the Old Covenant was able to effect (10:11-14; cf. 7:25ff.). This aspect of the picture of Christ as high priest is also in agreement with the prophecy about the New Covenant because this covenant grants forgiveness of sins (10:16f. = Jer 31:33f.). Where there is forgiveness, there is no further need for any sacrifice (Heb 10:18). Accordingly, this group of ideas also flows into the comprehensive idea of the new divine order (10:15-18). The fact that the exposition is summed up in this central idea is another indication that Hebrews has the Mosaic period, the period of the first covenant, in mind as a type.

In the discussion of Christ as high priest, Hebrews is in no way pursuing speculative interests. Everything begins and ends in an urgent exhortation: Christ is the true high priest, he is the mediator and the guarantor of the New Covenant, through him alone can perfection be attained; therefore, leave the old behind and come to the throne of glory to which he has prepared the way and where he is interceding for us (3:1; 4:16; 6:19f.; 10:19-22). This redemption, however, is still hidden, and both external and internal temptations threaten to ruin the church. God's people in the Mosaic period are an example in type that should warn and strengthen the church in this struggle.

The exhortation in 13:10-14 comes immediately after the discussion of Christ as high priest. Christ's offering of himself had been compared with the sacrifice

---

27. Hebrews quotes from Psalm 40, one of the principal passages in the prophetic criticism of sacrifice in the OT. In this connection, see W. Loewenich, "Zum Verständnis des Opfergedankens im Hebräerbrief," *TBl* 12 (1933) cols. 167ff. He finds various approaches intertwined in the expositions in Hebrews: (1) a purely thetic approach, Heb 9:16-22; (2) a critical approach, Heb 10:4; (3) an approach based on typology and redemptive history; this is the one most characteristic of Hebrews; (4) the theory of type and antitype, Heb 3:1ff.; 8:1ff.; 9:1ff.; 9:23ff.; 10:1ff.; (5) the allegorical approach, Heb 7:1-10; 9:8. These appear to us to be partly subdivisions of the typology (as in Heb 1:2) and partly subsidiary (Heb 4:5) to it; the latter, however, not in the sense that they are needed by the typology.

on the great Day of Atonement (9:7, 25). The regulations for that sacrifice do
not give any portion of the bodies of the sacrificial animals to the priests; instead,
those bodies are to be burned outside the camp (13:11; Lev 16:27). Consequently, in order to be the true sin offering that sanctifies the people, Christ had
to suffer "outside the city gate," i.e., outside Jerusalem (Heb 13:12; cf. Matt
21:39 par. Luke; Mark is different). According to that regulation, those who
serve in the order of the Old Covenant have no share in this sacrifice (Heb
13:10).[28] We must "go to him outside the camp," i.e., we must separate ourselves
from Judaism; we must be altogether separate from the natural and legal bonds
of this world (13:14) and bear Christ's disgrace with him (13:13). For Hebrews,
Christ's death also meant the separation of the new church of God from the
people of the Old Covenant and from Judaism. Even if the exposition of individual unessential features that have nothing to do with man's relationship to
God does border on allegory, the whole is still a typology that connects the
realities of redemptive history with one another and indicates how the parenesis
that pervades the chapters that form the framework of the epistle is related to
the presentation of Christ as high priest.

3. GOD'S RULE OVER ISRAEL AS A TYPE THAT WARNS AND STRENGTHENS THE CHURCH

The exposition in Heb 1:4–2:4(9) must be interpreted within the framework of
the typology of the Mosaic period. The detailed proof of Christ's exaltation above
the angels as the Son (υἱός) and God (θεός) and Lord (κύριος) (1:4-14, we do
not know the occasion for this) leads to the exhortation in 2:1-4 (9). Because
(διὰ τοῦτο, 2:1) Christ has been exalted so much more than the angels, contempt for the salvation he has announced will result in a much more sure and
severe punishment than did transgression of the Law, which was only announced
by angels (Acts 7:53; Gal 3:19). This is not a reference to impending judgment
(cf., e.g., Gal 3:10), but to punishment that has already been carried out (Heb
2:2).[29] It is clear that the author has specific instances in mind, particularly the
fate of the Israelites in the wilderness (cf. Heb 3:8ff.), and he uses typology to
draw conclusions from these instances. Perhaps the author has the events of the
wilderness wandering in mind[30] when he emphasizes in 2:4 that God caused
miracles and gifts of the Spirit to accompany the proclamation of Christ's message of salvation.[31] The connection between this exhortation and 1:4ff. is confirmed by the transition that is placed at the end: It is not to the angels, but to
the Son that everything has been subjected, including the future world. Conse-

---

28. On this expression, see Michel, *Hebräer*, 226.
29. The aorist, however, may point as well to the unchangeable nature of the regulation.
30. See Acts 7:36, and possibly Heb 3:10 (Michel, *Hebräer*, on this passage).
31. Cf. also Heb 2:3: ἐβεβαιώθη—Heb 2:2: βέβαιος.

quently, contempt for his word means the certain loss of salvation (2:5-8). This warning and exhortation is necessary because we do not now see One who is exalted above everything, but One who for a little while was made lower than the angels—Jesus, who, as high priest, has become like us (2:8b-18). The broader context is obvious.

Before the nature of this salvation is portrayed in the typology of Christ as high priest, another exhortation is presented that is based on Mosaic period typology.

Moses and Jesus are compared, first, in order to show how the church is related in redemptive history to the people of God of the Mosaic period (3:1-6). The comparison of Moses and Jesus is good typology and is clothed in a subtle exposition of Num 12:7. Moses and Jesus, in faithfulness to God[32] their creator,[33] mediated God's revelation to the house of God, his church (Heb 3:5b; cf. 2:3; 1:1f.). Moses is only a member of the church. Christ, however, is the builder of the house, the creator of the church (3:3), and this includes the OT church as well. Every house is built by someone (3:4a), including the OT church. God, however, is the builder of all (3:4b), and he does this through Christ (1:2). This is the basis for the conclusion that Moses is related to Christ as creature to creator. As each had a different share in the erection of the house, so each has a different rank (3:5f.). Moses is a servant in the house.[34] Christ, however, has been put in charge of the house (here the author is no longer speaking of a building, but of a household); he is the Lord (χύριος) of the church (perhaps of the OT church too) because "we are his house" (3:6).

When Jesus and Moses are compared typologically, it is obvious that Jesus the true high priest was a greater gift to the church than Moses was to the church of the Old Covenant. This brings us to the warning and appeal that is based on the fate of God's people in the wilderness (3:7–4:13) and is presented as a free interpretation of Ps 95:7-11 (= Heb 3:7-11). This interpretation shows no trace of allegorizing, but is evidence of a clear view of Scripture as redemptive history. The fact that Ps 95:7-11 was written about Israel's experience in the wilderness is taken seriously (Heb 4:1-3), and, therefore, the application to the present church is developed typologically.[35]

It is appropriate that he begins by applying the word "today" (Ps 95:7 = Heb 3:7)[36] and the warning against hardening themselves in unbelief to the present time in which the church is being called by God (Heb 3:12-14). The cause of

---

32. Heb 3:2 = Num 12:7; here too the representative of the Old Covenant is portrayed very idealistically, not in accordance with Num 20:12.

33. Heb 3:2 may be an allusion to 1 Sam 12:6: God "appointed Moses and Aaron" (= the high priest).

34. Cf. 1 Cor 4:2; 2 Cor 3:7ff.

35. Ps 95:7f. was spoken by David at a specific time, according to Heb 4:7. It is clear that for Hebrews, Scripture is not merely a timeless inspired oracle.

36. The wording of the passage differs in several respects from the LXX; perhaps it is a free quotation.

Israel's downfall in the rebellion, by which they forfeited salvation, was their unbelief (3:15-19). The church of Christ must be on guard against unbelief because the good news has been proclaimed to them in the same way that it was proclaimed to Israel (4:1-3; cf. v 11b). The typological correspondence is made prominent for the sake of the parenesis, and the heightening is obvious. (We cannot find any better typological exegesis on which to base our proclamation.)

The exegesis of the positive side of the exhortation is culturally conditioned (4:3ff.). If the church perseveres in faith, it will enter the rest that Israel forfeited (4:3; cf. v 1). From Gen 2:2 the conclusion is drawn that God has a true rest (Heb 4:4; cf. vv 9f.), and from Ps 95:11 that Israel has not attained that rest (Heb 4:5). Because it is still possible to enter the promised rest (4:6), God, through David, addresses the word "today" to Christ's church long after those events (4:7). If the conquest of Canaan had brought the promised rest, this exhortation would have been superfluous (4:8-10). In contrast to Acts 7, God's true rest, not the promised land,[37] is considered to be the destination of Israel in the wilderness. There is a sublimation of the OT promise of salvation in Hebrews so that persons from the OT who have hope are placed on a par with the NT church so far as hope is concerned.[38] Because of the typological relationship between the church and Israel, the entire exhortation has been summarized as follows: "Let us, therefore, make every effort to enter that rest, so that no one of us will fall by following their example (ὑπόδειγμα) of disobedience." The reference to Christ as high priest is resumed now in Heb 4:14ff., and together with the jarring interpolation in 5:11ff. it leads directly to the description of Christ's ministry as high priest (7:1-10, 28).

The exhortations with which the epistle concludes are also based largely on the typology of the Mosaic period. The opening statement reminds us of the comparison of Moses with Christ (3:6; cf. Num 12:7): "We have a great high priest over the house of God" (Heb 10:21). Then this warning follows: "Anyone who rejected the Law of Moses died without mercy on the testimony of two or three witnesses (Deut 17:6). How much more severely do you think a man deserves to be punished who has trampled the Son of God underfoot (cf. Acts 7:35), who has treated as an unholy thing the blood of the covenant (cf. Exod 24:8) that sanctified him and who has insulted the Spirit of grace?" (cf. Numbers 12; Heb 10:28f.). This conclusion is also based on the typological relationship between the present time and the Mosaic period (cf. Heb 2:3; 12:25). The author may have been thinking of specific examples of the sin and punishment of Israel in the wilderness that illustrate this statement (see the references in the parentheses). At that time Moses' adversaries were consumed by fire (Num 16:35); therefore, a little earlier in this epistle the opponents of Christ were warned of judgment by fire in a supernatural sense (Heb 10:27 in dependence

---

37. See above on this passage.
38. See below on Hebrews 11.

on Isa 26:11, LXX).[39] God's words of warning at the end of the exhortation are taken from the Song of Moses.[40]

The picture of Israel in the wilderness seems to be in the background again when Prov 3:11f. (= Heb 12:5f.) is quoted to encourage the church to bear suffering and temptation as expressions of fatherly reproof and discipline (Heb 12:4-11). It was said concerning Israel in the wilderness that "as a man disciplines his son, so the Lord your God disciplines you."[41] The only words from this quotation that are used here are "son" (υἱός) and "discipline" (παιδεία).

The church must exert all their strength and hurry directly to the goal so that the weak among them, who otherwise would scarcely be able to keep up, might not perish on the wrong path (Heb 12:12f. in dependence on Isa 35:3; Prov 4:26, LXX). Surely the author was thinking of the people of Israel who were passing through the wilderness on the way to the promised land.[42]

A very effective comparison of the OT revelation with the NT (Heb 12:18-29) forms the conclusion of these sayings that warn the church about the possible loss of salvation. None of the sayings is concerned with individual sins, for all have the sin of apostasy in mind. The theophany of Sinai (described in accordance with Exod 19:16-19; Deut 4:11f.; 5:22f., most likely with the help of the haggadah) occurred on an earthly mountain surrounded by dreadful natural phenomena. Israel turned away in fear from the words of God, which were accompanied by these signs that were indicative of the dreadfulness and unapproachableness of God (Heb 12:18-20). Moses himself trembled at the terrifying sight (12:21). The church of the New Covenant, however, will come to Mount Zion and to the city of God, the heavenly Jerusalem (symbolic images for the place of God's perfect and gracious presence and the place for the gathering of his church),[43] to the joyful assembly of angels and the church of the firstborn, whose names are written in heaven (i.e., the church of God that God has been gathering since the creation),[44] to God who is judge and to the spirits of righteous men made perfect. This is certainly a glorious and inviting picture (12:22f.). All may come to it, because Jesus is the mediator of the New Covenant and his blood covers all sins. He opens the way to all the benefits of the New Covenant (12:24). The text, however, also reminds the church that "If they did not escape when they refused him who warned on earth,[45] how much less will we, if we turn away from him who warns from heaven" (12:25).

---

39. Cf. Heb 12:3 where Num 17:2, 3, LXX is applied to Jesus.
40. Heb 10:30 = Deut 32:35, 36; God's vindication of his people is mentioned also in Ps 135:14.
41. Deut 8:5: ὡς εἴ τις παιδεύσαι ἄνθρωπος τὸν υἱὸν αὐτοῦ.
42. Cf. Heb 13:14, and see above on 1 Peter.
43. See Zahn, *Hebräer*, 413.
44. Ibid., 415; Michel, *Hebräer*, 210.
45. T. Zahn, *Hebräer*, 420; Strathmann, *Hebräer* (NTD III) 128; however, see Michel, *Hebräer*, 213: Moses is not compared with Christ here or in the preceding discussion.

Although this comparison is not typology in the strict sense of the word,[46] it is a powerful and comprehensive expression of the typological relationship between the first time of salvation and the time of fulfillment, between the Old Covenant and the New. The first was earthly and temporal; the latter is heavenly and eternal. The difference between the earthly and the heavenly is not descriptive of some kind of metaphysical relationship, but the theological interrelationship of things in redemptive history. This is indicated by the final statement in the comparison (Heb 12:26-29): At that time the mountain was shaken; at the time of the end, according to Hag 2:6, God will shake not only the earth, but heaven also. In other words, he will transform everything that has been created (ὡς πεποιημένων, Heb 12:26f.; cf. 1:10-12).[47] Therefore, the "heavenly" which remains is not some higher part of creation; it is God's eternal kingdom (12:27f.). Christ is the high priest who is exalted higher than the heavens (4:14).[48]

The exposition in Hebrews 11 completes the description of the relationship between the church of the Old Covenant and the church of the New. The comparison of a cloud of witnesses with the church of Christ seems to have taken the place of the typological relationship. This, however, is merely due to a difference in point of view. Up to this point, the center of attention has been the gifts of redemption and their acceptance or rejection; consequently, the contrast between the old and the new was emphasized.[49] Now, however, faith, which is necessary because of the hiddenness of God's redemptive acts, is being illustrated.

From the very beginning[50] to this present hour, it has been possible to comprehend God's activity only by faith.[51] It is not the content of this faith but its outward expression that is presented here by means of witnesses from the Old Covenant. Faith is always a confidence in God alone. It is confidence in invisible things, especially things in the future, that God has promised and that he calls into existence by his creative power (Heb 11:1f., 19).[52] As can be seen in the lives of the patriarchs, believers confess that they are strangers on this earth (11:9f., 13-15) who are waiting for God's eternal city (11:9f.). They are dying persons who are waiting for life (vv 17-19; cf. vv 13ff.). Because they are

---

46. There is no proper correspondence or prophetic relationship of the one to the other; also cf. "the blood of Abel" instead of the expected "the blood of animals."

47. Accordingly, Sinai is not only a type of the present revelation of redemption but also a type of the end.

48. Cf. Michel (*Hebräer*, 214): "A new eschatological realism forces its way in Hebrews whose connection with Greek thought is obvious, but it has overcome the basic tenets of the Greek world view (the divorce of spirit and flesh, the dualism of an earthly and a heavenly world, and the eternity of the cosmos)."

49. See above on Heb 3:1-6; 12:4-11.

50. Heb 11:3: from creation itself.

51. Hebrews 11 does not contain a survey of redemptive history; it presents a series of specific examples, which are enclosed in parentheses. The author presents his view of redemptive history using concepts from the Old and New Covenants, i.e., in terms of God's revelation. The description of these witnesses to faith is not really exegesis, although it is a profound interpretation of the history recorded in Scripture in relationship to Christ.

52. See above on Romans 4: Abraham's faith.

strangers, they are afflicted by the world in many ways (vv 35-38), but they are not afraid (vv 23, 27). They overcome all opposition and so they obtain salvation (vv 33f.).[53] The church of Christ shares this experience with the witnesses to faith who were called before Christ came (9:15). Consequently, what 13:13 describes as the greatest honor for the Christian[54] can be said of Moses: he bore "disgrace for the sake of Christ" (11:26, in dependence on Ps 89:50f.; cf. Ps 69:9). It is possible to say this about Moses, not because the psychological processes were the same then as now,[55] but because he suffered for his profession of faith in the same God who accomplishes in Christ the salvation that is hidden under the cross.[56]

In keeping with the objective of this exposition, the major emphasis is placed on the things the two ages have in common; nevertheless, the differences that have resulted from the coming of Christ are not overlooked, nor is the fact that these differences require that the two ages be related typologically. That entire band of witnesses to faith, from creation to the time of the Maccabees, is obviously considered to be a fellowship that has been separated from the church by the coming of Christ (οὗτοι—ἡμεῖς, Heb 11:39f.; cf. 3:6; 4:2; etc.). The blessings that accompany that faith are often raised to the level of Christian faith, higher than the original meaning would allow. No attempt has been made to conceal the fact that because they are part of a salvation that had already been experienced and are also shadowy types of the salvation that appeared in Christ, those very blessings are promises that are fulfilled in Christ. The salvation that Noah accomplished for his family by his faith (σωτηρία τοῦ οἴκου) was primarily the deliverance from the flood (11:7; cf. Acts 16:31). It is very clear that when Abraham, who believed in the God who raises the dead, was given back his son, it was a (shadowy) type (παραβολή, see Heb 9:9) of the resurrection of the dead (11:19). We must not stretch these statements in the process of our research; they are much more significant when, in this context, it is not the substance of faith that is being considered, but the nature of faith, and that nature remains the same because it is always directed to the same Lord.

Once again it is evident that there is an eschatological tension in NT typology. Salvation has come in Christ; therefore, the church possesses what the fathers longed for (9:15). This salvation is hidden with Christ and is coming; therefore, the church, together with the fathers, waits for the perfect antitypes to be revealed. (The idea that the churches of the Old and New Covenants stand around Christ on equal footing like two sections of the same choir is based on the second factor, but it overlooks the first, which is decisive for the NT.)

---

53. The references to the church's situation (Heb 10:32ff.; 12:3ff.; 13:33) explain the emphasis placed on these features.

54. Cf. Acts 5:41; Rom 15:3; etc.

55. Moreover, Hebrews found this idea suggested already in Ps 89:50f.

56. Cf. Heb 1:2f.; this was certainly true of redemptive history; see on Heb 3:4; cf. 1 Cor 10:6; 1 Pet 1:10f.

4. CHARACTERISTICS OF THE TYPOLOGY IN HEBREWS; COMPARISON WITH PAUL; TERMINOLOGY

The details of the exposition in Hebrews make it more or less evident that there is a typological background throughout with scarcely any exception. It is significant that Hebrews, the NT book that has the most quotations from the OT, makes the most intensive use of typology.

Hebrews contains the most thorough development of the typological approach to the Mosaic period, especially to the covenant of Sinai and its cultic order. The typological relationship between the covenant of Sinai and the New Covenant, between Moses (Aaron) and Christ, between the Law and the redemptive work of Christ, does not have the character of an antithesis as it does in Paul, but the character of a comparison. When Hebrews looks at the Law contained in the covenant of Sinai it does not see the ethical command primarily, as Paul does, but the cultic order of atonement. The type is not found in the contrast with the old that calls for its abolishment, but in the inadequacy of the old that points to the perfect. In Hebrews the significance of the covenant of Sinai is more similar to what is attributed to it by way of allusion in the words of institution in the Lord's Supper. (The quotation of the Mosaic words of consecration in Heb 9:20 may be a direct allusion to the Lord's Supper.)[57] This difference in comparison with Paul, however, is only a difference in perspective and not a material change in the overall typological relationship. Hebrews too emphasizes that the Law has not made anything perfect, not even in this cultic sense.

Christ is not present in the OT sacrifices. Hebrews does not regard those sacrifices as a temporary substitute for Christ's sacrifice by virtue of their having been commanded as a part of God's redemptive order and certainly not by virtue of what they are in themselves. Only Christ's offering of himself takes away sins, including those that were committed under the Old Covenant (Heb 9:15; cf. 9:9f.; 10:4; etc.). For Hebrews too, Christ would have died in vain if there had been any salvation apart from the historical reality of his death. A type is not the mechanically reduced prototype of something greater; rather, it presents some basic element in the relationship between God and man that was not fulfilled in the Old Covenant, but is fulfilled in Christ.

Hebrews stresses consistently and emphatically, as Paul does, that the new completely abolishes the old; there is no compromise between Christ and the order of salvation on Sinai. For Hebrews, as for Paul, all typology is formed with reference to Christ. There is no systematic exposition of the basic features of the Old Covenant here either; there is a bundle of light rays which issue ultimately from the focal point—Christ and his body—and are reflected back,

---

57. Heb 9:20 = Exod 24:8. Hebrews has: τοῦτο τὸ αἷμα τῆς διαθήκης as in Mark 14:24 par. Matthew; whereas Exod 24:8, LXX, has: ἰδοὺ τὸ αἷμα. . . ; however, see Zahn, *Hebräer*, 276 n. 42.

augmented by the statement that the church "shines in a dark place" (2 Pet 1:19).

Hebrews develops no new terminology for its typology. This indicates that the typology is not viewed as a method of interpretation, but is supplied totally by the content. Terms that are traditional and figurative are used to designate the typological relationship. The Law, i.e., the OT cultic order, has only the shadow (σκιά), the outline without any content. It does not have the completed picture (εἰκών), i.e., the full expression of the thing itself (Heb 10:1).[58] This same terminology is used to describe the relationship between the earthly sanctuary and the heavenly one. The earthly tabernacle is a shadow (σκιά) and copy (ὑπόδειγμα, 8:5; cf. 9:23; ἀντίτυπος, 9:24) of the heavenly prototype (τύπος, 8:5). The other two terms that occur here are also used to express the typology of redemptive history: the church must be careful not to fall by following the example (ὑπόδειγμα) of Israel in the wilderness (4:11; cf. 2 Pet 2:6: contrast John 13:15).[59] The arrangement of the first tabernacle is a παραβολή, a type, pointing to the present perfect tabernacle (Heb 9:9). Abraham received Isaac back as a παραβολή, a type,[60] that points to the future resurrection (Heb 11:19).

We do not find these terms used in an unambiguous or technical sense. Similar terms are found in Philo. The words σκιά, ὑπόδειγμα, ἀντίτυπος/τύπος, and εἰκών are used to depict the relationship between the earthly and heavenly sanctuaries, and this makes it obvious that these terms, like many other expressions in Hebrews, have been borrowed from Alexandrian philosophy. But even in this the contact is minimal. For example, Philo usually uses τύπος, in the technical sense, to designate the more insignificant copy, not to designate the more important prototype, as Hebrews does (Heb 8:5, quoting Exod 25:40).[61]

From the way these terms are applied to the typology of redemptive history, we can discover important clues about the nature of typology that confirm our discussion above. These terms indicate that typology is a comparative relationship and is arranged qualitatively rather than quantitatively. The type is not essentially a miniature version of the antitype, but is a prefiguration in a different stage of redemptive history that indicates the outline or essential features (σκιά, παραβολή—εἰκών) of the future reality and that loses its own significance when that reality appears. Finally, when we consider the way these terms are used to describe the relationship between the sanctuary above and the sanctuary

---

58. Cf. Col 2:17 where the figurative language is even stronger: the cultic law is only the σκιά of the σῶμα, of the real, i.e., of the worship of the church.

59. For ἀντίτυπος, see on 1 Pet 3:21.

60. BAG (2d ed. rev. by F. Gingrich and W. Danker, 1979) 829f., "τύπος."

61. Cf. Philo: After Moses had entered the cloud on Sinai, i.e., "the archetypal essence of existing things" (τὴν . . . τῶν ὄντων παραδειγματικὴν οὐσίον, Vit. Mos. 1.158), among other things he perceived "the shape of the model" (ὁ . . . τύπος τοῦ παραδείγματος) of the construction of the sanctuary (Vit. Mos. 2.76). Cf., however, Holtzmann, Lehrbuch 2. 332f., esp. p. 333 n. 1. The meaning of σκιά corresponds with its use in Philo (see BAG, 755; cf. Michel, Hebräer, 130).

below, we may conclude from Hebrews alone, totally apart from any connection with Alexandrian philosophy, what we have encountered repeatedly from the start: the appearance of the antitype indicates that a new *heavenly* world has already begun in this age.

Chapter Eight

THE GOSPEL OF JOHN

1. THE RELATIONSHIP OF JOHN TO THE OLD TESTAMENT AND THE NATURE OF JOHN'S TYPOLOGY

The question about the use of OT typology in the Gospel of John is part of the larger debate about the general character of this Gospel. Does it belong to the OT world of ideas or to Hellenistic thought?[1] Frequent attempts have been made to find different sources in the Gospel in order to resolve the tension between apparently contradictory statements in it relating to this and other issues.[2] We will have to work with the Gospel in its present form, however, and make our contribution to the discussion of sources in the appropriate places.

The canonical form of the Gospel reveals an attitude toward the OT that largely corresponds with what we have observed in the Synoptic Gospels and the rest of the NT.[3] This attitude presupposes a typological approach. Jesus emphasizes that Scripture testifies about him (John 5:39, 46), and he refers to various details in Scripture to justify his claims (8:17; 10:34) and to interpret the salvation that he has brought (6:45; 7:38; cf. 7:15; 10:35).

His interpretation of Scripture stands in sharp contrast to the interpretation of the Jews. They use Scripture to test Jesus' claims (6:31; 7:42; 12:34) and come to this conclusion: "According to our law he must die" (19:7; cf. 7:42ff.). Their law, however, is the very same Scripture which Jesus says testifies about him.

---

1. For a discussion of the general character of John, see P. Feine, *Theologie des Neuen Testaments* (Leipzig, 7th ed. 1936) 335-56.

2. E. Hirsch, *Studien zum vierten Evangelium* (Tübingen, 1936); cf. P. Feine, *Einleitung in das Neue Testament* (Leipzig, 8th ed. rev. by J. Behm, 1936) 95f. = *Introduction to the New Testament* (trans. from 14th ed. rev. by W. Kümmel [Nashville, 1966] 151f.). On this particular problem, see A. Faure, "Die alttestamentlichen Zitate im 4. Evangelium und die Quellenscheidungshypothese," *ZNW* 21 (1922) 99ff.; F. Smend, "Die Behandlung alttestamentlicher Zitate als Ausgangspunkt der Quellenscheidung im 4. Evangelium," *ZNW* 24 (1925) 147ff.

3. On the question of the OT text used by John, see A. Schlatter, *Der Evangelist Johannes* (Stuttgart, 1931) 59: "It is the Greek text predominantly which determines John's use of Scripture, but the Hebrew text has had some influence, as is true also in Matthew and characterizes both as Palestinian."

There is special emphasis on the fact that Jesus, particularly after his resurrection, opens the eyes of the disciples to understand the Scriptures and to interpret his life in that light. He does not do this through instruction, as in Luke 24, but by the very fact of his being glorified (John 2:17, 22; 12:16; 20:9). This point of view is certainly indicative of the original situation, and it is the reason why John makes a much more explicit appeal to OT passages to prove that the necessity of the Son of Man's being lifted up is revealed in Scripture as God's redemptive decree (3:14; 12:34; 20:9; etc.).[4]

A trend that has been evident from the very beginning reaches its conclusion in John. Jesus' words and the apostolic record about him are becoming "Scripture." The same terminology is applied to them as is used for the witness of the prophets in the OT.[5]

This particular evaluation and use of Scripture that preserves traditional ideas includes a typology that is marked by the character of John's Gospel. John is the spiritual Gospel.[6] The nature of Jesus' person is the central concern that dominates everything else. The details of his life and the events surrounding it are not spiritualized, but are transparent in this one respect: Everything is so comprehended in him that one can speak of the church and its redemptive gifts only in direct relationship to him and, therefore, not in an explicit way. Furthermore, John does not mention the initial stages of salvation nor its hiddenness in the course of history. He describes the glorious fulfillment of salvation that the disciples saw with the open eyes of faith. Jesus is not compared with individual phenomena in OT prophecy or with prophetic types in a colorful variety of historical events,[7] but he is proclaimed as the one who with creative power brings all to fulfillment. This is what ultimately lies behind the witness to Christ in the Synoptics. The basic orientation of this Gospel accounts for the fact that Jesus' work moves exclusively on the level of creation typology. It also explains why the mediators of salvation are not related to Christ as types. Only the redemptive gifts of the Old Covenant that give life and, therefore, announce the

---

4. John 2:17 = Ps 69:9; John 3:14 = Num 21:8f.; (John 12:15 = Isa 40:9; Zech 9:9); John 13:18 = Ps 41:9 (cf. John 17:12); John 15:25 = Ps 35:19; 69:4; John 19:24 = Ps 22:18; John 19:28 = Ps 22:15; John 19:36 = Exod 12:46; Num 9:12; John 19:37 = Zech 12:10; John 20:9 and with greater detail in John 12:38-40: Jesus fulfills the destiny of the Servant of the Lord (Isa 53:1 = John 12:38), and the hardening announced in Isa 6:9f. (= John 12:40) is fulfilled in the Jews. The prophet saw Christ's glory (Isa 6:1ff.; cf. John 12:41), just as Abraham did (John 8:56), and, therefore, there is a common bond between them. The Jews, however, cannot find this redemptive plan in Scripture (John 12:34).

5. John 18:9, 32: "so the words he had spoken would be fulfilled," i.e., Jesus' words (cf. John 2:22); 20:30f.: γέγραπται is used of this Gospel (see Schlatter, *Johannes*, 363); cf. 21:24; cf. also the use of γράφω in the Johannine epistles and Revelation; see G. Schrenk, "γράφω," *TDNT* 1. 745ff.

6. Clement of Alexandria, quoted by Eusebius *Hist. eccl.* 6.14.

7. To be sure, all the titles of honor are heaped on him; cf. John 1:35ff. There is a summary of these in W. Bauer, *Das Johannes Evangelium* (HNT; 2d ed. 1925) 37.

new creation are related to him typologically and they are related to him exclusively. Consequently, types have arisen in two interrelated categories.

Nowhere is the typology developed explicitly as it is in Hebrews or, in a rudimentary way, by Paul. For the most part, the allusions are even more carefully hidden than they are in the Synoptics because of John's original style.[8] Rather than balanced individual typologies, we find continuous indications of a comprehensive typological approach in terms of creation typology. These types, however, frequently shade over into typological symbolism.

2. JESUS, THE PERFECTER OF CREATION

The basic characteristics of the Gospel are visible in the prehistory, the so-called prologue (1:1-18). The introduction to the Gospel reminds any biblically informed reader of the opening verses of the Bible (Gen 1:1-5).[9] The Word (λόγος) through whom "all things were made" is an allusion to the creative word of God which the OT views as the agent in the creation of all things (cf. Ps 33:6). Only of the Word may it be said: it "was in the beginning." Philo's λόγος and the concept of wisdom are very similar to John's idea of the λόγος (John 1:14; 1 John 1:1; Rev 19:13), except that it is possible to say that they were created, or, at least, that "there was a time when they did not exist."[10] Undoubtedly John is alluding to these and similar ideas, but the essence of his concept of the λόγος is developed on the basis of the OT from his knowledge of Christ. This is not speculation; it is proclamation. There is no dualism in John that would place the λόγος between God and the world so that the λόγος would rank somewhat lower than God. He who "speaks the words of God" (John 3:34) bears witness as the eternal Word of God who "became flesh and lived for a while among us" (1:14).

These statements bring us to another kind of typology. The coming of the Word to tent among us signifies the in-breaking of the new age. In the Mosaic period the glory of God came down in the tent (σκηνή, Exod 33:9; Num 12:5) and the OT predicts that this grace will come again in perfection in the new age.[11] Moreover, the coming of God's glory (δόξα, Exod 33:22), together with love (חֶסֶד) and faithfulness (אֱמֶת),[12] was celebrated in the Mosaic period and

---

8. See n. 3.

9. Gen. 1:1: ἐν ἀρχῇ ἐποίησεν ὁ θεός . . .—John 1:1: ἐν ἀρχῇ ἦν ὁ λόγος . . .; also cf. φῶς—σκότος in Gen 1:3f. and John 1:4.

10. Bauer, *Johannes*, 9; Schlatter (*Johannes*, 1) refers to the Jewish idea that the Law was given by God before the creation of the world. There is a thorough comparison in G. Kittel, "λέγω," *TDNT* 4. 131f. (It seems unlikely to us that John would have formulated his thought concerning the Logos in a kind of typological antithesis to rabbinical speculations about the Law; cf. ibid., 134f.)

11. Zech 2:10 (2:14, LXX): ἰδοὺ ἐγὼ ἔρχομαι καὶ κατασκηνώσω ἐν μέσῳ σου. Schlatter (*Johannes*, 23) assumes that John 1:14a is formulated directly from Zechariah. Moreover, the first part of the saying from Zechariah is echoed in John 14:3, and both parts are found in Revelation (22:7 and 7:15; 21:3).

12. Exod 34:6 (δόξα occurs shortly before in Exod 33:22); of course, the LXX has ἔλεος καὶ ἀλήθεια, not χάρις; however, see n. 3.

was expected to reoccur in the last days.[13] In Jesus these things are now visible to all who are able to see (John 1:14).[14]

Any reader familiar with the typological approach will find the prologue announcing that the new age has begun; God's glory has appeared, full of grace and truth; God's mighty creative Word, who makes persons children of God and creates new life, lives among us (1:12f.). The combination that Deutero-Isaiah had already seen (Isa 41:17ff.; 43:14-21; 49:9-13)[15]—the second, perfect deliverance and the new creation—is now here (cf. John 6:34 with Isa 49:10; Rev 1:7). This combination is characteristic of the typology in John (it confirms our interpretation which has been supported solely by a few similarities). In Jesus the redemptive gifts of the former salvation time come in perfected form, and this signifies that the first creation is being perfected in a new one.

We will begin our discussion with the second consideration, for it includes and defines the first. It is prominent in Jesus' conversation with Nicodemus (John 3:1-21), and, significantly, it includes the other idea as well. The new birth (or, birth from above, ἄνωθεν γεννηθῆναι) that Jesus requires, promises, and offers is not "an idea that has grown up on the soil of syncretism."[16] It must be interpreted on the basis of creation typology (and so must ἐκ θεοῦ γεννηθῆναι, 1:13). Very likely the promise in Ezek 36:25-27 is behind the summary of Jesus' demand in John 3:5. In the new age the people will be cleansed by the sprinkling of water and will be created anew inwardly by the Spirit.[17] The truth that is presented in 3:6 (also in Johannine formulation) to explain this demand is one that is common in the OT and in Judaism.[18] Nicodemus is reproved because any teacher in Israel (a teacher of the redeemed people)[19] should certainly know this (3:10, 7; cf. Eccl 11:5 with John 3:8).

The background of this passage is the OT promise of the new creation. Therefore, the new birth should not be interpreted as another natural birth, as in the mystery religions, but it must be understood in a typological sense as a renewing of creation. This assumption is substantiated in a remarkable way by the rabbinic idea of new birth: "When someone brings a creature (i.e., a man [who prior to this is simply a creature]) under the wing of the Shekinah (i.e., wins him to Judaism according to Cant. r., 1 on 1:1), then it is counted to him (i.e., by God) as though he had created (Gen 1:1, 27) and fashioned (cf. Gen 2:7; Ps 139:6) and formed (cf. Ps 139:15) him."[20] Only by conversion to Judaism does the creature become a man because the Law alone makes it possible for

---

13. Isa 35:2; 66:18: ὄψονται τὴν δόξαν.

14. See the comparison of Jesus with Moses in John 1:17.

15. See above, p. 39.

16. Bauer, *Johannes*, 48: When he uses γεννᾶν, John is thinking of an "act which causes human beings to share the divine nature through fertilization with heavenly semen."

17. John 6:45 is an allusion to the prophecy in Jer 31:33f., which is parallel in subject matter.

18. Cf. Ps 51:7 and 12, which is in close agreement with Ezekiel 36.

19. See below.

20. *Cant. Rab.* on 1:3, quoted by K. Rengstorf, "γεννάω," *TDNT* 1. 666.

him to live a life that is suitable for man who is the image of God. Therefore, a proselyte is considered to be like a newborn child.[21] This is a concept of new birth that is far different from the mystery religions and that has the characteristics of creation typology. Therefore, from the Jewish point of view, Jesus' demand that Nicodemus the Pharisee be born again could be compared only with John the Baptist's offering to the children of Abraham (Matt 3:9) the cleansing bath which, up to that time, was known only as proselyte baptism.[22] The simplest explanation is that in both instances the concept has been transformed through the influence of OT prophecy, especially Ezekiel 36.[23] This also explains why John's Gospel emphasizes the connection between the water baptism of John the Baptist and the announcement that the new creation through the Spirit is imminent (cf. John 1:26, 31, 33).

There are obvious relationships to the history of religions here. They confirm our assumption that, as in the case of John 1:13, we should not compare this with ideas from the mystery religions, but with the promised new creation that comes by means of the mighty, creative word of God, the word that is now present in Christ. To be born again means nothing other than to become a child of God (1:13), not to be condemned (3:18), and not to perish (3:16), but to have eternal life (3:15). In order for this to happen (3:9), "the Son of Man must be lifted up, . . . just as Moses lifted up the snake in the wilderness" (3:14). Only because he fulfills God's redemptive history does Jesus become the one who creates everything new. For John too he does this by his cross and resurrection.[24] When Christ's being lifted up to the Father by the cross is compared with the snake's being set up on a pole in the wilderness, the significant thing is that in each instance a symbol of redemption was set up so that it could be seen by everyone and could help everyone (cf. 12:20-23). The reference is too brief to indicate whether or not John finds anything more here than a parallel or a prophetic type.[25] Later in *Barn.* 12:5-7 the raising up of the snake on a pole is seen as a type predicting that it would be necessary for Christ to be lifted up on the cross. This cannot be the correct interpretation in John where the word "lifted up" (ὑψωθῆναι) has such a profound double meaning. It would be completely out of keeping with the rest of typology in John; nevertheless, it is appropriate to compare these two redemptive symbols.

What is recorded at the end of the Gospel (20:22) confirms our classifying the new birth as a new creation (ἀνῶθεν γεννηθῆναι) with the ideas of creation typology and justifies our associating it with the lifting up of Christ. By breathing into the lifeless lump of clay, God made it a living being (the same word is used, ἐνεφύσησεν, Gen 2:7). In this same way, the one who was lifted up by the

---

21. Ibid.

22. A. Oepke, "βάπτω," *TDNT* 1. 537.

23. Ibid.

24. See above, p. 135; on ὑψωθῆναι see p. 91 n. 137.

25. καθώς is used for evidence from past redemptive history, John 6:58; 1:23.

cross and resurrection breathes on his disciples and, by this efficacious sign, he imparts to them the life-giving Spirit.[26] Only the glorified one is able to bestow this Spirit (John 7:39; 16:7). What Jesus had proclaimed in word and sign[27] becomes a reality when he gives them the Spirit. Through the Spirit of the exalted one they are given a new relationship with God,[28] and with that new relationship they are given eternal life (cf. 6:63). As persons who have been brought into a vital relationship with God and Christ, the disciples can lead others to life also. Through them (17:18) Jesus completes his mission to bring life into the world (1:4; 3:15f.; 17:2; 1 John 1:1). The allusion is unmistakable, and it clearly indicates that although the word "life" is fully compatible with Hellenistic concepts, it conveys the idea of the new creation in this context. Of course, the incarnate and glorified Christ, who brings about the new creation, is not God's antitype; he is his λόγος. His task is not merely the improvement of the world. He is to fulfill the first creation by its renewal (i.e., the typological renewal of creation). Something really new is breaking into this world. This is clear because it is separated from this world by Jesus' death and it comes in fulfillment of the redemptive gifts of the OT that come from the milieu of an old world and point to this salvation.

---

26. Cf. Ezek 37:5f., 14; Isa 44:3f.

27. In general, the seven miracles of Jesus that John records (2:1-11; 4:43-54; 5:1-9; 6:1-13; 6:14-21; 9:1-7; 11:1-44) are free of any secondary purpose and are signs (σημεία) of the fact that Jesus is the one who renews life (John 11:25f.), i.e., the perfecter of creation (this is true already in the miracles in the Synoptics; see J. Schniewind, *Das Evangelium nach Markus* and *Das Evangelium nach Matthäus* [NTD I; Göttingen, 3d ed. 1937] 312). The miracle at Cana is one of these. Like all miracles in John it has a deeper symbolical meaning. This, however, is not achieved by allegorizing (Bauer, *Johannes*, on the passage) any more than in the other passages in John, but is derived from the literal meaning. Schlatter (*Johannes*, 65) says that Jesus by this action wants to demonstrate that "that which has been offered to the world is fulfilled by him." (The idea that the dating in John 2:1 locates this act on the seventh day after the beginning of Jesus' ministry [John 1:29, 35, 43, + 3], the day when creation was complete, is too artificial.) J. Jeremias (*Jesus als Weltvollender* [Gütersloh, 1930] 29) states that John 2:11 is saying, "The disciples understand what Jesus wants to say to them by this, when he changes water to wine and, as his first sign, he brings them the fruit of the new age (cf. *Did.* 9:2). The miracle at Cana is the first revelation of Jesus' greatness as the renewer of the world (δόξα) in the figurative language of the Bible" (cf. John 3:29f.; 15:1ff.).

A few allusions in the miracle stories show that the typological comparison of Jesus' miracles with those of the OT has meanwhile been further developed: John 6:9 differs from the Synoptics in reading ἄρτους κριθίνους, probably from 2 Kgs 4:42 (cf. John 6:14f. and Luke 7:16; in this case it is likely Moses and not Elijah who is meant); John 9:7 is clearly alluding to 2 Kgs 5:10. It is not likely that in the prayer of Jesus that precedes the raising of Lazarus (John 11:41f.) John was thinking of Elijah in 1 Kgs 18:36f.; nevertheless, the comparison is instructive.

John does not appear to place any special value on these relationships. All that issues from them is what the people are professing: This one is *the* prophet. The disciples know more; they know that he is the perfecter of creation who is godlike in essence. They experienced this also when he walked on the water: Jesus comes to them, stepping across the waves, and the boat is brought to land (John 6:21). Both elements, especially the latter, which is characteristic of John, are attributed to God in Ps 107:28-30.

28. The expression "forgiveness of sins," which occurs this one time in John, is in complete accord with the meaning of John 1:12; 3:17f.

3. JESUS, GOD'S PERFECT GIFT

a. Jesus Fulfills the Gifts of the First Age of Salvation

In connection with John's prologue, we already touched on the idea that in Jesus the redemptive gifts of the Mosaic period have come in their perfect form. In him God's glory, grace, and truth—God's very Word—lives for a while among men.[29]

In the discourse that follows the sign (σημεῖον, John 6:26) of the miraculous feeding in 6:1-13, the people are reminded of the manna.[30] If Jesus wants them to believe, let him give them bread from heaven[31] (vv 30f.). Jesus replied that the manna was not the true bread from heaven (v 32), nor was it the bread of life, because those who ate it still died (v 49). It is nothing more than an allusion to the true bread from heaven that gives eternal life (v 33). The redemptive gifts are being compared, not the givers—Moses and Jesus. "I am the bread of life" that has come down from heaven (vv 35, 41, 48, 50f.). This, however, is what he becomes later by the Spirit through the cross and resurrection[32] (vv 51ff., 63). Moreover, the inclusion of this sign and this discourse between references to the Passover and to the meal of the New Covenant[33] (vv 4, 53ff.) shows that the author is not simply using certain figurative expressions; he has the typology of the Mosaic period in mind.

It is not certain what the connection is in the sayings about the water of life (7:37f.; cf. John 4). Jesus associates 7:37f. with the customary ritual at the Feast of Tabernacles. "Every celebration of the Feast of Tabernacles, every time the ceremonial water is poured out at that feast, is a prophecy of the stream of blessing that the sacred rock will pour out over the earth in the new age."[34] The background for all these ideas is the memory of the rock in the wilderness from which Moses made water gush forth to the people. This miracle from the Mosaic period was expected to reoccur in the new age.[35] When, in response to what Jesus says, some of the crowd call him the prophet (Deut 18:15; John 7:40), "this can only mean that they see Jesus' proclamation as the fulfillment of the promised messianic Horeb-miracle."[36] This is true whether John 7:38 (αὐτοῦ) is applied to the believer[37] or is considered as a quotation (perhaps from an

---

29. Cf. above on John 1:14, 17.
30. Schlatter, *Johannes*, 174.
31. John 6:31; cf. Neh 9:15a; Pss 78:24; 105:40.
32. See Schlatter, *Johannes*, on John 6:63.
33. See below, pp. 190f.; cf. John 6:45 = Isa 54:13; cf. Jer 31:33f.
34. Jeremias, *Weltvollender*, 48.
35. See above, p. 39; cf. Jeremias, *Weltvollender*, 50.
36. Ibid., 50; however, cf. Bauer, *Johannes*, 30 on John 1:21.
37. Schlatter, *Johannes*, 200f.; Schlatter also says, "Very likely John was thinking of the Scripture that tells of the giving of water through Moses. Christ brings again in a more glorious manner what Moses once gave the people. Now the thirsty are effectively and fully satisfied." (Since Isaiah's invitation to the thirsty was clearly engraved nearby, Isa 44:3 could have had an influence, as well as the idea of a stream flowing from the temple in Ezek 47:1; Zech 14:8.) Schlatter's view is

apocryphal passage) and applied to Christ.[38] In either case, Christ is, once again, not being compared with Moses, but with the water of life, or the rock from which that water flows (cf. 1 Cor 10:4).[39] In the first instance it refers to the continuation of the work of Christ through his own people in accordance with John 20:22.[40] It is unlikely that there is any direct reference to the Mosaic period here.[41] Undoubtedly, the basis is Mosaic period typology, but it seems to have shaded over into typological symbolism.

The concepts of the living water and the sacred rock are not confined to Mosaic period typology, but involve relationships with patriarchal history as well (1:51; 4:4-30). The saying in 1:51 seems to have been developed from Gen 28:12 (it is strange that the word "ascending" [ἀνέβαινον] occurs first in both instances). What appeared once to Jacob in a dream will occur regularly in the experience of the Son of Man. Here again, Jesus is not being compared with Jacob, but with the place where the ladder stood. Jacob said, "How awesome is this place! This is none other than the house of God; this is the gate of heaven" (Gen 28:17; cf. v 16). The similarity to the ideas in John 7:37f. is even greater if the contemporary interpretation can be accepted. In that interpretation, the stone on which Jacob lay his head (Gen 28:11, 18) was the place of ascending and descending, and that stone is identified with the sacred rock in the sanctuary in Jerusalem as the gate of heaven and the place where God is present.[42] It is likely that Jesus is being compared also with the sacred rock where God was present in glory and saving power in the crucial periods of Israel's history—the patriarchal age and the Mosaic period.

There is a more obvious connection with Jacob in the discourse about the water of life (John 4:4-30). The close parallels between the principal statements in this chapter and those in chap. 6 clearly indicate that John intends to make a comparison here similar to the one in that chapter: compare 4:14 with 6:27 and 4:15 with 6:34 and 6:35; both chapters are reminiscent of Isa 49:10 (cf. John 4:14a with Rev 7:16). Just as in chap. 6, it is the physical setting (4:5) which is the basis of the comparison. "It is no accident that Jesus rested at Jacob's well rather than by Jacob's grave which was nearby. Jesus did not lead his disciples to the graves of the patriarchs and prophets (Matt 23:24)."[43] He

---

supported by the fact that this saying made the same impression on the people (John 7:40f.) as did the miraculous feeding in the wilderness (John 6:14f.).

38. Bauer, *Johannes*, 108f.; Jeremias, *Weltvollender*, 48.

39. J. Jeremias ("Golgotha und der heilige Felsen," *Angelos* 2. 124; cf. pp. 120ff. on John 7:37f.) states, "The comparison with the sacred rock is carried out feature by feature, the one, by virtue of the dole of water offered at the Feast of Tabernacles, gives water to the whole world, and in the messianic age the other will fulfill the promise of obtaining water from the springs of salvation and will dispense the water of life, the Holy Spirit. 'I am the sacred rock that dispenses the water of life'—this is the content of John 7:37f." Cf. Jeremias, *Weltvollender*, 49.

40. See above on this passage.

41. See n. 37.

42. Jeremias, *Weltvollender*, 51; idem, "Golgotha," 93.

43. Schlatter, *Johannes*, 116.

does not propose to venerate the dead but to carry on their work. The earthly and religious life of the Samaritans was founded on what their "father Jacob had given them."[44] The field he had acquired gave them title to the land (John 4:5). The water from his well is the source of their life. They expect God to give them the earthly goods needed to sustain their lives for the sake of their father Jacob. Jacob's well is merely a symbol of their religion. (Of course, this adherence to the type as if it were the final reality is also characteristic of Jewish religion.) Therefore, Jesus is not referring to any particular OT passage, but to a tradition, and a Samaritan one at that (cf. 4:22), when he offers the woman living water (4:10) that, like a continually flowing spring, satisfies all thirst forever (4:13f.; cf. Hebrews). The woman asks in astonishment, "Are you greater than our father Jacob?" (4:12).[45] Jesus' answer is intended to help the woman understand that drinking living water and believing in Jesus are the same thing. He is not merely the one who gives the water; he is the water. The allusions in 4:14 to OT prophecies about living water indicate, once again, that everything is conceived in the framework of this typological symbolism.[46] Perhaps the author overlooked the difference between biblical narrative and imaginative tradition and saw a true typology here that is carried by type and prophecy the same as in John 6. In any case, this dialogue has to be presented as another example of John's comprehensive typological view.

Whenever John compares the new age that has come in Christ with the crucial periods of the past, it is characteristic that he compares the redemptive gift only with Christ, and not the human mediators of redemption, and that this gift is always *life*, i.e., the new creation.[47] This is why the question answered itself when this outsider asked—"Are you greater than our father Jacob?" (4:12).[48] Jesus, who is the life, stands far above those who have only been given a shadow of that life.

This is the way John describes the relationship between Christ and John the Baptist, the last man of God before Christ's coming, a relationship that has been thoroughly discussed by others[49] (cf. 1:6-8, 15, 19-27, 30; 3:25-32; 4:1). Christ is the light; John, like all who preceded him, "came only as a witness to the light" (1:6-8). John is a man who was born in history; Jesus is God's incarnate and eternal Logos.[50]

The allusion to Jesus' preexistence is discussed when he is compared with Abraham. This comparison is a response to an objection the Jews raised that is

---

44. Ibid., 122; H. Odeberg, "Ἰακώβ," *TDNT* 3. 191.

45. On μείζων cf. Matt 11:11.

46. Cf. John 4:14a with Isa 49:10 and 55:1; John 4:14b with Isa 58:11: καὶ ὡς πηγὴ ἦν μὴ ἐξέλιπεν ὕδωρ; see above, p. 39 and n. 37.

47. "Jesus' promise is always the same: being born anew, drinking living water, eating the heavenly bread, are all the same promise" (Schlatter, *Johannes*, 173).

48. Analogous to John 8:53; cf. 6:31f.; 7:40f.

49. Cf. A. Schlatter, *Die Theologie der Apostel* (Stuttgart, 1922) 151.

50. Cf. John 1:1: ἐν ἀρχῇ ἦν ὁ λόγος with 1:6: ἐγένετο ἄνθρωπος; cf. also 1:15, 30.

similar to the question asked by the Samaritan woman (4:12). The Jews object, "Are you greater than our father Abraham? He died and so did the prophets. Who do you think you are?" (8:53). Jesus insists that Abraham, like Moses (5:45f.), was on his side, not on the side of the Jews. Abraham was glad that he could see the day of Christ (the very same person whom the Jews are rejecting, 8:37ff.)—either he saw Christ in the prophetic word he was given (cf. 12:41) or else Abraham was now present (8:56). The statement that Abraham had in some way seen Jesus is so incomprehensible to the Jews that they quite naturally turned it around: Does Jesus claim to have seen Abraham (8:57)? There is no speculation in the answer; to faith it is certain that Jesus, the incarnate Word, existed "before Abraham was born." Christ stands above Abraham in the same way that God, the eternal creator, stands above the creature.

The consideration of Christ's relationship to Moses leads us to the second category of types. As giver of salvation (cf. 6:32; [7:22]; 3:14) and witness to salvation (5:45f.), Jesus is considered to be like Moses. Nevertheless, as giver of the Law, Moses has no counterpart in Jesus. John 1:17 is comparing what is historically parallel but is antithetical in content: the Law was given through Moses; grace and truth were given through Jesus Christ. The Law is revered as having been instituted by God, but the Jews' appeal to Moses and the Law (9:28f.; cf. 19:7) is invalid. The Jews' claim that they are Moses' disciples, like their claim to be Abraham's descendants (8:39-44), is viewed as being nullified by their rejection of Jesus (7:19b). The relationship of a person to Christ is the measure of his relationship to God and to all that comes from God. It is also clear that through the grace of Christ his disciples have been introduced to the true worship of God, which breaks through the institutions and regulations of the Mosaic Law and is the reason why that Law is consistently called "your law," i.e., the Jews' law.[51] The details will become clear now when we see how John portrays Jesus as the fulfillment of the institutions of the Old Covenant.

b. Jesus Fulfills the Institutions of the Old Covenant

Schlatter has pointed out that the Gospel of John gives a detailed description of the way in which the institutions of the OT are renewed by Christ. He affirms that "the sacrifices are the first part of Jewish ritual that the Gospel of John says must be renewed and are renewed through Jesus. . . . After the sacrifices come the temple (2:19; 4:21), the Sabbath (5:17), Scripture (5:39, 47), the sacred Passover meal (6:4), the holy church (10:1), and the divine command (13:34)."[52] What he says is generally correct, although we may not be able to follow him in every detail. John does not present this material because he has any special interest in these institutions, but in order to show the glory and importance of Christ. At any rate, it dovetails with the other characteristic of the Gospel that we have already considered.

---

51. Schlatter, *Johannes*, 207.
52. Ibid., 48f.; cf. p. 289.

John the Baptist's testimony about Jesus is summarized by John in the statement: "The Lamb of God who takes away the sin of the world" (1:29; cf. v 36). This idea is "undoubtedly" derived from the OT.[53] There are three ways this could be done.

(1) It may be derived from the sin offerings in general, or, as Schlatter supposes, it may be derived from the two lambs that were offered daily in the temple and were the most important part of the ritual of sacrifice (Num 28:3f.).[54]

(2) In Isa 53:7 the Servant of the Lord, who suffers patiently, is compared to a lamb. This comparison is specifically applied to Christ in Acts 8:32 (= Isa 53:7; cf. 1 Pet 1:19f.; 2:22-25). No comparison is being made here, however, and it is hardly a metaphor. What we have is a very clear statement about the lamb of God.[55]

(3) In 1 Cor 5:7 Jesus is compared explicitly with the Passover lamb. (This connection is not ruled out by the fact that kids were also acceptable.)[56] This comparison is also common in John.[57]

None of these three possibilities provides a satisfactory explanation for the "highly singular genitive combination"—the lamb of God (ὁ ἀμνὸς τοῦ θεοῦ).[58] A good solution is proposed by Jeremias, who suggests that this phrase is based on "the Aramaic טַלְיָא דֶּאֱלָהָא in the sense of עֶבֶד יְהֹוָה," since in Aramaic טַלְיָא has a double meaning: (a) lamb and (b) boy or servant.[59] "In terms of Isa 53 the Baptist was calling Jesus the Servant of the Lord who takes away the sin of the world (cf. Isa 53:12), and thus thinking[60] of the substitutionary suffering of the penalty of sin by the Servant of God."[61]

Not only is the meaning of טַלְיָא changed when translated into Greek, but so is the meaning of the word that is behind αἴρειν. John usually understands αἴρειν as "take up" in order to carry something away (John 2:16; 11:39), and then, simply, as "take away" (10:18; 11:48; 15:2; 19:31). The use of αἴρειν in 1 John 3:5 also encourages us to interpret our passage in this way.[62] In Isaiah 53 it is affirmed that the Servant of the Lord "took to himself" the sins of many.[63] The effect of αἴρειν is the same in both cases—it is "the setting aside" of another person's sin and guilt—but the way in which this is done is different.

Consequently, it is not Isaiah 53 that John has in mind; he is thinking either

53. Bauer, *Johannes*, 33.

54. Schlatter, *Johannes*, 46ff.

55. Advocated in H. Cremer, *Biblico-Theological Lexicon of New Testament Greek* (Edinburgh, 1872) 78, 79.

56. Schlatter, *Johannes*, 47; J. Jeremias, "ἀμνός," *TDNT* 1. 339.

57. See below; advocated, e.g., by Bauer, *Johannes*, 33.

58. Jeremias, "ἀμνός," *TDNT* 1. 339.

59. Ibid.

60. Jeremias, "αἴρω," *TDNT* 1. 186.

61. Idem, "ἀμνός," *TDNT* 1. 339.

62. Bauer, *Johannes*, 33.

63. Isa 53:4, 12: נָשָׂא = LXX φερεῖν; 11: סָבַל = LXX ἀναφερεῖν. For αἴρω in this sense see Jeremias, "αἴρω," *TDNT* 1. 185.

of the lamb of the daily sacrifice or of the Passover lamb. The daily sacrifice had been discontinued long before John wrote, and John's church was not acquainted with it from personal experience. John and his readers were familiar, however, with the idea of comparing Jesus with the Passover lamb. And so, without being able to attribute any unambiguous idea to this traditional formula, one must think of the Passover lamb (cf. Exod 12:7, 13, 22, 27; Heb 11:28a; 1 Pet 1:19) which delivers from death and destruction by the atoning power of his death (and in this way brings in the new age).[64]

The statements in John about the day and the hour of Jesus' death that differ from the Synoptic tradition are another indication that John viewed Christ as the true Passover Lamb. According to the Synoptics Jesus celebrated with his disciples on the evening of the Passover.[65] According to John, however, he died on that day at the hour specified by the Law for the slaughtering of the Passover lamb (John 18:28; 19:14, 31).[66] The great emphasis John places on the particular moment proves that he had this relationship in mind even if this was actually the time of Jesus' death and John has not altered the Synoptic tradition to enhance the typology.

This assumption is confirmed by 19:33, 36. The fact that Jesus' legs were not broken (19:32f.) is seen by John as the fulfillment of the Scripture that says, "Not one of his bones will be broken" (ὀστοῦν οὐ συντριβήσεται αὐτοῦ, 19:36). It is not likely that he is thinking of the passage about the redeemed righteous ones in Ps 34:20, where there are significant differences in wording. It says that he protects "all their bones, not one of them will be broken" (LXX [33:21]: πάντα τὰ ὀστᾶ αὐτῶν, ἓν ἐξ αὐτῶν οὐ συντριβήσεται). What John has in mind is the regulations concerning the Passover lamb in Exod 12:46 (Num 9:12) where it is commanded, "Do not break any of the bones" (ὀστοῦν οὐ συντρίψετε [συντρίψεται A] ἀπ᾽ αὐτοῦ). By this he does not intend to say that the slain body of Jesus was granted divine protection in accordance with the promise,[67] but that "Christ, our Passover lamb, has been sacrificed" (1 Cor 5:7).

Moreover, John has retained the same connection between the Lord's Supper and the Passover that we have already observed in the Synoptics. John, however, is the only one who indicates that the miraculous feeding took place on the Passover. No particular time is specified in the Synoptic parallels. To the story of the miraculous feeding, the discourse about the bread of life (John 6:25ff.) is added as the sign (σημεῖον). According to 6:29, 35 the bread of life is appropriated by faith, but there is also a literal eating and drinking according to 6:52-58. These verses point unmistakably to the Lord's Supper. Here Christ, the incarnate and glorified one, gives himself to his own as the bread of life. The

---

64. Jeremias, "ἀμνός," *TDNT* 1. 340.
65. See above.
66. Bauer, *Johannes*, 209.
67. As Schlatter, *Johannes*, 354.

time designated in 6:4 indicates that John viewed the Lord's Supper as the antitype of the Passover, and, for any reader who is familiar with this idea, it indicates that John is disclosing his interpretation of the Lord's Supper. The suggestion that he would have compared the elements of the Lord's Supper with the Passover lamb must not be brought in here from our consideration of the manna and the water of life. And yet, we should point out that by associating the reference to the feeding with manna, the prototype of the messianic banquet, John implies a connection between the messianic meal of deliverance and the messianic banquet. When the new Passover meal is described as a distribution of the bread of life, it is placed on the level of the new creation.

We have already observed that Jesus' attitude toward the temple in John is the logical development of statements in the Synoptics. In the account of the cleansing of the temple (2:13-22) the parallels to the actions of the prophets are suppressed (the allusion to Isa 56:7 and Jer 7:11 has disappeared from John 2:16; cf. Mark 11:17). The action is made a distinctive work of Christ. The fulfillment citation (John 2:17 = Ps 69:9) is from a psalm about the righteous sufferer that had been interpreted messianically. The citation views the cleansing of the temple as a work appropriate for the Messiah who is on his way to the cross. It also shows that the destiny of the temple is bound to the destiny of Christ. The same thing is indicated by the conflict that follows (John 2:19-22). When questioned about his authority, Jesus answers with a saying that is similar to Synoptic tradition (Mark 14:58 par. Matthew; 15:29 par. Matthew): "Destroy this temple, and I will raise it again in three days" (John 2:19). The evangelist understands the saying to be referring to Jesus' body as the temple (2:21f.). The raising of Christ is the sign (σημεῖον; cf. Matt 12:38ff.) that shows Jesus' right to perform this action (which proclaims the messianic renewal of the temple). When the resurrected one himself is designated as the newly erected temple, these words carry the additional implication that the death of Jesus signifies the end of the temple. It is the Jews themselves who will cause its downfall. The place of the temple will be taken by the resurrected one who "brings God's dynamic presence and forgiveness to the church."[68] As the incarnate one, he already is God's sanctuary in which God's Word "lives for a while" among God's people (John 1:14) and to which God's glory comes.[69]

What is implied in this passage is clearly stated in 4:21, 23: "A time is coming when you will worship the Father neither on this mountain nor in Jerusalem." "A time is coming and has now come (for all who profess 1:14) when the true worshipers will worship the Father in spirit and truth." As the woman says (4:25), it was expected that the Messiah would resolve the debate about the temple. When Jesus professes to be the Messiah (4:26), he is indicating that his proclamation is not merely the conjecture of a scribe nor the prediction of a

---

68. Ibid., 79.
69. See above on John 1:14.

prophet. It is a present reality that he himself has brought about. Jesus produces the true worship for which the prophets were striving in all their criticism of temple ritual. Once again it is in keeping with the general outlook of John when Jesus sets this new worship completely free from Jerusalem and in so doing goes beyond the universalism of prophecies like Isa 2:4 and Jer 3:17.[70]

It is no longer the course of redemptive history in this world that is the concern of Jesus' work, but the fulfillment of redemptive history in the new creation. This is made very clear once again by Jesus' breach of the Sabbath. In John too, this action represents Jesus' attitude toward the Law (John 7:19-24). There are two accounts of Jesus' healing on the Sabbath, and they are so structured that they become public violations of the Sabbath command (5:8-10; 9:6f., 14, 16).[71] Jesus justifies this breach of the Sabbath by declaring that his work is identical with God's work (5:17); his healing is a sign (σημεῖον) of God's eschatological work that is being fulfilled by him. It is the giving of life (= creating anew) and judging (5:21f.). The new creation abolishes both the Sabbath and the Law. This is implied even in the regulations of the Law itself, as is further explained in 7:21ff. Circumcision was commanded by Moses and was performed even on the Sabbath, which was protected by the same Mosaic Law (7:22f.). If the Sabbath is nullified by this insignificant ritual, how much more is it nullified by the great thing Jesus did—the healing of an entire person (in the fullest sense of the word). The Law is not broken by Jesus' action any more than it is by the performance of circumcision.[72] On the contrary, it is fulfilled in keeping with its intended purpose through the coming of that which is perfect, the new creation, and this belongs completely to God because when the new creation comes, the judgment is past (5:24, etc.).

None of these institutions from past redemptive history are replaced by better ones. All are replaced by the one new institution, Christ, and by the new creation that is found in him. This is no Platonic idea; it is a divine reality that is breaking into history. Jesus is proclaiming this reality in word and sign and, as the exalted one, he brings it to pass. Consequently, more than any other NT writing, John bridges the gap between the coming again of the resurrected one that is perceived by faith and the coming that will be visible to all.

The new command (καινὴ ἐντολή, 13:34; cf. 1 John 2:7f.) that Jesus gives his disciples is not a new law. It is the expression of the relationship that is

---

70. Here it should be noted that, according to John 19:23, Jesus wore a χιτὼν ἄρραφος. The robe of the high priest is described as "unsewn" by Josephus (*Ant.* 3.7.4 §161; quoted by Bauer, *Johannes*, on this passage). But John is not thinking here of comparing Jesus with the high priest, but of Ps 22:18 (John 19:24). The same thing applies to the relationship to Joseph's coat (Gen 37:3, 23; cf. *Angelos* 4. 55).

71. "If he had healed by his word alone, it could remain questionable whether any work had been done. The making of mud, however, in the jurisprudence of the Pharisees was clearly a work that profaned the Sabbath" (Schlatter, *Johannes*, 225).

72. Cf. John 7:23: ἵνα μὴ λυθῇ ὁ νόμος with 10:35: οὐ δύναται λυθῆναι ἡ γραφή.

possible only in the new creation (καινὴ κτίσις).[73] This relationship unites God, Christ, and Christ's disciples in a living fellowship (cf. John 13:34; 14:21, 23; 15:10; 17:11, 21ff.). What is spelled out here in John was already implicit in the Sermon on the Mount in the commands that burst the order and the possibilities of this world. John also mentions "commands" in the plural (ἐντολαί, 14:15, 21; 15:10). These are nothing more than "the radiating of the one ἐντολή out into the manifoldness of the obedient life."[74] There is nothing that resembles coercion here in ἐντολή, as can be clearly seen when the concept is applied to the relationship between the Father and the Son (15:10; cf. 17:21). Because this is not a mystical-physical fellowship, it is brought into being by the Word. Here again, the new is so high above the old that no direct comparison can be made.[75]

The new command presupposes God's perfect church and God's Christ. The calling and nature of the church are described in John with the traditional metaphors of the flock (chap. 10; 21:15ff.), the field (the vine, 15:1-17; cf. 4:35ff.), and the bride (3:29f.; cf. 2:1-11).[76] No direct comparison with the OT people of God is perceptible (10:8, 10 is referring to the present Jewish leaders). The old figurative titles lose their pregnant coloring when they are used in extensive parables that are not derived from the OT. The calling of the Twelve is dealt with very briefly (6:67, 70f.; 20:24). John uses the name Israel as a religious stereotype to designate the people of God who are waiting for the Christ and whom he clearly distinguishes from the Jews (1:31, 49; 3:10; 12:13; cf. 1:47).[77] It is very significant that he never applies this honored name to Christ's church. This peculiarity of Johannine typology is explained by the general outlook of the Gospel. The church has no independent existence apart from Christ, any more than the means of grace do. Jesus calls them "his own" (οἱ ἴδιοι, 10:3, 4, 12; 13:1) and the ones "you have given me" (17:6, 9, 24; cf. 10:14; in addition to the rather bland term "disciples," μαθηταί). It can also be said that, as persons who have life through fellowship with Christ and who are the newly created ones, the church moves far ahead of the people of the Old Covenant. As the ἴδιοι of the Logos,[78] Jews and Greeks are all called in the same way to be

---

73. Cf. Rev 21:2; see J. Behm, "ἐπικαλέω," *TDNT* 3. 449f.

74. G. Schrenk, "ἐντολή," *TDNT* 2. 553f.; cf. pp. 554f. on 1 John.

75. The emphasis in 1 John (2:7f.; 2 John 5) on the fact that this command is an old one does not mean that it comes from the OT, but that it has governed Christian living from the beginning (cf. 2 John 5; G. Schrenk, "ἐντολή," *TDNT* 2. 554). However, in 1 John something else takes from καινή the full meaning that it has in the Gospel, i.e., primarily the failure to state the reason found in John 13:34b (cf. ibid.).

76. See above, pp. 109f.; Schlatter refers John 10:7 to Ps 118:20 (gate), John 15:1 to Jer 2:21 (vine); cf. John 3:29f. with Jer 5:7 (God as husband of his church) and in the NT with Mark 2:19ff. par.; 2 Cor 11:2; Rev 21:2, 9; 22:17 (allegorical interpretation made it possible to retain Canticles in the canon and this guaranteed the spread of this concept; cf. Schlatter, *Johannes*, 107). Bauer, *Johannes*, et al., wish to see an allegorical representation of the church in Mary (John 2:1ff.; 19:26f.); since allegory is generally foreign to John, it should not be assumed here either.

77. See W. Gutbrod, "Ἰσραήλ," *TDNT* 3. 385.

78. See Schlatter, *Die Theologie der Apostel*, 163; cf. John 1:10f.; 10:16; 11:52.

"his own." (In view of the creation typology which is dominant here, Israel's advantage in redemptive history, though acknowledged throughout, appears to be a relative matter more than in the rest of the NT.)

4. THE UNITY OF JOHN'S USE OF SCRIPTURE AND ITS RELATIONSHIP TO THE REST OF THE NEW TESTAMENT

When we compare the Gospel of John with the Synoptics, we find further development in the various kinds of explicit proof from Scripture that are presented for the exaltation of the Son of Man rather than development in the scope of that proof. This is true also of the assimilation of the narratives to OT stories, and it is apparently due to the progress of the tradition of the church. In addition to this, the typology is diminished in extent and in form. Christ is still compared with the saviors of the OT, but he is presented exclusively as their Lord, and no longer as their antitype. He is described as the mighty perfecter of creation and as the perfect redemptive gift, but the redemptive gifts and institutions of the OT with which he is compared become typological symbols rather than true types. Seldom is there any explicit reference to the church and its redemptive institutions, and for this reason such things are rarely, if ever, compared with any OT types.

The special character of the typology in John is not the result of any lesser regard for the OT nor of a different theological position on this matter; it is the result of a different point of view. John is accentuating different aspects of the redemption that has come in Christ. The basic features of John's typology can be explained as the expression of the general trend in the content of the Gospel that we described at the beginning. The Synoptics focus on the ministry and destiny of the Son of Man who walks on this earth incognito and whom faith struggles to know; they also focus on the formation of his church. Hebrews is interested primarily in the Christ who was made perfect through suffering and in the church that bears his disgrace. Paul is concerned with the church that is under the cross on a pilgrimage to perfection and that is striving to gain a proper understanding of its salvation. John's interest is centered on the person of the Son of God whose glory he has seen, full of grace and truth; he who is God's salvation incarnated. Therefore, John's typology presents Christ as the redemptive gift of God that includes the new creation in itself.

This typological view of Christ is very similar to Paul's. The only way he can describe the tremendous significance of Christ is with the concept of the second Adam that is a part of creation typology. When Jesus is portrayed by Paul as the second Adam and by John as God's incarnate Logos, these are really two sides of the same figure. It reflects the difference between a Pauline and a Johannine view of salvation and is congruent with the fact that the metaphor of the struggling church is developed in great detail by Paul, but scarcely at all by John. It is very significant that the antithesis to the present condition of the first creation that is implicit in the concept of the second Adam is not missing from the figure of the world perfecter that is found in John. Only through his being lifted up does Jesus become the bread of life and giver of the Spirit who brings about the new creation. For John, as for the rest of the NT, his being lifted up stands under the necessity that Scripture reveals to be part of the divine plan of salvation.[79] Christ fulfills redemptive history by dying, and only in this way does he become the maker of the new creation.

At first the evidence from Scripture for Jesus' being lifted up appears to be traditional and superficial, but it fits into the overall picture together with the unique typology of the snake that was lifted up. These are united in a single portrait along with the typological relationship to the redemptive gifts of the OT, a relationship that seems rather coincidental at first. If in the midst of a wealth of religious imagery Christ can only be presented as the perfecter of the miracles and institutions of the Old Covenant, then it is obvious that a light is shining in him whose radiance can be seen only in this unique history of a nation—God's redemptive history that takes place in this world. This light shines forth solely as the fulfillment of this history of the condescending grace of God that has issued from humiliation, cross, and resurrection. If this idea is in the background here in one way or another—of course, independent of our conceptualization of it—then the metaphors of the bread of life, etc., are not merely typological symbols; they are true types.

John's typology presents a unity with Christ as its center. It is in harmony with the rest of the NT because all are speaking of the same Christ. By disregarding everything else, John has developed what is the greatest certainty about Christ and was already in the background of the picture presented in the Synoptics. Our study began with the astounding assertion in the Synoptic Gospels that anticipates the "great joy" (Luke 2:10): this one is greater than a prophet. As we conclude our study, the conviction is evolving that this one is not simply a bearer of the Word; he is himself the Word of God. None of the testimony about Christ and his church that comes in between should be depreciated. Like "a light shining in a dark place until the day dawns," it all serves to illuminate the church. Faith can see the radiance of that day in the face of Christ, as John does, but we are still waiting for the day to come.

APPENDIX: TYPOLOGY IN THE NEW TESTAMENT PICTURE
OF THE FUTURE
(A Consideration of the Apocalyptic Portions of the NT)

The eschatology of the OT and late Judaism often presents the future fulfillment of redemption as the typological restoration of the former time of salvation. By applying these types to the present moment, the NT announces that the fulfillment of redemption has come. We have seen repeatedly, however, that the NT types are themselves open to a future salvation. The present fulfillment in type

---

79. See above, p. 179.

is fully comprehended in Christ. Therefore, it has come with him, but like him it is still hidden and awaits its revelation in the future. It is the object of faith and hope, not of sight. There is a tension between the present reality of the fulfillment of which faith is certain and the fact that that fulfillment is hidden with Christ. This is stated repeatedly in terms of the blessings of salvation being reserved in heaven—a methodology which does not conflict with the eschatology of redemptive history, but supplements it. Consequently, we have already presented everything that can be said about the typological relationships which compose the nucleus of NT eschatology.

Some passages go beyond this nucleus of hope—the certainty of the future revelation of Christ and of the salvation that is found in him. In order to comfort or to warn the church, these passages give a more complete description of the coming of the end—its sudden, unexpected coming, the signs of its nearness and the outline of what must happen prior to that time, the events at the time of the end and the consummation. In order to describe the ideas in the last two categories, the NT employs primarily the language of apocalypticism, particularly in the so-called apocalypse of the Synoptics (Mark 13 par.) and more extensively in the Revelation of John. The nucleus, however, remains unchanged: The Lamb that was slain is the only one worthy to open the seals of the course of world history (cf. Revelation 5).

The language of Revelation (and of Mark 13 par.) is the figurative and symbolic language of apocalypticism, and it borrows extensively from OT accounts of revelations and descriptions of the future, especially from Daniel, Ezekiel, and Zechariah. It also develops its own means of expression parallel to the language of rabbinical eschatology and of noncanonical apocalyptic literature, a means of expression which it derives primarily from OT narrative. Because of the incompleteness of our materials, we cannot be sure how much of this development, which goes beyond the OT, is the NT seer's own creation and how much he derives his means of expression from late Judaism.[80]

Perhaps the use of certain details from descriptions of past judgments and deliverances to sketch a picture of the future can only be called typology in a limited way. For the most part past events are not regarded as types which point to something greater in the future; certain details are simply borrowed for use

---

80. Schrenk, "γραφή," *TDNT* 1. 760: "In Rev. the OT provides an instructive treasury of images for the portrayal of the final denouement to which the community looks forward, except that there is now an undreamed of heightening of what is therein narrated." On the relationship to Jewish eschatology, see A. Schlatter, *Das Alte Testament in der johanneischen Apokalypse* (Stuttgart, 1912); what Revelation has that is more than the common Jewish heritage (esp. the Palestinian haggadah, cf. pp. 104f. and the whole treatise) comes from its confession of Jesus (pp. 105f.). Its points of agreement with apocalypticism arise from the fact that here and there the same exegetical tradition is developed in a similar direction (pp. 106f.). Cf. *Die Apokalypse* (THKNT; Leipzig, 1928ff.) 5: "None of the apocalyptic documents that have been preserved and that are known is cited explicitly or can be demonstrated to have been used, while the biblical literature preserved in the OT has been used extensively." For an extensive collection of parallel material from apocalypticism see Bousset, *Die Apokalypse* (MeyerK; 6th ed. 1906). For a collection from the haggadah see Schlatter, *Das Alte Testament*.

in sketching the future. Moreover, it is never certain whether the seer himself has transferred these details or has utilized the symbols that were available to him and painted with the colors that were at his disposal. For a proper understanding of these prophecies, it is important to research the provenance of the apocalyptic metaphors and symbols, and they are largely of typological origin. But this study of the symbolic language of apocalypticism must be carried out with careful consideration of the symbolism of the OT and late Judaism. Such a study exceeds the bounds of our task. Moreover, we could not expect to find any important contribution to the typology that developed in the NT and is the concern of our study. For this reason, a few references in a footnote will have to suffice to illustrate what we have said.[81]

---

81. On the Synoptic apocalypse: Mark 13 par., like Revelation, stands under the guiding principle of the apocalyptic prophecy in Dan 2:28; Matt 24:6 par.; Rev 1:1; cf. v 19; 4:1; 22:6. OT material for the Synoptic apocalypse is collected abundantly by Schniewind, *Markus*, on the passage; on Jesus' figurative eschatological language, see Jeremias, *Weltvollender*, 72-74.

On the Revelation of John: For an interpretation of the entire book, it is important to note that the seer, in conformity with the OT passages of which the description of his revelatory experiences is reminiscent, likens himself to the prophets of the OT without hiding behind the pseudonym of one of them as the other apocalyptic writers do (cf. Rev 1:9: "I, John"; 1:10—Ezek 3:12 [the following vision has features from Ezekiel]; its effect in Rev 1:17 as in Ezek 1:28; Isa 6:5; Dan 8:18; 10:9, 11; Rev 4:1 is reminiscent of Ezek 19:16, 24 [for the rabbis, Moses' ascent up the mountain becomes a translation to heaven; see Schlatter, *Das Alte Testament*, 72]; in addition cf. Rev 10:9f. with Ezek 2:8; 3:1-3; Rev 10:11 with Jer 1:10; on the whole matter, see ibid., 71f.).

In the apocalyptic images which contain prophetic material, the symbols taken from the sphere of Mosaic period typology are most conspicuous. The devastations which introduce the end of the world are portrayed in colors derived from the plagues in Egypt (on this whole matter, see Schlatter, *Das Alte Testament*, 84f.):

Rev 8:7—cf. Exod 9:24 (the 4th plague); cf. 7:19ff.	Rev 16:2—Exod 9:10f. (the 6th plague)
Rev 8:8f.—Exod 7:20 (the 1st plague)	Rev 16:3—Exod 7:17, 21; cf. Rev 16:4
Rev 8:10f.—cf. also Exod 7:20ff.	Rev 16:10—cf. Exod 10:21
Rev 8:12—Exod 10:21 (darkness)	Rev 16:21—Exod 9:23; cf. Isa 8:22

Moses and Elijah appear as the two witnesses who come before the end (Rev 11:3-6; references are given by J. Behm, *Die Offenbarung des Johannes* [NTD III], on this passage; J. Jeremias, " Ἠλ(ε)ίας," *TDNT* 2. 939f.). These witnesses, however, are no longer historical persons; they are symbols "of the power of witnessing" (see Behm, *Offenbarung*, on the passage). The world powers hostile to them are figuratively called Sodom and Egypt (Rev 11:8; similarly, they are called Babylon in Rev 14:8, etc.). The protection of the church from Satan is accomplished by its removal to the desert (Rev 12:14; cf. Schlatter, *Das Alte Testament*, 77f.). Its salvation here and in the consummation is described with attributes of Israel in the wilderness (Rev 1:6; 5:10 [cf. 8:3f.]; cf. Exod 19:6). The victory song of the righteous is at once the Song of Moses (Exod 15:1—Rev 15:3) and of the lamb, for now the work of salvation that was prefigured has been fulfilled (through the new Passover lamb? See Schlatter, *Das Alte Testament*, 62f.). God's σκηνή is among the perfect (Rev 21:3) so that what was promised in Ezek 37:27; cf. Zech 8:8 (which clearly have the Mosaic period in mind) is fulfilled.

Israel typology is being alluded to when the perfected church is described according to the pattern of the twelve tribes (Rev 7:4; 14:1, 3; 21:12, 14) or as the "new Jerusalem."

Here too, the new age is described as a return of the primeval period. The overcomer not only receives the manna to eat (Rev 2:17; cf. Schlatter, *Das Alte Testament*, 590), but at the same time is permitted to eat from "the tree of life, which is in the paradise of God" (Rev 2:7; 22:2; cf. Ezek 47:7, 12; see Gen 2:9). As is true already in Deutero-Isaiah, so here also the spring of water in the desert is combined with the river in paradise (Rev 7:16—Isa 49:10; Rev 21:6 and 22:17; cf. Isa 55:1; Zech 14:8; Rev 22:1, cf. Ezek 47:1, 7 and Zech 14:8). With the "new Jerusalem" there also appears a "new heaven and a new earth" (Rev 21:1 in accordance with Isa 65:17).

Chapter Nine

THE NATURE OF OLD TESTAMENT TYPOLOGY IN THE NEW TESTAMENT

Our study of OT typology in the NT has introduced us to a comprehensive and profound view of redemptive history. This is not a modern or more sophisticated justification of the NT use of Scripture that is based on a more recent view of history; it is a point of view that is integral to the NT itself. In contrast to most of the earlier works mentioned in the Introduction, we have not sought simply to present a plausible explanation for the use of the OT in the NT. We have been determined to present the NT's own view. Although we may have modified the question and restricted its scope, we can still affirm that typology is the method of interpreting Scripture that is predominant in the NT and characteristic of it. This should be obvious even though we have not been able to present an exhaustive treatment of the nontypological uses of Scripture.

The extent to which this method of interpretation is used in the NT can be perceived only when one is acquainted with the forms in which it appears. In previous studies of the NT use of Scripture, far too much emphasis has been placed on actual quotations, and these have been considered apart from the other allusions to the OT. The NT use of Scripture is not restricted to the direct quotation of OT passages. Continual allusions to Scripture are found in the exposition of the writers as well as in the actions of Christ and his church. They did not regard this as a collection of proof texts, but as a word that was living in their hearts and minds and was intended for their time. This fact has been overlooked or has been evaluated negatively and used as a criterion for judging the historicity of biblical statements. Much of the NT abounds with allusions to the OT that have little resemblance to the exact wording. These allusions make up the larger portion of the NT use of Scripture and form the heart of its view of Scripture. The typology in the Synoptic Gospels is usually a simple reminder of the OT parallels by means of the names that are given to NT phenomena or by allusions that are included in the narrative. These allusions may be simply the use of figurative language or the author's unintentional imitation of familiar narratives. Most of them, however, are intended to evoke comparison with the OT passages that they bring to mind. The evangelists were not the first to perceive these parallels or to call attention to them. Jesus himself formulated many of his sayings and arranged various events in such a way as to make the connection with OT parallels obvious (e.g., the calling of the disciples and the institution of the Lord's Supper).

The conclusion that is to be drawn from this comparison with the OT is enunciated in the relatively few passages where the typology is presented in the form of a direct statement. These passages declare that there is something here which corresponds to the substance of the OT parallels and yet is *greater*. This something greater is what constitutes a genuine typological heightening, and this is especially clear in the inferences that are drawn from this fact. The things that are compared are related to each other in redemptive history; therefore, this is not the same as the parallels that are observed in the history of religions. The relationship in redemptive history is taken for granted by the evangelists and the rest of the NT because they are convinced that there is a continuity between OT history and Jesus Christ in the sense of preparation and fulfillment. This is clearly emphasized in their use of Scripture to account for Jesus' death. Type and antitype are interrelated as prophecy and fulfillment in the Gospels also, and this is a genuine typological relationship.

The external form of the typology in John is the same as in the first three Gospels. There is one difference, however, because John has fewer direct allusions to OT events. He uses symbols from OT prophecy instead. He makes no explicit comparisons in the form of parallels; he simply observes that, compared with the salvation that has now come, the preparatory salvation is not worthy of this lofty name.

In addition to the typology in allusions and parallels that is so common in the Gospels, there is a more narrowly defined typology in Paul and in Hebrews. Type and antitype are explicitly compared; the common elements and the heightening are emphasized, and prophecy is used to indicate how they are related to each other. In Hebrews special emphasis is placed on the fact that already in OT prophecy there are inadequate prototypes that point to a fulfillment. (The earliest example of the use of OT prophecy to interpret an OT phenomenon typologically may be the incident where Jesus gave a typological interpretation to the figure of the Son of David in Psalm 110.)

A truly typological exposition states explicitly how an OT type in a specific Scripture passage is referring to something greater. There are only a few examples of this kind of exposition in the NT (primarily in Hebrews and Acts). This is evidence that the writers had no intention of reading NT salvation into the OT type. The OT type retains its own independent status as something God has ordained, and this is why it can serve as a true type.

There is a way of undergirding the relationship between OT prophecies and NT salvation that goes beyond the original meaning. This is especially common among the exegetes of the nineteenth century, but it has very few antecedents in the NT.[1] In general, the NT authors interpreted such OT passages as direct prophecies. They did not view them as predictions that could be checked, i.e., as signs (σημεῖα) like the ones mentioned in 1 Cor 1:22, because that kind of sign is rejected by the entire NT. They regarded them as σημεῖα in the Johannine sense of the word, as witnesses that give clarity and certainty to faith. It is only for faith that scriptural evidence can eliminate the offense of the cross. The typological use of Scripture places the other uses of Scripture in the larger context of redemptive history and demonstrates that they are not merely an application of oracular proofs. We have only been able to illustrate this in a few passages from the Gospels. We have established that typology is the basic method used to interpret Scripture in the NT. Individual monographs are needed that will study the various NT writings and determine the extent to which the other uses of Scripture are related to typology.

Our consideration of the way typology was used by contemporary Judaism to interpret Scripture confirms the fact that a typological approach underlies the external forms of their interpretation of Scripture. This is another impressive proof that, from the frequency of its use and from its very nature, typology is the method of exegesis that is the characteristic use of Scripture in the NT. Typology is found in only a small portion of contemporary Judaism's usage of Scripture and solely in the development of its eschatology. It lacks the theological depth that typology has in the OT and especially in the NT. In the NT, typology is the means regularly employed to relate the present to redemptive history in the past. What this means in essence is that the messianic fulfillment has come of the provisional redemptive events that are recorded in the OT. There is no other way to interpret those seemingly insignificant references in the NT writings.

Everything we have been able to infer from the form in which typology is used indicates that the NT does not regard it as a formal hermeneutical technique (there is no technical terminology and no appropriate formulas to indicate sources, etc.). It is simply an indication of the relationship that results from the fact that salvation is a present reality in the NT. The kind of typology that is found in the individual NT writings (its scope, its method, its content in types and antitypes) must always be interpreted in the light of the primary concern of the particular writing. The typology in the various NT books is carefully adapted to this primary concern, and it bears the impress of these books.

The results of typological exegesis are primarily statements about NT salvation, not statements about the OT. The typological heightening indicates that something new is breaking in and shows the importance of this event; it discloses the typological equivalent in the nature and destiny of the new. To each of these is added a warning (also based on typology) against contempt for or desecration of the new. Typology helps faith to recognize the greatness of Jesus. He who by

---

1. See above, pp. 122f.

his word and actions is greater than any of the OT heralds of salvation is the Christ of God. In this way, typology also justifies Christ and his disciples when their actions violate the regulations of the Old Covenant, because the Old Covenant itself is pointing to this something greater by which it would ultimately be abolished. Typology also gives certainty and clarity concerning Christ's destiny and the corresponding destiny of his church. The Son of Man must suffer, die, and rise again. It is no strange thing which happens to the church and its servants when persecution from without and various temptations from within oppress them. Typology removes the redemptive history of the NT from simple fortuitous factuality and places it under God's eternal redemptive decree. This does not lead to complacency but to obedience. Typology indicates the necessity of Christ's destiny, and in doing so it also indicates the meaning of Christ's destiny and the nature of all institutions based on it—the church and its means of salvation. The lifting up of Christ signifies the atonement which neither cult nor intercession by the OT men of God was able to accomplish. In Christ's church, the new people of God and the new humanity have become a reality. It is necessary to part with the old because the church's means of salvation makes shadows of all OT institutions. Typology not only brings the assurance of salvation, but it always provides a rationale for its warnings against contempt for this salvation. It clarifies the nature of salvation and justifies the warning against its misuse. The typological relationship to the punishment of Israel under divine forbearance (ἀνοχή) indicates that contempt and misuse will result in the eternal loss of the true salvation. These statements which continually arise out of the typology correspond to the basic elements in the NT message of salvation and, like that message of salvation, are revealed throughout the entire NT. It is only the choice of individual features that varies according to the basic concern of a particular writing.

The use of typology to illuminate the NT involves a series of interpretations of individual OT passages, the basic elements of a comprehensive approach to the OT, and the essential elements of an appropriate method for interpreting it. The individual interpretations are always secondary inferences. Typology begins and ends with the present salvation. NT typology is not trying to find the meaning of some OT story or institution. It compares Jesus and the salvation which he has brought with the OT parallels in order to discover what can be learned from this about the new and then, perhaps, what can be learned also about the old. There is nothing in the NT to compare with Philo's running commentary on the OT, nor is there any unified system of interpretation. The same events and institutions are related to a variety of NT phenomena (and vice versa); furthermore, the position of the individual events in the totality of OT history and the position of particular institutions in the totality of the OT covenant order are not considered unless they are important for the illumination of NT salvation. (Therefore, Hofmann's two principles for the identification of individual types are not observed in the NT.)[2] NT typology does not have a closed system of detailed interpretations or any appropriate rules for their discovery.

Typology is not a hermeneutical method with specific rules of interpretation. It is a spiritual approach that looks forward to the consummation of salvation and recognizes the individual types of that consummation in redemptive history. Nothing more than this can be determined other than certain hermeneutical principles which are dictated by the subject matter. These principles presuppose once again a corresponding basic approach to the OT and are evidence of such an approach.

Each typology includes typological correspondence and heightening. Accordingly, every typology presupposes that the God of the OT is the Father of Jesus Christ and that Jesus of Nazareth is the Christ, the one who fulfills OT redemptive history. The OT is an entity in itself distinct from the history of religions and distinct from the fulfillment of salvation in Christ. The typological correspondence arises from the first presupposition and the typological heightening from the second. The NT does not disrupt the order of the OT or its redemptive history by introducing its own ideas, as Philo does, for example. The NT values the OT as a true, though merely provisional, redemptive history which in its literal meaning originated from God.

The discovery of individual typological relationships is governed by the following principles (unconsciously, of course, and simply as a consequence of the nature of the subject matter): Persons, events, and institutions are interpreted only insofar as they express some aspect of man's relationship to God. Consequently, typology does not deal with inherent or external features in the events and accounts in the OT. Because Christ alone is the fulfillment of this relationship to God, another principle is always added that arises from the subject matter. This principle specifies that all typology proceeds through Christ and exists in him. From these two principles it follows as a matter of course that the antitypes, like the types, are not merely inherent or external features, but are the important elements in the perfect relationship between God and man.

The OT is not the inspired letter to the extent that it is for Judaism. It is a witness to a redemptive history, to a provisional and inadequate salvation, and a prophecy that points beyond these things. (This is Hofmann's basic thesis about Scripture and it is firmly based on the NT view of Scripture.) What is important about the history which is recorded in the OT is its description of man's relationship to God. The OT declares what God's attitude is toward man and how man appears in the eyes of God. It portrays man's relationship to God under God's provisional and gracious condescension and man's judgment by God under divine forbearance (ἀνοχή). It is clear, especially in Paul, that Christ's coming is the ultimate expression of God's gracious condescension and that his coming signifies something that could only be accomplished through him—the healing

---

2. See above, p. 12.

of the breach between God and man that was inherent and inescapable in the OT relationship. This is why the antitypes sometimes seem to be the positive fulfillment of those divine ordinances (the new creation, Abraham's children, the election of a new people as God's own possession) and at other times seem to be the antithesis that abolishes those ordinances (the second Adam, the New Covenant as opposed to Sinai).

The importance of these basic principles is obvious when we look at the way Scripture is interpreted in the *Epistle of Barnabas*. In various ways, this book has been considered to be the logical development of the tendency in the NT to interpret the OT as a Christian document. As a matter of fact, however, *Barnabas* has abandoned the most important aspect of NT typology.[3] The OT is no longer viewed as an entity in itself, distinct from the history of religions and distinct from NT salvation; it is no longer regarded as a prefiguration of what has come in Christ. When interpreted correctly it is a collection of Christian doctrine, but when taken literally (which, of course, was the error of Judaism), it differs little from paganism in various respects (e.g., circumcision, *Barn.* 9:6; temple, *Barn.* 16:2).

This general attitude is expressed in the way the Mosaic covenant is interpreted. God wanted to give the Israelites the covenant he had promised to the fathers (*Barn.* 14:1), but this desire was frustrated by their conduct. In the meantime, the people had become apostate so that Moses did not give them the tablets of the covenant; instead, he smashed those tablets (14:2-4a; cf. 4:6-8). Through the mediation of Christ the Lord, we now receive that covenant order (14:4b, 5). The *Epistle of Barnabas* does not seem to recognize any old covenant (as is often the case, the statements in the OT that contradict this view are arbitrarily suppressed). Accordingly, the entire OT is placed in parentheses.

The consequences of this are clear, primarily in the attitude of the *Epistle of Barnabas* toward the OT Law. The Law has not been totally cancelled through Christ, as in the NT, but it has been transformed in the new law that Christ brought (*Barn.* 2:6). This *Christianization* of the Law is accomplished by means of allegorical reinterpretation, such as was practiced by Hellenistic Judaism, and by quoting the criticism of the prophets in a one-sided manner in which any contradictory OT statements are suppressed. Rarely are there any references to the idea that the OT is replaced by something greater, and these references are very superficial.[4]

---

3. Similar things could be pointed out concerning the use of Scripture in the other writings of the Apostolic Fathers; cf. O. Michel, *Paulus und seine Bibel* (Gütersloh, 1929) 201-9, especially concerning the naive way *1 Clement* treats the OT as Scripture, which, unfortunately, many Christian preachers have followed; A. Harnack, *Einführung in die alte Kirchengeschichte* (Leipzig, 1929) 66-71. On the position of Ignatius, which is closer to the NT in this respect, see E. Goltz, *Ignatius von Antiochien als Christ und Theologe* (Leipzig, 1894) 80-86.

4. The dietary laws are reinterpreted allegorically as moralistic instructions, as is done in Aristeas, except that the observance of the literal meaning is rejected even more than in Hellenistic Judaism as being a perversion of the divine command (*Barnabas* 10). The prophetic sayings about

When the OT cultic institutions are interpreted as types referring to Christ, it is not a genuine typology because the OT types are not regarded as expressions of a true divine order.[5] The structure of Scripture is understood simply as a concealed prophecy of Christ, and its details are interpreted accordingly. In reality, typology is not used to compare two institutions that are expressions of the divine order. Although the events being compared may have been regarded as historical, the literal meaning is interpreted allegorically.

Even when the *Epistle of Barnabas* applies historical events "typologically" to Christ's destiny, these applications are fundamentally different from the ones found in the NT.[6] Now it is superficial details that are compared, not basic theological elements. The *Epistle of Barnabas* is trying to provide scriptural proof for the crucifixion of Christ.

In its search for a scriptural basis, the NT considers the cross to be central; however, it does not find the fulfillment of Scripture in the external reality of the crucifixion, i.e., in the act itself, but in the lifting up of the Son of Man— in the disgrace of the cross. Perhaps it is more than a methodological difference when the *Epistle of Barnabas* carefully demonstrates the typical nature of the events that are being interpreted. It may indicate a corresponding rationalization of the witness of Scripture as *proof*. This superficial typology is parallel to an equally superficial and artificial use of prophecy as scriptural proof.[7] (It is obvious that there is a certain intrinsic connection between the conception of NT salvation and both the typological and the direct proofs from Scripture.)

On the whole, the attitude of the *Epistle of Barnabas* toward the OT is more like the position of enlightened Judaism than the position of the NT.[8] When Christian salvation is read into the OT, both the OT and the reality of Christ are distorted. In the *Epistle of Barnabas*, the OT witness to a provisional redemptive

---

circumcision of the heart are pitted against circumcision (*Barn*. 9:1-5); Abraham's practice of circumcision is justified in that he did it while looking to Christ in the Spirit (*Barn*. 9:7-9; see n. 6). The same one-sided and arbitrary selection of prophetic witnesses is used to justify the rejection of the Sabbath (*Barn*. 15:8), temple (*Barn*. 16:1-5), and sacrifice (*Barn*. 2:1-10). (The statement that Christ, when he returns, will be the true temple appears to be a faint reechoing of similar statements in the NT [*Barn*. 16:6-10; cf. 4:11; 6:14f.].)

5. Cf. the application of the Day of Atonement (*Barn*. 7:3-11) and the sacrifice of the red heifer (*Barnabas* 8) to Christ's sacrifice.

6. "The serpent that is placed upon the tree" and "though dead is able to give life" is compared with the crucified one (*Barn*. 12:7; as τύπος τοῦ ᾿Ιησοῦ, 12:6). The prophetic meaning of that sign arises from the fact that Moses made it in spite of his prohibition of images (*Barn*. 12:6; on Christ's destiny, cf. John 3:14f.). In the same way, Moses' praying before the people with outstretched hands (cf. Exod 17:8-13) is interpreted superficially as a reference to the cross (*Barn*. 12:2ff.). (The only typology in *1 Clement* is similar—the application of the red cord in Joshua 2 to Christ's blood [*1 Clem*. 12:7].) Finally, even the gematria must serve as a means of detecting a reference to Christ and his crucifixion: Abraham circumcising his 318 servants (based on Gen 14:14 arbitrarily combined with Gen 17:23, 27) refers to Christ, because 18 = IH (᾿Ιησοῦς) and 300 = T (a reference to the cross) (*Barn*. 9:7-9).

7. Cf. *Barn*. 5:13; 6:6f., 16f.; etc. The passages that are quoted also in the NT provide a favorable contrast to these; cf., e.g., *Barn*. 5:1-4, 12b, 14.

8. Cf. H. Windisch, *Der Barnabasbrief* (HNT; 1920) 395.

history becomes a collection of obscure oracles, and the divine reality which breaks into this world in Christ becomes a system of theology and ethics.

This summary of the way Scripture is interpreted in the *Epistle of Barnabas* indicates how important our conclusions concerning the typological interpretation of the OT in the NT are in the contemporary search for an understanding of the OT, the concern with which we began. Our approach provides no specific guidelines for the exposition of the OT, and the NT interpretation of individual passages cannot be made authoritative for our exegesis. Nevertheless, NT typology gives us a comprehensive view of the OT and establishes certain boundaries. Of the approaches outlined in the Introduction, those of Hirsch and Vischer are shown to be outside the boundaries of the NT point of view. This is acknowledged by Hirsch, but is denied by Vischer. It is not our task to extend these boundaries to the present-day discussion or to impose the NT viewpoint on them. The suggestions which typology offers for the interpretation of the OT deserve serious consideration because they are rooted, as the typology is, in the basic concern of the NT.

Not only does this study of the typological approach in the NT provide important suggestions for our interpretation of the OT, it also makes an important contribution to our understanding of many individual passages in the NT and of basic theological elements. Typology bears the stamp of the NT's primary concern. We have indicated in various ways that it is an important witness to the basic tenets of the theology of the NT. It is an excellent witness to the NT's consciousness of its own place in redemptive history. The NT knows itself to be in some way the fulfillment of the types found in the redemptive history of the OT and to be a prophecy in type concerning the future consummation. As Hofmann has emphasized, the NT must be understood and explained in this twofold relationship. NT exegesis in the twentieth century has often overlooked the relationship to redemptive history in which the NT exists in favor of a comparison with parallel phenomena in the history of religions; this is, of course, a comparison that is needed and profitable. The numerous allusions and references to the OT in the NT are not the remnants of an obsolete system of scriptural proof—nor are they passages that are exegetically embarrassing and unproductive. Although their form is culturally conditioned, they are evidence of a comprehensive and profound view of redemptive history that discloses the nature of the salvation that has come in Christ and protects it from distortion. They are meant to present this view, not only to the exegetes, but also to the church of Christ—it is for this very reason that Luther thought to put them in bold print—in order that in the light of the prophetic word, the church might become aware of the glory and the nature of the salvation that has come in Christ and of the glory and the nature of the church's mission.

Part III

APOCALYPTICISM AND TYPOLOGY IN PAUL[1]

---

1. This is an article from *TLZ* 89 (1964) cols. 321-44 that was appended to the 1969 reprint of this book with the permission of the publisher.

Chapter Ten

APOCALYPTICISM AND TYPOLOGY IN PAUL

1. TRADITIONAL APPROACHES TO THE RELATIONSHIP BETWEEN THE TWO TESTAMENTS

In the most recent theological discussions in Germany, apocalypticism and typology have become catchwords for two ways of viewing the relationship between the OT and NT and of understanding each individually.

By way of introduction, we will trace the way in which these two points of
view arose in the history of NT research in order to give a clear indication of
their importance. Before the rise of the historical study of Scripture, it was
generally assumed that Jesus and the early church acquired their self-understanding from OT prophecy just as the NT references indicate that Jesus was the one
promised by the OT and that he was understood in this way. In the early nineteenth century, however, the historical study of Scripture revealed that most of
the NT references to the OT are not in harmony with the historical meaning of
the OT passages.[2] In the course of research, it became increasingly clear that
the NT interpretation of Jesus' advent has much in common with the ideas of
the Jewish and Hellenistic environment. These two observations lead to the
question that is our primary concern in this chapter. It is the question about the
structure of the NT interpretation of Jesus. Since this question first arose, scholars have suggested two different solutions. One of these was given its classical
formulation in the nineteenth century by J. von Hofmann. In this approach a
more profound theological understanding of both text and context is sought in
order to defend the NT's use of the OT as being basically a historical view of
Scripture[3] and in order to interpret the NT on the basis of its own self-
understanding.[4]

---

2. See above, pp. 8f. By accurate historical exegesis of the OT quotations in the NT, H. Braun
has again identified this discrepancy ("Das Alte Testament in Neuen Testament," *ZTK* 59 [1962]
16-31).

3. See above, pp. 9-17.

4. J. Schniewind is typical of contemporary interpretations: ". . . time and again the uniqueness
of Jesus' situation involves a minimum of authenticity." It is necessary to ask "whether any part of
Jesus' ethical prophecies can be understood except from the standpoint of the 'last days' " ("Zur
Synoptiker-Exegese," *TRu* 2 [1930] 186f.).

Historical observations, however, seemed to favor the other solution, which was most carefully developed by the history-of-religions school. In their opinion, the NT interpretation of Jesus was developed from contemporary Jewish and Hellenistic ideas. The use of an artificial and culturally conditioned scriptural proof to relate this to the OT was a later development.[5] They analyzed the NT texts exclusively in the light of contemporary thought, primarily that of apocalypticism and Gnosticism. They derived the theological meaning of these texts either by eliminating such mythical ideas or by interpreting them existentially.

When theological work was resumed in Germany after the Second World War, the advocates of these two solutions were divided in a different manner. The second solution was favored in NT research. In OT research, however, the work of Gerhard von Rad was a major factor in winning wide acceptance for the hermeneutical principle that the OT should be interpreted the way it is interpreted in the NT. This method of interpretation proceeds typologically on the basis of the fulfillment by Christ, and is, therefore, fundamentally in agreement with the OT itself.[6] This hermeneutical principle challenged the one which was predominant in NT exegesis. The NT must not be interpreted merely by "analogy and correlation," but in accordance with its own claim to be the fulfillment of the OT. In order to meet this challenge to his own hermeneutic, Bultmann made typology the theme of his presidential address at the first German theological conference after the war. He characterized typology as a variation of the idea of restoration that was a common theme in antiquity. He did this in order to justify his remark that John, the principal pillar of his theology, "easily carries (in John 6:31) his typological thinking to absurdity," i.e., to the idea of restoration found in Jewish eschatology.[7] Unfortunately, in the discussion that followed it was not made clear that the conception of typology which Bultmann developed and dismissed was not the same as the typological approach of the NT—the approach which von Rad discovered in OT prophecy and used in his interpretation of the OT.

In the decade between 1950 and 1960, von Rad's historical and typological exposition of the OT and Bultmann's interpretation of the NT, which is based on the history of religions and existentialism, were the center of theological interest in Germany. Both approaches were vigorously discussed in isolation without any consideration of their interrelationships.[8] At this time a group of younger theologians from these two schools who had gathered around the systematic theologian W. Pannenberg attempted a solution that maintained the ob-

---

5. E.g., W. Bousset, *Kyrios Christos* (Nashville, 1970) 45ff., 149f.

6. H. J. Kraus, *Geschichte der historisch-kritische Erforschung des Alten Testaments von der Reformation bis zur Gegenwort* (Neukirchen, 2d ed. 1969) §87 and §94; von Rad, *Old Testament Theology* (New York, 1962-65) 2. 400; see below, n. 8.

7. R. Bultmann, "Ursprung und Sinn der Typologie als hermeneutischer Methode," *TLZ* 75 (1950) 206-11, especially p. 210.

8. C. Westermann, ed., *Essays on Old Testament Hermeneutics* (Richmond, 1963); H. W. Bartsch, *Kerygma and Myth* (London, 1953-56); G. Bornkamm, "Die Theologie Rudolf Bultmanns in der neueren Diskussion," *TRu* 29 (1963) 33-141.

jectives of both men.[9] In opposition to Bultmann, they appealed to theology to affirm the inseparability of biblical revelation and biblical history, and they appealed to exegesis to affirm the continuity of redemptive history, in both the OT and the NT. Contrary to von Rad, they found the historical bridge between the two Testaments in apocalypticism, not in typology. In their opinion, OT tradition reached its legitimate conclusion in apocalypticism, and apocalypticism was decisive for Jesus' interpretation of the revelation which was being fulfilled in him, just as it was for Paul. This conception differed from that of Bultmann primarily in its historical and theological ideas; it differed from von Rad in its hermeneutical approach. Bultmann considered apocalypticism and Gnosticism to be equally important as means of interpretation in the NT, and he justified his existential approach because of the tension between the two. He viewed apocalypticism not only as being more widespread in the NT from the standpoint of the history of religions, but also as being legitimate from the standpoint of theology.

Even though Bultmann's disciples have raised many appropriate objections,[10] the weakest point in Bultmann's hermeneutical approach is still this: the breaking down of the relationship between the OT and NT, the elimination of the NT's understanding of itself in redemptive history, and a corresponding way of thinking about revelation and history. At the present time this weakness has been widely publicized in the objections of the group around Pannenberg so that efforts to find new approaches are being made on a wider front. Moreover, the concept of apocalypticism and, more especially, the concept of Gnosticism, which is the basis of Bultmann's analysis of the NT, have been fundamentally altered by developments in the study of the history of religions. Therefore, it is now necessary to ask anew: in what sense and to what extent was apocalypticism used in the NT as a means of interpretation? It is even more important to ask how this method of interpretation is related to typology. This is the form in which we are confronted today with the question which has been posed ever since the beginning of the historical study of Scripture—the question about the structure of the interpretation of Jesus and the corresponding question about the interrelationship of the two Testaments.

In Paul we find the outlines of apocalypticism and typology side by side. We will endeavor to further clarify the characteristics of each of these approaches and their interrelationship in Paul's writings.

2. THE CHARACTERISTICS OF APOCALYPTICISM AND TYPOLOGY IN PAUL

In recent years various schools in NT research have emphasized that Paul the Christian was also an apocalyptist. Not only does this mean that he adopted

---

9. W. Pannenberg, ed., *Revelation as History* (New York, 1968).

10. G. Klein presents the relevant material in his article, "Offenbarung als Geschichte?" *Monatsschrift für Pastoraltheologie* 51 (1962) 65-88.

apocalyptic ideas and concepts, sometimes directly and at other times through the mediation of early Christian tradition, but also that his theology was shaped significantly by apocalypticism. This thesis has been presented in three very different forms. In each of these, apocalyptic features of Pauline theology are viewed from a different vantage point. H. J. Schoeps attempts to view Paul from the standpoint of the history of Jewish religion.[11] U. Wilckens interprets Paul from the viewpoint of the theological scheme of "revelation as history."[12] E. Käsemann is guided by the concept that has controlled his thinking for a long time and which leads away from Bultmann; it is the conviction that NT theology must be approached in terms of the lordship of Christ, not in terms of a kerygmatic anthropology.[13] Each of these three positions works with a different concept of apocalypticism. From the standpoint of the history of religions, Schoeps understands apocalypticism as the form of Jewish eschatology that was predominant in the NT period and that was represented by the apocalypses and the rabbis with substantial agreement between them.[14] For Wilckens, apocalypticism is the theological system delineated by D. Rössler into which OT theology flows; i.e., a panoramic view of history oriented to the end, such as is found in the classical apocalypses[15] (Daniel, *1 Enoch*, 4 Ezra, and *2 Apocalypse of Baruch*). Finally, with Käsemann, apocalypticism is what systematic theologians designate a futuristic, cosmic eschatology that is shaped by a sense of imminence.[16] Moreover, their opinions vary as to the way in which Paul uses apocalypticism as a means of interpretation.

Schoeps explicitly adopts Albert Schweitzer's ingenious construction according to which Paul was given the key to his theology through his experience at Damascus.[17] This key is the insight that Jesus has been exalted as messianic Lord. He explained Jesus' present messianic reign by means of the two-stage eschatology with which he was familiar.[18] Schoeps, in opposition to Schweitzer, emphasizes that this is the eschatology that is found in some apocalypses and in the Tannaim. According to this scheme, the coming age which begins with the general resurrection will be preceded in history by an intervening messianic

---

11. H. J. Schoeps, *Paul: The Theology of the Apostle in the Light of Jewish Religious History* (London, 1961).

12. U. Wilckens, "The Understanding of Revelation within the History of Primitive Christianity," in *Revelation as History* (ed. E. Pannenberg; New York, 1968) 82-90.

13. He develops his programmatic statement: "Apocalyptic . . . has been the mother of all Christian theology" ("Die Anfänge christlicher Theologie," *ZTK* 57 [1960] 180, and "Gottesgerechtigkeit bei Paulus," *ZTK* 58 [1961] 378) in the essay: "Zum Thema der urchristlichen Apokalyptic," *ZTK* 59 (1962) 257-84.

14. Schoeps, *Paul*, 40ff.

15. Wilckens, "The Understanding of Revelation," 62f., where he refers to D. Rössler, *Gesetz und Geschichte* (Neukirchen, 1960).

16. E. Käsemann, "Urchristlichen Apokalyptik," *ZTK* 59 (1962) 257 n. 2.

17. A. Schweitzer, *The Mysticism of Paul the Apostle* (London, 1931).

18. Schoeps, *Paul*, 97-101.

reign,[19] a time that "is the consummation of that which is corruptible and the beginning of that which is not corruptible" (*2 Apoc. Bar.* 74:2). In contrast to apocalypticism, Jesus views his resurrection as standing at the beginning of the messianic reign. The resurrection of Jesus drives Paul to the conviction that the citizens of the kingdom already "live in the resurrection mode of existence." He expresses this concept and the corresponding notion of the superterrestrial position of the Messiah by means of Hellenistic ideas that represent this transcendence mystically or in terms of the mystery religions.[20] Paul develops what can be considered an "eschatological mystical sacramentalism" (p. 115). Schoeps calls his picture of Pauline theology a "Christ metaphysic" (p. 109). According to Schoeps's reconstruction, Paul simply transferred the name Jesus to ideas from the apocalyptic anticipation of the end and used Hellenistic ideas to reformulate these in the light of a purely formal concept of Jesus' resurrection. Paul already believed in Christ, even before he had the vision of the risen Jesus (p. 43, following W. Wrede).

This reconstruction of Paul's theology on the basis of apocalypticism underscores the crucial problem: for Paul, the resurrection of Jesus signifies that the eschaton is already present and yet, in terms of his parousia, it has not yet come. For apocalypticism, however, the eschaton is characterized by the resurrection of the dead and is associated with the end of the cosmic world order. The apocalyptic ideas concerning the woes that come before the end and concerning the intervening messianic reign are not compatible with Paul's statements that the eschaton is already present. Furthermore, the notion of a shadowy (intervening) messianic reign is not documented unambiguously until the period after Paul. All that it has in common with the reign of the exalted one—the content of which has been formulated on the basis of the resurrection of the crucified one and has been augmented in the process of preaching—is the time of the end, and this does not interest Paul in the least (1 Thess 5:1f.). Although Schoeps's reconstruction of Pauline theology with the methods of classical history of religions clearly indicates what the problems are, it does not solve them.

The difficulty with deriving Paul's theology from apocalypticism is very clear when Wilckens presents his position in vigorous contrast to the viewpoint of Schoeps.[21] His position can be described as the exact antithesis. (1) Paul did not transfer the name Jesus to the apocalyptic Messiah. He made Jesus the warrant of election instead of the Law which was central in apocalyptic theology and he made the Law the warrant of rejection.[22] Paul does not share the view of the Messiah found in Jewish apocalypticism, although he fully agrees with the struc-

---

19. *2 Apocalypse of Baruch* 29–30; 72–74; 4 Ezra 7:26-33; cf. *1 Enoch* 91:12f.
20. Schoeps, *Paul*, 104-9.
21. U. Wilckens, "Die Bekehrung des Paulus als religionsgeschichtliches Problem," *ZTK* 56 (1959) 287-93.
22. Ibid., 290-93; cf. Schoeps, *Paul*, 33.
23. Wilckens, "Die Bekehrung des Paulus," 289.

ture of the course of the history of election as such.[23] (2) For Paul, Jesus' death and resurrection mark the beginning of the apocalyptic events of the end, not the beginning of an intermediate kingdom.[24] In the Hellenistic church Jesus' death and resurrection, the presence of the church, and the future judgment were all seen together as the final apocalyptic event. It was the practice of viewing all these as one event that led to the gnostic dehistoricizing of Christianity in Corinth in which the resurrection of believers was interpreted as a spiritual experience. Paul refuted this idea by reemphasizing the difference between the Christ event in the past, the present, and the future. This was his important contribution to the theology of Hellenistic Christianity, and it has its source in the ideas of apocalypticism and redemptive history.[25]

When one examines Wilckens's analysis, it demonstrates even more clearly than that of Schoeps what Paul considered to be the limits of the possibility of interpreting Jesus' coming on the basis of apocalypticism. The two principal statements of Wilckens that we have underscored are an attempt to use apocalypticism to explain the eschatological annulling of the Law and the eschatological character of the present Christ event. Schweitzer and Schoeps contend that Paul obtained his thesis concerning the end of the Law directly from the apocalyptic notion that the Law would pass away with the old aeon.[26] Nevertheless, Wilckens is correct when he objects that this idea cannot be documented in Judaism and asserts that Paul derived the content of his thesis from Jesus' earthly ministry. While Jesus ministered on earth as mediator between God and man, he took the place of the Law.[27] Paul does not explain this displacement of the Law theologically as being the supersedure of the Law by Christ, as Wilckens assumes, but as its eschatological annulment (in this Schweitzer was correct). Paul used Abraham typology (Romans 4; Galatians 3) to develop this interpretation, not the apocalyptic theology of history. The Law continues to be the center of a course of history viewed apocalyptically, but only as a means of condemnation (Rom 4:15)—to this extent Wilckens's first statement is correct. Paul, however, did not discover the relationship of Jesus' resurrection to the course of history and to the Law in an apocalyptic thought pattern, unless typology can be considered to be such.

Wilckens's second statement makes this even more clear. 1 Cor 15:20-28 has been cited repeatedly as evidence of the apostle's apocalyptic thinking. This passage seems to indicate that Paul viewed Jesus' resurrection, the gathering of the church, and the imminent parousia as the final cosmic event which will occur in the way it was destined according to apocalyptic principle. However, it was

---

24. Ibid., 290.
25. Wilckens, "The Understanding of Revelation," 84-90.
26. Schoeps, *Paul*, 171f.
27. Wilckens, "Die Bekehrung des Paulus," 291.

in this very framework, which is clearly apocalyptic, that Paul developed the decisive relationship of Christ to history from Adam-Christ typology (1 Cor 15:21f.). Righteousness and life come through Jesus' righteous act. They are not established through a cosmic process in some predestined manner nor are they established by some decision rather than a law. They come through preaching that initiates faith and delivers unbelief to judgment.

Käsemann also emphasizes this passage, and for him the cosmic breadth of righteousness and life in Pauline thought is evidence of the apocalyptic basis of that thought.[28] Käsemann, however, is not dealing with the question that we have been considering and with which we are concerned here. He does not ask how extensively Paul used Jewish apocalypticism as a means of interpretation, but to what extent Paul shared the apocalyptic eschatology of early Christianity. He reaches the conclusion that for Paul this is the cosmic form of Christ's reign and, as such, is a basic tenet of his theology and anthropology and that it cannot be restricted to his anthropology alone.

At the present time, various schools are beginning to recognize once again that apocalypticism was the most important contemporary factor in the construction of Pauline theology. We will now attempt to describe this recognition more precisely. From a historical point of view we must define apocalypticism as consisting primarily in the common theological elements that are found in the classic apocalypses (Daniel, *1 Enoch*, *2 Enoch*, 4 Ezra, and *2 Apocalypse of Baruch*). Although careful analysis of this many-layered phenomenon in terms of genre, history of religions, and theology is an urgent task for research, we cannot go into it here.[29] We are concerned with the question as to how Paul viewed apocalypticism in relationship to Jesus' coming. To illustrate this relationship we can use a circle to represent apocalypticism, with Jesus' advent as its center. How the two are interrelated is a debated issue.

First, we will trace the effect of the center on the circumference. Undoubtedly, the cosmic and historical framework in which Paul views Jesus' advent and his church originated largely in apocalypticism. Nevertheless, this framework is not the same as the apocalyptic view of the world and of history. The difference is not due to the introduction of other factors from Hellenistic ideas, for example, but is clearly due to the alteration of the circumference by the center. The changes caused by the center can be summarized in the following differences: (1) The fantastically developed cosmology and the careful and detailed

---

28. Käsemann, "Urchristlichen Apokalyptik," 282f.

29. For bibliography, see O. Eissfeldt, *The Old Testament: An Introduction* (New York, 1965) 571f. and 617-36; H. H. Rowley, *The Relevance of Apocalyptic* (New York, 3d ed. 1963); idem, *Jewish Apocalyptic and the Dead Sea Scrolls* (London, 1957); M. Black, *The Scrolls and Christian Origins* (New York, 1961) 129-42; J. Bloch, *On the Apocalyptic in Judaism* (Philadelphia, 1952); M. Noth, *Das Geschichtsverständnis der alttestamentlichen Apokalyptik* (Cologne, 1954); see also n. 16 and n. 70.

calculations of the course of world history are not found in Paul. This is no accident, and the material omitted should not be supplied from Jewish apocalypticism as E. Stauffer attempted to do.[30] Paul has Jesus as his authority for ruling out all manner of calculating (1 Thess 5:1-3). It is obvious that Paul used a concept of faith that is determined by the center to consciously and unconsciously refine the apocalyptic picture of the world and of history. He did this by removing its content of divine law that had been shaped by the OT revelation of God. (2) To this circumference of the remaining cosmic and historical ideas, Paul added new points of view from the center that penetrate it in various ways and significantly change its overall character. Faith is waiting for the consummation as the fulfilling of the reign of Christ (1 Cor 15:24). It is even more true that faith is waiting for believers to be gathered to be with the Lord; consequently, "the first resurrection," which represents this gathering, becomes the focal point of the consummation (1 Thess 4:13-18; 1 Cor 15:22-29, 51-57). The first resurrection is a concept foreign to Judaism, but apparently it had been developed in Christianity before Paul by means of apocalyptic forms of expression.[31] Later the certainty of being with the Lord after death was added to further round out the cosmic events without sacrificing any of them (2 Cor 5:8; Phil 1:23). Just as the expectation of the consummation was placed in a new perspective by the new center, so also was the picture of the course of history. The corruption of history appears so radical in the light of Christ's cross that it can only be portrayed in terms of the lostness of the Adamic race (Rom 5:12-21; 7:7-25) and no longer in the form and sequence of the world empires. In spite of this emphasis on anthropology, the cosmic universalism which had developed from apocalypticism is preserved by the concept of "this age," for one thing. Finally, it is particularly clear that the imminent expectation of the end, which is characteristic of apocalypticism in this literature, is subordinated by the new center. This is evident in its use in pareneses: The instructions given in 1 Cor 7:25-31 and Rom 13:11f. are derived from the imminent expectation of the end, but the parenesis which has been derived from the finished act of atonement is much more important (1 Cor 7:17-24; Rom 12:1f.).

After all, Jesus' coming is fitted into the circumference of the apocalyptic picture of the world and of history in such a way that this circumference is purified, changed, and frequently penetrated by the new center. Much of this particular apocalyptic view of the world and of history was not developed by Paul from Jewish apocalypticism, but was adopted by him from a tradition of

---

30. *New Testament Theology* (London, 1955). In a similar way Wilckens introduced the conceptual structure of apocalyptic vision into the Damascus revelation in Gal 1:15 in his article, "Der Ursprung der Überlieferung der Erscheinungen des Auferstandenen," *Dogma und Dankstrukturen* (ed. W. Joest and W. Pannenberg; Göttingen, 1963) 90-93.

31. A. T. Nikolainen, *Der Auferstehungsglaube in der Bibel und in ihrer Umwelt* (Helsinki, 1944-46) 2. 175f.

early Christian apocalypticism which till then had not been written down.[32] It is very characteristic of apocalypticism, in contrast to OT prophecy, that it does not develop its view of history from the notion of God's election in redemptive history.[33] For Paul, however, the divine election in Jesus is the dominant theme.

This influence is a reciprocal one: Jesus' advent not only had its effect on the circumference, but was also interpreted by it. Apocalypticism handed down important means of interpretation for understanding Jesus' advent and its consequences. For example, it introduced the idea of resurrection into the early kerygma, and Paul actually understood the resurrection of Jesus in the apocalyptic sense as the beginning of the eschatological awakening of the dead to a new life in the body (1 Cor 15:20-28). Of course, he used Adam-Christ typology to explain this consequence of Jesus' resurrection (1 Cor 15:20f.). Apocalypticism presents the world and history as a general unity and in terms of epochs that supersede one another; it also indicates that both are ordained by God. Paul develops them both in a typological framework (Romans 4; 15:12-21; Galatians 3). Apocalypticism presents the eschaton strictly as an other-worldly phenomenon in the hereafter. Paul, however, used typology to demonstrate that the eschatological is a contemporary phenomenon that he perceived as being already present within history (e.g., 2 Cor 5:17).

These and other means of interpretation that Paul derived directly or indirectly from apocalypticism are elements in the structure of his theology and not merely a mode of expression. They are more comprehensive and important than any means of interpretation derived from other spheres. But there is another interpretation that Paul develops explicitly—the typology. It is not really a different interpretation, but one underlying them all. Its relationship to the apocalyptic approach is the most crucial problem concerning the structure of Pauline theology. This problem is not widely recognized in current discussions because in Paul, as in the Jewish apocalypses, typology often appears in conjunction with apocalypticism[34] and is viewed simply as an apocalyptic way of thinking.[35] An analysis of typology reveals at once that it is an approach which arose before apocalypticism and independent of it and that it is essentially different from it, insofar as it is possible to compare the two. There is one crucial point in which these two very different phenomena—apocalypticism and typology—can be compared, since both interpret history as pointing to the eschaton. Apocalypticism interprets history as a course of events leading to the consummation; typology interprets it as a prefiguration of the consummation. Emphatic scriptural

---

32. It is clear that there was an independent stream of early Christian apocalypticism, because apart from the book of Daniel, Revelation does not agree directly with any Jewish apocalypse, but it certainly takes up elements of early Christian apocalypticism, e.g., the idea of the first resurrection (Rev 20:5; cf. above, n. 31).

33. See below, n. 75.

34. See above, pp. 33ff.

35. E.g., Schoeps, *Paul*, 42: "Thus he derives from that source (the apocalyptic writings) his theory of aeons, which lies behind his typological exegesis."

accounts of the history of Israel (e.g., Dan 9:2) are used for this purpose not only by typology, but also by apocalypticism.

The problem outlined above assumes a more definite form when the structure and origin of Paul's typology are explained more fully.

3. THE STRUCTURE AND ORIGIN OF PAUL'S TYPOLOGY

First of all we will attempt to give an exact definition of Paul's typology.[36] In doing so, one necessarily moves somewhat in a circle methodologically because the decision as to where typology is found in Paul depends largely on one's definition. For this reason, we will begin with an attempt to deduce the characteristics of typology from two passages which are generally recognized as typologies—Rom 5:12-19 and 1 Cor 10:1-11. In both passages typology consists in the relating of OT events to NT ones. To comprehend the structure of this relationship, we will determine what is the OT pattern or the type, what is the NT copy or the antitype, and, finally, what is the relationship between the two.

The patterns or types, which are used in these two passages, are not OT texts, but events that are described in loose dependence on the texts.

This is one way in which typology is different in principle from allegorizing. Allegorizing works with the exact wording of the text. It interprets the words metaphorically without being concerned about their literal meaning or even their historicity; rather, it usually keeps aloof from both.[37] Although allegorizing has been used in the religious sphere since ancient times for deriving philosophical truths for the present from traditional mythologies, it was especially common in the Hellenistic age. Typology, by contrast, belongs to the biblical world;[38] it searches the records thoroughly for the types, i.e., the recorded events, and applies them to other events.

The structure of the types will become clear if we do a history-of-religions analysis of our two passages. The verbal correspondence indicates that the presentation of the Mosaic period in 1 Cor 10:1-13 uses primarily the relevant

---

36. For information about special studies of Paul's typology, see above, pp. 7-17; H. Müller, *Die Auslegung alttestamentlichen Geschichtsstoffes bei Paulus* (diss., Halle, 1960) 1-10; and K. Galley, *Alte und neue Heilswirklichkeit bei Paulus, Ein Beitrag zur Frage der Typologie* (diss., Rostock, 1960) 1-10. Of the literature published between 1940 and 1960 in addition to what we have referred to already (see n. 7) the following studies should be mentioned: J. Daniélou, *From Shadows to Reality: Studies in the Biblical Typology of the Fathers* (London, 1960); G. W. H. Lampe and K. J. Woollcombe, *Essays on Typology* (London, 1957); E. Ellis, *Paul's Use of the Old Testament* (Grand Rapids, 1957); S. Amsler, *L'Ancien Testament dans L'Église, Essai d'herméneutique chrétienne* (Neuchatel, 1960; contains additional bibliography).

37. E.g., in John 3:14f. the erection of the bronze snake in Num 21:6ff. is applied typologically to the "lifting up" of Christ. In Philo, on the other hand, the text is explained allegorically as follows: "If the mind (= Israel) when bitten by pleasure, the serpent of Eve, shall have succeeded in beholding in soul the beauty of self-mastery, the serpent of Moses, and through beholding this, beholds God Himself, he shall live" (*Leg. All.* 2.81). See above, p. 18; L. Goppelt, "Allegorie: II. Im Alten Testament und Neuen Testament," *RGG* (3d ed. 1957-65) 1. 239f.

38. See below, pp. 225f.

pericopes from the Pentateuch. In several places it follows the wording of the traditional OT summaries of the wilderness wandering that differs from the wording of the Pentateuch.[39] Finally, it takes up the midrash on the Pentateuch that states that the rock "accompanied them," and perhaps it also adopts the traditional Hellenistic-Jewish interpretation which compared the rock to such intermediaries as *Sophia*. Consequently, the picture of the Mosaic period in 1 Corinthians 10 is augmented from the stream of OT-Jewish tradition in which Paul stands. For Paul, however, this is not simply a matter of augmentation. The situation of the Christian church has guided the selection, assembling, and shaping of his material. For example, the phrase "they were all baptized unto Moses" is patterned after the formula for Christian baptism.[40] It is even more apparent that the saying about spiritual food and spiritual drink is taken from the Christian antitype. Jewish traditions are used to develop the picture in Romans 5 of the disastrous effect of Adam's fall beyond what is recorded in Genesis, but none of those traditions indicates that Adam's fall resulted in all being subject to the reign of sin and death.[41] Rom 5:18f. indicates that Paul derives this idea from Adam's antithetical relationship to Christ. Paul's theology is not simply informed by tradition; rather, he is using tradition to formulate something new. Paul was familiar with the hermeneutical principle which states that ultimately the meaning of the OT type can only be comprehended on the basis of the NT antitype. He believed that the meaning of Scripture (i.e., of the OT) is only unlocked by faith in Christ (2 Cor 3:15f.).

The genetic structure of the type corresponds to its theological structure. In 1 Cor 10:11 Paul emphasizes three things: (1) "These things (the events of the Mosaic period) happened to them as examples" (τυπικῶς). Accordingly, all that happened in creation and in history are not types, but only those acts of God in grace and judgment that point to the final salvation. (2) These special acts of God are written down in Scripture. It is clear that Paul does not restrict himself to the text of Scripture. In principle, however, he does not consider everything that is reported in a tradition to be types, but only what is testified in Scripture by divine command. This kind of testimony is only possible when the type was an act of God accompanied by a revelatory word. (3) This divine act does not

---

39. 1 Cor 10:1b = Ps 105:39; 1 Cor 10:5b, 9 = Ps 78:31, 18; the summary in 2 Esdr 19:9-20 (= Neh 9:9-20) follows the order of 1 Corinthians 10 up to v 4, but without verbal agreement, so that, as we have already stated, this passage was not the immediate source.

40. The idea that the Israel of the wilderness wandering had been baptized may have been suggested by rabbinic discussion (J. Jeremias, "Der Ursprung der Johannestaufe," *ZNW* 28 [1929] 317f.).

41. Consequently, R. Bultmann, *Theology of the New Testament* (New York, 1951-55) §15,4b; §25,2, following the history-of-religions school (R. Reitzenstein, W. Bousset), traces these statements to the idea of the fall of the gnostic primitive man-redeemer which supposedly were taken over by the Hellenistic church (1 Cor 15:44ff.). So also E. Brandenburger, *Adam und Christus* (Neukirchen, 1962). This idea, however, is no longer held in this form in the history-of-religions school (C. Colpe, *Die religionsgeschichtliche Schule* [Göttingen, 1961] and it contradicts the structure of the thought in Romans 5.

refer to any other events in history and was not written down for all subsequent generations in general. The type refers to the church of the last days and it was recorded for their sakes. Accordingly, a type is something that happens between God and man and that points to the salvation which has come in Christ. It is testified to by the Scripture and it prefigures a corresponding event in the last days.

Accordingly, the antitype in 1 Corinthians 10 and in Romans 5 is something that concerns God and man and is fulfilled by Christ. Paul does not derive any doctrine from the type; it simply indicates that God will act in the last days and how he will act. Moreover, the type does not enable Paul to predict some particular divine intervention that could be expected to happen in Corinth; it merely indicates the characteristics of the divine action which the church of the last days could anticipate. For this reason the section uses the pronoun "we" in a general sense.

What then is the nature of the relationship between the events of the OT and NT that Paul describes in 1 Cor 10:6, 11; Rom 5:14 with the terms "type" (τύπος) and "typical" (τυπικῶς)? That God's action in the Mosaic period prefigures his action in the new age is something Paul found in the OT and in Jewish tradition. This correspondence was announced by prophecy[42] and was eagerly antiticipated in Jewish eschatology.[43] The form and content of the relationship are also specified by the tradition.

The formal correspondence that relates type to antitype includes heightening also. According to Deutero-Isaiah the second exodus will be far more glorious than the first.[44] In Romans 5, in addition to setting forth the correspondence between Christ and Adam with the conjunctions "just as"— "so also" (ὡς—οὕτως) which occur twice in 5:18f., Paul develops forcefully in 5:17-19 the heightening which is expressed twice (vv 15f.) with the words "not like" (οὐχ ὡς—οὕτως) and twice (vv 15, 17) with the words "how much more" (πολλῷ μᾶλλον). In 1 Corinthians 10, the correspondence is emphasized for the sake of the parenetic objective (καθώς occurs four times in vv 6-9; καθάπερ in v 10); the difference is only implied. For Paul, manna and water from a rock are spiritual gifts in a different sense than the Lord's Supper is, and the impending fall of the church has a different character, i.e., the character of the last days, as is implied in v 11.

The formal characteristics of the relationship arise from the nature of the content. Both of the following statements are found in Deutero-Isaiah: "Yes, and from ancient days I am he . . ." and, "See, I am doing a new thing" (Isa 43:13, 19). God's prophetic word makes it clear to Deutero-Isaiah that God is

---

42. Primarily in Deutero-Isaiah according to von Rad, *Old Testament Theology* 2. 243-47.
43. See above, pp. 34-36.
44. Von Rad, *Old Testament Theology* 2. 246f.

the same in both past and future even though he will do a new thing (Isa 44:7f.; 45:21). Revelatory word and the corresponding historical event stand in a reciprocal relationship that cannot be broken. For Deutero-Isaiah, a new promise of salvation makes the first a reference to the second and at the same time gains content and certainty from it. From the time that Jesus Christ was revealed to him at Damascus, Paul found a similar reciprocal effect between the "Yes" to every announcement of salvation and the goal of all God's saving acts. Now in retrospect, he sees all the announcements of salvation in the OT as a unity, boldly subsumes them under the term "promise," which was still unknown in Scripture, and "develops in the light of the goal the idea of a single divine history."[45] Its unity, for Paul, is not a consequence of historical continuity, but of the divine plan of redemption that he had comprehended by faith.[46] This conviction is called into question by Israel's unbelief toward the gospel (Romans 9), but is ultimately assured by the prophetic revelation of Israel's future salvation (Rom 11:25f.).[47] On the strength of this revelation, he is able to confess, not just postulate, that "God has bound all men over to disobedience so that he may have mercy on them all" (Rom 11:32). Because this is God's will, Adam, in his destructive work, is a type ($\tau\acute{u}\pi o\varsigma$) of the one to come (the coming Adam) (Rom 5:14). (In Rom 5:18f. the strange "all," which occurs again in 11:32, is indicative of the correspondence between Adam and Christ.)

For Paul, the relationship between type and antitype is not provided by the regular conformity of history to natural law. *1 Clement* discovers in historical events the "order" that prevailed in creation and draws analogous conclusions for the present (*1 Clement* 4–6; 19; 24ff.). Types, however, are not historical analogies. Paul does not find the relationship in cyclical thought either, although it certainly had its effect on Jewish eschatology. It is no accident that terms from this school of thought appear here and there in the NT, but are not used by Paul. He makes no mention of either the coming aeon or the rebirth ($\pi\alpha\lambda\iota\gamma\gamma\epsilon\nu\epsilon\sigma\acute{\iota}\alpha$). The word "type" ($\tau\acute{u}\pi o\varsigma$), which he introduces as a hermeneutical term, designates a situation which moves in a straight line to make its impression on a

---

45. J. Schniewind and G. Friedrich, "ἐπαγγέλλω," *TDNT* 2. 579-81; cf. O. Michel, "οἰκονομία," *TDNT* 5. 151-53.

46. This problem was discussed in Romans 4: U. Wilckens, "Die Rechtfertigung Abrahams nach Römer 4," in *Studien zur Theologie der alttestamentlichen Überlieferungen* (ed. K. Koch and R. Rendtorff; Neukirchen, 1961) 111-27, and G. Klein, "Rom. 4 und die Idee der Heilsgeschichte," *EvT* 23 (1963) cols. 424-47. According to Wilckens, Abraham is united with the believers by a continuum in the history of election (p. 127). Klein, however, sees the connection sometimes positively under the timeless aspect of example and sometimes negatively under the historical aspect of a chronological distance that profanes and paganizes the history of Israel and frees the believer from the control of history. For Wilckens the continuum approaches the old biblical tradition; for Klein it approaches historical-critical contemporaneity; for Paul it is given in accordance with Rom 4:23 (col. 333). Both only mention in passing this sentence, which is the most crucial statement in the chapter.

47. See below, p. 227.

corresponding situation.[48] τύπος is a dynamic word. In its basic meaning it designates the impression left by a mold, the imprint that a seal leaves in the wax, for example. Paul more often uses this term, which is rich in meaning, for the stamp that leaves its imprint. Consequently, it does not refer here to an exact copy, but to a correspondence in form that may even be the antitype. The term designates a relationship that is foreordained in God's redemptive plan. God's plan bestows the same features to his saving acts in the realm of promise as it does to those in the realm of fulfillment (Rom 9:6; 11:29; cf. Ephesians 3).

Since by virtue of God's redemptive plan the type points to the antitype, the character of typology is not changed if the correspondence is antithetical in Romans 5 and positive in 1 Corinthians 10. In cyclical thought the first would signify restoration and the latter recurrence. Because of God's redemptive plan, however, the judgment which falls on those who refuse God's commands points to the final revelation of grace just as much as do the provisional manifestations of grace. Moreover, God's judgment in the Old Covenant is a warning concerning the final judgment which will fall on those who refuse God's grace.

In keeping with the nature of this relationship, Paul does not seek the correspondence between type and antitype in superficial similarities but in the theological essence of the events. Israel's experience at the Red Sea, for example, is not a type of baptism because both involve passing through water, but only because each is a fundamental saving act of God. Only in the early Christian writings that come after the NT is there a shallow typology that is based on superficial similarities; for example, Rahab's red cord is interpreted as a reference to Jesus' blood (1 Cor 12:7).[49]

The structure of the relationship between type and antitype is also indicative of the theological significance that Paul attributes to it. He does not develop a typology in order to give examples from history or to bring scriptural proof from a sacred document or to develop a historical and theological construct. He does so in order to reveal a relationship that God ordained in history and had recorded in Scripture for the sake of the church (1 Cor 10:11). This relationship should enable the church to understand its own situation by faith. 1 Corinthians 10 is written to a church that has become lost in mythology and syncretism. Due to Hellenistic ideas of God, this church has misunderstood the sacraments as something magical or mystery-like. In that chapter, Paul uses typology to show this church that God's redemptive act encounters them in the sacrament as it encountered Israel in the wilderness, revealing the life that issues from faith, although it does not confer any elemental heavenly powers. Just as the

---

48. The word is used as a technical term from this time on in the early Christian writings: 1 Pet 3:21; *Barn.* 7:3, 7, 10f.; 8:1; 12:2, 5f.; 13:5; cf. *Herm. Vis.* 4.1.1; 4.2.5; 4.3.6; *Sim.* 2.2. We can best translate the Greek word with the loanword "type" or "typical." For the corresponding method of interpretation, we use the customary term "typological." On the following discussion, see my article on τύπος in *TDNT* 8. 246-59.

49. For similar examples from *Barnabas*, see above, pp. 203-5.

correspondence indicates that the God of the OT is seen in the God and Father of Jesus Christ, so the heightening indicates that in Jesus one can see that God's eschatological acts show the characteristics of the last days. The heightening is not relative; it is absolute: In contrast to the miraculous feeding with manna, the Lord's Supper is the meal of the New Covenant (1 Cor 11:25), and Christ's redemptive act completely cancels the ruinous effect of Adam's fall.

Finally, with Paul, typology is not a hermeneutical method to be used in a technical way to interpret the OT. It is a spiritual approach that reveals the connection ordained in God's redemptive plan between the relationship of God and man in the OT and that relationship in the NT. The focus oscillates between the present divine-human encounter and the one in the past that is recorded in Scripture. Each points to the other and is interpreted by it, and thus they describe man's existence under the gospel. This description cannot be achieved by philosophy or by mythology or even by apocalypticism. The result is not a typological system but is clearly an insight into the important features of God's redemptive act and of God's redemptive plan.

4. THE EXTENT OF TYPOLOGY IN PAUL

The definition of typology that we have derived from Romans 5 and 1 Corinthians 10 will be further clarified if we survey the occurrences of this kind of typology in Paul. Of course, the boundaries of such occurrences are not fixed. Typology is found not only in the form of detailed comparisons, but is also implied in allusions to OT texts (e.g., 1 Cor 5:7) or incorporated in titles such as "the Israel of God." Therefore, we cannot be certain in individual passages whether or not any typological reference is intended. We will not need to deal with such questionable cases here. We will have to give special attention to those references to the OT whose typological character is contested on the basis of the definition of typology. These are not simply peripheral references; rather, they constitute entire sections in the categories of OT ideas which Paul uses typologically and which were often used that way in the OT and in Judaism. We will divide our survey according to these categories.

There is no question that the comparison of Adam and Christ is typological (Rom 5:12-21; 1 Cor 15:21f., 44-49). It is not simply mentioned occasionally in order to underscore some particular statement; rather, it is one of the aspects with which Pauline theology begins. In 1 Cor 15:20ff. the formula "in Christ" (ἐν Χριστῷ) is developed as the antithesis to "in Adam" (ἐν Ἀδάμ), and in this way the two possibilities of human existence are described. The positive correlation between the first and second creations that is presented as typology in 2 Cor 4:6 and also in 2 Cor 5:17 must be distinguished from the antithesis between Adam and Christ.

The next category of ideas is controversial: In Romans 4 and Gal 3:6–4:7 the justification of Christians by faith is related to Abraham's justification. According to Bultmann, Abraham is "an ideal and a pattern of the believer, as he was already in Jewish literature," but not a type, because "the idea of recurrence does not play a part."[50] Paul, however, views Abraham in a basically different way than Judaism does. He summarizes the conclusions he draws from his comparison in Rom 4:23f. as follows: "The words 'it (faith) was credited to him' were written not for him alone, but also for us, to whom God will credit righteousness—for us who believe in him who raised Jesus our Lord from the dead." What he says in this passage about the statement in Scripture concerning Abraham's faith is almost the same, word for word, as what he says in 1 Cor 10:11 about the texts that he uses typologically concerning Israel in the wilderness. It is obvious that Paul finds the same use of Scripture here as he does there, namely, typology. In fact, the justification of Christians by faith is the heightened analogy of Abraham's faith. In spite of his unfruitfulness, Abraham believed that God would raise up descendants for him. Christians, in spite of the cross, believe in the God who has raised Christ. These two phenomena are bound to one another through the promise concerning Abraham's children, i.e., through God's redemptive plan (Rom 4:16f.; Gal 3:6ff.). It is not important to Paul that a concept of recurrence resonates in primeval period typology and wilderness wandering typology that originated in the OT and in Judaism, but does not resonate in the Abraham typology which he develops. For him, type and antitype are always related in terms of God's redemptive plan and never by a cosmic cycle. The type expresses the promise (this is stated clearly in the case of Abraham); the antitype expresses the fulfillment[51] (Rom 4:16; Gal 3:17). Therefore, the decision whether or not the passages that deal with Abraham are typological is really nothing less than a test of one's understanding of typology. The interpretation of the relationship of Ishmael and Isaac in Gal 4:21-31 is only tangential to this section; it is a typology that in large measure passes over into allegory.

A third category of ideas, those of the Mosaic period, is used typologically as a positive correlation in its redemptive aspects (1 Cor 5:6ff.; 10:1-11). The Mosaic period was also a time of the covenant of law and its administration, and, in this respect, it is used in antithetical correlation (2 Cor 3:4-18; 1 Cor 11:25). Moreover, literal and figurative titles for the people of God in the OT are transferred to the church so that the church is designated as the new people of God. But the typological background of these titles is even more clearly intended in a few primarily polemical passages, e.g., "the Israel of God" in Gal 6:16, and "the circumcision" in Phil 3:3 and Col 2:11.

---

50. Bultmann, "Ursprung," 210. Galley, *Alte und neue*, 8 objects to designating the use of Abraham as typology; however, such a designation is supported by Müller, *Auslegung*, 114 and, with qualifications, by Ellis, *Paul's Use of the Old Testament*, 130; see above, n. 46.

51. Of course, Paul does not speak of a "fulfilling" of the promise nor even of a fulfilling of Scripture; he speaks of God's "yes" to the promise which has been uttered in Christ (2 Cor 1:20; cf. Rom 15:8) and of the guaranteeing of the promise (Rom 4:16); cf. G. Delling, "πληρόω," *TDNT* 6. 295-97; on πλήρωμα in Gal 4:4; Eph 1:10, see ibid., 305.

This last title brings us to the category of the cult. When Paul designated the church (1 Cor 3:10-17; 2 Cor 6:16; cf. Eph 2:20ff.) or even the individual Christian (1 Cor 6:19) as the true temple of God, he was using a metaphorical expression whose typological background is no longer apparent. Nevertheless, there may be an important typology from this category in Rom 3:25 that presents Good Friday as the eschatological Day of Atonement. For the most part, the characterization of the Christian's obedience as a sacrifice in Rom 12:1 passes over into metaphor.

Of the many references to the OT in the Pauline epistles, the typologies are only a small portion numerically, but they are characteristic of his overall use of Scripture and set a pattern for it. Paul views all of Scripture in a framework that arises from these typologies and is, therefore, the first to designate Scripture as the "Old Testament" (τῆς παλαιᾶς διαθήκης, 2 Cor 3:14). This framework can be called redemptive history if the term is defined in accordance with typology.[52] As we saw in 1 Corinthians 10, Paul uses this framework to gather the individual statements of Scripture in groups as pictures of a single divine redemptive act that has been carried out in history, but which has now been surpassed, i.e., set aside. He does not view the OT as a book of laws or as a collection of oracles. Finally, this approach has influenced his use of individual sayings from Scripture; for example, Paul, like the rest of early Christianity, applied Psalm 69 to Christ (Rom 15:3). He knew that in Jewish exegesis the psalm was usually applied to David;[53] consequently, he defends his interpretation with the words "For everything that was written in the past was written to teach us" (Rom 15:4). Perhaps this principle, which is in harmony with Rom 4:23f. and 1 Cor 10:11,[54] expresses ultimately a typological conviction. Though the psalm spoke originally of David, it really refers to Christ. Accordingly, the typological approach has put its stamp on the apostle's total understanding of Scripture. It shows conclusively how it also controls his whole theology. The nature of this typology must be fully determined, first of all, by inquiring about its origin and legitimacy.

5. THE ORIGIN AND LEGITIMACY OF THE TYPOLOGICAL APPROACH

Concerning the origin of the typological approach, three things are certain: (1) Typology is unknown in the nonbiblical Hellenistic environment of early Christianity. (2) It is found exclusively in the Jewish environment, but only as a principle of eschatology. (3) The typology that is found in Judaism had a prior

---

52. See below, p. 237.
53. In rabbinic writings Psalm 69 is usually related to David (b. Zebaḥ 54b in Str-B 2. 410).
54. Even in the opinion of the rabbis, only that prophecy which was needed by future generations was written down in Scripture (ibid. 3. 12f.). It was commonly thought in early Christianity that all prophecy applied to the present: Acts 3:24f.; 1 Pet 1:12; cf. 2 Cor 1:20.

history in the eschatology of the OT.[55] Where the historical and material roots of this approach lie is a debated issue.

Bultmann traces the origin of typology to the concept of recurrence that was widespread in antiquity, but he does not include the prior history of typology in the OT in his analysis.[56] He believes that typology arises through the "eschatologizing of the recurrence motif,"[57] the instant the old returns in a new form and no longer as it used to be. Methodologically this explanation is an abstract construction in religious phenomenology; it adds conceptual elements, but it does not explain the motivations for the rise of such a distinctively biblical approach. Most importantly, Bultmann deals only with the contemporary idea of typology in general and overlooks the important differences that exist, for example, between Paul and the *Epistle of Barnabas*. Thus the idea of recurrence, which is the basis of his reconstruction of typology, is indeed emphasized in the *Epistle of Barnabas* (6:13), but it is not found in Paul.[58]

How the typological approach actually developed is clear from its first occurrence. We have already seen in Deutero-Isaiah[59] that the eschatology of the OT prophets whose development and structure is unusually complex contains a motif that is reminiscent of typology.[60] In the predictions of the prophets, the coming new age is frequently portrayed in colors from the past; there will be a new Exodus, a new covenant, a new David, etc.[61] What is the significance of this return to the past? Do the past experiences of redemption simply provide a medium of expression so that the new beginning can be described in terms of the idea of recurrence?[62] I prefer the position of von Rad, who understands this

---

55. See above, pp. 32-41.

56. Bultmann, "Ursprung," 205-8.

57. Ibid., 207.

58. See above, pp. 221f.

59. See above, pp. 220f.

60. W. Eichrodt, *Theology of the Old Testament* (Philadelphia, 1961-67) 1. 385f.; A. Jepsen, "Eschatologie in Alten Testament," *RGG* (3d ed. 1957-65) 2. 655-62; von Rad, *Old Testament Theology* 2. 116-24; see below, n. 62.

61. This material has been collected by H. Gressmann, *Der Messias* (Göttingen, 1929) and W. Staerk, *Die Erlösererwartung in den östlichen Religionen (Soter II)* (1938); for a summary, see p. 38 n. 99.

62. Stimulated by H. Gunkel's *Schöpfung und Chaos in Urzeit und Endzeit, Eine religionsgeschichtliche Untersuchung über Genesis 1 und Offenbarung 12* (Göttingen, 1894; 2d ed. 1921), especially pp. 366-69, Gressmann (*Der Messias*) attempted to trace OT eschatology to the recurrence motif. Staerk, "Erlösererwartung," added abundant material, but he also emphasized the fundamental difference between OT eschatology and the eschatology of the ancient east (p. 178). In his review of research, E. Rohland (*Die Bedeutung der Erwählungstradition Israels für die Prophetie der alttestamentlichen Propheten* [diss., Heidelberg, 1956] 1-23) shows how recent research has gone beyond this view of the origin of OT eschatology. Rohland himself prefers the view that we mentioned above: "It is only for the sake of characterizing the future as a new beginning that it is pictured as a renewal of the past acts of election, and not because these were considered divinely ordained types of the future." Therefore, he does not want to call this motif a typology. A different analysis of the correlation motif in "eschatological prophecy" (i.e., beginning with Deutero-Isaiah according to his view of prophecy) is presented by G. Fohrer ("Die Struktur der alttestamentlichen

return to the past primarily as an expression of the idea of redemptive history.[63] It is this which set Israel apart from its environment in the ancient East where cyclical thinking was predominant. The idea of redemptive history, together with certain other motifs, was influential in shaping the eschatology of the prophets. When the prophets were confronted with the complete shattering of the previous relationship between God and man, the divine oracles renewed their expectation of a new relationship that would be full and final. This new relationship between God and man is the eschaton. (Therefore, prophecy is fully able to conceive of the eschaton within history; at least it cannot be defined as the end of history.) The more emphasis prophecy places on the radical breakdown, the more important it is that the older experiences of salvation are not obliterated, but are "present in the new in the mysterious dialectic between what is valid and what is obsolete. The prophets set great store by this typological correspondence because they work it out in their prophecies and, in so doing, they are very careful to show how the new overtakes and surpasses the old. The new covenant will be better. . . ."[64] Perhaps the underlying thought can be illustrated from Romans 11: Paul, too, sees a radical breakdown between the unbelief of Israel and the gospel (Romans 9–10), but the new election which has happened to them as the remnant of Israel (Rom 11:1-10) and God's new promise that is given them (Rom 11:25) make it possible for the original election of Israel to become the basis of hope for their full and final deliverance in spite of the breakdown (Rom 11:2, 28f.). Such a concept of redemptive history enables prophecy to view the eschaton as a new Exodus, a new covenant, a new David, etc. The concept of recurrence,[65] which arises from the observation of nature and was familiar especially in the river countries of Egypt and Mesopotamia, has certainly been a stimulus for this, but it is not the basis of it. Consequently, this motif in OT eschatology can be designated typological, even in the Pauline

---

Eschatologie," *TLZ* 85 [1960] cols. 401-20): "This view is not based on cyclical or teleological thought but on thought that deals with typical events. Situations experienced in an earlier time are considered as typical of God's action (cf. Hos 13:4) and of the conduct and destiny of the world and humanity, so that they can be expected to recur in a corresponding manner." "The concrete and figurative manner in which OT man thought and expressed himself is another reason. In general, he used every possible metaphor to present his thoughts and ideas clearly and concretely; consequently, he chose specific historical events to prefigure metaphorically the things that were anticipated in the future. Finally, especially for Isaiah . . . Yahweh's action in creation and his direction of history to which he refers is founded on the action that redeems. Everything belongs together and forms a unity. . . . Accordingly, the correlation motifs demonstrate the continuity of God's redemptive will" (col. 418). Certainly these points of view are prominent also in our motifs. In my opinion, however, Fohrer generally is too inclined to view this as an expression of analogous thought such as is found in *1 Clement* (cf. above, n. 46).

63. Von Rad, *Old Testament Theology* 2. 269-77.

64. Ibid., 272.

65. M. Eliade, *The Myth of the Eternal Return* (New York, 1954); G. van der Leeuw, *Urzeit und Endzeit* (*Eranos-Jahrbuch* XVII; 1949); cf. above, n. 60.

sense. This typology is not to be distinguished from prophecy; rather, it is a principle that forms and upholds it.

The degree to which cyclical thought and the idea of redemptive history have influenced the typological approach varies. In general, it can be stated that the typology in Jewish eschatology subsequent to the OT is affected more strongly by the concept of recurrence than by the idea of fulfillment. The eschaton is fancifully portrayed as the restoration of a better paradise (primarily in the apocalypses) or the return of the Mosaic period in a better form (primarily in the rabbis).[66] The typology is always related to a future eschaton, not to the present. In the Essene texts also[67] the present is never viewed as the typological equivalent of OT phenomena,[68] although the present is interpreted in various ways as the initial fulfillment of OT prophecy.[69] This is in agreement with the basic pattern of Essene thought. The ideas of the sect are based on the literal wording of Scripture, not on a redemptive history, and the sect understands itself to be the preserving holy remnant that endures and is always present, not as the heir of a new election in fulfillment of the old.

In the Jewish world, it was nothing new when Jesus related his person and his work typologically to the divine history of the OT by saying, "Now one greater than Jonah is here"—in other words, here is a call to repentance that is more important than the call of the prophets (Matt 12:41 par. Luke). "Now one greater than Solomon is here"—in other words, here is a wisdom that is more significant than the wisdom of Solomon (Matt 12:42 par. Luke). One greater than David is here (Mark 2:25f. par.); one who is greater than the temple (Matt 12:6). The righteous one is here; his dying is the blood of the (new) covenant (Mark 14:24 par.). All evidence suggests that these sayings originated with Jesus himself. Apparently, the ideas of the righteous one and the eschatological prophet that were current in his environment provided a point of departure for Jesus' self-understanding, as the more recent history-of-religions analyses

---

66. See above, pp. 32-41.

67. Black, *The Scrolls*, 135-42.

68. A. S. van der Woude (*Die messianischen Vorstellungen der Gemeinde von Qumran* [Assen, 1957]) is of the opinion that the sect understood its stay in the wilderness, i.e., in Qumran, as the eschatological recurrence of the Mosaic period: "As Moses was mediator of the old covenant, so the teacher of righteousness is mediator of the new covenant (cf. CD 8:21 and 6:4ff.); in the wilderness the way is prepared for God's coming and for the final redemption from evil (1QS 8:12ff.): Now, as then, people live in camps (CD 7:6; 12:23)" (p. 84; cf. p. 48). However, behind these contacts, which are very doubtful in the case of the teacher of righteousness, there is no reflection on a recurrence or renewal of past history, but basically there is a biblicism that identifies the present with the word of Scripture: the new covenant (CD 6:19; 8:21; 20:12) is no new covenant, nor even a renewed covenant; it is simply a reinstated covenant. Accordingly, these statements are not based on any reflection on a salvation-time in the past or present nor on any typological thought. Müller (*Auslegung*, 126 n. 5) comes to a similar conclusion.

69. Therefore, as 1QpHab and fragments of other commentaries on the prophets teach, they apply prophetic writings to their own time. According to 1QS 8:13-16, Isa 40:3 is fulfilled in the migration to Qumran.

demonstrate.[70] The logia mentioned above indicate that he did not simply clothe himself with these ideas, but in dependence on them he placed himself in direct relationship to the divine history of the OT. This means that he did not proclaim himself to be a figure from the Jewish anticipations of the end, but uniquely and in elemental immediacy as the one who fulfills the OT revelation of God. All these logia point in a straightforward and meaningful way to a correlation that surpasses God's dealings with his people in the past. They are, if we use the term in the Pauline sense, an expression of a typological approach. In this way they demonstrate the eschatological character of what happens "here," i.e., through Jesus. Typology brings a new revelation in a new form. It has been molded by the concept of fulfillment just as the revelation in prophecy was. This way of interpreting the present corresponds precisely with the nature of Jesus' acts. He brings salvation in a hidden form, i.e., he brings it for faith. Therefore, the fulfillment character of what has happened through Jesus cannot be demonstrated from prophecy. That character is revealed to his followers by means of typological comparison and a corresponding use of the essence of prophecy (Matt 11:2-6). In this way, Scripture discloses the things that really happened in Jesus' teaching and action that outwardly were no different from the work of a rabbi or a prophet. Whoever permits his faith to be tested is called into a relationship with God that corresponds typologically with the OT relationship. When we find a typology in Paul that interprets the present as an eschatological fulfillment, we know that in this respect too Paul developed an approach theologically which Jesus himself used.

6. TYPOLOGY AND THE HISTORICAL-CRITICAL METHOD

For more than a century it has been asserted that the historical-critical method has invalidated this important interpretation of the revelatory event which was fulfilled in Jesus. Historical criticism considers the OT account of history to be a description of faith that is different from the actual course of history. Therefore, it is necessary to ask: Does Mosaic period typology, for example, become invalid if, from the historical point of view, the way the events happened was different from the OT's witness of faith? In the last decade, F. Baumgärtel has not tired of calling attention to this problem from the standpoint of OT research and he has developed the thesis that the NT interpretation of Jesus that is based on typology and prophecy is no longer valid for us.[71] All that has been fulfilled in Jesus is the promise, "I am the Lord your God," which underlies the entire OT.

---

70. E. Schweizer, *Erniedrigung und Erhöhung bei Jesus und seinen Nachfolgern* (Zürich, 2d ed. 1962) 21-33, 56-62; cf. F. Hahn, *Christologische Hoheitstitel* (Göttingen, 1963) 219, 380-404, who states that the earliest Palestinian church interpreted Jesus on the basis of Moses typology. For earlier literature, see ibid., 381.

71. F. Baumgärtel, *Verheissung. Zur Frage des evangelischen Verständnisses des Alten Testaments* (Gütersloh, 1952), especially pp. 83f., 140f.

S. Amsler has dealt comprehensively with this and other objections to typology and he has defended typology in a very convincing manner.[72]

Today the discussion generally favors the position that neither the critical reconstruction of history nor the viewpoint of faith can be made absolute. Both must be taken seriously and must be reconciled with one another from a higher point of view.

This is the position of R. Rendtorff, who offers the following balanced solution: "If we examine the history theologically, we are not confronted with the alternative of a historical-critical picture of history or a confessional-kerygmatic one. Instead, we encounter the tradition which stands above any such distinctions. When we speak of God's action in history, we cannot mean that he has only been concerned with certain historical facts, and that these facts are now reinterpreted again and again. Rather, the tradition of God's action in history is itself history." The continual "progress of the tradition reveals the character of this history which is always pressing forward. It has not reached completion in the last stages of the Old Testament tradition; apocalypticism follows immediately after it."[73] Those who follow this view usually build the bridge between the OT and NT with a stream of tradition, i.e., the apocalyptic literature, and reject typology with the following words: If "the relationship between the Old and New Testaments is found in analogies, in typological correlations," then the relevance of the course of history is given up, because "the continuity of the history in which the events stand becomes meaningless." But this continuity is crucial because it is the distinctive mark of history.[74] Prior to this, tradition history was used as a principle of analysis, but this remarkable concept gave it a definite significance in the theology of history. In fact, tradition history is an important connecting link between the historical fact and the kerygmatic recital of history; it frees both from unrealistic isolation and combines them in a unity of historical event. To be sure, tradition history, like typology, remains in large part dependent on the historicity of its approach. This is a question that requires more careful attention. Furthermore, Rendtorff's article on how this occurs fre-

---

72. S. Amsler, *L'Ancient Testament*, 220-27. He deals primarily with three objections: (1) Typology introduces a meaning of Scripture other than the literal meaning that was not found in the text. (2) Typology is based on the events which are recorded in the OT, events that have been called into question by historical criticism. (3) Typological interpretation takes away what is characteristic in the OT witness, leads to an arbitrary selection of OT material, and gives the OT a meaning that is unfamiliar to the OT itself. To the first and third objections, we must reply with Amsler and G. von Rad ("Offene Fragen in Umkreis einer Theologie des Alten Testaments," *TLZ* 89 [1963] cols. 401-16) that the OT itself points continually beyond itself. The most difficult objection is the second. F. Hesse has asserted emphatically: "God's history with Israel which reaches its goal in Jesus Christ must be traced where history has really happened, and not where certain ideas about an event are present that may at times prove to be incorrect" ("Die Erforschung der Geschichte Israels als theologische Aufgabe," *Kerygma und Dogma* 4 [1958] 11; cf. Hesse, "Kerygma oder geschichtliche Wirklichkeit," *ZTK* 57 [1960] 17-26). We will deal with the second objection below.

73. R. Rendtorff, "Hermeneutik des Alten Testaments als Frage nach der Geschichte," *ZTK* 57 (1960) 27-40, especially p. 39.

74. Ibid., 32.

quently in the analytical use of this principle gives too little consideration to the discontinuity of tradition history. This is evident in a rather conclusive passage: Apocalyptic literature with its many layers and many interpretations can scarcely be called the legitimate successor of the OT and even less can it be considered the standard for understanding Jesus and the earliest Christian theology.[75] Early Christianity appealed to the OT to counter Jewish traditions, just as Jesus did, and even more harshly than the Essenes.[76] Of course, from the standpoint of history, this theological self-understanding did not make either of them free from Jewish tradition. As a matter of fact, however, they accepted no direction from Judaism without at the same time making a fundamental break from it, and they used their own interpretation of the OT to defend themselves against the Jews. Of Jewish traditions that helped to shape the teaching of Jesus and the theology of Paul in this dialectical antithesis, we should emphasize Pharisaism before apocalypticism in the stricter sense.[77] The discontinuity of the material is itself reflected in the history of the concept: Jesus' message about the kingdom of God is more like the apocalyptic concept than the rabbinic-Pharisaic concept. It is not identical with the apocalyptic concept, although J. Weiss and many others have assumed so on the basis of the idea of analogy in the history of religions.[78] These and other observations make it impossible to find in the complex historical relationship of Jesus and early Christianity with OT-Jewish traditions any definite continuity in the history of religions that builds the theological relationship between the OT and NT.[79] The true relationship between the content of the two Testaments must be sought, as the NT does, in God's faithfulness. God fulfilled through Jesus the events which happened to Israel without being bound to any

---

75. Opinions about the relationship of apocalypticism to prophecy vary greatly. Von Rad reaches this conclusion about apocalyptic literature as a child of prophecy (O. Procksch; H. H. Rowley): "To my mind, however, this is completely out of the question. . . . The decisive factor, as I see it, is the incompatibility between apocalyptic literature's view of history and that of the prophets. . . . This view of history lacks all confessional character; it no longer knows anything of those acts of God on which salvation was based and in the light of which previous accounts of the nation's history had been constructed" (*Old Testament Theology* 2. 303f.). Even Daniel does not begin with a definite tradition of election; of course, salvation is found in holding on to Israel's traditional commandments, but the commandments are freed from any relationship to redemptive history (pp. 308f.). Nevertheless, K. Koch ("Spätisraelitisches Geschichtsdenken am Beispiel des Buches Daniel," *Historische Zeitschrift* 193 [1961] 1-32) identifies the positive side of the relationship of apocalypticism to the prophets: "The thoughts of the prophets concerning the events of their time were now bound to a system; the divine prophecies . . . were now spread over an extended period of time. Consequently, a universal outline of history arose along with the acceptance of myths of the ancient east—the first in the history of the world. There are good reasons to assert that in this way the book of Daniel has carried out the testament of the prophets" (p. 31).

76. E.g., Mark 7:9-13 par. Matthew; Acts 7:51ff.; 2 Cor 3:12-18; John 5:39, 46f.

77. For a discussion of this question in research, cf. L. Goppelt, *Jesus, Paul and Judaism* (New York, 1964) 45-52.

78. L. Goppelt, "Reich Gottes in Neuen Testament," *Evangelische Kirchenlexicon* 3 (1959) 555-59.

79. See above, pp. 215-18.

sequence or development in history, i.e., he fulfilled them in the relationship of promise and fulfillment, of type and antitype.[80]

Now it is even more necessary to ask: Is typology invalidated by the discrepancy between the historical and the kerygmatic presentations of history in the OT? At the present time it seems that this discrepancy has largely been eliminated for typology. This is as much a result of the nature of the biblical type as it is a result of a newer view of history. We have shown that for Paul the OT type is not interpreted history nor is it historical analogy. It is God's self-manifestation expressed in historical events that are communicated by the revelatory word and are preserved in the confession.[81] By its nature, this revelation of God is inseparable from the historical events and is not valid as timeless truth. It is valid only in the framework of those events. For this reason, it can be used in other situations only if these historical events are included. On the other hand, this revelation of God allows considerable latitude for its becoming effective in history. It assumes a relationship between man and God or expresses some basic element in this relationship so that this revelation applies to a broad historical situation and is not exhausted in individual events. Therefore, for example, the details about the type in 1 Corinthians 10, such as the concept of a traveling rock, are bound to the exegetical methods of the NT period.[82] These are methods that we find unacceptable, or were doubtful already in the OT accounts from the historical perspective. This does not mean, however, that the statement is merely one of Paul's theological ideas whose basis in redemptive history is invalid for us. A type has validity also for us if a historical event in the Exodus or in the wilderness wandering that was governed by a revelatory word made a life from God possible for Israel, and if contempt for this experience resulted in judgment. The validity is not diminished even if many details in the description of the wilderness wandering are a reflection of subsequent divine revelations to Israel. If it is true, as we have indicated, that the OT type has not been molded by the church's experience of redemption, then that experience only confirms the significance of the type. Accordingly, the validity of a typology does not depend on the historicity of individual scenes, but on the truth and reality of God's

---

80. Cf. Matt 3:9 par. Luke; Matt 8:11f. par. Luke; Rom 9:6-8; this must not be watered down through a use of the figure of the olive tree in Rom 11:16-18 that was not intended by Paul.

81. W. Zimmerli (" 'Offenbarung' in Alten Testament, Ein Gespräch mit R. Rendtorff," *EvT* 22 [1962] 15-31, esp. p. 29) skillfully uses the incident of Israel's deliverance from Egypt to show how proclamation of revelatory word, historical event, and confessional presentation of history are intertwined in the OT: "This faith (Exod 14:31) understands that the historical act of deliverance over which the name Yahweh is proclaimed is an intentional event which cannot be understood in connection with history as a whole, but must be heard in the present as a summons in the name of Yahweh and must be interpreted and responded to in worshipful and believing obedience."

82. How much Paul in his exegetical thought forms concurs with contemporary rabbinism is indicated in the following books: J. Bonsirven, *Exégèse rabbinique et exégèse paulinienne* (Paris, 1939); J. W. Doeve, *Jewish Hermeneutics in the Synoptic Gospels and Acts* (Assen, 1954); W. D. Davies, *Paul and Rabbinic Judaism. Some Rabbinic Elements in Pauline Theology* (London, 1955); D. Daube, *The New Testament and Rabbinic Judaism* (London, 1956); Müller, *Auslegung*, 64-179.

revelation of himself in history and on a standard for the historicity of the historical phenomena that can only be developed from the subject matter. In principle, typology is not dependent on a greater amount of historicity than any other biblical revelation, as long as one maintains that true typology represents an important element in God's relationship to man.[83]

These considerations of the revelatory events of the Bible have been aided by a search for a view of history that has recently been revived. This search attempts to overcome both historicism and the flight from history in the historicity of existence that underlies existential interpretation.[84] It is clear from this that historical events carry a meaning in themselves that points beyond the bare unrepeatable historical fact to another event and cannot be restricted to an existential understanding.[85]

These insights into the relationship between revelatory events and history and into the nature of history permit us to affirm that the typological approach of the NT is, in principle, historically and theologically legitimate even in the light of historical criticism.

7. THE RELATIONSHIP BETWEEN TYPOLOGY AND APOCALYPTICISM IN PAUL

We have presented an outline of Paul's view of typology, just as we did for his apocalypticism. This is as much as we could accomplish within limitations of

---

83. Cf. Amsler, *L'Ancient Testament*, 221f.: "Typological interpretation does not deal with the literal historical sense of an event, but with its theological meaning. Of course, the way in which the events of the Old Covenant happened is not unimportant, but their typological interpretation in the church depends on the revelatory scope of the events that is attested by the texts and not on their accurate reconstruction. . . . The theological truth of the events recorded in the texts is not placed in doubt even when the historical reconstruction indicates that the events happened in a way different from what is presented in the texts of the Old Testament, as, for example, the entry of Israel into Canaan."

84. An informative account that deals with the subject more thoroughly is found in the article by J. Moltmann, "Exegese und Eschatologie der Geschichte," *EvT* 22 (1962) 31-66. On the earlier discussions see: K. Löwith, *Weltgeschichte und Heilsgeschehen* (Stuttgart, 1953), and O. Cullmann, *Christ and Time* (Philadelphia, 1950), especially pp. 17-33.

85. Moltmann ("Exegese," 61) reaches the conclusion: "We do not fully understand an event until we perceive its significance for its own future and not only for our present and future. . . . I understand typology to be the quest for the continuity of thought which eludes a consideration of the bare factuality of the events because typology seeks the finality and intentionality of the things that happened. . . . It does not seek to present an uninterrupted sequence of all the events, but only sets forth those which are themselves an announcement of future happenings." H. W. Wolff ("The Understanding of History in the Old Testament Prophets" in C. Westermann, ed., *Essays on Old Testament Hermeneutics*, 344-46 n. 14) states the question even more clearly as to how far "typology . . . goes hand in hand with historical interpretation. In our theological and hermeneutic considerations we have paid too little attention to the meaning which typology gains in the present-day science of history, which has recognized the limits of the one-sided individualized approach of historicism. . . . By inquiring into the typical we overcome the non-obligatory comparison of partial phenomena, the capitulation before the 'omnipotence of analogy' (Troeltsch). . . . But, faith in Jesus of Nazareth finds its basis as the final Word of God in history because the types of the two Testaments help interpret each other and together stand in contrast to that which is typical in the surrounding world."

a comprehensive treatment such as this. Now we can attempt to answer the question with which we began, and it is a key question in NT research: What, for Paul, are the respective roles of typology and apocalypticism as means for interpreting the Christ event? In spite of much overlapping, each has proven to be an independent means of interpretation, and, in spite of their different origins, each can be compared with the other. When we do compare them, we find a very profound difference between them in spite of their many similarities.

(1) The OT and Jewish antecedents of typology and of the portion of apocalypticism that is crucial for our study are interpretations of historical events with reference to the consummation. Apocalypticism, however, interprets the course of those world events that center around the elect people who are faithful to the Law. Typology, on the other hand, interprets the individual announcements of God's plan of salvation that are contained in historical events, primarily in God's acts of election.

(2) Both means of interpretation were developed from the OT revelation of God and have, therefore, a different theological flavor than, for example, means of interpretation from the Hellenistic world. Nevertheless, typology is the central motif of prophetic eschatology. Apocalypticism, on the other hand, is the successor of prophecy and carries on the purposes of prophecy in a universal and radically eschatological way. At the same time, however, it brings a certain amount of alienation from prophecy.

(3) Both approaches were adopted from Jewish traditions by Jesus and by early Christian theology. They were transformed and reshaped in various ways so that a truly Christian tradition developed for each.

(4) Paul uses both as means of interpretation, similar to the way Jesus and early Christianity had used them, to present and to interpret the entire history that leads to Christ and, especially, the eschatological character of Jesus' coming, its consequences, and its consummation in the parousia. The manner in which each was used for the presentation and interpretation of the history and the eschaton reveals how they differ as means of interpretation.

The crucial difference is evident in their interpretation of the eschaton. It is the nature of apocalypticism throughout to combine the coming of the eschaton with the course of cosmic and historical events and in this way to comprehend these in their entirety. Therefore, Paul, like early Christianity before him, uses apocalypticism to state that the coming of Jesus which would occur in the near future means the end of this world and the beginning of a new one, and that this world should definitely be called "this (passing) aeon" (1 Thess 4:15ff.; 1 Cor 15:20-28; cf. 2 Thess 1:4-10; 2:1-12). In particular he uses the apocalyptic term "resurrection" to designate what has already happened to Jesus as an eschatological event and, in keeping with this idea, he uses the apocalyptic terms "to reign" (βασιλεύειν) and "new creation" to show that the consequences of his coming are eschatological phenomena (1 Cor 15:25; 2 Cor 5:17; Gal 6:15;

cf. 4:27). In what sense, then, can Paul view these events as eschatological while this aeon still continues?[86]

Apocalyptic thought makes it possible to understand these phenomena of history as being eschatological in two ways. (1) Paul can regard Jesus' resurrection and the gathering of the church as eschatological events because he views them as parts of an eschatological drama that has already begun. This is what 1 Cor 15:20-28 seems to imply. This very passage, however, does not present the reign of Christ that begins with the resurrection as an apocalyptic event, i.e., an event that was predetermined by cosmic events, although it certainly has cosmic effects.[87] For Paul the eschaton is not present in the form of an eschatology that unfolds step by step in an apocalyptic drama, but it is present in the dialectic of the "already" and the "not yet" (Rom 8:24). There is, therefore, another more plausible explanation: In apocalyptic thought the eschatological phenomena are experienced as the impinging of another world—to be a Christian means to be released from the world. This understanding of the present eschaton could lead to a gnostic self-understanding. For Paul, however, the eschatological existence is a life of faith while still in the flesh, i.e., in historical life and in obligation to it (Gal 2:20; 1 Cor 7:20). One's obligation to this historical life does not end for Paul in the same sense that his obligation to the Law does (Rom 10:4).[88] For Paul, therefore, the presence of the eschaton does not mean removal from the world. How the eschaton is present for him in history cannot be explained on the basis of apocalyptic thinking.

It is no coincidence that Paul, like Jesus, explains the presence of the eschaton by means of typology. Adam typology and Abraham typology make it clear that Jesus' resurrection is an eschatological event because it presupposes a new relationship to God that cancels Adam's fall and fulfills Abraham's relationship to God in accordance with the promise (1 Cor 15:22; Rom 4:23ff.). The eschaton is present, therefore, in the new relationship to God that the one who is justified by faith enjoys (Rom 4:24; Gal 3:29). It is present also in the New Covenant

---

86. A good survey of the discussion of this problem is given by F. Holström, *Das eschatologische Denken der Gegenwart* (Gütersloh, 1936), and W. Kreck, *Die Zukunft des Gekommenen* (Munich, 1961) 14-76. R. Bultmann (*Geschichte und Eschatologie* [Tübingen, 1958]) tries to explain the eschatological self-understanding of early Christianity on the basis of apocalyptic thought. Because of the apocalyptic expectation of the end, early Christianity prior to Paul understood itself "not as a historical phenomenon, but as an eschatological one." That is, "it no longer belongs to this world, but to the coming aeon which lies outside history and is now breaking in" (p. 42). "Therefore, the individual believer has no responsibility for the world that still exists or for its regulations . . ." (p. 41). This conclusion contradicts the socio-ethical statements of the NT all the way from Jesus' saying concerning the paying of taxes to Caesar to Romans 13 and the household codes, and, therefore, casts serious doubt on Bultmann's conclusions. (Cf. L. Goppelt, "Die Freiheit zur Kaisersteuer," in *Ecclesia und Res Publica* (ed. G. Kretschmar and B. Lohse; Göttingen, 1961) 40-50.

87. See above, pp. 216f.

88. Cf. E. Käsemann: "It becomes much more clearly evident here that Paul simply cannot and will not speak of an end of history that has already come, although he views the end-time as having begun" ("Urchristlichen Apokalyptik," *ZTK* 59 [1962] 280).

(1 Cor 11:25; 2 Cor 3:3, 6) and in the church as the Israel of God (Gal 6:15f.). This new relationship to God is the center of God's entire work of redemption. It is ordained by God in various ways through Jesus' death and resurrection, through Christ's reign, through the work of the Holy Spirit, through election and calling, and through baptism which faith perceives as "already" but "not yet," i.e., something pointing to a visible, bodily fulfillment (Rom 6:2-11; 8:23, 29f.; 1 Cor 15:25; 2 Cor 5:7, 18ff.). This way of thinking is informed by typology, and it transforms the means of interpretation that have to some extent been developed from Hellenistic ideas. The "dying with" and the "living with" are not meant in a mystical sense nor in accordance with the mystery religions; they refer to the creation of a relationship to God that is begun through faith (Rom 6:11). Being in Adam (ἐν ᾿Αδάμ) and being in Christ (ἐν Χριστῷ) are divinely ordained certainties, not natural relationships (Rom 5:18f.).[89]

Paul uses these two means of interpretation to describe and interpret the historical event with reference to Christ, just as he did with the eschaton. Apocalypticism provides the outline of a world view, principally, the overall view, and a way to express it. Typology, on the other hand, supplies the central theological position.[90] In reality, Paul does not begin, as apocalypticism does, with a historical-theological picture of the history of mankind; instead, he uses typology to sketch episodes from the history of election (Romans 4; Galatians 3). To be sure, this history of election has universal significance for him; therefore, its preparation and substructure is Adam typology. Adam typology is more important than the apocalyptic concept of the aeon with its destructive powers. Paul is not really interested in the entire course of all the events, but in God's plan of salvation; he is not concerned about the continuity of history, but in God's faithfulness. The context of events in which he thinks of Christ can be called redemptive history, and then this concept with its varied meanings must be defined for him in terms of the typological approach. Redemptive history is that context of events within history that is determined solely by God's plan of

---

89. According to Bultmann, Paul acquired his definition of the present, eschatological salvation as righteousness and freedom through a transformation of the apocalyptic view of history and the eschatology of early Christianity into anthropology (*Geschichte*, 46-49). Moreover, this deduction is also called into question by the conclusion that Bultmann draws from it: "Since Paul interprets history and eschatology from the standpoint of man, the history of the people of Israel and the history of the world has vanished from his sight and something else is discovered instead—the historicity of human existence, i.e., the history that each human being experiences or can experience and in which he first gains his being" (p. 49). In reality, however, Paul is led to the history of Israel in the very place where he concentrates his proclamation most intensively on man, in Romans 7–8. The theme of Romans 9–11 (9:6) places the highpoint of his concentration on man in Rom 8:29f. Accordingly, the concentration on anthropology is the result of an understanding of history and eschatology that is based on typology, i.e., based on an orientation toward man's relationship with God. Anthropology is a consequence, not a principle!

90. Bultmann puts the emphasis the other way around. The apocalyptic view of history is the beginning point for Paul, inasmuch "as Paul views past history as the history of mankind (by no means Israel's history) and as a history that is controlled by sin and whose end is ordained by God" (*Geschichte*, 47).

salvation and his election which is characterized by a revelatory word and is visible to the apostle by faith in terms of its goal, i.e., Christ.

There is an obvious objection to this: Does this description of typology as a means of interpretation really do justice to its use by Paul? Yes, it does in a remarkable way. Paul does not use typology in the way that we might expect. He does not use it as an exegetical method to develop a running commentary on the OT. It is certainly no accident that we never find any such midrash in his epistles. Rather, he uses typology as a spiritual approach in terms of redemptive history in order to expound the present salvation as a whole by sketches of redemptive history based on Adam or Abraham, or in order to give a central theological interpretation of the cross, the church, its sacraments, its offices, etc.

Accordingly, the typological approach is most important for us as a central theological interpretation of the present salvation in Paul's writings and in the rest of the NT. It is crucial for our understanding of the NT that we give serious consideration to this method of interpretation, apply it in a manner appropriate to our own thought forms, and interpret the coming of Jesus and his church in the light of their being events in fulfillment. Typology does not exclude the apocalyptic approach, but it must be related to it in a manner that is appropriate to Paul's thought. Both approaches have a history-of-religions and a theological side, although the theological side is predominant in typology.

For our understanding of the OT, typology provides a framework that is determined not only by the NT but also by the OT itself; one that unites the two Testaments with one another and that facilitates the understanding of each by pointing to the other.[91]

---

91. Within the framework of this comprehensive view the individual OT passages are to be related to the Christ event, whereas isolated typological interpretations easily drift into allegorizing. It seems remarkable to me that although the general outline of von Rad's *Old Testament Theology* is oriented typologically, he develops very few specific typological interpretations.

INDEXES

INDEX OF SUBJECTS

INDEX OF NAMES

INDEX OF SCRIPTURE

THE OLD TESTAMENT

NEW TESTAMENT

APOCRYPHA

PSEUDEPIGRAPHA

APOSTOLIC FATHERS